AmPress

FIGHTER GENERAL

The Life of Adolf Galland

by
Colonel Raymond F. Toliver
and
Trevor J. Constable

INTRODUCTION

by
Gen. James H. Doolittle, USAF Ret.

AmPress

AmPress Publishing
Zephyr Cove, Nevada

Published by AmPress Publishing, Inc., Zephyr Cove,
Nevada 89448

AmPress and colophon are trademarks of AmPress Publishing
Book design and production by Robert Wenkam
Photos from the collection of Raymond F. Toliver
Manufactured in the United States of America

Quality Printing and Binding by:
Berryville Graphics
P.O. Box 272
Berryville, VA 22611 U.S.A.

This book is dedicated to the ground crews
of all air forces, in both war and peace,
the unsung heroes of air power.

CONTENTS

ACKNOWLEDGMENTS

Numerous kind people have contributed in various ways to the compilation of this book. Their knowledge, experience, and capabilities have provided the authors with invaluable help and guidance. General Galland's former *Luftwaffe* comrades saw him from many different angles and perspectives, in a wide variety of military circumstances. Most of them have known him well in postwar times, adding to their insights.

Former foes who became peacetime friends with General Galland have added their special contributions. We are grateful as well to have had access to General Galland's war diary. The German fighter pilot community as a whole has been most helpful.

Detailing the aid we have received would require many pages. We are, therefore, listing alphabetically all those who have helped with technical and research assistance. For any unintentional omissions, we apologize. We have been helped by:

The late Sir Douglas Bader, Cajus Bekker, Hans Heinrich Brustellin, Joseph Buffer, Harley Copic, Robert T. Crow, James H. Doolittle, Anne-Marie Drinhausen, Wolfgang Falck, James J. Finnegan, Erich Hartmann, John H. Kirby, Walter Krupinski, Gerhard Meyer, Nathan Miller, Johannes Mohn, Eduard Neumann, Heinrich Olemotz, Douglas Pitcairn, Hans Schmoller-Haldy, The late Werner Schroer, Eduard Schroeder, Robert H. Stanford-Tuck, Johannes Steinhoff, Ray Waddey, Anton Weiler, Dr. John M. Whitten, Frank Wootton

In their totality, the contributions of these people have been indispensable, and the authors are duly grateful.

Col. Raymond F. Toliver, USAF Ret
Trevor J. Constable
Los Angeles, California

A SPECIAL NOTE FROM GENERALLEUTNANT ADOLF GALLAND

Many opportunities and offers came to me through the
decades for the preparation of an official,authorized
biography.None of these proved appropriate or timely,
until my friends Colonel Raymond F. Toliver and Trevor
"Sailor" Constable proposed this biography to me several
years ago.All the necessary elements were present at this
time.

These American authors know personally all the successful
Luftwaffe fighter leaders who survived the war,and have earned
their respect for integrity and fairness.The Toliver-Constable
literary team has been able in past works,to capture the
inner spirit of the Luftwaffe Fighter Arm and make it comprehensible to future generations.They have told history
what happened,minus the biases and distortions of wartime
propaganda.

Many years of research by the authors into Luftwaffe WW II
records,secret wartime code decrypts and Allied interrogation
reports,material declassified just a few years ago,has gone
into the assembly of this new book.Such official documentation
was not available to me thirty years ago,when "THE FIRST AND
THE LAST" was published.I must admit that through the authors I
learned things about WW II history and also the Luftwaffe,that
were new to me despite my central involvement.Additionally
my close friends were indeed under my skin for a long time.
Most of the photographs in this book furthermore,are from
my private collection,and have never previously been published.

ADOLF GALLAND
Lt. General (ret.)

BONN, WEST GERMANY
September 1989

INTRODUCTION

The largest single obstacle to the success of the allied strategic daylight bombing of Germany was the German fighters. The name of General Adolf Galland was directly associated with that force.

I took command of the United States Eighth Air Force in early January 1944. At first we had a shortage of long-range fighter planes and our bomber losses were heavy. As we got more long-range fighters, our bomber losses were reduced. Finally we had enough fighters to risk putting part of them directly against the German fighters. This greatly displeased the bomber commanders but delighted the fighter pilots and the fighter commanders.

Events soon proved, nevertheless, that free-hunting fighter sweeps ahead of and sometimes far afield from the bomber boxes resulted in serious and irreplaceable losses to the *Luftwaffe* Fighter Arm. This in turn allowed daylight strategic bombing to reach its full potential. Mortal damage was then inflicted not only on German air power but also upon their industry, through destruction of fuel supplies, transportation, and other key targets.

General Galland foresaw these developments as early as 1942, including the eventual strangulation of German war potential. Repeatedly he warned his superiors. He urged strong fighter reinforcement of the Western Front so decisive losses could be inflicted on the Americans before daylight bombing found its strength. His warnings went unheeded.

By one of those strange parallels that often occur on opposite sides in war, the measures I took with Eighth Air Force fighters were essentially identical with those that Galland had urged on Goering during the Battle of Britain. As a successful fighter ace and leader, Galland believed that free-hunting fighter sweeps were tactically essential against RAF Fighter Command. Goering insisted, instead, on close fighter escort of German bombers, thereby robbing his fighters of both battle initiative and flexibility.

Galland's rise to General of the Fighter Arm at age 30 was truly meteoric.

History acknowledges now the broad accuracy of his tactical insights and of his gifted understanding of fighter aviation in the overall structure of modern air power. In my view, these wider attributes mark him larger than do his high decorations. The *Luftwaffe* produced many outstanding aces but only one Adolf Galland.

Frequently it has been borne in on me how fortunate it was for the Allies that General Galland did not have full operational authority over the *Luftwaffe* Fighter Arm. In the event, the years of war between our countries were mercifully brief. The decades of friendship since, extending over the whole range of constructive human activity, have brought us all closer together than we ever were in the past.

General Galland became a peacetime businessman, like myself. Through the years we have met in friendship on this common ground, as well as having our memories of the past when we were opponents in war. This authorized biography gives us new insights into the forces that shaped Adolf Galland, that built his character, and that gave him the strength to face his unusual military challenges. Written by two respected American historians, this book is not only a worthy addition to the history of air power but also contributes to the mutual understanding of our two nations.

James H. Doolittle
General, USAF Ret.

PROLOGUE

Personal property of enemies may be confiscated by the State, but never by individuals.

—Winston Churchill, 1940

The luxurious former home of screen star Joan Crawford in Brentwood, California, was the scene of a dramatic ceremony on 16 October 1980, centered on General Adolf Galland. The guests present and awaiting his arrival were aware of what was about to happen, but not Galland. Thirty-five years after the end of World War II, the leader of Germany's wartime fighter pilots was about to receive the surprise of his life.

The Joan Crawford mansion belonged now to Robert T. Crow, son of the Dallas-based Trammel-Crow Corporation family. Several of Crow's friends eagerly awaited the arrival of General Galland and his party. Mr. and Mrs. C. Allen Colley, Mr. and Mrs. Joe Buffer, Ronald Cox, the Hayden C. Eaves, and author Ray Toliver and his wife, Jen, were among the welcoming group.

Just as the second round of drinks was being served, Galland arrived in characteristic style—a lady on each arm. Virginia Bader and Norma Bert were both radiant. Galland nevertheless became the immediate focus of attention, a human magnet automatically establishing the center of any gathering.

Screenwriter and historian Joe Buffer introduced everyone, while Bob Crow stood quietly beside a long leather chest. A brass plate mounted on the chest was inscribed with the *Luftwaffe* eagle and the number 12. Crow made sure that Galland had a drink, figuring that he would soon need one. Then Crow rapped on the table and called for attention. As conversation faded, he made his announcement.

"General Galland, I have something here that belongs to you. I want to take this opportunity to return it to your now, to the rightful owner."

Shoving the case towards Galland, Crow motioned to the general to open it up. Galland stood transfixed, staring at the brass plate with its number 12. He was like a man magically teleported to another time and place.

Hands trembling with excitement, Galland slipped the catches and swung back the lid. Eyes wide, mouth open in astonishment and wonder, he stared down at the matched pair of Merkel trap shotguns. Inside the lid was the original yellowed paper with numbers of the guns and the owner's name: First Lieutenant Galland. The guns had been presented to him by the *Luftwaffe* at Suhl, now in East Germany, back in 1936.

In the surrender maelstrom of 1945, these guns had been stolen from storage by a lieutenant colonel of the U.S. Army. They had been "liberated" in the parlance of the times. Galland had lost hope of ever seeing them again. Still without a word, he scooped up the first gun and assembled it as though he had done so daily for the past 35 years. Aiming along the barrel over the sights, he swung the gun as though tracking a skeet pigeon, then dropped the weapon to his side.

"My God! My guns! My guns! My guns!"

"Yes, sir, General" said Bob Crow, "your guns once more. They are hereby finally returned to you with my compliments, sir."

The following evening, Galland was entertained at a dinner in Santa Ana, California, hosted by former naval aviator Wilbur F. Bettis, at the latter's famous Nieuport 17 restaurant. Present also on this memorable evening was General James H. Doolittle, one of America's most famous flyers and Galland's chief wartime adversary as the 1944 commander of the mighty 8th USAAF. General Curtis E. LeMay of B-29 & SAC fame, General Kirk Armistead of the U.S. Marine Corps and Midway Island action, and General Jay Hubbard of U.S. Marine Corps completed the array of distinguished air generals.

American fighter aces James L. Brooks and Robert M. DeHaven represented the U.S. fighter pilot fraternity. Other notable guests included aircraft designer and aviation artist R. G. Smith, James T. Burton of McDonnell-Douglas, former *Luftwaffe* interrogator Hanns Joachim Scharff, Colonel Al Osequerra, USMC, screenwriter Joe Buffer, and author Raymond F. Toliver. Virginia Bader and Norma Bert were again in the company of the guest of honor—*Generalleutnant* Adolf Galland.

Before this glittering assembly, financier Bob Crow once more presented the long-missing guns to Galland. This time there were two other enthusiastic shooters and hunters on hand—Doolittle and LeMay. Throughout the evening, these two historic personalities could be seen picking up the guns, sighting them at imaginary targets, and hefting each weapon to admire its balance and workmanship. Both American generals were intrigued by these exquisite examples of the gunsmith's craft. Equally intriguing to them was the chain of events by which the guns had been returned to their rightful owner—35 years later and half a world away in California.

The guns dated from early 1936, when Galland was a member of the *Luftwaffe* clay pigeon shooting team. World War I ace Ernst Udet, a passionate hunter, gun enthusiast, and master marksman, had organized the team to help improve marksmanship and morale. Each of the ten young officers on the team was presented with a matched pair of Merkel shotguns as a personal gift. Their cost was out of reach for all save the wealthiest sportsmen.

Trap and skeet shooting was not a 1936 Olympic discipline. Parallel with the Olympic Games in Berlin, nevertheless, a World Shooting Championship was organized at excellent new facilities in Berlin-Wannsee. Using these superlative guns, the *Luftwaffe* team surprisingly outscored the best German civil teams. The exultant Udet presented every team member with a season pass to the entire Olympiad.

Galland kept the guns with him during the war. In April 1945, he placed these guns and others from his extensive collection in the care of Mr. Erich Vollmer at Hohenpeissenberg in Bavaria. He was Galland's wartime cigar manufacturer and also a major of the reserve in JV-44, the jet fighter unit that was Galland's last command. U.S. Army occupation forces after the surrender compelled Vollmer to hand over all Galland's guns. The Merkel pair were personally appropriated by the lieutenant colonel. Galland in the meantime had become a prisoner of war at the surrender.

He learned of his loss when his principal American interrogator, Captain John M. Whitten of the U.S. Army, escorted him on a sub rosa visit to Vollmer. Whitten and Galland had become fast friends, and it was relatively easy for Whitten to learn the identity of the officer who had stolen the guns and who had already returned to America, guns and all. In the temper of the times, nothing could be done. Galland had to accept losing the guns and all his other personal property as part of the price of defeat.

Many years later, the former colonel tried to sell the guns in America for an exorbitant price. Galland's 1953 memoirs, *The First and the Last,* had in the meantime made him internationally famous. This automatically boosted the value of the guns, although they were not sold at this time due to the excessive price. Galland made every effort to get his guns back, but there was no response of any kind from the man who now claimed ownership. A resident of the southeastern United States, he ignored all correspondence.

The guns were eventually sold to Dr. Frank Hannon, a physician in Washington State. Through a friendly female employee of the American Consul General in Frankfurt, Galland learned of the sale and also the name and address of the "new owner." Contacting Dr. Hannon by letter and telephone, Galland made him a substantial offer for the guns, which was turned down. The doctor argued that Galland had offered him only one third of the present value of the guns, and the physician had his eye on tomorrow.

"The price will triple" he said, "when you pass away in the near future, General Galland."

After the doctor died, leaving Galland still in this world but minus his guns, the weapons were left in Hannon's estate. Advertising for the estate sale caught the eye of Joe Buffer of Malibu, California. A collector himself, and a

German arms and collectibles investment expert, Buffer knew he had a find. A former Marine Corps master sergeant who had voluntarily served in both World War II and Korea, Buffer had equipped himself with a detailed knowledge of German history. He, therefore, had no doubt about the potential value of the Galland guns. He bought the guns from the Hannon estate for his own collection, at a price he described as "a little staggering."

Shortly after his return to California with his prize, Buffer was lunching with Robert T. Crow, then president of Trammel-Crow Corporation, Los Angeles Division. Crow turned out to be a longtime admirer of Adolf Galland, with a strong desire to personally meet the former General of the *Luftwaffe* Fighter Arm. When Buffer told him about the Galland guns, Crow was ecstatic. The executive knew that he finally had the key to a meeting with the German general— provided he could get Joe Buffer to part with his prize.

Bob Crow made Buffer an offer that he could not refuse. The price this time was more than a little staggering. The guns thus began the final phase of their journey back to Galland. Crow returned these irreplaceable weapons to their rightful owner with absolutely no strings attached. Such a gift places him among the most big-hearted of men. The authors asked Crow why he performed this generous act, which could not bring him any material return—the acid test of a true gift.

"These guns were the looted property of a man of honor and integrity, he replied. If they had been picked up by an agency of the state, then law would dictate that they should be returned to their rightful owner.

"A deeper motivation was to do something proper, honorable, and nice for a man of his stature. It has always pained me to see the way that the German people have flagellated themselves over the acts of a few. General Galland was a man of destiny, placed in a point in time of great events. His qualities as a man and as a warrior served his people very well.

"He never allowed his duty as a soldier of Germany to force him to violate those higher principles of mankind which the German people—in the overwhelming balance—hold dear and exemplify in their lives as well as any other people on earth. These principles of truth, compassion, and mutual respect among people are based upon belief in the inherent goodness of man.

"I believe that a generation of self-flagellation for the heinous acts of a few, by the German people as a whole, is penance enough."

Bob Crow's action is perhaps the ultimate expression of a phenomenon that has been evident internationally for several decades. Adolf Galland brings out the best in people. Their good qualities and impulses appear kindled by him, despite his being a former enemy general. He generates their warmest respect.

Drawn to him in social groups and similar settings, they want if possible to speak with and to touch this most famous of all German flying men. Those able to receive a handshake sometimes walk away looking at their own hand as though it were something blessed. A gathering may contain many famous aces and aviation personalities from numerous nations, but if Galland is present it is to him that people gravitate. Even the heroes crowd around him. All this occurs with no effort on his part, as an automatic reaction to his presence.

Charisma is the buzzword for what Galland has, but it explains nothing. Adolf Galland is a man of body, soul, and spirit who brought all three principles into high function in a life of drama and challenge. How he directed his talents and gifts, developed his character and abilities, and survived his triumphs and tragedies is the subject of this narrative. Those who stay the course will agree at the end that he certainly deserved to get his guns back.

CHAPTER ONE

The retired *Luftwaffe* general and fighter ace who criss-crosses planet Earth in the 1980s is a combination of businessman and international ambassador of the world fighter pilot community. He deals with high technology in the aerospace epoch, but he began in the era of helmet and goggles. Adolf Galland was already six years old when Baron von Richthofen was shot down, yet Galland remains involved in matters of aerospace. Like a towering old German oak, it is his roots that have enabled him to endure.

When he was growing up during and following World War I, there was no "counterculture" to menace his development. Anything of such a nature thrusting into his boyhood would have faced immediately a hostile and aggressive foe—his father. Adolf Felix Galland ruled his household and his sons with an iron hand, in the fashion of that age. Permissiveness was unknown. His goal was to raise men of character and integrity who would become capable citizens. Adolf Galland the younger was raised in accordance with the trusted principles of tradition.

The presence of the Galland family at Westerholt in Westphalia, where the future General of the Fighter Arm was born on 19 March 1912, was itself a tradition. Galland is a French name. The first Galland in Westerholt was a Huguenot refugee from France, who sought a new life in Germany in 1742. Appointed bailiff to the estate of Count von Westerholt, the *emigré* Galland began a tradition that handed the office down continuously from father to son.

Americans are accustomed to the term *bailiff* almost exclusively in the sense of a minor court official. The bailiff of the Westerholt estate held a far wider range of responsibilities. Adolf Galland's father supervised and administered the work of more than 100 persons carrying out agricultural, mechanical, domestic, and maintenance pursuits, as well as the functions of forestry. (Management of such vast holdings today would classify the bailiff as an agribusiness executive.)

His authority on the Westerholt estate was unquestioned, just as it was in his own home, located just outside the gates of Count von Westerholt's castle.

Galland's mother came from a successful business family in Bochum. Both parents were from the upper middle class of their own day. They were devout Roman Catholics, and the family was run along completely traditional lines. (Young Adolf would live his whole life and raise his own children under basic Christian principles. In his boyhood home, an authoritarian father was accepted unquestioningly by everyone. Equality of the sexes would never have been accepted in the Galland home, even if anyone had dared suggest such a thing 70 years ago.)

Discipline for boys was a central family principle. Adolf and his elder brother Fritz caught the main force of their father's convictions about discipline. He drove all this home to them with blows of a stick. They were sternly warned to avoid even minor infractions of their father's rules. Adolf and Fritz were afraid of their father.

Frau Galland exemplified the feminine principles of giving, softness, and caring. Consoling her sons after their thrashings, she would also gently remonstrate with their father against excessive severity. (Adolf Galland remembers his mother with deep fondness and warmth. A man who normally avoids superlatives, he indulges in them regarding his mother. "She was absolutely the best mother in the world. I loved her very much.")

Two younger brothers came after Adolf, named Wilhelm-Ferdinand and Paul. Papa Galland had pet names for all family members. His wife he called "Anita" instead of Anna. Fritz was "Toby," Adolf was "Keffer," Wilhelm-Ferdinand was nicknamed "Wutz," and Paul was called "Paulinchen" or sometimes "Paula." When he arrived as the youngest family member, everyone was expecting a girl.

The arrival of Wutz and Paul diminished, through thinning out, the disciplinary pressure their father could exert. Perhaps Mother Galland's importunings for more leniency had an effect as well, but life was easier in a disciplinary sense when there were four boys instead of two. Wutz and Paul had things relatively easy.

Papa Galland was not all severity and discipline. A hunter and outdoorsman of consummate skill, he had spent his life on the Westerholt estate. He made sure that his knowledge and skills were passed on to young Adolf—an eager pupil. He was taken on his first hunting trip at age five. He shot his first hare at age six. Safe gun-handling and correct shooting technique became part of him. Opportunities were provided for the steady practice that is essential to the development of a master marksman.

All the great fighter aces of the air wars have been excellent marksmen. Those among them who learned to shoot under expert guidance early in life almost invariably found quick success in aerial combat. Galland's training had another crucial component. Less ponderable than the ability to hit the bullseye, this faculty was developed by having a game preserve at his back door in boyhood

1925–1926: Class at
Gelsenkirchen-Buer. Galland
is fifth from right in third row.

Adolf "Keffer" Galland on
Christmas Eve, 1912, at the
age of nine months, had yet
to light his first cigar.

At Christmastime, 1949, Anne (nee Schipper) Galland and Adolf Galland, mother and father of Lt. General Galland.

At left is mobile trailer designed and built by Galland. His motorcycle is being attended by a friend, Hermann Selm, and his glider STROLCH is at the right. Trailer provided tools and camping quarters for the glider group.

and by plenty of invitations to the hunt. Galland had a fine ''hunter's nose''—
the ability to smell out his quarry. Open-cockpit aces of World War I claimed
it was literally possible to ''smell out'' the enemy; but in World War II the
hunter's nose was an intuitive capacity to find the enemy, developed by years
of hunting game.

When Galland arrived on the Channel Front in June of 1940 to take command
of III/JG-26, he was already a widely known ace. He also brought with him
from the woods of Westerholt that all-important hunter's nose. Leading his fighters
down to lower altitudes he located RAF aircraft with uncanny consistency. His
hunting talent and the success that sprang from its wartime use changed the
fortunes of III/JG-26 and boosted their morale.

The Great War, later to be known as World War I, made only a superficial
impression on the young Galland. He was six years old when it ended. The
only glory surviving amid its horror seemed to be the heroic status of fighter
aces. He read about Immelmann, Boelcke, and Udet. He knew who Hermann
Goering was (and would find out what he was really like in due time). Von
Richthofen was an ace he could identify with, because the immortal Red Baron
was also a hunter and woodsman. From this beginning, Galland's interest in
aviation expanded to admiration of the great international pioneers of the twenties.
Bored stiff by classical academic subjects at Westerholt Public School, and
later at the Hindenburg *Gymnasium* in Buer, Galland's boyhood interests were
almost exclusively technical. Studying only enough Latin, Greek, and other deadly
dull subjects to scrape through his grades, he educated himself in the subjects
of his own interest. Fascinated by electricity, he rigged up numerous experiments
to demonstrate its laws and capabilities. He built radios and rockets and became
an expert motorcycle mechanic.
Energetic involvement in athletics, especially sprinting and the high and
broad jumps, ensured the development of a sound and healthy body. (Trap-
shooting sharpened his marksman's eye to the point where he would later easily
qualify for the *Luftwaffe*'s first trap-shooting team.) Motor cycles, car driving,
and girl chasing were all part of his versatile youth. Model aircraft rapidly turned
his interest towards the burgeoning sport of sailplaning, and in a short time the
air and aircraft became the dominant passions of his life.
Papa Galland had been watching his second son's technical abilities developing. He took a sort of gruff interest in the youngster's enthusiasm for sailplaning.
Part of the vast Westerholt estate was the Borkenberge, a sprawling heath east
of the Haltern-Munster railway. The Gelsenkirchen Flying Club had set up a
camp on the Borkenberge for sailplaning, about 20 miles from Westerholt. Papa
Galland stunned Adolf by buying him a small motorcycle. (A tremendous unfoldment would result from this act of paternal generosity.)
While his brothers were enthusiastic horsemen and cantered about the Westerholt estate, Adolf sped over to Gelsenkirchen and continued his chosen education.

Classes were held by the flying club in aeronautics, including practical training in the design and construction of sailplanes, the theory of flight, meteorology, and kindred subjects. Galland absorbed this knowledge eagerly.

His relationship with his two younger brothers was one of fraternal love and respect. Different feelings were evoked by his elder brother and these hovered between bare tolerance and dislike. Fritz then made the mistake of seeking to take away from Adolf an exceptionally attractive girl who had attached herself to the would-be sailplane pilot. (Antagonism was awakened in Adolf towards Fritz that was to have far-reaching consequences in shaping his character and approach to life.)

Adolf told himself repeatedly that he would always be better than his brother, and that no matter what sacrifices were necessary he would make himself excel by sheer merit. (This resolution went deep. Long after he had won back his girl from his brother, the drive to be number one remained. Minus any objective connection to his brother, the resolution came to apply to his life as a whole. He would find it impelling him to achievement and sustaining him through the darkest times of his life. He had tapped a profound wellspring of his will.)

Sailplaning became a passion. Every weekend he was out on the Borkenberge toiling with the launching and retrieval of sailplanes. With other boys, he would haul the precious and fragile birds up with heavy catapult ropes and then stand open-mouthed as they went rushing away on the wind. He dreamed of the day that he would go aloft. Hard physical work while improving their rough encampment and hacking out roads with picks, shovels, and wheelbarrows hardened his resolve even more.

Galland made a rocky beginning as a pilot in 1927. His first sailplaning effort ended in a crash shortly after he became airborne. A second start went better and, with thumping heart, he experienced for the first time the seemingly magical solidity of air when penetrated by a wing at the proper angle. Each flight saw his skill improve. He was hooked on the adventure of flying.

Life's proudest moment at this time was passing his sailplane pilot's "A" license. The treasured lapel badge that he was now entitled to wear showed a white gull on a dark blue field (and it would remain the most exciting of all the pilot's badges he would ever earn). He had stayed aloft 34 seconds to win the right to have the badge in his lapel.

Five more flights qualified him for the "B" test. The coveted "C" test was now within reach but required five minutes of sustained flight. That was difficult to achieve on the Borkenberge (before the physics of thermals—vertical air streams caused by temperature differentials—were understood by scientists and airmen). The Borkenberge soaring record was 47 minutes 45 seconds at that time. Galland assaulted this record after a detour to the Mecca of German sailplaning—the Rhoen.

His Rhoen trip almost slipped from his grasp. His interest in soaring brought about a nosedive in his classical schooling. His father was furious to learn from the *Gymnasium* in Buer that young Adolf did not meet the standards of his class. An ultimatum was issued: School work up to standard, or there will be no more flying.

The 19 year old maintained himself in school by a bare margin. He was therefore able to attend the Easter soaring meet at the Rhoen in 1931. The Rhoen mountains lie about 25 miles north of Frankfurt-on-Main. Highest among them is the legendary Wasserkuppe—the "water hill"—so named because its top is frequently swathed in clouds. The view from the crest in good weather is among the world's most spectacular. Gliding had begun there before World War I, developed into soaring, and by the middle 1920s the Rhoen had become a famous international soaring site.

A luminary of the 1920s on the Rhoen was a tall, dark, gaunt-looking designer of sailplanes and soaring machines—Willy Messerschmitt. Half designer and half artist, he learned and applied well the lessons of the Rhoen. Messerschmitt was famous as a sailplane designer long before he created his first fighter aircraft. (His later creations would figure significantly in the life of Adolf Galland.)

The legendary stars of German soaring had all made their names and records at the Rhoen. Galland now rubbed shoulders with some of these personalities, watched them in action, and took the course that would lead to his pilot's certificate. Enthusiasm and fellowship at the Rhoen were like champagne, bubbling and irresistible.

Galland was back at the Rhoen in the autumn, with members of his own club, participating in the International Soaring Competition. They had hauled their own best sailplane, designed as *Meyer II,* to the meet. The elated young Galland stayed aloft for an hour, thus qualifying for his official pilot's certificate. Only two other men in Westphalia held this certificate. The honor was sufficient to warrant its presentation to Galland by the President of Westphalia (the first of numerous similar ceremonies that would mark his life as a pilot).

He could now make cross-country flights, perform at air shows, and instruct other sailplane pilots. He was exceling his brother Fritz but nearly crashed educationally as a result. As his final examination (*Abitur*) loomed, he had to literally force himself into familiarity with all the classical knowledge that did not interest him.

Count von Westerholt now provided special incentive. He had watched young Galland's progress as a pilot with interest. He offered him a sailplane of his own as a reward for successfully passing his final examination at Buer. Young Adolf knew how to take advantage of an opportunity. His final composition described the design and construction of a trailer for sailplane transportation to soaring sites. The trailer was designed to provide overnight shelter for the soaring team, including their food supply, and the unit also provided storage for the sailplane when it was not in use.

Galland passed his finals. He had won his heart's desire—a brand-new sailplane built to his specifications at the factory. His choice was the Grunau Baby (a popular and durable craft that enjoys classic status today among sailplane enthusiasts). Excitement ran high at the Gelsenkirchen Flying Club as Galland

Sailplane Grunau Baby in 1932; STROLCH means "imp" or "scamp." This is the sailplane flown by Galland to new records at Borkenberge.

Soaring greats at Wasserkuppe, 1932. Kronfeld, world record holder at the time, is lying on the ground facing camera, second from left. Professor Georgii lies with back to camera. Theo Keweloh is standing fourth from left.

drew up his specifications and sent them to the Grunau factory.

Galland began to notice in himself a developing trait (and a portent of his military future). The sailplaners all pitched in to help build the trailer he had designed. He became aware that his comrades were increasingly looking to him for leadership and came to him with ideas for his approval. When he spoke, they listened receptively, as though intuitively aware that he knew more than they. The entire group worked naturally and efficiently under his direction in memorable harmony. All the discipline required came from within them. He was their naturally chosen leader, without any election or badges of rank.

Years later, with the Condor Legion in the Spanish Civil War, Galland would again encounter this phenomenon. As a squadron leader in his middle 20s, he had over 140 men under his command. The squadron ran smoothly and successfully. He would remember with pride that, despite his own youth and operations in a foreign country, he never had to punish even one member of his squadron.

Club members on the trailer project contributed both labor and savings. When they were short of funds, they borrowed from parents, relatives, and friends to complete the job. Arrival of the sailplane *by rail* crowned this venture with an amusing touch of practical idealism. The proper craft was in their hands to prove the merits of the Borkenberge as a soaring site, and for Galland to make his attempt on the Borkenberge record of 47 minutes aloft.

"Calvary" was the nickname given to the high launch point on the Borkenberge, since it always involved heavy loads and sacrificial labor. Labeled Rauher Hang on the map, the site was wreathed in freezing murk early on the morning of 27 February 1932. The club members battled the precious Grunau Baby into position in zero visibility, and Galland was strapped in, already frozen to the bone by a biting northeaster.

Visibility lifted slightly. Galland gave the starting signal, and his comrades launched him into the soup. He immediately vanished from sight. The near-blizzard was as bad as it looked. He felt the frigid pinch of ice on his face. His goggles fogged. The sailplane's wings quickly developed an ominous frosty mantle. A lull in the wind decided the issue, and the would-be record breaker crunched back down on the icy heather. With diminished enthusiasm, the comrades hauled the craft back to the launch point.

By 9:25 AM, in better visibility, he was catapulted again, rejoicing at the responsiveness of the new sailplane. Higher and higher he rose in a series of steep turns. Facial detail of the hopping figures below disappeared as he passed the 30-minute mark. Navigating carefully to catch the upwind, nursing his kite through air pockets, he felt as though born to the air. Surviving 47 minutes, he smashed the old Borkenberge record and swept on. He was determined to make it a decisive improvement.

Turbulence amid the fresh breeze jarred the Baby, pushing Galland to the limit of his piloting skill. Far below, his comrades were in ecstasy—distant pygmies prancing and waving sheets in salute. He reached a triumphant two hours aloft. Part of him wanted to continue the intoxicating majesty of his victory over the air. Intellect nevertheless ruled emotion. He could feel the slackness that had worked into the aileron cables from more than 300 turns.

When he landed back on the Borkenberge, he had been aloft for 2 hours, 6 minutes, and 5 seconds. He had not only shattered the old Borkenberge record but also had established a new regional soaring record for northwest Germany. The legend of Galland the pilot had begun. His feat was hailed and he became famous in soaring circles (a success that would continue until he became the most famous German pilot of his time).

The Borkenberge was now established as an excellent soaring location for good sailplanes. Local enthusiasm boomed. The Westerholt Soaring Club, affiliated with the DLV (*Deutscher Luftsport Verband*), was formed to give this enthusiasm a focus. At the foundation meeting of the club, Galland's record-breaking sailplane was christened The Imp (*Strolch*). He had proved that he could make things happen through his resolution always to be number one—the best.

His father was enthusiastic over this success but highly skeptical about aviation, other than as a sport. He was taken aback when, in a fatherly interview about the direction of young Adolf's future, the latter said immediately that he wanted to become a commercial pilot. (Such an ambition would be normal in today's world, but Westerholt in 1932 was another world.)

Europe was then served by numerous air-taxis. Small aircraft transported businessmen and were used in medical emergencies and in similar functions. Hermann Goering had run an air-taxi in Scandinavia. Galland Senior equated commercial piloting with taxi-driving. He could not envision an airline operating like a steamship line, even though Lufthansa already operated on long international routes.

Papa Galland had been born in the 19th century. Expectation on his part that young Adolf would follow him as bailiff was normal and natural. Galland Senior would have been fully in character had he tried to persuade his son to follow some orthodox and recognized profession. He showed, instead, a practical wisdom, urging his son to choose the profession for which he truly felt the call. Funds were available to young Adolf for any higher education he needed.

When his son still came out unswervingly for a career as a commercial pilot, Galland Senior stilled his misgivings and supported him fully. He could do little in a practical way, but he provided plenty of moral support, which earned him young Adolf's warm respect. Moral support was essential in such a discouraging situation: Chances for a young man to become a commercial pilot in Germany in 1932 were close to zero.

The German social scene in this period bordered on anarchy in the big cities. The most populous, energetic, and technically skilled nation in Europe was living a nightmare of unemployment, soup kitchens, and lethal street riots between warring political factions. Most of Galland's contemporaries would go from Germany's *Gymnasiums* directly into the ranks of the more than six million unemployed.

Qualified, mature, and capable men—the citizenry that should have been making the country prosperous—were living desperate lives. The German nation was a gaunt shadow of itself. The National Socialist Party led by Adolf Hitler daily drew attention to the monstrous irrationalism of a great nation in degradation. Hitler's unrivalled oratory, and the social situation itself, swept him onward towards political mastery of Germany.

With the German economy in low gear, 20-year-old Adolf Galland wanted to be an airline pilot. (His chances were approximately the same as a young American today wanting to be an astronaut.) The supply of human material grossly exceeded the demand. The national popularity of soaring had made German youth air-minded, and all the country's best young men wanted to fly.

The German Air Line Pilot School (*Deutsche Verkehrsflieger Schule*) had branches at Braunschweig, at Warnemuende, at Schleissheim, and at List on the island of Sylt. There were 20 vacancies for beginners; 20,000 applications inundated the school. Odds of 1,000 to 1 against Galland dropped steeply when the school itself weeded out all save 100 exceptional young men.

This elite would be privileged to sit for a gruelling ten-day examination. Galland was among them. A battery of exhausting physical, academic, psychological, and technical tests was applied at Braunschweig with relentless thoroughness. Galland's sailplaning experience was a substantial help. He was among the 20 survivors of the ordeal. He was keeping his resolution to always be the best.

The spirit in which he was approaching life at this time is exemplified in the following excerpt from a sailplaning article that he wrote in 1932:

> The dashing sailplane is flying like an arrow into the ether. Moments before, it was indifferent, heavy on the earth. Now it is in its element and flies noiselessly, carried by a magic force, climbing to enormous heights with entrancing boldness, obedient to the will of its master, the pilot.
>
> One is affected by the beauty of Nature, the grandeur of soaring, the almightiness of our Creator. Flying is foolproof, but it must first be learned thoroughly. There is always a way for a healthy person to become a pilot— when there is will power, consistent direction, and love and idealism for flying.

Fortified by this spirit, he was about to begin living his boyhood dream.

CHAPTER TWO

The gruelling tests that selected 20 elite young men from an application list a thousand times larger characterized life at the German Air Line Pilot School in Branschweig. Issued blue civilian clothes and quartered in modern barracks, the future airline pilots found themselves under tight discipline. (They did not know it at the time, but Galland and his fellow students were becoming part of the "Black *Luftwaffe*.")

Generaloberst Hans von Seeckt had laid the basis for this shadow air arm more than ten years previously. An air service for the Army was regarded as essential by the planners working under von Seeckt's direction. While there was no vision of a massive and completely independent Air Force (such as the *Luftwaffe* later became), the secret aviation section within the War Ministry remained abreast of world aviation developments. This section also set in train the clandestine design and engineering work on the military aircraft denied Germany under the Versailles Treaty.

Preparations were also made to produce a new generation of military aviators and aviation specialists. Under a secret clause of the Treaty of Rapallo in 1922, a German Army aviation training program was set up at Lipetsk in the Soviet Union. This program operated from 1926 until Hitler came to power. More than 200 German officers, including such later *Luftwaffe* luminaries as Albert Kesselring, Hugo Sperrle, and Hans Juergen Stumpff, were given aviation training at Lipetsk.

The German Air Line Pilot School, to which Adolf Galland had now won entry, became a part of the Black *Luftwaffe*. Creation of a cadre of excellent pilots, around whom the new air service could be built when open rearmament began, was a major goal of the shadow force. The rigid discipline at Braunschweig had little to do with flying an airliner. A crushing scholastic load and the demanding physical and practical training drew out of the young Galland the best that he could produce. Fear of failure was used to spur the students to maximum effort.

Instructors repeatedly told the students that anyone who did not measure up would be dismissed from the school and be bundled into the first train to his home town. Thousands were waiting to jump into any vacancy. The stern, military-style training was under the general supervision of a famous military aviator, retired Colonel Alfred Keller. His background for training airline pilots was flying bombers in World War I. Keller had taken part in London bombing raids and had won the coveted "Blue Max," the *Ordre pour le Mérite*. Keller and all others wore civilian clothes, but his war hero's aura shone right through them.

Galland had direct personal contact with Keller after a couple of incidents involving aircraft damage and the loss of a Klemm trainer. The young man from Westerholt broke the undercarriage of an Albatros L-101, and this caused him acute anxiety due to the tight discipline at the school. Visions of receiving the humiliating rail ticket back to Westerholt marched before his mind's eye. Shortly afterwards things became even tenser. He was leading a three-plane formation of Klemm trainers and the other two fledgling pilots collided. One got home and the other bailed out.

The ensuing investigation and fuss upset Galland mightily. Investigators attributed the collision to unordered formation changes. The inference was that Galland was to blame—or so it seemed to him at the time.

Fearing expulsion, he moved to cover himself by applying for officer-cadet training with the 18th Infantry Regiment at Paderborn. Passing the necessary entry examinations without missing any schooling at Braunschweig, he was further depressed when the Army people were pessimistic about an opening, and his application went into a pile of similar papers. Hundreds of applicants were available for every officer-cadet vacancy.

To his astonishment, loss of the Klemm trainer seemed to be gradually forgotten at Braunschweig. He had expected the incident to be held against him. Things had completely cooled down at flying school when the Army suddenly summoned him to officer-cadet training in the autumn of 1932. Taking the Army order to Colonel Keller, Galland explained his predicament to the bomber pilot who had become a school principal and asked his advice.

Keller made it clear that Galland's flying career was in no danger. Training young pilots necessarily meant some crashes and losses. Galland's school record was good, and the school would support and assist him. Seeking refuge in the Army was out of the question. Keller would not release him.

Galland now knew that he was going all the way as a pilot. Gone was the dark impression that his stay at Braunschweig was marginal. (He would encounter Alfred Keller many times in coming years—as *Generaloberst* Keller, an Air Fleet Commander in World War II, and also as Chief of the National Socialist Flying Corps, NSFK—but his first meeting with Keller was the most memorable one.) He withdrew his Army application immediately.

The school handled not only beginners but also part-time released Army officers who were taking courses on special aircraft. These were a more obvious element of the Black *Luftwaffe*. Friction arose between Galland's group of blue-clad but authentic civilians and the *Reichswehr* officers who acted as though they had never been discharged. The civilians stoutly resisted being ordered about.

Powered flight was the focus of Braunschweig activities. The school had a sailplane available but no soaring program, even though all the students had interest and experience in the national aeronautical sport. Galland used the school sailplane to keep his soaring skills sharp. Word had reached him that his old soaring mates were busy building an all-new sailplane.

His comrades christened the new sailplane "Keffer"—his own nickname. Galland was invited to make the maiden flight at the 1932 autumn soaring meet on the Borkenberge. Takeoff was a time of high excitement. Fashioned by the hands of his comrades and designed by Georg Ismer, their instructor, the new craft looked sleek and beautiful. Looks were deceiving. When they hauled the sailplane aloft manually with rubber catapult ropes and Galland slipped the tow, he was shocked to feel the tail drop as though there were a sandbag in the rear fuselage. There was nothing any pilot could have done to correct the imbalance at such a moment.

Spinning in rapidly, the craft landed heavily. Dizzy and bleeding from facial cuts, Galland was pulled from the wreckage in the first of his several crashes as a pilot. Cuts on his face spoiled his dark good looks for the time being, and he had suffered a mild concussion. Resting for only a few days, he went back into the air at the controls of his own "Imp," and took second prize. Then it was back to the grind at Braunschweig.

By Christmas of 1932, half of the elite 20 who had begun the course with Galland had been dropped by the school. By securing his B-1 pilot's certificate in the summer, he had acquired the necessary 150 hours for his B-2 certificate by New Year 1933. Aerobatic training at Schleissheim, near Munich, had revealed his talent and passion for the art of aerobatic flying. His piloting expertise now included looping, diving, spinning, rolling, and inverted flying.

After a 25-hour course in seaplane piloting, combined with instruction in naval procedures and terminology at Warnemuende, Galland and four comrades were told to report to the Central Air Line Pilot School in Berlin. Officials there "invited" them to take part in "a secret training course for military pilots." All five accepted. This meant flying fighter aircraft and learning the skills required to handle high-performance machines. He was part of the Black *Luftwaffe*.

Maintaining external pretenses, Galland and his comrades reported to Schleissheim in civilian clothes. Training was under Major Beyer, an Army officer who had received aviation training under the Lipetsk project in Russia. The Schleissheim course was a poorly organized mixture of lectures and flying training. Oral material concentrated on military affairs, Great War air tactics, and aviation history. Galland enjoyed 25 hours in Albatros and Heinkel biplanes, including mock aerial combat and formation flying. High point in the course for the marksman from Westerholt was firing with live ammunition at ground targets.

All this activity was strictly prohibited under the Versailles Treaty, but in Germany things were changing fast. While Adolf Galland had been developing his piloting skills, men who would bulk large in his life and career were busy shaping 20th-century history. Hermann Goering had developed high skills as a political manipulator. These skills, combined with his status as an ex-officer and highly decorated war hero, were used on Germany's aging President, Field Marshal von Hindenburg, inducing him to appoint Adolf Hitler as Chancellor.

Hitler's first coalition government promoted development of the Black *Luftwaffe*. Goering was now not only President of the *Reichstag,* a post he was entitled to legally and electorally, but also Prussian Minister of the Interior. Through this latter office, he controlled the police. Hitler also made him National Commissioner of Aviation, a euphemistic title for Germany's first Air Minister. Behind the facade of civil aviation, Goering immediately began strengthening the Black *Luftwaffe*.

Goering wisely secured at this time the services of Erhard Milch as Secretary of State at the Air Ministry. An observer flyer who had finished the Great War in command of a fighter squadron, Milch had taken over the organization and direction of Lufthansa in the early 1920s. Proving himself an outstanding organizer and administrator, Milch also had business acumen and vision. Lufthansa became one of the world's most progressive and innovative airlines, despite the aviation restrictions of the Versailles Treaty. Milch's achievements were accomplished despite numerous high-level intrigues against Lufthansa within Germany. He was both capable and tough.

While building Lufthansa, Milch hired Goering as a lobbyist when the latter was serving in the *Reichstag.* Milch knew all about the Black *Luftwaffe*. He had seen to it that military aspects of aviation had been woven subtly into the courses at the Germany Air Line Pilot School. Airliner design and procurement kept military needs in mind. Milch had been reluctant to work for Goering— his former hireling—but the mind of the Lufthansa boss was changed by a personal interview with Hitler.

As State Secretary, Milch now became a sort of operating head of the Black *Luftwaffe* and all its workings. (Adolf Galland, the pilot trainee at this time, would get to know Erhard Milch well during World War II, and he would also see more than he wished of both Goering and Hitler.) The rise of the Black *Luftwaffe* accelerated almost by the month, as Milch increased production of the Ju-52 and many types of training aircraft. More obviously, old Goering flying comrades from the Great War began surfacing in significant posts.

Already prominent in national aviation was Goering's war comrade Bruno Loerzer, with whom Goering had broken in as an aerial observer before becoming a pilot. Loerzer had long been head of the DLV, the national body that governed soaring. Goering would certainly put Loerzer in a high rank in the new *Luftwaffe*.

Ernst Udet, as Germany's most successful living ace, was appointed a consultant to the Air Ministry. He was told that big things were coming. Goering's former adjutant, Karl Bodenschatz, who had loyally served him in the Richthofen Circus, again became his liaison officer. Other famous pilots of the Goering era were already serving in various Black *Luftwaffe* posts.

The energy pouring into clandestine preparations was making itself strongly felt when Galland completed his Schleissheim course in May of 1933. He was ordered to attend a meeting of some 70 young pilots, called by Goering at the *Behrendstrasse* in Berlin. Galland and 11 others were civilians. The rest were Army officers and NCOs, summoned from branches of the German Air Line Pilot School and from various clandestine training facilities. Goering soon made clear that the purposes of the meeting were military.

Goering's title of National Commissioner of Aviation was as harmless as calling him Lord of the Isles. His secret orders from Hitler, however, portended much harm. Civil aviation was to be strongly developed, and he was ordered to create a new German Air Force. The job was to be done as quickly as possible.

Goering had a forceful speaking style. Combined with his fame as an ace and hero, and the plans he outlined, Goering's oratory left Galland and the other pilots with a positive impression. Goering was also a cultivated man, in contrast to some of the coarse Nazis around Hitler. In the context of May of 1933, therefore, Goering appeared to Galland as a man worth following.

Goering told them that the shackles of Versailles were about to be removed. Training German pilots in Russia would soon become politically impossible. Hitler's friendship with Mussolini had nevertheless made it feasible for the fortunate young men present to train as fighter pilots in Italy. The project was politically sensitive. Secrecy and tight camouflage were essential to preclude adverse international reaction.

Goering had made all necessary arrangements through his friend Marshal Balbo, head of the Italian Air Force and an old fighter pilot. Galland found all this translated into orders to rendezvous at Frankfurt-on-Main in civilian clothes. After three boring days of security lectures and other instructions, the pilots split into two groups. One was assigned to Udine in northern Italy, while Galland's unit was headed for Grotaglie in the south. They would train at an Italian Air Force base.

Crossing the frontier at Brenner as South Tirolean recruits, Galland's party detrained at Bari on the Adriatic coast. Italian civilians greeted them. Army motor transports were waiting, thinly disguised as civilian buses. After several miles, the convoy stopped at a remote olive grove and their Italian greeters piled out and went behind some trees. They reappeared in the elegant white uniforms of the Italian Air Force and clambered back aboard the buses with an air of superiority that did not sit well with the Germans.

Jolting onto the Grotaglie airfield, which dated from the Great War, Galland and his fellow students were herded into a barracks and actually locked up. Frayed and worn-out uniforms of Italian Air Force officer-candidates were issued to them, and they were placed under close surveillance, almost like prisoners. Following this came recruit-style barrack drill, as though they were raw newcomers to military and aviation life.

Goering's way of doing things, combined with the language barrier, had misled the Italians. They failed to realize at first that they had three dozen fully trained pilots on their hands, most of them German Army officers. These newcomers had expected to go to work immediately, flying modern fighters and shooting live ammunition. Galland's aerobatic skill helped clarify the situation.

An Italian pilot had just set a world record for inverted flight. His feat had been headlined in the press, and it was the subject of some Italian boasting around the air base. The new record stood at about an hour and a half. When Galland's turn came to take up the flimsy Breda biplane trainer, he put the aircraft upside down and flew back and forth for about 45 minutes.

The deflated Italians ordered him down, and they were peeved. Their world record had been endangered before their eyes. The visitor from Westerholt never tried for the inverted flight record, mainly because he deemed this kind of flying only slightly less pointless than flagpole-sitting. His little exhibition nevertheless convinced the Italians that they had excellent pilot talent among their visitors.

The entire Grotaglie scene now improved. For hunter Galland, using machine guns was an exciting new dimension to marksmanship. For the entrenched Italians below, who were holding the strings of target balloons for the zooming pilots, things were also exciting—but in a different way. There was too much metal whizzing through the air for comfort.

Despite the enjoyable flying and shooting, Grotaglie began to drag after a couple of weeks. Social life was nonexistent. There were no girls for the secret visitors. Galland was glad to return to Germany in the autumn of 1933, his Italian experience of minimal value, either to him as a pilot or to the building of German air power.

Back in school at Braunschweig, he learned instrument flying and the special techniques of piloting required in handling heavy transport aircraft. After 50 additional hours of training, he passed his final examination and became a qualified airline pilot. (Assigned as voluntary second pilot on Lufthansa's Stuttgart–Geneva–Marseilles–Barcelona route, he began his long love affair with the Spanish way of living.)

Twice a week, he would fly a Rohrbach-Roland or a Junkers G-24 over the route that terminated in Barcelona. Layovers in the Spanish city were balmy idyllic interludes, but Galland's career as an airline pilot was itself little more than an interlude. Hermann Goering was galvanizing German aviation, and, in January of 1934, Galland was again ordered to a Berlin meeting, this time at the HQ of the German Air Line Pilot School.

The civil pilots who had trained in Italy were present. They were asked if they would like to go on the active list of the new German Air Force. Galland wavered inwardly when he thought about giving up his hard-won civilian job. The days of drinking and loving in Barcelona would have to be sacrificed. Going on the active list also meant a period of recruit training, with its monotonous "square bashing" drills and loss of personal freedom.

By the time recruit training was over, Galland reasoned, and had been followed by a War Academy course, Goering's new *Luftwaffe* would be out in the open. He would be on the ground floor. Weighing the chances for promotion in a new and expanding *Luftwaffe* against the relative stagnation of civil aviation, he decided to volunteer. The senoritas would have to wait.

When Galland reported to the 10th Infantry Regiment at Dresden in February of 1934, he at 21 was the youngest man in his group. His pilot comrades included Army veterans in their late 30s, ex-Lufthansa pilots, flying club pilots, instructors, and weather research flyers. Three months of basic infantry training instilled in them the importance of following orders and gave basic orientation to military life.

Promotion to officer-cadet (*Fahnenjunker*) marked completion of the infantry course. The subsequent War Academy course showed the basic conservatism of the German Army towards aviation. Air power as a potentially dominant tactical and strategic instrument was not contemplated. An Air Force as an independent and equal service arm was not discussed. The presumption throughout was that aviation would remain under the Army.

Goering was busy changing all this even as Galland was taking the Dresden course, from which he emerged on 1 October 1934 with a commission as a lieutenant. He was also immediately discharged from the Army. In the waning days of the Black *Luftwaffe,* he found himself reincorporated into civil aviation. In uniforms that foreshadowed the coming new force, they wore birds on their lapels as badges of rank. He became *Kettenfuehrer* Galland.

The Schleissheim branch of the German Air Line Pilot School was now being transmuted into the new *Luftwaffe*'s first fighter pilot school. Still under camouflage, the facilities along with the courses became steadily more militarized. The Black *Luftwaffe* was being phased out. A need rapidly developed for instructors—many instructors—to train the hundreds of new pilots and mechanics who would man the coming fighter squadrons.

Realizing that his present course at Schleissheim was not just a modernization course but a means of selecting new fighter pilot instructors, Galland subtly fumbled every exercise or test. This made him appear unsuitable for instructor duty, a groove in which he had no intention of getting stuck. His superiors passed him over. Assignment to a fighter unit within a short time was certain.

Goering came in February of 1935 to inspect the personnel and facilities at Schleissheim. At a subsequent meeting in the officers mess at Mittenheim Castle, Goering outlined the plans and preparations of the past two years for the new *Luftwaffe*. Included was Goering's design for the new blue pilot's uniform, modeled for those who would shortly wear it by Rittmeister Bolle—late of the Richthofen Circus and a *pour le Mérite* winner.

Goering told the eager pilots that all pretense would soon be dropped. The real *Luftwaffe* was about to be born. One month later, in March of 1935, the world public was shocked to learn that Germany's new *Luftwaffe* was an accomplished fact and not a paper proposal. Much was made of this in newspapers outside Germany, with emphasis on the clandestine preparations, as though it was somehow dirty of the Germans to do such things in secret.

The Black *Luftwaffe* had never been either a mystery or a secret to the intelligence services of the nations most concerned. No responsible leader in France, Britain, or Russia could honestly say that the *Luftwaffe* was a surprise. French intelligence had for years assembled a catalog of Versailles Treaty violations by Germany. The Russians had been hosts for over six years to German airmen training at Lipetsk.

Hitler had received, in February of 1934, a personal visit from F. W. Winterbotham (the remarkable British spy who later managed the distribution of *Ultra* intelligence throughout World War II). Hitler told the German-speaking Winterbotham almost casually in their conversation that the Versailles Treaty was dead. The *Fuehrer* added that his new Air Force was growing rapidly. He expected that, by the end of 1934 or early 1935, the *Luftwaffe* would have 500 operational aircraft. Winterbotham duly passed all this information along to the British authorities.[*]

All these political factors and machinations were well beyond the ken of Lt. Adolf Galland in April of 1935. He had achieved his immediate goal—assignment to a fighter squadron. Posted to the first official new *Geschwader* in the *Luftwaffe*, JG-2 *Richthofen,* he was a proud member of that formation's I *Gruppe.* HQ was at Döberitz, near Berlin, and Galland found it heady stuff after all his toil.

Hitler and Goering and all the rest of the things going on in Germany were even less important to him when he was reposted to the newly formed II/JG-2 as a foundation member. The unit was established at Jüterbog-Damm, and Galland was assigned as training officer—an honor for a pilot just out of school. The *Luftwaffe* was providing the opportunities for which he had hoped.

Flying the red-nosed He-51B-1 fighters, with their salty link to the Red Baron, was like riding in the stratosphere. The latest fighter type in the *Luftwaffe,* the Heinkel biplanes had a top speed of over 200 mph. Able now to indulge his personal passion for flying, thrilling to the joy of a powerful machine aloft, Adolf Galland thought about little else in 1935 but his own good fortune. Only a handful of young men in all the world could revel in the thrills—and spills— of flying.

---

[*] See *The Nazi Connection,* by Group Captain F. W. Winterbotham, CBE, pp. 50–53. Published by Harper & Row, N.Y., 1978.

CHAPTER THREE

Aerobatic flying was encouraged at Jüterbog-Damm. Assigned to specialize in aerobatics, and to train himself for appearances at air shows, Galland turned all his talent and energy to becoming an expert. Ernst Udet was at this time considered the greatest aerobatic pilot in Germany, and Galland modeled himself after the famous fighter ace.

"Aerobatics gave me great satisfaction," he recalled of this period. "After my earlier success in soaring, I realized for the second time in my flying career that I was better than most of the others."

His urge to be number one, combined with a natural talent for aerobatics, soon produced results. He became the kind of flyer that his fellow fighter pilots would gather to watch, dropping whatever they were doing to observe his spellbinding skills. He became a pilot's pilot, yet still he reached for more.

He modified the carburetor of the Focke-Wulf *Stieglitz* (FW-44) biplane that he flew aerobatically. His aim was inverted flight without fuel starvation. Seeking a further performance gain, he modified the horizontal stabilizer for more negative maneuverability—to help keep the tail down and the nose up in inverted flights. This modification was strictly against regulations and changed the spin conditions of the FW-44, but Galland did not know how much.

On a radiant October day in 1935, he took the modified aircraft up near noon for a tryout. Giving himself an extra margin of altitude, he took the little bird to 2,500 feet and put it through a sequence of maneuvers he had accomplished many times previously without incident. He intended to make three turns of a spin and pull out handily. This time his illegally modified horizontal stabilizer had significantly changed the spin characteristics.

Spinning quickly, the kite lost altitude far more rapidly than before modification. Galland had the aircraft under control as he came out of the third turn, but his sink rate was extremely high. There wasn't sufficient altitude left for him to complete recovery to level flight. Knowing exactly what had happened, yet unable to do a thing about it, he sat transfixed—awaiting the imminent, unavoidable crash.

Watching his display from the terrace of the officers' mess, horrified squadron mates groaned as the biplane went hurtling into the ground at nearly a 45-degree angle, breaking to bits in a shower of dust and turf. Impact and unconsciousness were for Galland mercifully merged. Jumping off the terrace and hurdling a fence, the shocked officers went sprinting to the crash, certain that their comrade could not have survived.

A ghastly sight awaited when they pulled aside the wreckage. The pilot's seat had separated from the fuselage upon impact, slamming Galland's head into the instrument panel and leaving his face a bloody mask. Gently they pulled him clear and stretched him out on the grass. Medical personnel took over. Sadness settled over the officers' mess that night, as the young pilot hung between life and death.

For three days and nights he lay in a coma. Summoned from Westerholt in the emergency, his parents maintained a round-the-clock vigil at his bedside. When he finally surfaced through the darkness, Galland heard his mother's voice, soothing, consoling, and encouraging him. He recognized the touch of her hand holding his, and he heard the reassuring voice of his father. Slowly it dawned on him that he had survived, and that his head was totally swathed in bandages. He was alive, but only just.

Galland was under a lucky star. The finest German surgeon of that time, Professor Dr. Sauerbruch of Berlin, happened to be at the Jüterbog hospital on military duties, together with another Berlin specialist. Their skills and devoted labor were largely responsible for his survival. He had suffered multiple skull fractures of a critical kind. Three months were needed for his injuries to heal.

Galland's face was permanently altered. His nose had flattened and broadened when it was broken and never regained its shape. He had been a handsome young man before this crash, as contemporary photographs show. As the British put it in a preface to one of their interrogation reports after World War II, "He is not entirely a pleasant looking man." The *Stieglitz* crash of 1935 gave the world the Galland face it knows.

Serious for a pilot was the damage to his left eye. Severe cuts and glass splinters in the cornea drastically weakened this organ. His final hospital discharge report certified him as "Physically unfit for flying duty." As a pilot, he was finished—according to the doctors.

The C.O. of II/JG-2 was Major Rheitel, a pilot from the Great War who had also trained at Lipetsk. He understood another pilot's problem. Galland was a gifted young airman of rich potential who had been in a crash. His abilities would be lost to the *Luftwaffe* if the doctors had their way.

Focke-Wulf FW44 "Stieglitz." This was the primary trainer of the Luftwaffe in the mid-'30s. Galland wrecked this aircraft and his own profile in an aerobatic crash.

In 1933, Galland flew this Albatros L-75 "AS" to East Prussia. His brother Fritz, a student at Königsberg, stands at the extreme left.

Rheitel was one of the good old eagles from an earlier era who were not overawed by regulations. He conveniently shunted Galland's medical grounding report under other papers and then claimed he could not remember seeing the report. "In the meantime, Lieutenant Galland," he said, "try to return to your normal flying duties until your medical report turns up."

At Jüterbog-Damm two technical eras came together when Galland got his first look at the new Me-109. A developmental prototype of Professor Messerschmitt's widely heralded new baby landed at Damm en route from the Augsburg factory to the Rechlin Test Center. The Me-109 was an all-metal low-wing monoplane with an enclosed cockpit. This was the new aerial epoch.

Milling around the new aircraft were curious pilots of two generations. In addition to Major Rheitel, all three squadron leaders in II/JG-2 were Great War veterans: von Schoenebeck, Osterkamp, and von Kornatzki. The first two had been combat pilots, and Theo Osterkamp had been a famous ace with 34 aerial victories and the Blue Max. These men carried enormous prestige because of their war experience, but they were highly suspicious of the Me-109's enclosed cockpit. Arguments arose about the high wing loading of the Me-109, which meant that it was not ideal for a turning dogfight.

Although he would later fly the Me-109 to glory and immortality, Adolf Galland was not too impressed by his first look at this historic aircraft. He would look back at age 70 and admit frankly that, at the time, he was not able to recognize the extent of the technical progress embodied in the Me-109. He could not then discern its virtues, despite an aeronautical background that already covered ten years.

The Me-109 test pilot was not permitted to demonstrate this developmental model. None of the II/JG-2 pilots was allowed to fly the machine. Similarly prohibited were comparison test flights against the He-51 biplane. Evaluations of the new bird, therefore, remained theoretical to Galland and his comrades.

His medical grounding report remained concealed for nearly a year. A disastrous test flight in an Arado-68 changed everything. With a misfiring engine, Galland swung around 180 degrees for a quick downwind landing directly into the setting sun. Tall light masts at one end of the Bernburg airfield marked a row of fruit trees between the end of the runway and a nearby parallel street. Galland failed to clear one of the masts.

His left wing slammed into the light post and was shorn off. Slewing down in what was left of the Ar-68, he crashed thunderously. Cutting his head and face yet again, splintering his shin, and bruising himself all over, he was carted off to the hospital. Doctors pulling his personnel file were aghast to find—from almost a year previously—his medical grounding report.

This time, the medical authorities intended to make his grounding order stick. His latest crash proved that he was a menace to other pilots, aircraft, and himself, according to the doctors. He was to be grounded permanently, and there was talk of a court martial for Major Rheitel for allowing a half-blind man to fly.

Galland took the offensive against this medical attack. Exemplifying his own later credo that a fighter pilot who does not at all times attack loses the initiative, he put on an energetic campaign to survive as a pilot. He lobbied and politicked with superior officers and comrades who visited him in hospital, seeking their assistance and support. Insisting from the outset of this campaign that his left eye vision was normal, he never stopped repeating this lie.

Prevailing upon a medical orderly to obtain for him the sequence of lines, letters, and numbers on the military eye chart, he lay for days in his hospital bed commiting the chart to memory. Every line and every possible sequence of letters and numbers was so burned into his memory that he could run them back and forth like a movie film. His doctors meanwhile scheduled him for a complete physical at the town of Magdeburg, where nothing would be overlooked.

His general physical condition was satisfactory, but the medics at Magdeburg had his personnel file and they quickly zeroed in on his damaged left eye. They found the glass splinters in the cornea and other indications of damage. He was asked to read the standard eye chart with his right eye covered. He could see the chart but the letters were blurred. Seeming to perceive them clearly, Galland began reciting them from memory.

As the dark-haired young pilot reeled off the numbers and letters with precision, the doctors stood gaping. On down the chart he went, reaching the final row without a single error. An incredulous examiner swallowed hard.

"Read the letters again, please. This time from the bottom row to the top, and *backwards,* please."

Out of Galland's mouth came the sequences. Making a slight pause here and there for effect, he made it sound as natural as possible. Even the doctors themselves could hardly boast of such eagle vision. They certified him fit for flying duty. (He would enter the eighth decade of his life with the glass splinters still in his left eye, but by then he had hundreds of combat missions behind him.) His return to the pilot roster of II/JG-2 was duly celebrated.

The period between Galland's two crashes with JG-2 was a time of signal international events in Europe. Hitler overrode the advice of his Army generals in 1936 and German troops reoccupied the demilitarized Rhineland. France and Britain enjoyed a marked superiority in every military category at this time. Only one *Gruppe* in JG-2, out of all the new *Luftwaffe* fighter formations, was thus far equipped with machine guns and ammunition. (When the Allies backed down before Hitler's bluff, the *Fuehrer* gained a psychological edge over his highest generals that was to set the pattern of the years immediately ahead.) In July of 1936, the Spanish Civil War broke out and further darkened the European scene. (The political background to the Spanish conflict remains to this day one of the most complex and thorny sequences in modern European history. Contemporary political biases, furthermore, make it even more difficult to view the Spanish Civil War dispassionately and objectively.)

The final general election of the Second Spanish Republic was held in February of 1936. Socialists of all shadings united with anarchists, separatists, syndicalists, and the Communists to form the so-called Popular Front against a coalition of Rightist parties and factions. With a large majority of the seats in the Spanish parliament, but an extremely narrow margin in the total vote, the Popular Front nominally had complete control of parliament.

Street violence, massive property damage, and political murders erupted almost as soon as the votes had been counted. (The extreme Rightist Falangists and the extreme Left Communists are generally credited with the main responsibility for the violence.) By the time this savage scene degenerated into civil war, more than 250 political murders had been committed, in a country riven by factionalism in mind-boggling complexity.

General Francisco Franco finally emerged as the strongest personality on the Right after the civil war broke out, and he became the rallying point for the Nationalist or Rebel forces. Franco sent a three-man delegation to appeal directly to Hitler on 26 July 1936, and the *Fuehrer* received them personally at Bayreuth. He agreed to their immediate request for air transport.

That same evening, Special Staff W was established in Berlin to manage and expand the aid program in secret. Soviet aid to the Spanish Left on a large scale was also secretly going forward. The British, German, Italian, and Soviet governments nominally all subscribed to a French proposal that other powers maintain a policy of strict nonintervention in Spain.

Air power was the cutting edge of German aid. In history's first major military airlift, German-flown Ju-52s ferried 2,500 Moroccan soldiers from North Africa to Spain early in August 1936. The sudden appearance of these troops at the front, and their professional capabilities, probably saved the Nationalists from defeat. Further aerial participation in the war was also being organized in Germany, in a project under General Wilberg.

An impenetrable factionalist tangle to most people even today, the details of the Spanish civil war were certainly incomprehensible to Adolf Galland in 1936. He was 24 years old and had grown up without any interest in politics. The idealism that permeated the soaring sport had touched him, and National Socialism had seemed like its political expression. His passion nevertheless was planes and piloting, not politics.

Galland had pursued his passion in difficult times for aviation. Conditions had required him to be single-minded, and so politics had no soil within him in which to take root. This was true of his own country, and it was certainly true of his attitude towards the Spanish civil war.

When Galland's flying comrades in late 1936 began here and there to disappear suddenly from squadron life, as though swallowed into black holes, rumors soon abounded that they had gone to Spain as volunteers. Fighting in Spain against Communist takeover provided the conditions for military adventure. When some of these pilots reappeared six or eight months later, with sun-tanned faces and large rolls of money, the existence of the Condor Legion was no longer secret. Everyone wanted to volunteer. Adventure beckoned with the chance to test themselves in real combat.

Galland knew Spain well enough from his Lufthansa days to want to return. The experience and the high pay that went with such service were added incentives. He also wanted to get to grips with the realities of aerial warfare after so much training, theory, and mock combat. He appeared at Special Staff W in Berlin, where Condor Legion volunteers were processed.

Civilian clothes, credentials, and money were provided, and Galland joined a "Strength through Joy" tourist group of the Union Travel Society. This "excursion" group of 370 young Germans was ostensibly bound for Genoa. Embarkation was at Hamburg, where they boarded a battered 3,000-ton tramp steamer flying the flag of Panama.

Romantic ideas about tramp ship voyaging were soon dispelled by the overpowering stench aboard the vessel. Franco's navy had captured the wreck when she was running guns to the Loyalists. There had been only minimal conversion for carrying troops. Makeshift bunks had been hammered together out of old dunnage and roughly secured in the holds and tweendecks. *Luftwaffe* men accustomed to decent living conditions at their new bases in Germany found the ship a devastating blow to their pride.

As the senior officer present in terms of service, Galland was assigned by the ship's master, Captain van Ehren, to take command of the troops on board. The crude accommodation and facilities, heavy seas, and confinement below decks in stale air created disciplinary problems. Civilian clothes contributed to disciplinary breakdown. Galland ordered officers and NCOs to wear colored armbands.

Weather and engine trouble extended the voyage from 7 to 12 days. Short rations and then exhaustion of the water supply brought the volunteers to the brink of mutiny. Violent characters had to be tied to the mast in some cases until they cooled down. This reality was a far cry from the propagandist version of the Condor Legion's arrival in Spain. When the ship wallowed into El Ferrol on 7 May 1937, Galland gladly laid down his first command assignment with the Legion. Life ashore in Spain just had to be an improvement.

Condor Legion personnel were issued distinctive olive-brown uniforms similar in design to those of the National Socialist Labor Service. Fur boots were a feature of this new garb. German officers were promoted to the next grade above their *Luftwaffe* rank, so Galland wore the three stars of a captain. Placed in command of the Staff Company of the Condor Legion's Fighter Group in Avila, Galland found himself flying less than if he had stayed in Germany. So much for the life of adventure that he had visualized in Spain.

The Condor Legion, in primitive conditions in Spain, and Galland in particular, helped develop modern techniques of tactical air power. Painter Charles G. Hodgson of Newhall, California, realistically depicts an attack on Nationalalist ground troops by an He 51 of Galland's unit.

Mickey Mouse in Spain. Galland's He 51 sported this squadron insignia during the Spanish Civil War. It was the logo of 3/J88.

Dive bombers in Spain. Heinkel 51 (He 51) of 3/J88 on the flight line during the Spanish Civil War.

CHAPTER FOUR

Soon acquiring the nickname of "Capitano" among his brother officers, Captain Galland was in charge of maintenance and repair for the Condor Legion's three fighter squadrons. A fourth squadron was to be added early in 1938. His responsibilities included assembly and testing of new aircraft from Germany, repair and testing of combat-damaged aircraft, major overhauls, vehicle maintenance, repair and improvement of ground support equipment, and provision of spare parts and tools to the squadrons. He had essential and time-consuming tasks, but they were unexciting.

The Staff Company was quartered in an ancient monastery, with Galland and his staff living in a small nearby hotel. In due course he discovered the Parador de Gredos, a stylish hotel some 60 kilometres distant in the Gredos mountains. The Parador became a beloved retreat for Galland and other pilots. He hunted ibex and partridge and went horseback riding. In the evenings he lazed with his comrades around the open fireplace. They drank red wine with young Spanish girls, who sang folksongs happily for their German companions. Relations with the Spanish villagers and the Spanish military were warm and affectionate and deepened Galland's enchantment with the Spanish way of life.

The Condor Legion was a relatively small force. Flying units consisted eventually of four bomber squadrons, four fighter squadrons, and a strengthened reconnaissance squadron. Four heavy and two light anti-aircraft batteries, signals units, and miscellaneous support detachments completed a force that never exceeded 5,600 men. Communist propaganda nevertheless tried to convince the world that half the *Luftwaffe* was in Spain. By the time Galland arrived on the scene, the Legion had proved itself highly effective, and its command had significant influence on military decisions.

As the first C.O. of the Legion, Lt. General Hugo Sperrle set the tone for the unit. He celebrated his own arrival in Spain in dramatic fashion. On 15 November 1936, he personally led three squadrons of Ju-52s in a massive strike against Loyalist ships and port installations in Cartagena. Leadership of this forceful style impressed Franco's generals profoundly. Sound cooperation ensued between the Legion command and the Nationalist leaders. The Germans were called upon like a fire brigade when Franco's forces ran into difficulties.

An emergency situation gave Adolf Galland his first taste of combat. Both formally and informally he had applied for transfer to a fighter squadron, but the Legion command had taken no action. He organized his maintenance and administrative duties so well that he was occasionally able to fly on operations. When the Battle of Brunete was joined in July of 1937, the Condor Legion had a critical task and every available pilot was needed for combat.

The Loyalists under General Miaja timed their Madrid offensive well, because Franco's main strength and virtually all his air power were absorbed in northern Spain, at Bilbao, in preparation for an attack on Santander. Miaja's goal was to free Madrid from the besieging Nationalist forces, which would have been a psychological if not a strategic catastrophe for Franco's armies.

The Red thrust resulted in a breakthrough past Brunete to a point near Navalcarno, shattering the Nationalist Front. The gap in the Nationalist line continued to widen. Alarmed at this sudden reverse, Franco halted his northern offensive and ordered his able Navarre brigades to the Madrid Front immediately.

The Condor Legion was ordered to redress the aerial balance on the Madrid Front, in the fire brigade style to which the Germans had become accustomed. The Reds enjoyed solid air superiority in the Madrid area, due to the presence there of about 60 modern fighters—mostly Russian Rata and American Curtiss types. These aircraft were actively harassing Nationalist troops in the breakthrough area when the Condor Legion arrived, including the eager Galland temporarily assigned to flying duties.

The Loyalists had moved numerous anti-aircraft guns into the breach in the Nationalist line. These weapons were ready to chop up the slow-moving Ju-52 transports that were assigned to bomb Loyalist troops in the breach. The Condor Legion's 3J-88 Squadron, under Captain Harro Harder, was to silence these guns so the Ju-52s could bomb without prohibitive losses.

Flying with Harder's squadron, Captain Galland got his so-called baptism of fire in one of the most intense and stubbornly fought air battles of the Spanish conflict. Their He-51 biplanes were no match for the Rata and Curtiss fighters of the Reds, but they were highly effective against small ground targets like flak batteries. Such close-support attacks, combined with Ju-52 bombing strikes, halted the Loyalist attack on 12 July 1937.

The way for Franco's counterattack was open. The struggle continued as Franco sought to evict the Loyalists from the breach and reestablish his lines. In the ensuing two weeks, Franco's counterattacks were repulsed, and every He-51 in Harder's squadron was pocked with bullet holes. Galland knew the hair-raising experience of flying through hails of bullets that punched into his biplane.

On 25 July 1937, the Condor Legion again struck strongly against the Loyalist forces, targeting on reserve units grouped in narrow valleys near Brunete, ready to enter the battle on Loyalist call. Galland was in the thick of repeated attacks driven home against the brave and stubborn Loyalist troops. All available artillery was simultaneously directed on the same targets, including the 88mm flak guns of the Condor Legion.

The Loyalists collapsed. Abandoning their positions, they retreated—a rabble. The He-51s strafed the retreating troops and frustrated their efforts to dig in and form a new front. The Loyalists suffered 30,000 casualties and Madrid was again besieged by Franco. The Condor Legion was decisive in the Battle of Brunete (in which it has been said that Franco actually won the civil war without being aware of his victory).

Numerous missions in the Brunete struggle had provided Adolf Galland with an intense and indelible first taste of combat. A return to maintenance and repair duties commanding the Staff Company was now out of the question. The young captain's outstanding flying skill had shown vividly in the close-support strikes, and his further urgent request for transfer to a fighter squadron was approved. He was given command of the Condor Legion's 3rd Fighter Squadron.

He took over command from Captain Douglas Pitcairn, one of the officers who had witnessed his near-fatal aerobatic crash at Jüterbog-Damm. When Pitcairn had helped pull Galland from the wreckage of the *Stieglitz*, he never expected him to survive, let alone emerge as a combat leader in Spain. (The two men would remain friends right through into the 1990s.)

Galland's new unit was the "Mickey Mouse" squadron. Their aircraft had the pistol-waving Disney caricature painted on the fuselage. (Galland continued painting this insignia on all his personal aircraft in World War II and believes that it brought him luck.) His fighter squadron was now the only one in Spain still equipped with He-51 biplanes. The long-awaited Me-109 had come on the Spanish scene, but the new era had thus far reached only the other two squadrons.

Captain Joachim Schlichting and Captain Guenther Luetzow were the fortunate commanders of the two Me-109 squadrons. They were soon cleaning up the skies with their new machines, which were superior to all Loyalist fighters.

Both officers became fighter aces in Spain, with five aerial victories apiece, and both would also later fight in the Battle of Britain. Galland formed a friendship with "Franzl" Luetzow that was to endure until 1945. Luetzow was killed flying the Me-262 jet in Galland's elite JV-44, less than two weeks before the end of World War II. Luetzow had a lifetime score of 108 aerial victories.

Galland's admiration for the tall, haughty-looking Luetzow was never to dim from its beginning in Spain. Both were dedicated to their profession with the utmost seriousness. Both nevertheless had a fine sense of humor. This attribute prevented them from losing their humanity amid the often inhuman challenges of the war that was to come. Galland came to regard Luetzow as the finest leader in the *Luftwaffe*.

During the Spanish adventure, Galland found it a little frustrating that his friend Luetzow in an Me-109 was winning air-to-air combats, while he flew close-support missions in a biplane. The Mickey Mouse squadron was due to get Me-109s, too, but the aircraft never seemed to arrive from Germany. Galland had no option but to fly his No. 78 biplane through hails of lead and explosive from ground fire, while the Me-109s went hunting for enemy aircraft. A hunter, Galland was sure that he would be able to find his quarry aloft.

The Me-109B and the Me-109D, the latter a longer-range variant that came to Spain in due course, were more than a match for any Loyalist aircraft. They quickly dominated the aerial scene.

An invaluable lesson was thereby provided the *Luftwaffe* on the importance of technical superiority in tipping the balance of air power. Two squadrons of Me-109s shifted the balance in Spain. Galland absorbed this lesson, never forgot it, and in later years would fight for technical advances against officers and leaders who either failed to learn the lessons of Spain or forgot those lessons for political reasons.

In the overall development of Adolf Galland as an air force officer, he benefited immensely from his close-support operations in the He-51. He probably learned more in Spain this way than he would have flying the Me-109, which he later rapidly mastered in World War II. The He-51 by contrast, was an obsolete machine unable to contend with Loyalist fighters and thereby restricted to close-support operations. Many significant lessons were thus learned about tactical air power, and Galland's analytical talents and experience allowed him to make substantial contributions in this area.

While the Condor Legion was effective in Spain, the propagandist idea that they went there already knowing what to do and how to do it is completely erroneous. The Spanish civil war has often been described as a "curtain raiser" for World War II, but in the history of air power it is more accurate to say that the conflict was a *transition* from World War I to World War II. Galland's experiences provide an illustration.

When their slow biplanes were occasionally intercepted by Rata and Curtiss fighters, the Germans would form a Lufbery Circle in the pattern of World War I. Each He-51 would protect the tail of the He-51 immediately ahead. In this protective circle, the slower biplanes would gradually work their way back to their own territory. There was no radio communication between the aircraft in Galland's Mickey Mouse squadron. Visual signals were the means of control and command in the air. In these and other respects, World War I was repeated, but the new epoch loomed in the way the Germans learned to use tactical air power in close support.

The Ju-52 and He-111 bombers used by the Condor Legion were both unsuited to such pinpoint tasks as eliminating enemy artillery, mortar, or flak positions, or for attacking troop columns—especially in the absence of accurate bomb sights.

The sluggish Ju-52 was vulnerable as well as ineffective on such operations. The He-51s, by contrast, could punish such targets accurately at low level with machine guns and bombs and yet were fast enough to avoid too heavy an attrition from ground fire.

Adolf Galland as a boy had always been interested in finding out how things worked. Examining cause and effect in electricity, gasoline engines, rockets, sailplanes, and motorcycles had developed his analytical abilities. These talents were turned in Spain to developing the new era of close-support flying. The Great War had provided a slender tactical legacy, because of the static nature of that conflict. Unimaginative generalship and the butchery of millions of men in the mud had been a poor scenario in which to comprehend the tactical importance of air power.

Spain was a vastly different military milieu. Ground warfare was much more mobile and open. Air power came into its own as a new military dimension that could control and dominate the ground—provided that correct tactics applied air power effectively. Modern tactical air power had its birth in Spain, and Adolf Galland was one of the attending physicians.

Flying in his battered No. 78, often wearing only swimming trunks in the hot weather, he flew more than 300 missions as a squadron leader. Quickly he saw the crucial importance of coordinating his strikes in time space with the ground forces he was assisting. Lack of radio communication, both air to air and air to ground, heightened the need to know the exact time and place to put in a strike. A target bombed and strafed could be rapidly overrun and captured with minimum losses if the ground forces moved in immediately. If stunned enemy troops were allowed to recover, or given time to bring up reinforcements, the air strikes were wasted.

A pilot hurtling through the air at around 200 mph, with bullets perforating his aircraft, had little chance of telling friend from foe on the terrain below. Marking of the most advanced lines and troops with colored cloths, therefore, became a fundamental principle. Marking the direction of strongest enemy resistance became another basic stratagem. As techniques of timing and control improved, the tactical value of the aging He-51s increased. Their power was being focused instead of scattered.

Galland encouraged his pilots and ground crews to suggest and try out innovations that would make their aircraft more effective. His squadron was a smooth-running unit with high morale and strong spirit. Everyone seemed infected by and committed to their young C.O.'s continuing drive for excellence. (His mechanics devised a fire bomb that was a precursor of the napalm weapons that appeared in World War II.)

Filling a 25-gallon drop tank with a mixture of old crankcase oil and aviation fuel, his mechanics then attached a fragmentation incendiary bomb. When dropped from an He-51, the flammable mixture spread widely, ignited by the incendiary bomb. (While the results did not compare with those later obtained from napalm, in Spain they contributed to the air power that helped Franco decisively.) Galland wrote numerous reports on his tactical experience, innovations, and findings, sending them through official channels to Berlin.

He would live to regret this diligent reporting. The *Luftwaffe* was now fully committed in its doctrine and constitution to being an essentially tactical air force. (Galland's reports from Spain were like a running commentary on the actual development of modern tactical air power. They fell into eager hands at the Air Ministry in Berlin. His expertise and experience in close support were almost to cost him his career as a fighter pilot.)

Mobility is essential to modern military success. Galland made his squadron the most mobile air unit in Spain. The former sailplane pilot was appalled by the amount of labor expended in their frequent shifts from one operating base to another. The accompanying administrative turmoil reduced efficiency. The Spanish war was fluid, compared with the 1914-1918 slogging matches. Galland conceived the idea of putting his entire squadron aboard a train, complete with sleeping quarters, offices, kitchen, repair facilities, and recreational space. His squadron could then move itself rapidly on rails.

Galland acquired the necessary coaches through the Nationalist army. Franco's officers and troops were fond of the airmen who protected them and were glad to provide the rolling stock. In the spirit of No. 3 Squadron, everybody waded into the task of conversion. In a few days the needed modifications were completed, and thereafter the squadron rolled from base to base behind a locomotive. The aircraft flew to each new base, and, in a matter of hours, complete ground facilities and personnel were available.

This lesson learned in Spain was later applied in World War II on the Eastern Front. The *Luftwaffe* had only one night fighter *Geschwader,* NJG-6, available in that vast war theater. As with Galland's pioneering effort in Spain, NJG-6 assigned one squadron to each train. The resultant mobility multiplied the effectiveness of NJG-6 by rapid movement of its squadrons to sectors where they were needed. The units were able to go into action immediately, with complete administrative and command continuity.

The volunteer beginning of the Condor Legion was soon replaced by a more systematic rotation of personnel. New arrivals were still volunteers, but tours of duty were limited. Berlin wished to give combat experience to as many future *Luftwaffe* leaders as possible. When Galland's time was up, a replacement arrived whom he knew would not work well with the efficient squadron he had shaped. The officer was sent back to Germany.

A second replacement was assigned. This time Berlin sent an elderly pilot that Galland promptly disqualified. Before this officer could be returned to Germany, he collided in mid-air with one of Galland's best pilots, killing both of them. Busy preparing for the Sudetenland challenge, the *Luftwaffe* High Command urgently needed its experienced leaders from Spain. Galland's return was overdue. The Condor Legion command received a curt teletype from Berlin: Galland's relief was on the way. This replacement was the best man they had. Galland was expected to accept him and hand over the command promptly.

A lull in hostilities shortly afterwards allowed Galland some days of relaxation in Seville. He shared this interlude with his C.O., Gotthard Handrick, his friend, Eduard Neumann, and some other Condor Legion comrades. They were enjoying some glasses of wine in the bar of the Hotel Christina when a slender, dark-haired young man approached and asked to speak to the C.O. and also "to the squadron commander, Adolf Galland."

There was something steely and serious about this man. He introduced himself as 1st Lieutenant Werner Moelders, the new commander of Galland's No. 3 Squadron. Galland felt himself stiffen. A sudden current of resentment rose within him, which he immediately had to suppress. Galland was attached to his squadron and concerned for their welfare. He felt himself challenged—as a man dedicated to being number one—by Berlin having rated this man Moelders so highly. Could this newcomer handle the important task of squadron command in this foreign land, with all its complexities? Galland was not happy when he shook the hand of Werner Moelders for the first time.

In the ensuing days, Moelders showed all the qualities of leadership and flying skill that made him one of Germany's air heroes. Their instructional flights together quickly convinced Galland that his squadron and his men would be in the best hands. With Moelders came the long-awaited Me-109s. The old He-51s became No. 4 Squadron, led by Captain Eberhard d'Elsa (and carried on their tactical tasks until the end of the war). Moelders in the Me-109 soon started downing Loyalist aircraft.

By the end of the war Moelders had 15 victories—the top score of the Condor Legion. His tactical innovations with the Me-109 laid the basis for the wide-open "finger four" fighter formation, with much separation in altitude. This formation was adopted eventually by both the RAF and the USAAF.

The fighters flew in two elements (*Rotten*) of two aircraft each. All four made up a *Schwarm*. The combat flexibility and mutual protection provided by this formation were a tactical quantum jump that lasted until the jet age. Moelders was unsurpassed as a tactical innovator.

Galland missed out completely on the Me-109 in Spain. He was not finished with Werner Moelders by any means, and he would walk into history with him both as a rival and as a friend. For the moment, Galland was a young leader with 15 months of Condor Legion service, and that made him invaluable. The possibility of war over the Sudetenland was the impelling force behind his gloomy return to Germany, where new challenges impended. He would have been even gloomier had he known that certain people in Berlin were planning to have him fly a desk.

CHAPTER FIVE

By August of 1938, when Adolf Galland returned to Germany from Spain, Hitler had acquired more political and psychological momentum than any European leader since Napoleon. Announcing the new *Luftwaffe* and military conscription in 1935, the *Fuehrer* followed up on 7 March 1936 with his daring occupation of the Rhineland. He set up the Rome-Berlin Axis, intervened in Spain, and, in March of 1938—a scant two years after his Rhineland bluff—Hitler took over Austria and brought its 6,750,000 people into his Third *Reich*. The stage was thereby set for the dismemberment of Czechoslovakia, with Hitler now both head of state and supreme commander of the armed forces. Feverish propaganda detailed the alleged sufferings of 3,500,000 Sudeten Germans under Czech rule. This was the crisis scenario when the dashing young close-air-support specialist from Spain arrived back home.

Vigorous military preparations attending all Hitler's ploys automatically involved *Luftwaffe* expansion. Experienced leaders were sorely needed, and this also was one reason why *Luftwaffe* HQ had gone to such lengths to bring Galland home from Spain, despite the imminent end of that conflict. His detailed reports on close-support tactics and techniques, written by an operational pilot and squadron commander, reinforced the current service-wide emphasis on tactical air power. His expertise had entrained him with the march of events in Europe.

Reporting in with the Air Ministry in Berlin, Galland was sent home for a two-week leave. The contrast between renascent Germany and war-torn Spain was staggering to the young officer as he crossed Germany. Newspapers from home, which he had devoured in his off-duty times in Spain, could convey no real impression of the physical and spiritual changes in Germany. People were vigorous and busy. Financial difficulties for industry had seemingly evaporated. New factories had appeared everywhere. Even the landscape seemed to reflect a new and vital beauty. He was drinking in these good aspects of his country when an abrupt telegram ended his leave four days early. He was ordered to report to the Air Ministry in Berlin immediately.

Assigned to help work out directives for the raising and training of new close-support *Gruppen* (*Schlachtgruppen*), he found himself flying a desk in the new Air Ministry building. Goering had erected this edifice at the corner of the Leipzigerstrasse and the Wilhelmstrasse in Berlin as the command and power center of the *Luftwaffe*. Designed by the famous architect Dr. Sagebiel, the building had a cathedral-like entrance hall and contained 1,500 rooms and suites.

The place seemed to Galland like a vast formicary. He was just one of hundreds of officers who crawled ant-like in and out of and through the place every day. The elevators did not stop and start to let people out but were run instead on a continuous basis. Passengers waited by an opening and stepped into the moving elevator car, stepping out again when they reached their desired floor.

Gone was the uplifting comradeship of his squadron. Absent also was the freedom of action he enjoyed under the distinctive operating procedures of the Condor Legion. He yearned for the cozy functionality of his HQ in the converted Spanish railroad car, and he especially missed the front line informality with which he had run his efficient unit of war.

Nobody in Spain paid the slightest attention to oil spots on their trousers—not even the squadron leader. Such things were irrelevant in a fighting squadron. Trousers were important in Berlin. Staff types wore knife-edge creases in their distinctive crimson-striped trousers, as they scurried from office to office and braved the hazards of the elevators. All of them were much older than Galland. Some of them were so perfectly attired and immaculate they looked as though they had been varnished. The *Luftwaffe* uniforms were nevertheless among the most attractive and fashionable of all services world-wide.

Many of these staff officers professed interest in his experiences in Spain, but Galland repeatedly gained the impression that, when this experience ran counter to their own ideas from the past, they simply turned off mentally. His own tendency to informality in personal contact also contrasted sharply with their rigidity and consciousness of rank. The atmosphere of the Air Ministry was intellectually stifling.

Galland's boss was Lt. Colonel Dr. Gnamm of the General Staff, who had flown as an observer in the Great War. In the interim he had been a doctor of dentistry, without intimate contact with aviation. While Gnamm was a correct and hard-working officer, he exemplified a practice of Goering and the General Staff that Galland was to find all too common: unqualified officers in leading positions. (This was Galland's first direct experience of this phenomenon, but he would encounter it frequently as he worked his way up into the *Luftwaffe* hierarchy.)

Together Gnamm and Galland buckled down to writing the necessary directives, infusing into them all the most recent experience from Spain. The work went well for a few days. The real world then intruded on their labors. They were ordered to stop writing about it and actually go out and raise and train two brand-new *Schlachtgeschwader*. These formations were needed immediately. The Sudetenland crisis was putting heavy pressure on the armed forces. Every available combat aircraft had to be incorporated into a unit that could help support the Army. Galland put away his papers with glee. Cutting through peacetime red tape was to his liking, and short-cuts had to be made to raise the new *Schlachtgeschwader* in minimum time.

Improvisation had been a great part of life in the Condor Legion, and Galland now found this experience valuable. Raw young recruits and obsolescent aircraft had to be made into operational close-support units. The aircraft were second-class performers but still useful in close support. He-51s, Hs-123s, and He-45s were gathered from all over Germany. Pilots came from the training schools. Recruits were whipped into some semblance of efficiency by inexperienced NCOs. There were many flying accidents and crashes, but on the scheduled day the two *Schlachtgeschwader* were available for operations.

Lt. Colonel Gnamm was transferred from his steady desk job in the Air Ministry to become *Kommodore* of one of these *Schlachtgeschwader*. Fully aware now of Galland's abilities and expertise, Gnamm had him assigned as his adjutant and operations officer. Galland protested mightily, but to no avail. The ex-Condor Legion expert wanted to be a fighter pilot more than anything else in life, but he could not escape the close-support involvement. A major war was coming, whether over Czechoslovakia or otherwise, and Galland hated the thought of flying in such a war exclusively in direct support of the Army.

The new *Geschwader* was moved into Silesia at full mobilization tempo. The group was to provide close support for an airborne operation near Jägerndorf, should Hitler give the order to invade the Sudetenland. Czechoslovakia was dismembered at Munich, and the Sudetenland was occupied without a shot being fired.

After Munich, the scheduled operation was nevertheless carried out as an exercise. Confusion abounded in the new *Geschwader*, and Galland thanked heaven that the operation was not taking place in anger. Instead of strafing the Czech front lines, he was able to watch Germany's elite paratroops landing with precision. Examination of the massive Czech fortifications close up was sobering. He wondered about the outcome had Britain and France stood firm with the Czechs.

Persistent requests by Galland for transfer to a regular fighter unit were finally answered, in a compromise fashion, in the autumn of 1938. He was assigned to a fighter formation called *Jagdgruppe* Böblingen, with its preliminary HQ at Ingolstadt. Unfortunately the *Gruppe* did not yet exist. As a squadron leader in this new unit, he would help raise and train it from zero. His recent experience in creating two *Schlachtgeschwader* almost out of thin air was going to be useful.

The *Gruppenkommandeur* was Captain Count von Pfeil, who soon fell ill. As the oldest of the three squadron leaders, Galland therefore temporarily took command of the nonexistent new unit. When von Pfeil recovered from his illness, he got married, which further extended his absence. Working initially with 1st Lieutenant Alfons Klein and Lieutenant Wolfgang "Pequeño" Ewald, Galland soon had a harmonious situation with his subordinates. Klein was unfortunately killed in a flight crash, and he was replaced with 1st Lieutenant Kuehle, but the organizational work continued. Galland got tremendous satisfaction from seeing the *Gruppe* arise from nothing.

At last he was involved with a real fighter unit. *Jagdgruppe* Böblingen, to which village near Stuttgart the formation soon moved, was equipped with the Me-109D. Here was a fighter pilot's dream come true, and Galland was living through it as an acting *Gruppenkommandeur*. He led the unit's formation in mock combat, squadron against squadron. His early doubts about the Me-109, the first time he saw the prototype, seemed an odd memory as he thrilled to the flying qualities of Professor Messerschmitt's gift to the *Luftwaffe*. Here was a machine to revolutionize aerial combat.

The new squadrons were gradually worked up into an efficient fighter *Gruppe*. Galland taught them what he knew about ground attack operations, and, in full *Gruppe* strength, they made mock assaults on bomber formations provided by the Bomber Arm. Ammunition was now plentiful, so the pilots got all the air-to-ground firing practice they needed. In March of 1939, when Hitler occupied the rest of Czechoslovakia, Galland's formation sat with full gunbelts and engines warm on the Böblingen airfield. Bad weather socked in the field, and they never did take off. They were not needed. All Europe and Russia as well sat still for the final absorption of Czechoslovakia.

With the return of the last Condor Legion personnel from Spain, a Decorations Commission was set up at Döberitz to judge the order of merit of the recipients. Galland was ordered to join this commission. An eight-day "Victory Festival" began with the award of these decorations and was followed on 6 June 1939 by a march past in front of the Technical High School—with the *Fuehrer* on the reviewing stand.

In appalling early summer heat, the parade went through the Brandenburger Gate and up to the Lustgarten in Berlin. The "Spaniards," as former Condor Legionnaires were known in the *Luftwaffe,* were drooping badly at the end of this ordeal. Galland and others, in order to assure similarity in uniforms, had to wear thick and warm uniforms borrowed from the Labor Service, which resembled Condor Legion olive-greens. In this makeshift garb, Galland was part of a small group received by the *Fuehrer* in his new Chancellery.

Galland's first meeting with Hitler was confined to hearing a short speech and receiving a brief handshake. The *Fuehrer* drank tea with the "Spaniards," but they were all forbidden to smoke. This annoyed Galland profoundly, for long before he had cultivated a taste for large black cigars, with which he enhanced both his working power and his times of relaxation. (He was destined to see Hitler many more times in the future—certainly far more than he wished—and the *Fuehrer* always found time to chastise him about his cigar smoking. "You could approach him with a pistol as part of your uniform, but never with a cigar in your hand," said Galland of this Hitler quirk.)

The Condor Legion parade also brought Galland into reunion with Werner Moelders, who had relieved him as squadron leader of 3.J/88 in Spain. Moelders had become the most successful of the new generation of *Luftwaffe* fighter pilots, with 15 aerial victories in the Spanish war. Like Galland, he had written reports on his experiences. When Moelders returned to Germany on 5 December 1938, he also was given an Air Ministry desk to fly. His assignment was to write parallel directives for the Fighter Arm to those that Galland was commissioned to prepare for the close-support units. They were able after the parade to commiserate about desk flying, as well as joke about the decorations they had just received.

Chief among these decorations was the Spanish Cross in Gold, which was a German decoration. They also received the Medalla Militar and Medalla de la Campaña from the new Franco government of Spain. Goering considered that the Decorations Commission on which Galland had sat had been stinting in its awards. Two weeks after the victory parade, Galland was summoned by Goering to the island of Westerland, together with his Condor Legion friend Wilhelm Balthasar. Goering awarded them the Spanish Cross in Gold with Diamonds, the highest order of the decoration and much more impressive in appearance. Goering took their plain Spanish Crosses from them as he handed over the diamond-encrusted variant. He put the plain crosses in his pocket.

Only nine participants in Condor Legion campaigns were given this special Spanish Cross in Gold with Diamonds. Galland, Moelders, Balthasar, Luetzow, Schellman, and Oesau were all fighter pilots. Martin Harlinghausen was the lone bomber pilot recipient. The other two crosses went to Hugo Sperrle and Wolfram von Richthofen, both commanders at different times of the Condor Legion. (In years ahead, Galland would find that Goering's passion for diamonds would eventually provide him with a dinner story, on which he would dine out around the world. Goering at this moment in Westerland, was at his paternal best, exchanging new Spanish Crosses for old.)

Busy training days with *Jagdgruppe* Boblingen continued and were a happy fulfillment for Galland. This was what he wanted to do—to be a fighter pilot and be the best. Relentless training improved efficiency. By mid-summer of 1939, Galland would have put them in the air against any fighter formation in the world, confident that they would operate effectively.

His father took great pride in Keffer, his second son. Adolph's mother never ceased urging him to take more care of himself, and his brothers Wutz and Paul were themselves eager to become pilots. Wutz received a bonus out of his older brother's Spanish adventures. The money from Spain was substantial, and while with the Condor Legion he had spent relatively little. Now he splurged on a special new BMW cabriolet for himself. Wutz got Adolf's old Opel sportscar and could hardly have been happier.

The charming fighter pilot with the typically bent nose, thick black hair, and magnetic personality was already attractive to women, and the attraction was mutual—especially with beautiful women. With the BMW cabriolet thrown

Jm Namen
des
Deutſchen Volkes

verleihe ich
dem Oberleutnant
Adolf Galland

in Anerkennung
ſeiner ganz hervorragenden Leiſtungen
als Freiwilliger im ſpaniſchen Freiheitskampf
das
Deutſche Spanien-Kreuz
in
Gold mit Schwertern und Brillanten

Berlin, den 6. Juni 1939

Der Führer
und
Oberſte Befehlshaber
der Wehrmacht

Adolf Hitler signed this certificate of award of the German Spanish Cross with Diamonds, awarded to Galland after return of the Condor Legion from Spain This decoration was awarded to only nine members of the Luftwaffe

Legion Condor parade before Hitler upon return from Spain, in searing heat and wearing uniforms borrowed from the Reich Labor Service

in, Galland could hardly go wrong. Summer of 1939 was an idyll of satisfying work and happy leisure times. Early in August, the roof fell in.

A teletype advising him of his transfer back into the ground-support flying units was something that Galland had to read repeatedly in furious disbelief. All he had built up with this superb new fighter *Gruppe* was to be torn from his grasp. He was being denied the fruits of his labors—the opportunity to lead the fighter unit he had raised and trained into the clearly imminent war.

He was being drawn again into an eddy created by his expertise in ground-support flying. Assigned to replace a squadron leader in II/SLG-2, he made his way to Tutow where the unit was stationed. Major Werner Spielvogel was the *Gruppenkommandeur*. Galland was transferring from the Me-109D to the Henschel 123, another open-cockpit biplane, designed as a dive bomber. He stepped out of the future and back into the past, a time warp.

He took part in a massive exercise east of Cottbus in mid-August, an obvious rehearsal for the invasion of Poland. In command of air units was a familiar face from Spain—tough and energetic Lt. General Wolfram von Richthofen. The most noteworthy event in this exercise was the loss of 13 Ju-87 Stuka dive bombers, which flew into the ground *en masse* in a deceptive fog; 26 of the *Luftwaffe*'s best-trained airmen were killed.

Amid these feverish August days, Galland was ordered to Rechlin to test two new types of ground-attack fighters. The Air Ministry Technical Department had requested his services. They remembered the detailed Galland reports from Spain. The Hs-129 had the luxury of a bullet-proof cockpit, and the FW-189 was a sturdy gun platform. Both were twin-engined machines. Testing them was full of interest but did not console Galland in the least. He felt like a youngster whose favorite toy had been confiscated by his parents. His favorite toy at 25 years of age was the Me-109D.

Diplomatic maneuvers over Poland came to a head with the signature of the German-Soviet trade agreement, and four days later the German-Soviet Non-Aggression Pact was signed on 23 August 1939. This pact secured Hitler's rear while he absorbed Poland and dealt with Britain and France. The Russians signed with Hitler largely because their protracted efforts to join an alliance with Britain and France and, earlier on, with Czechoslovakia, had been consistently rebuffed. Stalin was in no doubt that Hitler would eventually attack Russia. He bought a little time.

Although the differences between nazism and communism were mortal, a secret additional protocol to their 1939 pact divided between them not only Poland but also the Baltic states. Germany invaded Poland on 1 September 1939, and two days later France and Britain declared war on Germany. Russia invaded Poland from the east on 14 September, four days before the end of Germany's Polish campaign.

At dawn on 1 September 1939, Adolf Galland was among the first German pilots to go into action in World War II. A successful strike was made against Polish Staff HQ, about 85 miles east of the German-Polish border. Weeks of tension before the invasion had adequately warned the Poles, and they had moved their important air units away from normal bases to makeshift and emergency airfields. When the Germans made their initial strikes against Polish airfields and hangars, with great success against Polish aircraft on the ground, the latter were obsolete types left behind by the Polish Air Force. The Poles had concentrated on preserving their better fighters and bombers.

Initial German air attacks caused such wide disruption of Polish communications, nevertheless, that the Polish Air Force could not be properly directed and controled. Polish fighters scored some successes against Me-110s on 2 September 1939, and Polish bombers and ground attack aircraft harassed the German XXI Army Corps later that same day as the invaders moved against Graudenz. Polish air strikes on 3 September against the 1st and 4th *Panzer* Divisions at Radomsko caused heavy losses.

The *Luftwaffe* was called on to suppress this Polish air activity. These efforts, in combination with the hopeless state of Polish communications, ground down Polish air power in the ensuing week until it was a handful of bombers. Even these units were shortly withdrawn to Rumania. The Polish Air Force could not cope with the *Luftwaffe*. The Poles fought their best but were overwhelmed.

Galland's perspective from the cockpit of his Hs-123 allowed him to see airborne Polish machines only a few times. His squadron had no contact or combat of any important kind with Polish fighters. They were part of a fast-moving campaign that linked highly mobile ground forces and air power on a scale not seen before. Galland had experienced it in miniature in Spain.

General von Richthofen applied with great skill the lessons learned with the Condor Legion, amplified now to the scale of Army Corps operations and all the more deadly because of their larger scope. Fighting for their native soil, Polish Army soldiers were individually brave and valiant; but the modern, well-integrated war machine that came thundering over the German border needed more than brave infantrymen and horse cavalry to halt its advance. Five Polish armies were overwhelmed. Ground-attack units contributed significantly to this German success.

The Polish Army capitulated on 18 September 1939, although the Poles continued to defend Warsaw and Modlin until 27 September. In the course of ceaseless air action by his unit, Galland flew 87 missions in his Hs-123. These operations included bombing and strafing airfields, bridges, troop concentrations, and trains. Where Polish flak appeared, it proved effective and accurate and much more dangerous than in Spain. Galland's *Gruppe* lost ten pilots, including Major Spielvogel, the *Gruppenkommandeur*.

During the campaign, Hitler visited Galland's squadron. The young pilot got his second close-up impression of the *Fuehrer*. Hitler was subdued and somewhat withdrawn amid the unit's personnel. He took a meal with them in the field, vegetable soup without meat. Galland's reaction to the visit was to wonder if this small and normal-looking man was really possessed of the leadership qualities claimed for him by Dr. Goebbels. (Galland was unaware at this moment that he would have abundant opportunity to experience the quality of the *Fuehrer's* military knowledge. On an airstrip in Poland in 1939, Hitler did not impress Galland as someone who could rock the world.)

Blitzkrieg, or lightning war, was already a part of international language by the end of the Polish campaign. German propaganda made extensive claims for *Blitzkrieg,* and Galland could reflect that he had made a substantial contribution to its development in the close-air-support sphere. He was nevertheless unhappy with trends that he saw developing amid this climate of staggering military triumph and success.

The tendency became marked in Poland for the German Army to use air power to attack the enlarged enemy front line. Aircraft were being employed like concentrated airborne artillery. When his squadron had driven home attacks against bridges and railroad junctions, Galland could see from his perspective in the air that such targets behind the front were the nervous system of the enemy army. When a rail junction was made unusable, enemy supplies and ammunition would soon be found backed up behind the blockage, and these could then be destroyed.

If a bridge were knocked out, enemy transport would shortly be involved in fording operations and could be attacked and destroyed while in this vulnerable state. With his analytical faculty, Galland began having some critical thoughts about the growing tendency to substitute close-support aircraft for field artillery. His mind was developing a strategic turn for the broader war.

After Poland, Galland's unit was transferred to Braunschweig, and he was awarded the Iron Cross, Second Class, for his efforts in the recent campaign. On 1 October 1939, he was promoted to captain; and, amid his thoughts on strategy and tactics he developed a means to free himself from close-support flying and get back in a fighter unit.

During operations in the summer heat of Spain, he had flown the He-51 naked except for swimming trunks. From a health point of view, this had been unwise. Drastic temperature changes and the blasts of air in the open cockpit had afflicted him with periodic rheumatism, one bout of which hit him at Braunschweig. He was sent down to Wiesbaden to take the cure. When he returned to his squadron, he had an interview with the medical officer, explaining to him his Spanish medical legacy.

"*Doktor,* you see that, every time I fly now in these open cockpits, this rheumatism gets worse. The pain this last time was intense. *Doktor,* could you recommend my transfer to an Me-109 fighter unit, so I do not have to fly in any more open cockpits?"

Galland was at his charming and persuasive best, to which most people are inclined to succumb. The doctor was not really fooled, but he was an understanding fellow. He took up Galland's medical dossier. "Captain Galland is not to do any more flying activities in open cockpits, on account of rheumatic complaints," wrote the doctor.

Wheels within the *Luftwaffe* bureaucracy were set in motion by these words.

Bf 109, also known as Me-109. Willy Messerschmitt and his aircraft design team at Bayerische Flugzeugwerke produced the first series of this outstanding fighter plane. It was known as the Bf 109 until midway through the Bf 109 "D" model, and known as the Me-109 from the "D" onwards. Above is an Me-109-1 model in France.

Me-109s on alert. These 109s have external fuel tanks, giving them extra range and combat time. Photograph taken in France.

major general, and served as liaison between Fighter Arm combat units and the Air Corps or Air Fleet of which they were a part. The downed *Jafü* was not happy at being shot from the sky by his own side.

Since the Fw-58 was an innocent-appearing aircraft, known in its ambulance version as "the sticking plaster bomber," the nervous pilots had to justify their attack. The situation was the same as if the RAF fighters had downed one of their lumbering all-purpose Avro Ansons. "How can a *Jafü* fly around in such a ridiculous plane?" said Galland's pilots, in self-defense.

Higher directives at this time instructed *Luftwaffe* fighters to stay strictly on their own side of the border. Only intruders were to be engaged. The frontier became indistinct at 15,000 feet and at over 300 mph, and it sometimes was obscured by clouds. Along this border, in an echo of World War I, aerial jousting occurred. French and German fighter pilots tested each other's machines and mettle. Most combat was joined in the "four borders" area, where France, Germany, Luxemburg, and Belgium came together.

Werner Moelders was there in the thick of the action. Now a *Gruppenkommandeur* with JG-53, and recognized as the leading German fighter pilot in every respect, he was adding to his score. Moelders was also implementing the tactical innovations that he had just codified during his Air Ministry assignment. This was unbearable for Galland. Moelders was adding to his aerial victories, while Galland struggled with the JG-27 paper mill and had to use ruses to get away on operations.

Galland wanted action, too. He also wanted to pick the fertile brain of Werner Moelders. Arranging through channels for a temporary transfer to JG-53, he soon was flying into action with Moelders and taking factual and practical lectures from him on the lethal art of shooting down aircraft in air-to-air combat.

Moelders covered the full spectrum of fighter combat knowledge. Tactics, flying approaches, firing, angles of approach, seeing and distinguishing friend and foe, pressing home attacks, and separating enemy units after the attack were all covered by Moelders.

"Everything was given to me by my admired friend Werner Moelders," said Galland of this time. "He was one year and one day younger than I, but I respected him as the superior tactician. Later we had strong competition in the number of aerial victories."

The basis for Galland's own later success in aerial combat was thus laid during this fortunate association with Moelders during the lull before the storm. Flying with the gifted pilot who was to be his great rival, Galland found that Moelders had a secret weapon—his eyesight. Moelders had phenomenal vision. He could pick out enemy aircraft in the sky before anyone else in the formation. Even after Moelders called out their location, most of the other pilots still could not spot the enemy aircraft. As Erich Hartmann, the greatest fighter ace of World War II, would say in later years:[*] "He who sees the enemy first already has

---

[*] Erich Hartmann shot down 352 enemy aircraft on the Russian front, becoming the top fighter ace of all time. He survived the war as well as 10½ years imprisonment in Russia after the war.

half the victory.'' That was certainly true of Moelders. Galland took note of it, aware all the time of the scars from splintered glass in his own left eye.

Impressive also was Moelders's ingenuity in planting a small spotting unit on the ground near the border. The unit maintained contact with Moelders in the air, reporting recognized types, numbers, course, speed, and altitude of any incoming or passing enemy aircraft or unit. This aided Moelders in making his remarkable interceptions. (And it was probably one of the first efforts at fighter control in the *Luftwaffe*—a function in which the Germans were woefully behind the RAF. Little further was done along this line, because in 1940 the German political authorities still considered Germany safe from air attack. In those days, it was.)

Galland and Moelders were temperamentally opposites, with Moelders an extremely serious young man who smiled but little and rarely laughed. Galland's affability, sense of humor, and penchant for the good life made him a typical fighter pilot. Moelders tended by contrast to concentrate intensely on his duties and on the larger functions of fighter aviation.

Moelders's bearing and demeanor evoked instant obedience, as though he were a mature general instead of a major in his 20s. His subordinates nicknamed him "Daddy" Moelders. Galland got to know Moelders well during their four-borders association in 1940. If Moelders was the master tactician and teacher, then Galland was the more enthusiastic hunter, and the teacher when it came to the good life—to the art of being human amid inhuman events.

Galland chided Moelders about his monkish lifestyle and his abstinences. Galland's young pilots prepared a lavish "girl party" at a special suite in Paris, and Galland persuaded Moelders to attend. Probably stung by Galland's chidings, Moelders was the first pilot to make his choice. Galland followed immediately with his choice, and left the room with his famous ear-to-ear grin that appears on such occasions. Moelders had unbent.

When the German offensive moved forward on 10 May 1940, JG-27 went into action, providing air support for the Army's successful crossing of the Maas River and the Albert Canal. On the third day of the campaign, Galland was leading a *Rotte*—a flight of two aircraft—five miles west of Liege at 12,000 feet, when he spotted eight Hurricane fighters 3,000 feet below him. He had not been seen.

He had the classic advantages of higher altitude and surprise in initiating a bounce. He was flying a superior aircraft and was the recipient of a long and careful training, crowned by over 300 combat missions. He had all the advantages a fighter pilot could possess.

The bounce had been practiced in mock combat until it was part of him. No hunting fever rose in him as the Hurricane in his gunsight grew larger by the second. The instant he pressed his firing buttons, Galland knew that he had opened fire too far out. All that competition trap shooting still paid off. His bullets went right to their target. Taking evasive action immediately, the victim flew right into the fire of Galland's wingman, as the Hurricane formation split in all directions.

Pressing a second attack on his now rattled quarry, Galland saw the rudder break off and the Hurricane went spinning down, shedding debris and parts of its wings. Leaving it to fall, Galland raced after another Hurricane in a diving chase. Closing in to 100 yards, he was about to fire when the Hurricane half-rolled and disappeared into the clouds. Mentally calculating what the British pilot might do, Galland followed suit in his Me-109E. Seconds later he was behind the Hurricane again—but closer. A short burst sent the Hurricane zooming to a stall, followed by a vertical dive from 1,500 feet directly into the ground.

A third Hurricane fell to his guns near Tirlemont later that same day, when he bounced a formation of five machines. Despite his having spent a decade preparing himself as a combat pilot, these first three victories brought him no elation. He had experienced none of the thudding excitement that seized him when he was flying through hails of lead in Spain. His conscience pricked him over the ease with which these first three victories had been won. Excited congratulations from his fellow pilots and the ground crews after he landed somehow were hollow praise to him.

His duties as operations officer precluded for a time any more missions. JG-27 moved forward with the Army. Numerous base changes and the paper chase and administrative turmoil that came with these moves were absolute anathema to Galland. He fought to get back in the air, and on 19 May 1940 he scored his fifth aerial victory. He was an ace.

He ran his victory tally to eight on 20 May, and was awarded the Iron Cross, First Class, by General Erhard Milch, Goering's Inspector General and deputy. (As Milch pinned the decoration on him, Galland was not to know that he would be seeing plenty in the next few years of this captain of industry turned *Luftwaffe* general.) Milch was freshly returned from commanding the *Luftwaffe* in the successful Norwegian campaign.

Battle lust was at an all-time peak among the JG-27 pilots, riding above a tremendous ground victory by the German Army. Colonel Ibel kept flying with his young pilots. Nothing daunted the crusty World War I veteran. Galland's duty when Ibel flew was to be his wingman, and this limited Galland's opportunities for further victories. The gallant Ibel evoked the admiration of his pilots, and Galland took good care of him in the air, except for one time when Spitfires caught them unawares. Ibel was shot down amid battlefield smoke and combat confusion. Galland was grateful when his haggard *Kommodore* trudged into their St. Pol HQ late that night, after a long and exhausting hike.

While operating out of Charleville, Galland tangled repeatedly with both Hurricanes and Spitfires of the RAF. He immediately realized that he was battling against high-quality pilots. Courage and skill characterized these British pilots, but these qualities were undermined by their outdated tactics. They clung to their clumsy three-fighter "Vic" formation. The Spitfire was a hot performer and a hard hitter, but Galland was certain at this time of the superiority of his Me-109E, compared to the Spitfire variants he was fighting.

The RAF was not hard to find. The pilots usually flew fighter patrols over British and French troops who were being compressed towards Dunkirk. High above the historic beaches, Galland and his pilots were in daily savage combat with the RAF. The gentlemanly games of the *Sitzkrieg* period against the French were gone. Combat was for keeps. Every attack was driven home fiercely.

Galland could count on finding RAF fighters over the Dunkirk beaches. The British were wading into the German bombers and Stukas with telling effect, especially when *Luftwaffe* fighters had to withdraw to refuel. This happened often, due to the bombers arriving late for rendezvous with their fighter escort. The fighters sometimes missed their rendezvous with the bombers due to their involvement in dogfights with the RAF.

The *Luftwaffe* attempt to destroy the escaping British Expeditionary Force, without major participation by the German Army or Navy, had been undertaken with impulsive enthusiasm by Goering personally. He believed that he could achieve this Douhet-style triumph of air power. Goering had some support for this in high *Luftwaffe* circles.

Galland's perspective on the battle was simple and direct. Too much was being expected of the available German air strength. RAF fighter opposition was ferocious, and the Spitfire a nasty surprise; 350,000 Allied troops escaped, and the *Luftwaffe* lost about 250 aircraft. German air strength, which had been held out of the Dunkirk battle to participate in the ongoing battle for France, could have provided a decisive margin. A Douhet-style air campaign demanded overwhelming strength. The *Luftwaffe* had been warned.

When Dunkirk passed into German hands on 4 June 1940, JG-27 turned its squadrons to the remaining French air units. The French Air Army was to be finally smashed through Operation "Paula," conceived with strategic overtones. Paula was planned to destroy French aircraft factories in the Paris area. No aircraft and no usable airfields meant the end of the French Air Army. The Germans prepared inadequately but still destroyed about 100 French aircraft for the loss of 30 of their own.

Leading a small unit, Galland got into a wild dogfight with a Morane squadron. In downing one Morane, he almost came into full collision with another. Shearing off his own antenna mast and damaging his vertical stabilizer, it was as close as he cared to come to a midair collision. Even after Operation Paula there were still brave French air units to be hunted down. The French claimed that Paula was a failure, but little attention was paid to the operation amid a continuing string of German triumphs. (The coming terrible years would prove that it takes a mighty air force to stop aircraft production.)

After Dunkirk, Galland was suddenly promoted to *Gruppenkommandeur* of III/JG-26—a substantial upward leap. Goering was giving scope to the best of his younger fighter pilots by retiring, to less-demanding assignments, the

World War I veterans who were still in combat commands. Galland's *Gruppe* was transferred to München-Gladbach for rest and refit at the end of the French campaign and then ordered to Döberitz—familiar to Galland from his fledgling days with JG-2. This was a special mission. JG-26 *Schlageter* had performed brilliantly in the Western campaign and earned the honor of flying fighter cover for a spectacular investiture of Germany's highest commanders in Berlin.

Hollywood is the only place to stage spectacles more impressive than the investiture in the Kroll Opera House on 19 July 1940. Hitler made an impassioned speech, culminating in a last, hopeless attempt to offer a peace agreement to Britain. With Adolf Galland leading his fighter *Gruppe* in salute overhead, Hitler promoted 12 of his generals to field marshals. Nineteen more became full generals. Amid the lavish pomp, the *Luftwaffe* was well represented.

Milch, Sperrle, and Kesselring became field marshals. Udet, Stumpff, Keller, Weise, and Grauert became colonel-generals. Jeschonnek, von Richthofen, Geissler, von Greim, and Goering's old squadron mate Loerzer were all raised to full generals (*General der Flieger*). Goering rose above them all, boosted to grandiose heights as Marshal of the Greater German *Reich*. An exalted new grade of the Iron Cross was instituted exclusively for Goering: no one else in Germany would ever wear the Grand Cross of the Iron Cross, and that briefly satisfied the *Reichsmarshal's* pathological vanity.

All these leaders moving up a rung or two all at once resulted in a promotional shockwave throughout the *Luftwaffe*. Galland said it was caused by the "common upward pressure for promotion." He was promoted to major at the age of 28, in recognition of his bravery in the French campaign, his 17 aerial victories, and his many aircraft destructions by strafing. Celebrations had hardly subsided when JG-26 was transferred back to the Pas de Calais. The war was still on.

Violent days lay ahead. Virtually all Galland's youth and adult life had been a preparation for this challenge. Leading an efficient fighter *Gruppe* in an historic operation of war completely filled his life. The award of the Knight's Cross, in addition to his promotion to major, left him overwhelmed. All this had begun back at the Borkenberge, in those simple days when he had first strapped himself into a sailplane.

Service in a top fighter unit, with the comradeship and spirit that made life zestful, was all he wanted professionally. When off duty, the rest of the good life beckoned, and he was off hunting in the woods and fields. There were always birds and hares for the pot. An active social calendar saw him indulge his taste for attractive women.

Overriding everything was the sense of being involved in something bigger than himself. Petty individual concerns withered away for lack of worthy dimension. Had it been left entirely to him, Adolf Galland would have added nothing more than he now had, at the beginning of the Battle of Britain. He was where he felt he belonged, doing what he knew best.

Seemingly unrelated chains of events, of which he was oblivious, were

The photographer caught Galland on a pheasant-hunting trip in Belgium. Note the cartridge pouch, both eyes open and the falling spent cartridge.

Galland, Rolf Pingel and Flak-officer Captain Wolfgram smile after Pingel was decorated with the Ritterkreuz on 14 September 1940.

nevertheless moving into a remarkable confluence. An historian's perspective of more than 40 years makes these connections readily discernible. Such insight is not granted a man while he is living his life at full throttle. In Galland's case, policies and decisions of human beings outside his sphere would soon saddle him with problems and pressures that would make a fighter cockpit seem by contrast a peaceful sanctuary.

Other human beings that he would not even know about until he was 65 years old would eavesdrop on his troubles. Information thereby gained would be used to make his way harder. Then there was one human being looming on his horizon who would put his tolerance, self-control, and soldierly fidelity to their limits.

To understand fully the high-command career of Adolf Galland, the three main elements mentioned need to be outlined before dealing with the Battle of Britain—the *Luftwaffe's* most crucial encounter. Decisions and policies of the *Luftwaffe* General Staff and High Command, and of the *Luftwaffe* Supreme Commander himself in the development of Germany's new air arm, profoundly influenced the outcome of the Battle of Britain. *Luftwaffe* fighter pilots caught hell not only in the air in combat but also on the ground, where they were blamed for many gross high-level failures. Galland's combat career in the Battle of Britain, and his later career in high command, circulated around the omissions and errors of others—mistakes that can best be described as techni-political.

While Galland had been an eager participant in the growth of the *Luftwaffe* from its birth, he was a young pilot and a junior officer. He was never privy to questions of policy, doctrine, or the structuring of the *Luftwaffe*. His contributions to the development of modern tactical air power had been considerable, but the *Luftwaffe* had been fashioned by Goering and by the mature leaders he had selected to work under his authority.

Fighter aircraft had always occupied a secondary role in the *Luftwaffe*. *Luftwaffe* policy was to rapidly acquire a Bomber Arm that would be sufficient to deter outside interference with German rearmament. The Fighter Arm was to receive attention only in a secondary way. The Bomber Arm thus enjoyed from the first days of the *Luftwaffe* both doctrinal and developmental primacy. Some officers in high *Luftwaffe* posts would persist in Bomber Arm primacy even when Allied bombers were laying Germany in ruins—that is how deeply this principle became ingrained.

Bombers as a key strategic weapon were understood and accepted by the *Generalleutnant,* Walther Wever, Chief of the Air Command Office, and, in all essentials save the actual title, by the first Chief of the *Luftwaffe* General Staff. A former Army General Staff officer who had been Ludendorff's adjutant in World War I, Wever was extremely capable, well-trained in military affairs, and gifted in his grasp of air power fundamentals. His leadership qualities and initiative included learning to fly at age 46, so he spoke with the added authority afforded him by his pilot rating.

He flew his own aircraft on visits to his troops. Galland met and was positively impressed by Wever when the latter made such a visit to I/JG-2 at Döberitz in 1936. Wever was progressive, with great vision, discerning as he did the four-engined bomber as the most important air weapon of the future. Only by this means could Germany strike strategically at Hitler's proclaimed foe—Communist Russia. Strategic blows against Russia would require a four-engined machine able to reach the Ural mountains and the main sources of Soviet material power. Wever intended to structure the *Luftwaffe* around this premier weapon, supported by the General Staff.

Presaging the coming epoch of the four-engined bomber was the giant Junkers G-38, completed in 1930. A four-engined passenger monoplane with a 150-foot wingspan, the G-38 also had copious freight and fuel space inside its wings. The machine flew a grand tour of Europe, including London. The famous editor of *The Aeroplane*, Charles Grey, would later call this aircraft the father of all big bombers. Germany had the aeronautical know-how to build strategic bombers.

General Wever's appreciation of the form that German air power would have to take—if Russia were the adversary—was based upon the *Luftwaffe* having time to build to full and balanced strength. A fatal plane crash on 3 May 1936, during one of Wever's routine troop visits, removed his vision and drive from the strategic bomber program. General Staff advocates of the program were thereafter unable to maintain its momentum against economic and political expediencies.

Political considerations virtually eradicated strategic considerations from *Luftwaffe* planning. Hitler's political goals required construction of the largest possible number of aircraft in minimum time. Although Dornier and Junkers built promising prototypes under Air Ministry contracts, Goering was persuaded by Milch and the Technical Office to abandon the long-range bomber. By the spring of 1937, German development of strategic air power had ceased.

With the strategic bomber dead, productive capacity was mainly concentrated on other bombers. Aside from the later innovations of Werner Moelders, only relatively minor resources and precious little vision were invested in the Fighter Arm. Dive bombing became a ruinous obsession of the *Luftwaffe* High Command—a veritable military neurosis—after Udet imported the dive bomber idea from America.

Udet gave up his cosmopolitan, carefree life and became head of the Technical Department at the Air Ministry for the sake of the dive bomber, his passion. Small and relatively cheap, dive bombers could be built quickly and in large numbers. They delivered their bombs accurately. No adequate weight was given by the *Luftwaffe* hierarchy to the dive bomber's vulnerability to fast modern fighters. Dive bombers meshed with Germany's political goals and purposes. Dive bombers were "in."

Amid shortages of raw materials, a stream of enthusiasm for dive bombers soon became a consuming flood. All bombers had diving capability written into their specifications, including the four-engined Heinkel 177. This edict had serious consequences. The speedy, twin-engined Ju-88 medium bomber, for example, underwent extensive structural strengthening for diving. Up went its weight, down went its payload. More powerful engines to compensate for the diminished payload were not forthcoming.

This diving orgy soon permeated the whole bomber program. Carpet bombing, as developed by Galland in Spain, was abandoned in favor of pinpoint bombing. Cancelation of the strategic bomber in April of 1937 began the shrinkage of the *Luftwaffe's* horizons. Concentration on dive bombing shrank what remained down to a dot.

A serious fighter procurement error influenced disastrously the fighter-to-fighter struggle that decided the Battle of Britain. The Me-109's competitor was the Heinkel He-112, marginally slower but more maneuverable. The He-112 also had a wide-track landing gear, the narrow landing gear of the Me-109 being a weakness that eventually led to thousands of wrecked and damaged aircraft. The He-112 had a 680-mile range, against 360–480 miles for the several Me-109 variants.

The short-winded Me-109 would never be able to stay more than ten minutes over London. (Galland would have bitter experience with this crippling handicap.) The Air Ministry chose not to produce both fighters, to the chagrin of Ernst Heinkel. The incensed professor then created the He-100, a faster and more advanced fighter that would be cheaper to build. Udet personally set a new world record 100-km circuit record in the V2 prototype, at 394.6 mph.

On 30 March 1939, the He-100 in the V3 version was flown to a world speed record of 463.93 mph by Hans Dieterle. The Air Ministry had authorized a series of prototypes, but, despite the imminence of war and the obvious supplementation of Me-109 deficiencies provided by this aircraft, mass production was never authorized. On the contrary, six prototypes were actually sold to Russia. Three more went to Japan. *Luftwaffe* fighter pilots were thereby denied the 559-mile range of the He-100 in their mortal clash with the RAF.

Adolf Galland was an extern to all these high-level decisions on policy, doctrine, procurement, production, and planning. The command arrangements and personalities who were responsible for creating the *Luftwaffe* as an exclusively tactical air force—like airborne artillery and minus any significant strategic capability—were also beyond his sphere as a young pilot. He would nevertheless have to cope with all the consequences arising from neglect of the Fighter Arm, and for numerous mistakes made by senior officers and planners in the 1930s.

The massive tactical *Luftwaffe* assembled at the beginning of the Battle of Britain had brought Hitler and Goering the greatest succession of victories in modern times. Success seemed to make everything right. The *Luftwaffe's* very existence had bulked large in the bloodless prior diplomatic triumphs, as well as in the victories over Poland, Norway, Holland, Belgium, and France. Victories are insidious. They conceal the weaknesses of the victor—especially from the victor himself. Top *Luftwaffe* leadership had an insufficient sense of weakness in July of 1940.

British conquest of German military *Enigma* ciphers was the second vital chain of events affecting Galland's war career. Even as the young *Gruppenkom-*

mandeur prepared for the Battle of Britain, British cipher teams at Bletchley Park near London were beginning to read regularly the radioteletype cipher traffic of the *Luftwaffe* in France. Immense·and ingenious labors by the British, based on the advantage given to them by the Polish cipher team and their smuggled *Enigma* machines, produced this breakthrough. Inadvertently aiding them was the *Luftwaffe* itself, through slackness in its enciphering practises and procedures.

Before the Battle of Britain started, the *Luftwaffe* Order of Battle was known to the RAF (Royal Air Force). The British knew the status of every participant *Luftwaffe* unit, including pilots, aircraft, spare parts, and fuel. This intelligence was protected by maximum security and given a classification, *Ultra Secret*. Security was tight enough to protect the secret by all involved until the mid-1970s—a marvel of both security and fidelity.

Extreme security measures were essential with *Ultra* during the war to preclude German realization that their ciphers had been broken. The high Allied officers who were authorized to receive *Ultra* decrypts remained tightly limited in numbers throughout the war. British master spy F. W. Winterbotham, the RAF Group Captain who had moved in high Nazi circles before the war, played a major role in the distribution of *Ultra* intelligence, including getting crucial decrypts to Fighter Command in the Battle of Britain. His experiences are recounted in *The Ultra Secret,* his 1974 book published by Harper & Row.

Winterbotham set up Special Liaison Units (SLUs) with the various high commands to which the *Ultra* intelligence was distributed. Part of Winterbotham's job was to brief high commanders on the origin of this remarkable intelligence, so they, in turn, could guard the secret. Winterbotham also was responsible for passing *Ultra* information personally to Churchill.

Early in August of 1940, Winterbotham established a small SLU at Fighter Command HQ at Stanmore. *Ultra* material relevant exclusively to the air battle that was about to begin could thus be sent directly to the SLU's soundproof subterranean cell in "The Hole" at Stanmore. SLU personnel would give German signals personally to Air Chief Marshal Sir Hugh Dowding, AOC Fighter Command. SLU personnel ensured that the written information was thereafter removed.

When Winterbotham also briefed Air Vice-Marshal Keith Park, AOC No. 11 Fighter Group, on the *Ultra* intelligence, the RAF was set for its historic aerial battle with the *Luftwaffe*. Park would know throughout the battle that orders emanating from Dowding were taking into account actual German radio traffic, crucial information that would reach Dowding almost as rapidly as it reached Goering, his Air Fleet chiefs, and his lesser operational commanders. Park's fighters were based in southern England. They would take the brunt of the *Luftwaffe* assault. *Ultra* thus became a subtle higher dimension of the Battle of Britain, through which the considerable qualities of Dowding's mind were further magnified. Galland across the Channel would have little other authentic information on the RAF than what he gleaned in action.

On the morning of 8 August 1940, when the HQ teleprinter at III/JG-26 on the Pas de Calais punched out an order of the day from Goering, Dowding was a recipient as well as Major Galland:

From Reich Marshal Goering to all units of Air Fleets 2, 3 and 5. Operation Eagle. Within a short period you will wipe the British Air Force from the sky. Heil Hitler.

From this time on until the end of the war, virtually every important radiotele-type message addressed to Galland would be simultaneously in the hands of the Allies. The losses suffered by the fighter units he would command in the coming battle would be known in Britain whenever he sent them via radioteletype to HQ. Constant possession of such information by his opponents would increase their ability to outwit him, multiply his difficulties, and partly nullify his bravery in action.

Allied air commanders opposing Galland would always have this beneficial intelligence when making their own decisions. *Luftwaffe* commanders like Galland would have nothing comparable concerning Allied leaders and their plans. The weight of *Ultra* gave unprecedented advantages to the Allied high commanders.

The vain man behind the Operation Eagle order of the day was the third force coming to confluence in Adolf Galland's life in 1940. Hermann Goering was Galland's direct superior when he rose to his highest responsibilities. The *Reich* Marshal was remote now from the young *Gruppenkommandeur*, but it was "his" *Luftwaffe* in which Galland held his commission. Soon it would be "his" Fighter Arm that Galland would command. Goering's authority in the *Luftwaffe* was unquestioned. There were no congressional committees to ensure that the *Reich* Marshal did not go too far.

Their relationship was to be a clash of strong men, strange in its many shadings. Goering stretched all the way from paternal mentor to abusive tyrant and swung unpredictably between these extremes. His bulky shadow would fall across everything Galland would seek to do in the years ahead. You had to go through Goering in the *Luftwaffe,* and nobody ever went around him—except Adolf Hitler.

Common historical impressions of Goering are disastrously simplistic. Galland was not to deal with this entrenched caricature of Goering but with Germany's number two man, whose authority was almost unlimited. Goering denied direct operational authority to Galland when he ushered him into the *Luftwaffe* hierarchy. This stricture and the clash of character that was inevitable between Goering and Galland was to influence the course of the air war. Before following Galland into the Battle of Britain, a realistic look at Goering is appropriate.

CHAPTER SEVEN

Four days after taking command of the Richthofen Circus in July of 1918, Lt. Hermann Goering summoned all leading pilots for a dressing down. He rebuked these aces for their sloppy flying discipline; but he also had an unspoken reason for blasting them. Even in 1918 Goering had a flair for personal politics and a determination to get his own way—if need be by browbeating.

Goering was an outsider from *Jagdstaffel* 27, who had been given command of the elite Flying Circus in preference to aces already serving with the unit. Living legends like Ernst Udet, Carl Loewenhardt, and Lothar von Richthofen—brother of the recently slain Red Baron—were all passed over for command. Naturally they resented Goering's appointment. He provoked a face-down with the veterans to assert his leadership. "Plucking the peacocks before they fall over their own feathers" was how Goering described his action to Lt. Karl Bodenschatz, his adjutant.

Twenty-two years later on the French coast, Goering as Supreme Commander of the *Luftwaffe* would again assail one of Germany's greatest aces. This time it would be Adolf Galland, *Kommodore* of JG-26. This confrontation took place in a new epoch, but it was the same old Goering, tough, forceful, and with his actions politically motivated.

Clashes between the two men were to continue, with increasing acrimony on Goering's part, until Galland's controversial dismissal from high command in January of 1945. These encounters were to be the most unpleasant in Galland's life. Antagonism between these two powerful personalities cannot be judged solely from a military standpoint. There was a characterological gulf between them that influenced profoundly their professional relationship.

Goering was at once Galland's sponsor and main antagonist. Goering was behind Galland's meteoric rise to high responsibilities, but, as his direct superior, he blocked most of the capable young man's recommendations. Sponsor and protege were almost always at loggerheads.

Goering survives in public memory as an overweight poseur, a flamboyant lover of uniforms, pomp, and personal adornment. Everyone knows he was a drug addict, but few know how his addiction began. He enjoys posthumous fame for plundering art works. As Hitler's closest associate and heir to the *Fuehrer's* power, he is stained by the excesses of the regime he helped create, engineered into place, and served to the end.

Goering was all these things, but to view him exclusively as a shallow sybarite is highly misleading. His capabilities were exceptional. One of the most formidable German personalities of the 20th century, his native brilliance and intellectual gifts were regained when the Allies weaned him from drugs at war's end. At the Nuremberg Trials, the world saw the real Goering. Unrepentant, eloquent, fearsomely logical, and armed with a photographic memory, his defense put the best Allied legal brains to their limits in coping with him. This was as a defeated captive, with all the legal rules and procedures drawn up by the victors, in trials under their total control.

Adolf Galland as a young general in his early 30s had to deal with this same personality on military issues. Goering was then in power—his direct superior. *"Der Dicke"*—the Fat One—was a heavyweight in more ways than one.

Galland developed in a solidly based family. Nothing disrupted the development of his character. From his boyhood interests, he phased smoothly into his flying career, armed with a strong character, sharp intelligence, and the personal equilibrium that stems from a sound upbringing. Hermann Goering, by contrast, had an emotionally rough childhood. He was disastrously influenced by his godfather, Dr. Hermann von Epenstein.

Right after Goering was weaned, he was placed with surrogate parents, while his mother went to join his aging diplomat father in Haiti. In his maturity, Goering would often complain to friends about the cruelty of such separations. His formative years were overshadowed by his mother's love affair with his godfather, while his aged natural father descended into senility. Hermann von Epenstein was the major influence in Goering's formative years, and he largely shaped the character of the man destined to become one of the lords of the Third *Reich*.

Von Epenstein was a lover of medieval pomp, and his example would induce Goering to live on a grandiose scale in the 20th century, while keeping one foot in the Middle Ages. Young Hermann Goering had a natural affinity for the folklore of chivalry, knighthood, and medieval splendor. Von Epenstein was so situated and disposed in life that he could infuse all these boyish fantasies with an overwhelming reality, a fairy tale translated into the here-now.

Acquiring a castle at Mauterndorf in Austria, von Epenstein moved the Goering family into lodges on the grounds of this romantic edifice. Von Epenstein had an arrogant, commanding method of speaking, with which he overpowered people in ordinary life. As the adored exemplar of all that young Goering admired and fantasized, von Epenstein was undoubtedly responsible for the way in which the adult Goering handled his military subordinates and his contemporaries in politics.

Von Epenstein introduced young Hermann to flamboyant manners and dress, which the youngster sought to emulate. All this was carried through into Goering's adult life. As *Reich* Marshal, he could indulge these tastes. Medieval grandeur sprang back to life at Mauterndorf. Uniformed retainers bowed and curtsied at von Epenstein's approach, surrounding him with groveling deference. Meal times were signaled with a hunting horn blast. Banquets in the great hall were laid on amid the trappings of bygone ages, including musicians playing in the gallery. This bizarre scenario sank into the receptive psyche of Hermann Goering like a draught of regal wine, evoking dreams in which he himself would swagger as the royal master. No atmosphere could be conceived that was less conducive to humility.

Von Epenstein was not content with one castle. He acquired Castle Veldenstein, 25 miles north of Nuremberg. Within its walls decades later, Goering would thunder at Adolf Galland and be heard in the village below. Von Epenstein moved the Goering family into the old fortress, which he restored and refurbished. A suite was reserved for von Epenstein's exclusive use when he was in residence. At those times, Hermann Goering's mother was in von Epenstein's bed. Her husband Heinrich and the Goering children were aware of these arrangements. Alcohol deadened the old diplomat's feelings. The children got used to it all, and Hermann continued to idolize his godfather.

Goering was shattered at age 11 when his school authorities informed him that von Epenstein was half-Jewish. Young Hermann had made the mistake of writing about his godfather in an essay assignment, "The Man I Admire Most in the World." Summoned to the headmaster's office, Goering was shown the listings in the semi-*Gotha,* which catalogued all titled Germans of Jewish blood—and there was the name of his hero. His fellow students added to his miseries by frogmarching him around the school grounds with a placard around his neck, advertising the Jewish origin of his godfather. He bolted from school. Jew or no Jew, Goering's loyalty to his godfather never wavered, and nor did his desire to model himself after his hero.

Von Epenstein's arrogant, domineering ways and his tastes, flamboyance, and assertiveness impressed themselves on young Hermann like a behavioral matrix. The boy would carry these impressions into adult life and find full expression when he rose to political power. All of it was nevertheless engrafted and tended to obscure his high native intelligence and outstanding intellectual capacity.

He was first class across the board in the elite Karlsruhe military academy, to which he was admitted through von Epenstein's influence as an ex-cavalry officer. His stellar performance at Karlsruhe got him an appointment to the cadet college at Lichterfelde, near Berlin, which trained officers for the German Army. Here he wrote a record of sustained brilliance, emerging with top honors and a commission in the Prinz Wilhelm Regiment.

Goering went into action as an infantry officer within a few hours of the

Navy visitor. Grossadmiral Erich Raeder visits Galland's JG26 base at Pas de Calais in 1940. The Admiral's Junkers transport, Ju52, provides the background for this photograph.

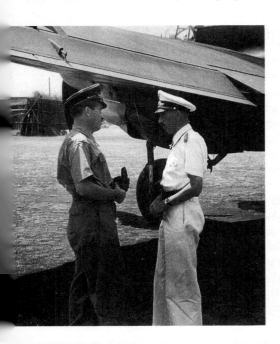

Two generations. The young ace talks to the elder ace; Galland and "Onkel Theo" Osterkamp meet during the Battle of Malta to discuss strategy.

outbreak of World War I. Fighting the Fatherland's wars was to Goering at 21 the highest challenge to his manhood. He proved himself resourceful, courageous, and capable, with plenty of initiative and daring. Rheumatic fever took him out of the trenches just before the Battle of the Marne.

While in hospital at Freiburg, his former regimental comrade Bruno Loerzer visited him. Loerzer was a pilot trainee for the new air service of the German Army. He was going to be flying over the mud of the battlefield, instead of wallowing in it as Goering had been doing. Fired by the adventure of flying, Goering immediately applied for transfer to the Freiburg flying school. While awaiting approval, he took some hops with Loerzer and thereafter was utterly determined to become an airman.

Goering's historic association with German air power began at this moment. His ambition was almost stillborn when his request for transfer was refused. Ignoring the order to return to his regiment when fit, he wrote fake transfer orders for himself and haunted the flying field. He went aloft at every chance to learn the task of observer-photographer, from which beginning he would make a later transition to pilot.

When his regimental authorities learned of his self-discharge from the hospital and his self-transfer to the air service, he was ordered to report for duty immediately. Any ordinary officer would have been frightened into compliance, for he had already committed court martial offenses. Goering was no ordinary officer. He reacted by telegraphing his godfather, who was well connected in royal circles in Berlin. Von Epenstein pulled strings.

Instead of a court martial, Goering was ordered by Crown Prince Friedrich Wilhelm, son of the Kaiser, to join the German Fifth Army's air detachment at Stenay in northern France, Loerzer along with him. Goering was to be a flyer for the rest of the war. As Loerzer's observer, Goering demonstrated an almost mystical quality of bravery. In the field he won the Iron Cross, First Class.

The Albatros in which Goering and Loerzer flew was not well suited to aerial photography. Goering compensated for that by hanging down out of the cockpit with his camera, taking photographs of fortifications and other targets. Stowing his camera after completion of photography, he would lean out again with a machine gun, hosing bullets into the entrenched troops below.

Nicknamed "The Flying Trapezist" for these exploits, his bravery made him into a legend in the German air service. Wild derring-do was in keeping with his extravagant tastes. (Memories of these days undoubtedly colored his judgments of *Luftwaffe* fighter pilots in World War II, when he berated Galland with accusations of their cowardice.) Goering's combat courage was of the highest order. (Only in Hitler's presence would he ever appear awe-struck.)

After unflawed pilot training in 1915, Goering was sent to the squadrons. By mid-1917 he had shot down 17 aircraft and earned two more medals, including the coveted Blue Max. He was not just a successful fighter ace but proved himself an excellent administrator. His all-around capabilities won him command of the Richthofen Circus after the death of the Red Baron in action. At the armistice, Captain Hermann Goering led the most famous aerial unit of the war. From chivalry, fame, and glory at the zenith of his flying career, Goering went tumbling into the social maelstrom of defeated Germany. His descent from life among the gods was sickening to his emotional and moral nature and spirit. Evidence of revolution and social disintegration was everywhere visible. Socialists and Communists on the left and numerous factions on the right locked themselves in verbal and physical combat all over Germany. War heroes were humiliated and spat upon.

Goering was revolted by what he saw. Soldiering and flying were all he knew. The winter of 1918–1919 became for him a personal nightmare. Anarchy threatened to engulf the country. Misery, poverty, and street violence were symbols of political chaos. Goering had not fought for four years for this. He began living a pillar-to-post life as a peacetime pilot; testing and promoting for Anthony Fokker, barnstorming, and operating an air-taxi.

The socioeconomic soil in postwar Germany was perfect to stimulate the growth of communism. The Communist Party was on its way to controlling Germany. A traditionalist and a professional officer like Goering could only react with rage towards these elements, until in November of 1922 the angry Goering found Hitler.

A spellbinding orator who articulated with precision the wrongs and shames of German life, Adolf Hitler seemed to be roaring Goering's own thoughts. Hitler also laid the pathway back to world respect for Germany. The Red betrayers, the Jews, and the Marxists would be eradicated. A new Germany would be built, proud and strong enough to tear up the humiliating Versailles Treaty. Goering was hooked. He had found a hero to supplant, in his own maturity, the godfather he had idolized in childhood. Hitler was a rising star to which Goering hitched his energy and ability.

Goering brought prestige to the Nazis, striving as they were for a respectable image. He was a member of the officer caste, a celebrated war hero, and a winner of the Blue Max. Hitler welcomed him and put him in charge of his 10,000 storm troopers, the SA (*Sturmabteilungen*). Goering turned them from a uniformed mob into dependable, smooth-working commandos. He infused them with high morale. Their public parades made good impressions. Their street operations against the hated Communists became highly successful.

Goering had entered a world not normally invaded by German officers— politics. Goering's high intelligence quickly grasped the intricacies of this new milieu, with its maneuvers and parlance. He was beside Hitler in Munich in November of 1923, when the Nazis tried to take over the government of Bavaria. This was a pivotal moment in Goering's life, because he took two bullets in the skirmish with the German Army.

One bullet in the hip was of no great significance, but the second shot entered his groin. Protracted and excruciating pain ensued and led him eventually to morphine addiction. Wounded, wanted, and hunted, the ex-hero was smuggled into Austria and thereafter led a desperate existence outside Germany. Hitler meanwhile languished as a prisoner in Landsberg Fortress, writing *Mein Kampf.* Goering was sustained in his ordeal by his wife Karin, whom he had met and married while operating his air-taxi into Sweden. They returned now to Sweden, where Goering had to face his unfortunate morphine addiction. At a hospital, his therapy was bungled and he became violent. Doctors straitjacketed him and committed him to Langbro Insane Asylum.

"Cold turkey" withdrawal followed in a padded cell, an ordeal guaranteed to weed out the nonsurvivors among drug addicts. Three months saw the return of his impressive mentality, and he was released, only to become readdicted and recommited. Two trips to hell and back nearly broke Goering's morale and spirit. Within he now carried a weakness, a mental wound as a counterpart to the gnawing presence in his groin. (He would not be free of dabbling with drugs again until dried out by the Allies after his surrender in 1945.)

Goering returned to Germany under a 1927 general political amnesty, over-weight, limping, and wasted. Hitler unenthusiastically told him to make a place for himself in commercial life, as a prelude to any further Nazi Party involvement. Goering bootstrapped himself up from zero in an epic comeback that verified his will power and gumption.

Landing a job as Berlin representative of BMW, he exploited every wartime friendship and connection. Bruno Loerzer gave him access to both Heinkel and Lufthansa. By energy and the shameless use of influence, the former Flying Trapezist was soon again riding high. He became a Nazi Party candidate in the 1928 *Reichstag* elections.

By studying Hitler, Goering had learned how to excite a mob through oratory. He put on a fierce political *Blitzkrieg* in Berlin and was elected. Only 11 other Nazis, including Hitler and Goebbels, sat in the *Reichstag* with him. Goering was on his way to the top.

Hitler put him on the Nazi Party payroll and sent him all over Germany as a spokesman and recruiter. Record crowds met him everywhere, and they started joining up. His hard financial times in exile faded behind him as his fortunes soared. Hanging onto his BMW agency despite his other responsibilities, Goering also became a paid political lobbyist for Lufthansa—courtesy of Erhard Milch.

Goering's background enabled him to influence the nobility in the direction of the Nazis. His aristocratic wife Karin, and his own social graces, gave the Nazis a respectability they needed. He promoted the Party with industrial and financial magnates. When the Nazis won 108 seats in the *Reichstag* in September of 1930, most of the credit for the Party's 96-seat gain belonged to Goering.

Despite the mortal illness of his wife, Goering maintained the pressure. His oratory repeatedly drew crowds in excess of 40,000 people in the bloody elections of 31 July 1932. Scores of people were killed in street battles, and hundreds were wounded as Reds and Nazis clashed all over Germany. When the dust settled, more than 13.5 million Germans had voted for Hitler, 38 percent of the vote. The Nazis now held the balance of power.

In the machinations that followed to make Hitler Chancellor of Germany,

Goering played a masterful role. His personal friendship with Germany's aged President von Hindenburg, dating from the war, allowed him access at will to the former Field Marshal. Von Hindenburg was opposed to appointing Hitler. Goering worked subtly on the old gentleman.

As President of the *Reichstag* Assembly, Goering first organized the ouster of Chancellor Franz von Papen through a *Reichstag* vote of censure. Goering then manipulated the Army and von Hindenburg's son to the side of the Nazis. The old Field Marshal himself thereafter acceded. Hitler was appointed Chancellor. Goering had completed a masterpiece of political engineering.

Goering's achievements up to this time were anything but dilettantism. He had become a master of politics. Once Hitler took office, Goering, as Prussian Minister of Interior and President of Police, ruthlessly purged the bureaucracies of all known anti-Nazis. He set up the *Forschungsamt*, the innocuous-sounding "Research Bureau," with monopoly control of wiretapping. Eventually to employ a force of more than 3,000 persons, the *Forschungsamt* eavesdropped on everything likely to be of use to Hitler and Goering. Foreign diplomatic traffic continuously in Hitler's hands contributed enormously to his prewar triumphs. Goering received daily digests of wiretapped information, ranging from foreign embassy intercepts to the scandal being traded by Nazi officials' wives. Goering used all this to protect his political position and to consolidate his grip on the vast range of offices that he assumed.

Under Hitler's first government, the new office of Commissioner of Aviation was created, with Goering in charge. He used this office to initiate the birth of the new German Air Force, which he had long envisaged as a separate, independent service arm. (As previously related, Adolf Galland met Hermann Goering for the first time during this period, and he was impressed by the new commissioner's vision of Germany's aerial future. As he sat in that May audience in 1933, Galland was not to know, or even dream, that his professional life and fortunes would be so directly and drastically influenced by this man.)

Goering initiated *Luftwaffe* development, but an Air Force could not be built with his enthusiasm alone. The actual work of creating the *Luftwaffe* from near zero was the responsibility of other men, far more technically capable than Goering. The prime mover was Goering's deputy and State Secretary, Erhard Milch, the tough ex-boss of Lufthansa. Goering wanted a *Luftwaffe* fast, and, when Milch obliged, Goering became jealous and acted to limit his power.

Several major reorganizations in the 1930s failed to prevent a destructive rivalry between Milch and the *Luftwaffe* General Staff. Instead of insisting on harmony, Goering allowed the friction to become chronic. The *Luftwaffe* suffered from these squabbles, but Goering obviously preferred that his main subordinates waste energy in rivalry. That way, there were no rivals for Goering.

His authority and political influence in Nazi Germany placed maximum resources behind the developing Air Force. Goering's ruthless energy smashed through bureaucratic barriers, securing priorities and precious raw materials for the *Luftwaffe*. This enabled the new Air Force to be created in minimum time, despite its inner weaknesses. Since Goering's numerous offices included Minister of the Four Year Plan, finance ceased to be a problem for building the *Luftwaffe*. Goering had no technical knowledge. Tuning in a broadcast on a radio taxed him technically, by his own admission. He nevertheless made himself Commander in Chief of the most highly technical of all the armed services.

He made technical decisions of far-reaching consequence, such as shelving the long-range bomber, and he allowed the dive bombing obsession to get out of hand. At critical wartime junctures, he brushed aside the advice of capable generals and sometimes took personal charge of operations for which he had no training. His high-command career is a catalog of miscalculation and disaster. Due to the nature of his upbringing in the shadow of Ritter von Epenstein, he was intoxicated by his desire to command.

Glory he regarded as his divine right. He demanded and basked in all the credit for the creation of "my *Luftwaffe*," and for its stunning early successes. Others were shut out. In defeat, he sought scapegoats, with unscrupulous zeal. He played favorites and was ill-served by the favorites he chose.

Envy often motivated him. Able subordinates in key posts were likely to find their authority and powers circumscribed by Goering. This was done with Galland. Goering once confided to Colonel Josef "Fips" Priller, a successor to Galland as *Kommodore* of JG-26, that he envied Galland's leadership talent and his ability to get the best out of subordinates. Yet in his own circle, Goering surrounded himself with toadies and sycophants of total transparency. They gave him poor advice. A realist like Galland, making recommendations based on logic, fact, and experience, usually found Goering's reactions entirely based on politics. His chief political goal was self-protection—the maintenance of his position.

Goering's emotions swung back and forth like a weighted cord. He could pass in seconds from friendly interest to abuse and invective, and he had done so since childhood. Drugs amplified this trait but caused a clouding of his superb intelligence. News of heavy aircraft losses could make him weep openly, yet he would persist in the unwise stratagems that caused numerous combat deaths.

Goering was cultivated, with an appreciation of fine art and elegant living, yet he associated politically with coarse individuals of the Nazi Party whose grossness revolted him. He was one of the most ruthless men in the most ruthless state of modern times, but he loved and protected animals. He was a conservationist of the first rank, a practical and yet visionary ecologist before that word ever became fashionable. The steps he took to protect German wildlife and forests showed both foresight and insight.

Goering was happily married. After his great love, Karin, passed away, he found marital peace with his second wife Emmy, and he was a loving and tender father. He sent many men to their deaths, yet he insisted on the chivalrous treatment of captured enemy flyers. His lifestyle was supported from many sources, including clandestine payoffs from industrialists seeking his influence and favor.

Fully awake to the magic of great paintings, he could not resist the temptation to plunder such works for his own collection.

Goering on social occasions was a man of great charm and charisma and a lavish host. He could rise to towering rages and bellow threats to Galland, and afterwards in cooler days he would apologize humbly for his conduct.

From this brief but realistic overview of Goering, his forcefulness will be seen as permeating all his errors and as the character trait that produced his grossest mistakes. Goering was something much more than the posturing clown whose portrait propaganda has left in the world.

When Galland's most important promotions were thrust on him by this complex and difficult man, Goering was old enough to be his father. To the Supreme Commander's high military rank was added his vast life experience, his maturity, and his status in the German state. All these things could overawe almost any young *Luftwaffe* officer. Against this lumbering bull in a technological china shop, Galland had only his intelligence, ability, experience, and integrity. Clash between them was inevitable, given Galland's resolve never to lick the *Reich* Marshal's boots or to meet him on any other ground than that of intellectual logic.

CHAPTER EIGHT

The young *Gruppenkommandeur* in the Pas de Calais had no inkling in the summer of 1940 of the pressures building up at high levels in Germany's armed forces. Galland was confident, superbly trained, and determined to do his best against the RAF. His combat experience and demonstrated competence united III/JG-26 behind him into one of the finest operational fighter units in the world. They were ready. That was not true elsewhere.

When Hitler on 16 July 1940 ordered his armed services chiefs to prepare for the invasion of Britain, the three high commands had little of the unity of purpose found in *Luftwaffe* fighter *Gruppen*. The Army immediately demanded sufficient shipping space of the Navy to transport troops, weapons, and supplies across the English Channel. The Navy demanded *Luftwaffe* air cover for the assembly of the invasion fleet in the Channel ports, and an air umbrella for the invasion itself.

The earliest date the Navy could agree to for the invasion, code-named Sealion, was mid-September. That set the time frame for all else. Air superiority was the central hinge upon which Sealion would turn, and air superiority was established by fighter aircraft. The Royal Navy could only be sunk or driven out of the invasion area by air action, since the German Navy was not strong enough on the surface or with sufficient U-boats for this task. Such air action required air superiority as basic protection for German bombers. If the Royal Navy could not be driven away from the invasion scene, certain death would await the German Army in transit.

If an invasion force were landed successfully, air superiority would have to be maintained over the beaches. Without this umbrella, German reinforcements and supplies would be halted by British air action. Germany's elite parachute regiments and other airborne forces might well wreak havoc if landed at strategic points in Britain, but they could not be delivered to such points through skies alive with Spitfires and Hurricanes. The air thus emerged as the dominant and

Katschmarek Hegenauer, Galland's trusty and loyal wingman, dismounts from his fighter after a flight.

Galland's ground crew helps him don his flying clothing as Crew Chief Gerhard Meyer gets the cockpit ready. His armament mechanic Heinrich Olemotz is far right.

decisive element. The Army and Navy found themselves dependent upon the *Luftwaffe*—the newest and least understood service branch—in forging strategy for a high-risk amphibious operation.

Germany's able planners were sobered by the magnitude and hazards of Sealion. Lack of professional enthusiasm for the operation followed. Hitler had personally ordered that Sealion was to proceed, although his main hope at that time was to force Britain into peace talks. This was not communicated to the planners, of course. Fear of Hitler's wrath drove professional pessimism underground, whence it emerged in the form of inordinate demands made by the services on each other. Resources and capabilities were pushed beyond their limits by these demands.

Three strategic missions for the *Luftwaffe* came out of Sealion planning. All three missions depended upon the Fighter Arm:

1. Britain had to be air blockaded in cooperation with the Navy, through attacks on shipping and ports. Such attacks required fighter protection.

2. Air superiority had to be won over southeastern England, to secure invasion areas against British air attack. Fighter Command had to be mastered in its own airspace.

3. Aerial bombardment of British targets by the Bomber Arm. Fighter escort and fighter protection were essential to such attacks.

This was a tall order for the *Luftwaffe*. Primacy had also come to the Fighter Arm, a status unforeseen by the *Luftwaffe* High Command. Given the strictly tactical structure of the *Luftwaffe,* enormous luck and substantial enemy errors would be necessary for successful discharge of its threefold Sealion mission.

Apprehensions over Sealion surfaced in high conferences. Well-founded professional misgivings made little impression on Goering. He was out to please his hero. Goering therefore assumed the responsibility for subduing Britain "with my *Luftwaffe*." Such total air war had been theorized by Douhet, embraced and touted by air power visionaries, and debated in war colleges. Never yet had it been seen in the real world.

Goering's penchant for exaggeration was a dangerous trait to have running amok in highly technical matters. The *Reich* Marshal committed the *Luftwaffe* to a truly immense operational task, motivated by a desire to please Hitler and to consolidate his own status. (Goering would soon have cause to regret this precipitate offering of his bright weapon.)

Only five days after issuing his Directive 16 for Sealion, Hitler told Field Marshal Walther von Brauchistch, C.-in-C. of the Army, to make immediate plans for invasion of the Soviet Union. This dampened Goering's enthusiasm for Directive 17, issued on 1 August 1940, calling for unrestricted air-sea warfare against Britain. Hitler wanted to see what the *Luftwaffe* could do to make feasible the tentative mid-September invasion of England—the technical feasibility of which the *Fuehrer* increasingly doubted.

Hitler's emotional commitment was to the conquest of Bolshevist Russia. England could be dealt with later. *Luftwaffe* forces required for invasion of the

Soviet Union would soon be removed from the West. Goering was meanwhile authorized to try and conquer the RAF. The Fat One was therefore under extreme pressure. Hitler was keeping his options open at *Luftwaffe* expense.

The largest aerial assault in history up to that time was to go westward, simultaneously with preparations for a land invasion of unprecedented scope— in the opposite direction. Hitler and Goering were involving Germany in a two-front war, and Goering was opposed to the attack on Russia. (This was all beyond the ken of young Major Galland in August of 1940. Like all other *Luftwaffe* pilots, he was completely unaware that Goering and Hitler were pointed in opposite directions.)

Galland's unit was part of Air Fleet 2, commanded by Field Marshal Albert Kesselring from his HQ in Brussels. Only these fighter aircraft, based in the Pas de Calais, could reach London and operate for 10 minutes before returning to their bases. Fighter units under Air Fleet 3, commanded by Field Marshal Hugo Sperrle in Paris, were on a shorter leash. From bases around Le Havre, they could make it only to the southern outskirts of London.

Jettisonable auxiliary fuel tanks were not available for the Me-109 at this time. They had been proposed to the Technical Office but not acted upon with sufficient energy or dispatch. Such tanks had been successfully improvised by the Condor Legion in Spain, and their feasibility had been firmly established on the Curtiss Hawk fighter in 1933. The Me-109s needed another 100 miles of range. (This deficiency would bedevil Galland and the rest of the Fighter Arm in their life-and-death struggle with the RAF.)

A third *Luftwaffe* strike force against England was Colonel-General Stumpff's Air Fleet 5, based in Norway and Denmark. Bombers of this force were to make outflanking attacks on northeastern Britain. Their long approach across the North Sea precluded Me-109 escort. Only the slower and less-maneuverable twin-engined Me-110 could cross with Stumpff's bombers. The *Luftwaffe* High Command intended such attacks to increase the pressure on Fighter Command. Through *Ultra* intercepts, Air Chief Marshal Dowding of Fighter Command knew of these plans. He took steps to deal with Stumpff's force.

Luftwaffe fighter pilots were operating in 1940 without any fighter-control system. German radar lagged technically behind the British. For the struggle in English skies, therefore, radar control of *Luftwaffe* fighters was nonexistent. In the first phase of the battle, when the *Luftwaffe* attacked Channel shipping, the absence of such control was not felt. The pilots were unaccustomed to such help. Airborne formation leaders controled operations. That is the way it was when German fighters began sweeping over the Channel and the southeastern English coast from 24 July 1940 onwards. (Nearly 50 years after these events, it is easy to grasp how extensively the *Luftwaffe* fighter pilots were disadvantaged by lack of proper fighter control.)

Leading his *Gruppe* over English territory, Galland took part in this first effort to engage RAF fighters in combat. The RAF rose to the challenge with its Hurricanes and Spitfires, making good interceptions through its fighter-control

The General makes a staff visit. Galland's crew chief Gerhard Meyer attends to the cockpit of the Siebl SH-104 while General Galland talks to Lt. Cols. Horst Geyer and Georg Christl.

When two stubborn and determined enemy pilots refuse to give way during a head-on pass, it takes a degree of luck to survive. "Wutz" Galland collided with a P-47 Thunderbolt and landed okay.

system. Unfortunately for the RAF, its obsolete three-fighter Vics were tactically eclipsed by the modern finger-four *Luftwaffe* formations developed by Moelders in Spain. When the British operated in squadrons in tight formation, the planes could be spotted at great distances. The advantages of their fighter-control system were thereby partially neutralized. Loose and widely strung out, the German formations were harder to see. Their staggered altitudes were a lesson to the RAF in the value of dispersal in sweep operations. British fighters waiting on the perch to bounce their incoming foes would sometimes be taken from behind by Galland's unobserved formation, because they had been spotted far away. This occurred despite British radar.

Galland found the Hurricane well outclassed by his Me-109. Spitfires of that period were marginally slower than the Me-109 but compensated for that with superior maneuverability. The Me-109's fuel injection pumps had an edge over the Merlin-powered RAF fighters, whose carburetors tended to produce engine misfiring during negative-G combat maneuvers. The *Luftwaffe* had first-class armament and ammunition that Galland felt were superior to those then in use by the RAF.

After about three weeks of combat, in which the RAF suffered heavier losses than the *Luftwaffe,* the British slowly switched to German-style formations. The British also rapidly adapted tactics to the new realities. RAF fighters made precise interceptions through their early warning and fighter-control systems. The British integrated chain of radar stations along the English southeast coast picked up Galland and his *Gruppe* shortly after their Pas de Calais takeoff. Once the Germans climbed to 2,000 metres, they were on the RAF plot.

Radar sets the electronically determined course, altitude, and speed of the raiders. These data were put on the central plot at Fighter Command in Stanmore. Such a comprehensive radar system permitted substantial economies as well as precision in the commitment of RAF fighters. Radar information was supplemented by reports of the Ground Observer Corps. The existence of such a sophisticated system gave the *Luftwaffe* High Command a nasty jolt, since it was making dispositions and decisions based on faulty intelligence.

Major Josef "Beppo" Schmid, the *Luftwaffe* High Command's Chief Intelligence Officer, had drawn up a study entitled "Comparative Survey of RAF and Luftwaffe Striking Power" on 16 July 1940—the day Hitler ordered Sealion. This study contained no mention of long-distance radio detection and ranging, and what it might mean to diminish *Luftwaffe* striking power. Schmid made other gross errors that were fed to *Luftwaffe* commanders via this study.

RAF fighter strength was overestimated by 30 percent. British aircraft production and repair capabilities were seriously underestimated. These erroneous appraisals became a fount of subsequent German miscalculations. (The German High Command went through the Battle of Britain without any accurate information about the status of RAF Fighter Command or the true results of their own operations.)

Using *Ultra* decrypts and other intelligence, the British captured more than

20 German agents dispatched to Britain by various means in the summer and autumn of 1940. These spies were either imprisoned or "bent" into double agents and used to feed disinformation to the Germans. The *Luftwaffe* thus went through the entire battle minus any worthwhile spies on enemy ground. The *Luftwaffe* attitude towards intelligence, furthermore, remains one of its more notorious failures.

Goering had a typical politician's talent for ignoring unwelcome or politically distasteful facts. This spirit spread downwards. Notably infected was General Hans Jeschonnek, chief of the *Luftwaffe* General Staff, among others. (Galland would in due course encounter incredible examples of the way in which crucial information could be ignored, shunted aside, or papered over if it ran counter to Goering's own politically based ideas. Goering dealt with adverse factual information by ordering that it did not exist.)

Air Chief Marshal Sir Hugh Dowding at Stanmore, meanwhile, was receiving priceless information from the *Ultra* decrypting teams at Bletchley Park. Immense skill and intellect went into the decrypts received by Dowding. The elaborate electromechanical decrypting was in itself a nightmare of complexity; but thereafter, translations, analyses, and assessments had to be made of the decrypts. There was not always a lot of material available, but what reached Dowding had high value because he knew how to use the information.

Almost from day to day, Dowding knew *Luftwaffe* intentions. He knew in advance the changes in strategy that Goering, Kesselring, and Sperrle were about to make. Information on the status of the Air Fleets across the Channel was sufficient to enable Dowding to orchestrate RAF fighter operations with consummate skill and subtlety. He husbanded his precious Spitfires and Hurricanes and his even more precious pilots—the latter his Achilles heel in the battle. Dowding had more factual information about the course of the Battle of Britain than all the German commanders facing him combined. He also had the training, mentality, experience, and judgment to interpret these facts correctly.

Dowding's career had started as a combat pilot with the RFC in World War I. He rose in the service in a varied career always close to fighters. The British were acutely conscious of their need for a strong fighter defense. Zeppelins and the German Gotha bombers of the first war had driven this lesson home. The secondary and limited role assigned to fighters in the *Luftwaffe* was something that Dowding did not have to struggle against, as Galland would have to do in Germany almost to the end of the war.

Between 1930 and 1936, Dowding was responsible with others for the development and acceptance of all-metal, eight-gun, monoplane fighters in the RAF. When he became A.O.C. Fighter Command in 1936, Dowding was intimately involved in the subsequent development of the British early warning radar system. He had been present at Dr. Robert Watson-Watt's first tests of radiolocation, as radar was initially called. Integration of this revolutionary development with Fighter Command control, took place under Dowding.

What came as a shock to Dowding's opponents across the Channel was long since woven into his mental fabric and incorporated into his management of events in 1940. The Germans had nothing to match Dowding's organic understanding of the complex weaponry involved in defending Britain. When the *Ultra* information was added to this, Dowding became the ultimate air general in 1940. His brave pilots, upon whom all would depend, had the best man in Britain to lead them.

Hermann Goering by contrast, was probably the most incompetent battle commander the *Luftwaffe* could have had at the most important moment in its existence. He had been disconnected from aviation technically since World War I. Although he had no background for the exacting responsibilities of high command, that did not stop him from shoving professionals aside and taking over personally.

None of these factors was even remotely in the mind of Adolf Galland during these hectic summer weeks. The battle simply came at him over the cowling of his Me-109, in a blazing maelstrom of kill-or-be-killed aloft. Strategy and military principles weren't considered. Leading III/JG-26 on up to four sweeps a day over southeastern England put him to his limit. The strain was almost as lethal as the RAF, putting the German pilots and their aircraft to the ragged end of their endurance.

As a *Gruppenkommandeur,* Galland was haunted by many other anxieties than the taxing presence of imminent combat. Newer and less-able pilots had to be watched over and, if possible, guided through to expertise. Always there was the damned English Channel, chewing up their fuel as they commuted to their few minutes of combat over or near England.

After combat, the leaden waters awaited them if they were shot up or ran out of fuel on the way back to France. Victories over the RAF were soured when German pilots went into the drink themselves, even when unwounded and with their fighters fully operational. The RAF sent Spitfires to finish off cripples and stragglers. At Udet's initiative, an air-sea rescue service was set up to save pilots from the sea, and buoys with survival gear were used by both sides. The Germans also set up "reception" operations, in which fresh Me-109s would fly out over the Channel to protect fighters and bombers returning to France.

Galland's own fighting spirit remained undiminished in spite of the cares of a *Gruppenkommandeur*. His wingmen could hardly stay with him as he hurled himself on the RAF. His old and finely honed aerobatic skills and his marksmanship proved invaluable. In the absence of radar, so did his hunter's nose. He found continuous combat success. Field Marshal Kesselring pinned the Knight's Cross to the Iron Cross on him at a field investiture in the Pas de Calais on 1 August 1940.

His fame as a fighter ace and combat leader was spreading. Magazines and newspapers began publishing articles on him and publishing photographs—

including a profile that vividly illustrated his bent nose. The Galland legend was taking form. The Germans needed success in the Battle of Britain, and their top-scoring fighter pilots epitomized success. They were the most dazzling feature on the German side, amid the many frustrations inflicted by the RAF. Galland's friend Moelders was still the *Luftwaffe*'s top scorer; but Galland, Helmut Wieck, and Wilhelm Balthasar were likely to overtake him if Moelders had to take a few weeks off for any reason. Rivalry was intense among these friends.

Dowding remained undeceived by German efforts to lure his fighters into massive battle with the *Luftwaffe*. A trait of fighter pilots all over the world is aggressiveness. They want to hurl themselves on an enemy aircraft as though their own lives depend on clawing the enemy machine down immediately. Dowding knew this, as an old fighter pilot himself. Commanders of large fighter forces cannot always afford to indulge this aggressive practice. Dowding had Britain's fate in his hands.

Knowing through *Ultra* the size and scope of the bombing attacks to be launched by the enemy Air Fleets, Dowding practised artistic restraint in using his fighters. Fighter sweeps by the *Luftwaffe,* or small decoy flights of a few bombers on isolated targets, could not seriously injure Britain. If Dowding rose to every challenge however, his fighters would be frittered away. England would be naked before the *Luftwaffe* Bomber Arm.

During the weeks of provocative German fighter sweeps over England, Stukas and Ju-88 bombers attacked shipping in the Thames estuary and off the English coast. Fierce fighter battles developed around these operations. Casualties among the Stukas were fearful. Escorting them was nerve-wracking, because the loaded dive bombers had a top speed of around 250 mph. With an approach altitude varying between 10,000 and 15,000 feet, down in denser air the Stukas drew the Me-109s out of their best element and into increased vulnerability to the controlled RAF interceptions. Stukas pulling up out of their dives were easy targets for the aggressive RAF fighter pilots.

Pilots of the much-vaunted Stukas had been largely drawn from the Fighter Arm before the war, in one of the numerous raids made by the High Command on fighter pilot personnel. They were among the best-trained flyers in the *Luftwaffe*. Irreplaceable now, they went down in dozens over England in a futile sacrifice that made Galland blanch. He knew many of them personally. He did not like seeing them massacred.

For the *Luftwaffe's* numerous dive bomber advocates in high rank, the Stuka slaughter over Britain was a stunning setback. (The Stuka survived to serve with distinction in close support of the German Army everywhere, but it did not belong in skies haunted by eight-gun British fighters. Unacceptable losses of Stukas and crews forced their final withdrawal from the Battle of Britain by mid-September.)

The RAF continued to come up for battle, never in large wings but always enough to give trouble. The British made operations expensive for the *Luftwaffe* and held their own casualties within tolerable limits. Flying two, three, and

Captains Joachim Müncheberg and Walter Schneider have just flipped a coin to see who rides the JG26 mascot next. Aboard is Robert Weiss. Fate was unkind to all three pilots, Schneider being killed 22 December 1941, Müncheberg killed 23 March 1943 and Weiss killed 29 December 1944.

Unteroffizier Meyer, Galland's loyal and efficient crew chief, help Galland don his Mae West.

Victory toast. Captain Walter Kienzle congratulates Lt. Col. Galland for a recent air victory over England, 1940.

sometimes four sweeps or escorts a day, Galland felt the mounting inroads on his own reserves of energy and morale. Individual successes by his *Gruppe* against RAF fighters continued as the only ray of light in a darkening situation. By switching stratagems and continually failing to lure the RAF into a fighter battle of annihilation, the *Luftwaffe* High Command was slowly eroding the confidence of its own pilots. Competent top leadership is essential to fighting spirit. No matter what the *Luftwaffe* High Command tried, RAF fighters just kept coming up in potent little packets, and they chipped away steadily at both *Luftwaffe* aircraft and pilot morale.

Bad weather gave occasional respite from the grind. Relief from battle tension acted on Galland like a tonic. His vitality would rebound. Fortified by extra sleep, he would take his shotgun and go hunting, bringing back pheasants and hares for the pot. Quarters were comfortable, usually in a pleasant country home that had been commandeered. Fresh food was plentiful, and so was good French wine.

He tried during these weather breaks to forget the war. Writing letters to the families of his dead pilots precluded that, and it was a depressing task. An optimistic weather forecast might mean operations on the morrow. That would mean more letters to write and new gaps at the mess table. Galland felt every loss personally.

Galland was strongly critical of himself and his own leadership, taking himself to task and analyzing every operation for mistakes and oversights. The system of escorting and protecting bombers was highly imperfect, and it was further complicated by the twin-engined Me-110 fighter. Despite its greater range and heavier firepower, the Me-110 itself needed fighter escort. The touted "Destroyer" could not fulfill its designed mission of protecting the bombers at longer ranges.

Procedures were set up in Galland's *Gruppe* under which an element leader who lost a wingman, or vice versa, had to report on why the comrade was lost. The young *Gruppenkommandeur* made a searching analysis of each such report. He hunted down inadequacies and omissions within his own *Gruppe* with the same determination as he hunted the RAF.

Goering and other high *Luftwaffe* personages, accustomed to quick and dazzling success, were upset by the RAF's continuing resilience. Goering for years had demanded prompt compliance with his orders. People jumped to satisfy each whim. The RAF was frustrating his wishes. Goering's irrational traits caused him to project onto others his failures as *Luftwaffe* Supreme Commander. He reacted to the frustrating situation over England by reproaching his warriors.

When the first recriminatory teletype was put in front of the nearly exhausted Galland, the tension of battle still shaking him, his reaction was an incredulous rage. He was doing his utmost. *Gott im Himmel!* The *Reich* Marshal could not possibly mean what he was saying. Further similar teletypes erased all doubt. Goering was laying blame. After scores of sorties over the damned Channel, one milling air battle after another—with the RAF always in the right attack position—Galland was being reproached. Worse than that, the courage of his pilots was being impugned.

Goering's actions made no sense to the battle-weary young *Gruppenkommandeur*. Orders then came through to attend a war conference at Karinhall, Goering's country estate northeast of Berlin. Good. Perhaps he would have the opportunity to explain to the *Reich* Marshal, in person, exactly what the Fighter Arm was up against. Galland knew that somewhere there had been a serious miscalculation.

CHAPTER NINE

Flying back to Berlin, Galland pondered while airborne the problems of the ongoing battle. He recognized that he could not see the whole picture, while commanding less than 40 fighters in daily operations. He nevertheless grasped intuitively that this mighty air battle was pivotal and must not be lost. Everything had come to depend on the *Luftwaffe* fighter pilots for a German victory. The High Command had not foreseen that development.

Nearly two weeks previously, the battle to subdue RAF Fighter Command had been activated on 8 August 1940 as "Eagle Day" (*Adler Tag*). Bad weather forced delays, but by 12 August Kesselring and Sperrle were putting 300 aircraft into the air. RAF forward airfields like Manston, Hawkinge, and Lympne were being hammered in a crescendo of strikes. German operations on 12, 13, and 14 August were not the real Eagle Day. From *Ultra* decrypts, Air Chief Marshal Dowding knew that 15 August 1940 would be Goering's maximum effort thus far to conquer Fighter Command.

The British commander once more was compelled to orchestrate his response carefully, avoiding premature overcommitment.

Goering planned staggered strikes against airfields and radar installations in southern England. This ruse would make the attacks seem to come from all directions. Goering intended to hammer at Fighter Command not only in the air, and through its airfields, but also through its morale. Goering's main goal was to so goad the RAF fighters skyward in force that they could be destroyed by the superior weight and tactics of the *Luftwaffe*.

Heavy pressure in the south of England would also draw down into battle the fighter units guarding northeastern Britain. Stumpff's bombers from Norway and Denmark, with their Me-110 escort, would come hurtling in to assault an undefended northeast coast. These blows would create additional strain on Fighter Command and help break its spirit. This was the plan for Goering's Eagle Day. (Over 1,700 sorties would be flown by the *Luftwaffe*.)

Sound in principle, the plan's defect was that it was known to Dowding. He turned Eagle Day into a *Luftwaffe* debacle by continuing his masterly handling of his fighters: 75 German aircraft were downed, for the loss of 34 RAF fighters. Goering's losses were neither irreparable nor out of proportion to his goal. The *Luftwaffe* reverse was nevertheless unexpected, hurt Goering's pride, and gave the British a propaganda binge, with their ecstatic overclaims of downings. British claims went as high as 182 aircraft.

Despite intense pressure on the RAF over southeastern England, Dowding did not strip the northeast coast of fighters. *Ultra* decrypts gave precise information on General Stumpff's Eagle Day bomber strikes. This advance information, in combination with radar, resulted in RAF fighters meeting their 100 uninvited visitors well out over the open sea. The British claimed 15 aircraft downed from this first formation. A second wave of 50 German aircraft was also roughly handled, with the RAF claiming eight downings, for no losses of their own. Stumpff's Air Fleet 5 contributed only casualties to Eagle Day.

Galland had been flying with his *Gruppe* in the August battles before, during, and after Eagle Day. He had seen how Goering's fighter escort policy had played into the hands of the RAF. The German fighter pilots in their majority were forbidden to wade into the RAF as they came up but were required under strict orders to stay close to the bombers.

Galland had found it bitterly frustrating to wait while he could see RAF fighters positioning themselves for attacks on the bombers he was escorting. Experience had already proved repeatedly in this war that attack by a fighter was its best defense. Going at the enemy hard and fast seized the psychological as well as the tactical initiative. *Waiting to be attacked* was the absolute negation of the purpose and mission of a fighter pilot. The strict close escort order led to heavy *Luftwaffe* losses—both bombers and fighters.

This third phase of the Battle of Britain struck Galland as basically unsound in concept. He had a shrewdness for what was effective against the enemy. Bombers may have been punching lines of craters in the turf at Manston in the morning, but, when the Germans returned in the afternoon, the British had filled the craters. The fighters had been able to take off. The bombers would punch more holes in the turf. The aerodromes and buildings were obviously being battered, but the undeniable reality was that the RAF fighters were still operating.

Amid the hot combat, Galland tried to keep a cool perspective. The airfields were being hit, but most British aircraft on the ground were cunningly parked behind high banks and revetments. Designed to frustrate strafing runs and to minimize splinter and blast damage, these shelters protected against anything except a direct hit. There were more airfields farther inland. The RAF could move to those. That would make it harder still for Galland and his pilots, cursed by their short fuel leash, to tangle with their foes.

The *Luftwaffe* fighters were flying escort missions of four kinds:
1. Direct escort.
2. Indirect or deployed escort.

3. Freelance patrols, coordinated timewise with and ahead of the fighter-protected bomber stream.

4. Supplementary escorts, to pick up and cover returning bombers and to protect air-sea rescue.

Direct escort missions involved squadrons split up into flights of two or four aircraft, these providing direct cover for the bombers. They used their superior speed to weave in zig-zag fashion around and among the bombers. This purely defensive mission was disliked by the German fighter pilots, and it was rarely effective against attacking RAF fighters. The Germans were robbed in these missions of the high-speed aggressive role—a serious drawback. Bomber crews favored such direct escort, which was reassuring to them in their near-defenseless state, and insisted that they be maintained.

Indirect or deployed escort missions were carried out in squadron strength at a higher altitude than the direct escort. The deployed escort flew in the general direction of anticipated British attacks. Their task was to jump RAF fighters before the latter could attack the bombers. The deployed escort remained in visual contact with the bomber force it was protecting. This meant that, in actual operations, these escorts could only engage in one combat before reforming and continuing the escort mission. Neutralization of imminent fighter attacks was the main object of this type of escort mission.

Freelance fighter patrols were sent ahead into areas through which the following bomber and escort forces would fly and also over the target itself. Flying on the approximate course of the bombers, but on that side from which RAF attacks were anticipated, freelance patrols were carried out in squadron or in *Gruppe* strength. Out of visual contact with the bombers, they were to seek RAF fighters and shoot them down, fighting the way clear for the bombers. German fighter pilots preferred freelance patrols to all other escort work.

After a mission, the freelance patrols were the rearguards. Dowding largely frustrated the freelance patrols by not rising to meet every fighter sweep. When RAF fighters were scrambled, they had to gather and climb up, at which time the Me-109s would press their attacks.

The supplementary escort missions were also carried out in squadron or in *Gruppe* strength. Their task was to counter the inevitable dispersal of the original formation of bombers and fighters after reaching their objective and after aerial battles. Supplementary escorts took station on damaged bombers limping home, and they usually met the returning main formation over the English coast between Manston and Dungeness. These escorts made it hazardous for British fighters to operate beyond mid-Channel.

Luftwaffe bombers and fighters made their rendezvous near the fighter airfields, usually over a prominent coastal landmark, at predetermined times and altitudes. Galland observed how frequently late-arriving bombers attached themselves to other fighter escorts than their assigned ones. The following bomber formations found themselves often with no escort. They had to face the RAF that way or abort the mission.

Kommodore of JG 27 in Africa. Lt. Col. Eduard Neumann says he is only a "little ace" because he had 13 aerial victories total. He was, however, considered to be one of the finest Kommodores in the Luftwaffe and he molded Hans-Joachim Marseille into becoming one of the best of Germany's aces.

Major Adolf Galland, Kommodore of JG26, affectionately pats his dog during a quiet moment on the front in 1940.

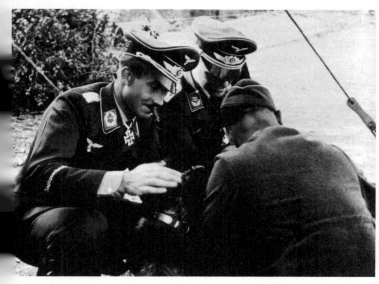

Incompatibility between bomber and fighter R/T equipment made it impossible for them to cooperate through air-to-air communication. Relays through ground stations were used between bombers and fighters, but it was a clumsy and inefficient arrangement. RAF communications were markedly superior. Special tactical rules or uniformities in planning were nonexistent in the *Luftwaffe* at this time for the task at hand. Each fighter *Geschwader* discharged its missions as it thought best. Wide disparities in performance were the result.

Galland chafed under these deficiencies and shortcomings in the escort "system"—if it could be dignified by that word—and especially at the way advantage in attack was usually passed to the RAF. The young major recalled ruefully that, in peacetime, practice missions escorting bombers had never been carried out by the Fighter Arm. The High Command had assumed for years that Germany's fast new bombers would not need fighter escort.

The excessively passive-escort system that had now spuriously evolved also allowed escaping British fighters a head start after their attack on the bombers. (Nearly half a century later, the error of rigorously restricting most German fighters to close bomber escort in this August period is easy to see. Goering's obstinacy in this respect tipped the battle balance away from the *Luftwaffe*.)

Adolf Galland could see the essential problems in the middle of the maelstrom. He was eager for the chance now imminent to tell Goering personally about the escort situation. Galland landed in Berlin with his thoughts well organized but with the strain of battle still in his body.

In Berlin the civilian scene was unreal. A flying soldier only hours from mortal combat, Galland gaped at carefree crowds splashing money around as though it were carnival time. Movies, nightclubs, and theaters were packed. Bars were jumping with people. Laughter rippled everywhere. The deadly struggle he had just left was as remote as the moon to these crowds. The Berlin scene depressed him.

Whisked by staff car to Goering's Karinhall estate, the woodsman lurking inside the young fighter ace revelled in the rural panoramas unfolding beside the speeding Mercedes. This was the Germany he loved. Then it was another dose of unreality—Karinhall.

A feudal monarch could not have dwelled in a more imposing forest stronghold. Reeded buildings surrounded an immense courtyard. Lily ponds, garden beds, and a statue of a nude hunter sighting his bow from horseback dominated the exterior. Inside the main hall, mighty oak beams soared overhead. Pine-lined walls were hung with stag heads and bearskin rugs lay about the floor. Almost the whole width of the room at one end was filled by a massive stone fireplace. As a hunter Galland could admire Karinhall. As a fighter leader, he could not help reflecting on how far all this was from the English Channel, and from the problems there needing urgent solution.

Colonels and generals present for the conference were optimistic and confident. Major Galland felt a certain shrinkage in his own concerns in the presence of such high-level confidence. These officers had unfortunately formed their opin-

Friends and rivals. Majors Adolf Galland and Werner Mölders meet on the veranda of JG26 Headquarters at Audembert. Galland often chided Mölders not to be so rigid in his social life.

Prosit! 1 November 1940 at Audembert, Galland as Kommodore of JG26 and Mölders, Kommodore of JG51, toasted each other's health and success. Galland had been promoted to Lt. Colonel and Mölders had tallied his 50th aerial victory.

ions on the ground. They had not experienced the resilience and skill of the RAF, or the way the British fighters just kept coming up.

Senior officers listened attentively and made suggestions. Their aides made notes. There was soldierly concern, but between the fighting pilots and their higher commanders there was a massive gulf. Galland was concerned that the operational problems of escorting bombers were not comprehended by the higher commanders or by the *Luftwaffe* General Staff officers present.

Goering was initially at his paternal best. Werner Moelders had also been ordered to attend this conference. Now the two rivals were taken aside by the Supreme Commander and an animated discussion ensued. Galland and Moelders between them gave Goering an accurate, up-to-the-minute summation of why Eagle Day and the battle to date had not gone well—from their point of view as fighter pilots and as combat leaders.

They explained the operational drawbacks of close-escort orders. They described from first hand the complex problems of rendezvous, station-keeping, communications, fuel limitations, and flak, which made the close-escort system the least-effective way to damage the RAF. Free chase of RAF fighters, by contrast, had been highly effective. These downed RAF fighters could not come up again to attack German bombers. Goering listened glumly. He had obviously already made up his mind.

Taking two small leather cases out of his pocket, the *Reich* Marshal presented Galland and Moelders with the massive Pilot's Badge in Gold, with Diamonds. Goering praised their bravery. The shimmering decorations symbolized Germany's gratitude for their accomplishments.

"You two have done splendidly, *as individuals,*" said Goering, "but I am not satisfied with the overall performance of my Fighter Arm. There isn't enough aggressive spirit. *That* is the real reason our escorts are letting the RAF through to shoot down our bombers. Our fighters must show more willingness to fling themselves on the enemy, just as we did in the first war."

Practical operational problems of crucial importance were thus avoided. In Goering's eyes, Eagle Day had failed because of the fighter pilots. When Galland and Moelders began responding to this slur, Goering curtly held up his hand.

"I'm going to revive the aggressive spirit of my Fighter Arm, no matter what steps I have to take," he said. "First step is to make both of you a *Kommodore*—give each of you a full *Geschwader* to command. I'm getting rid of all the older pilots. You young and successful ones are going up to command. Moelders, you will now command JG-51. Galland, you take over JG-26 right away—as soon as you get back to the coast."

Galland objected immediately to this promotion.

"If I am a *Kommodore,*" he said, "I will be stuck on the ground. I won't see the action I am seeing now."

"Don't worry about that," said Goering. "My new regulations are that each *Geschwader* must be led in the air by its *Kommodore.* He must be the most successful pilot. We've got to get some spirit into these fighter pilots somehow. Putting young men quickly into high rank and full charge hasn't been done before. Some won't be able to handle it. Others will. Now, any request to make before you go back to the front?''

Galland asked to be left in his present *Gruppe* command. Goering denied this request and stalked out. Galland was going to be a *Kommodore,* like it or not.

As they sped back to Berlin by car, Galland and Moelders discussed the new arrangements. Moelders disagreed strongly with his friend's wish to remain a *Gruppenkommandeur* for the sake of more combat action.

Moelders sought responsibility, and he told Galland that his abilities as a tactician would carry more weight if he were a *Kommodore.* Moelders met large challenges with ease and confidence. Galland already knew that his rival was an excellent organizer. Moelders would take larger responsibilities in his stride.

Galland, by contrast, was a hunter and fighter above all else. His hatred of desks and paperwork, and the personal paralysis they induced, was implacable. The hunt, the chase, and the victory dominated his existence. Conversation swung back to the First World War, when Oswald Boelcke and Manfred von Richthofen were the luminaries of the German Air Service. Boelcke was the master tactician, acting with development of the service uppermost. Von Richthofen was the supreme aerial hunter.

Moelders at this moment was the leading ace, but his aspirations were directed toward the development of the Fighter Arm. Moelders realized that this meant one day surrendering his top scoring spot to Galland or someone else. Galland always wanted to be the best, and now he wanted to be the best fighter pilot and the best *Kommodore.* Their conversation ranged over these matters.

''As far as I am concerned,'' said Moelders, with just a touch of indignation, ''you can be the Richthofen of the *Luftwaffe.* I prefer to be someday its Boelcke.''

These words of Moelders kept running through Galland's mind as he flew back to the Pas de Calais and his new command. The right elements were available to make him the new Richthofen. RAF fighters were waiting out there over southeast England, dozens of them. His mission was to find them and shoot them down. ''Anything else is nonsense,'' the Red Baron had once said. Galland believed that.

The young major knew well the colonel he was replacing in command of JG-26. Gotthardt Handrick was his old Condor Legion comrade and C.O. of J-88. They had enjoyed the good Spanish wine together too often for there to be any hard feelings over Handrick's relief. He was a sportsman of great merit, the Gold Medal pentathlon winner in the 1936 Olympiad. He took his removal from command in a sporting spirit. Handrick was able and experienced but had not been sufficiently successful in aerial combat to meet Goering's new standards. He had only ten aerial victories.

Galland immediately began remaking JG-26, putting his own ideas and experience into effect. He set high performance standards for his own Staff Flight, based upon his own eminence in aerial fighting. Handing over III/JG-26 to Gerhard Schoepfel, he moved himself to JG-26 HQ at Audembert. Schoepfel was an ace and an experienced leader. Galland further improved JG-26 leadership by putting Walter Adolph in command of II/JG-26 and Rolf Pingel in command of I/JG-26. Both officers were Condor Legion veterans and experienced fighter pilots and leaders. (Battles ahead would prove the soundness of these appointments.)

Galland made it his policy to command every JG-26 operation in the air, except when he was officially absent or wounded. His expectations of excellence were made known throughout the *Geschwader*. The highest bravery was expected of every pilot. Their C.O. exemplified what he was asking of them. Galland's Staff Flight became a model of efficiency and effectiveness. Where others might send warriors to war before the lash, Galland applied the "spiritual magic" of example. JG-26 was extremely popular with the Bomber Arm for escort duty and, under its young *Kommodore,* became the premier German fighter unit of the Battle of Britain.

Other units were revived under new leaders. Moelders took over JG-51 from the gallant Major General Theo Osterkamp. JG-51 became unofficially *JG-51 Mölders.* Galland's comrade of Condor Legion days, Captain Guenther Luetzow, was given command of JG-3. There was no finer leader in the *Luftwaffe.* JG-54 was blessed at this time by the appointment of big, convincing, and popular Captain Hannes Trautfloft as its *Kommodore.* Other appointments further helped each *Geschwader* with fresh new-generation leadership.

Galland was promoted *Kommodore* of JG-26 on 21 August 1940, after the Karinhall conference of the previous two days. Fighter Command at this time had been more seriously battered than the Germans realized. (Had the Germans enjoyed comparable intelligence to that provided Dowding by the *Ultra* decrypts, they would have been appalled by the toll they were taking of Fighter Command's precious pilots.) In the 12 days between 8 and 20 August, 94 RAF pilots had been killed or were missing, with a further 60 wounded. Pilot losses from drowning after ditching offshore forced the British to revamp and reinforce the scattered air-sea rescue efforts. Air Vice-Marshal Park had to take steps to keep his fighter operations within gliding distance of land.

Galland was still getting his replacement pilots, but they were filling the cockpits of irreplaceable experts. Young pilots coming from training school were green, and it showed in the air. Watching over them was a distraction for experienced pilots, and soon there were too many greenhorns in JG-26 and all other units for them all to be protected. Many of them went down before they had passed through their running-in period. Then there were more replacements. Galland knew that JG-26 quality was declining, and his *Geschwader* was almost always taking heavier pilot casualties than the bombers they were escorting.

Even amid the havoc of this terrible struggle, the traditional humor of German fighter pilots broke through often enough to keep them buoyed up. Taking off one morning with his Staff Flight, all four fighters moving out together, Galland was astonished to see his No. 4 pilot execute a wild ground loop. This was not hard to do in the Me-109, with its narrow undercarriage. In seconds the fighter was transformed into a smoldering pile of scrap, as though it taken a direct hit from a 500-lb bomb. Over the R/T came the Bavarian voice of his No. 4: "Adam 1 from Adam 4—I believe I have a flat tire."

Notoriously talkative when aloft, *Luftwaffe* fighter pilots found it hard to maintain radio silence. They were young men of high energy and strong spirit. Many fighter pilots of all nations confess to giving themselves pep talks when setting out on a mission. In a formation of 70 fighters from JG-26 one morning, there was such a pilot present, whose microphone was inadvertently left open. In this mode, he could not hear any commands to shut up or get off the air. Galland listened to the Britain-bound pilot's stream-of-consciousness pep talk.

". . . everything is fine. . . .

". . . still got plenty of fuel . . .

". . . no Spitfires in the blue, blue sky. . . .

". . . very soon I will be back home. . . .

". . . and in the evening, ho ho, I will need a girl."

Then came dirty songs. Galland's barked orders for silence went unheard. The entertainment continued until a wall of flak rose in front of them and a gaggle of Spitfires bounced them from superior altitude. Amid the milling battle, Galland could still hear the offending pilot, cursing now between gun bursts and breathing heavily as he hauled his Me-109 around the sky. In a lull in the battle, the offending microphone suddenly went off. A new and different voice came on the air. "Why don't you sing now, you son of a bitch?"

Humor helped both sides amid the high-altitude holocaust. As August rolled towards its end, Galland knew in his warrior's core that this greatest of all air battles would be decided in the next two to three weeks. Beyond that, the spirit might be willing to take off on more operations, but it was likely that the flesh would not obey, be that flesh British or German. All involved were nearing their absolute limit.

CHAPTER TEN

On 24 August 1940, Goering shifted the main weight of his bombing attacks on to RAF fighter airfields farther inland. This accorded temporary relief to the badly beaten-up airfields near the coast—but at a high price. What Goering did not know, due to the inadequacies of German intelligence, was that he was now assaulting the vital sector aerodromes of the RAF. From these electronic nerve centers, British fighters were vectored into tactically best contact with the *Luftwaffe*. Knocking out British fighter control would have ended the radar-based interceptions that allowed Dowding crucial economy in commiting his fighters.

The sector aerodromes now reeled under the thunder of bombs for two grueling weeks. Fighter Command's life was on the line, but the British were helped in their extremity by having additional time for interceptions before the bombers attacked. Galland and his pilots were again near the end of their fuel endurance with the deeper penetrations. Fuel worries added to the strain of ceaseless escort flying. Galland from the air could have a presentiment of the shambles being created by the bombers. He wondered how he would fare with JG-26 if Audembert and his other airfields were being plastered with bombs day after day. Keeping operational would tax all pilots, crews, and facilities.

This was exactly the situation for the RAF now. Main sector aerodromes like Biggin Hill were often reduced to handling a single fighter squadron. Sometimes they were lucky even to manage more than a squadron. When Goering took personal command of the assault on 30 August 1940, he immediately laid on a series of even more massive strikes. *Ultra* decrypts warned the British of these monster operations, but these warnings did not halt the torrent of explosives that pushed the RAF to desperation. Another two weeks of such blows and Goering would have Fighter Command on the very brink of defeat.

Dowding's practice of sending worn-out squadrons to the northeast for rest and refit, and of bringing freshened squadrons back to the south of England to replace them, was only good for a limited time. Worn-out pilots were soon

Galland relaxes between combat sorties, smoking his cigar and petting his hunting dog. Galland is wearing the winter flying suit taken from a downed energy bomber crew member.

In 1940 Göring came to the Channel Front in his special train, "Asia," to visit Kommodores Galland (JG26) and Mölders (JG51). There was later a fierce argument between Göring and Galland, when the latter asked for Spitfires for his squadron.

being replaced by pilots who were not quite so worn out. Fighter Command had sufficient aircraft but was approaching its human limits. Any able-bodied man in Britain who had flying experience was likely to be training as a fighter pilot. The *Luftwaffe* was pressing Britain's back to the wall.

Across the Channel, the Germans had their own acute difficulties. Replacement aircraft were down to a trickle. Supply and repair services could not stay abreast of the losses and damage. *Ultra* decrypts detailed for Dowding the woes of his opponents. The British leader knew better than anyone how narrow the margin had become. A major mistake by either side would unbalance the battle irretrievably. Goering was to make that mistake.

On 3 September 1940, while RAF sector aerodromes and fighter control were again being pounded, Goering summoned Kesselring and Sperrle to The Hague for a council of war. The *Reich* Marshal wanted to turn his bomber fleets onto London, the political and spiritual center of the British Commonwealth and Empire. Pressing his two Air Fleet chiefs hard, Goering wanted to know if the RAF had been badly enough stricken to permit the bombing of London with bearable losses.

Goering's sudden urge to switch strategy and targets had an overriding political dimension. RAF bombers had attacked Berlin at night on 25 and 29 August 1940. Minimal damage was inflicted, but the raids sent Hitler into a fury. Until these Berlin attacks, Hitler had personally ordered, under pain of court martial, that London was not to be bombed. Approximately ten off-course German bombers on the night of 24 August 1940 had mistakenly bombed London when haze and fog blanketed southeastern England. Prodded by Churchill, the RAF struck at Berlin in reprisal. (A mighty nocturnal holocaust, lasting four and a half years, was thereby ignited.)

Hitler canceled his restraining order. London was to be wiped out. Goering got the word from the *Fuehrer*. Eager to please Hitler and impatient to smash Britain quickly in view of the planned invasion of Russia, Goering passed all this pressure down to Kesselring and Sperrle. The *Reich* Marshal's historic questions were, Could London be bombed without prohibitive losses? and Was the RAF now hurt sufficiently to permit the London assault?

The towering, monocled Hugo Sperrle was among the most experienced leaders in the *Luftwaffe*. Command of the Condor Legion had taught him plenty about tactical air power. In Spain he had shown himself to be oblivious to personal risk and to be shrewd in assessing his enemy. He recommended that Goering continue assaulting the RAF airfields, pressing the attack until the weakening of Fighter Command became a collapse.

Kesselring was not as experienced in war command as Sperrle, but he was a former Chief of the *Luftwaffe* General Staff and an officer of great prestige in the service. Kesselring told Goering that, in his view, London could be attacked without excessive losses. In Kesselring's opinion, RAF forward airfields were expendable. Enemy fighters could be moved to bases on the far side of London. He argued that only by going for the heart of Britain could they provoke RAF fighters up in force and thus destroy them. Sperrle strongly disagreed.

Like all men of action, Goering's career abounded with mistakes, but his biggest was deciding to attack London. He sent a teletype to Kesselring, on 5 September 1940, ordering a raid on the London docks with full fighter escort. The *Ultra* decrypting teams delivered this key message to Dowding almost as quickly as it reached its official addressee. The hard-pressed head of Fighter Command saw in it the deliverance of his battered sector aerodromes and of their vital fighter control facilities.

Blasted and reeling, they were operating marginally with improvised hookups from emergency quarters. (Another dozen big raids would have done them in, and the history of the world altered. Now the fourth phase of the Battle of Britain was beginning, with the removal of this lethal and direct pressure from Fighter Command. The Londoners were going to catch hell, but Fighter Command would be able to come back from the brink.)

Across the Channel in the Pas de Calais, the black-maned Galland pondered the problems of escorting bombers over London. His fighters would have no more than ten minutes for combat before turning back to base. This meant that the entire force, bombers and fighters, would have fly in a straight line from the French coast to London and then straight back. This unvarying approach route made interception even easier for the RAF. The *Luftwaffe* was also aware that British radar was now picking up German formations as they assembled over France. Bombers and fighters would now have to mass during the climb, en route to the target.

Just before the big bomber assault on London (and the strategic error that was to cost him victory), Goering came up to the French coast to put some more fire into his fighter leaders. Galland and Moelders again stood facing an abrasive and reproachful *Reich* Marshal. "Fighting spirit" was lacking in the Fighter Arm, where it should be greatest, according to Goering. They were supposed to be *fighters*. Railing against his fighter pilots, Goering stalked up and down with his marshal's baton poking, waving, digging home his vilifications against the brave men Galland and Moelders were leading.

The new *Kommodore* of JG-26 stood enraged. In his soldier's mind, he saw the struggle not only in terms of strategy, tactics, and technical deficiencies but also in terms of the men he had led and lost. As unjustified allegations of cowardice poured out of Goering, Galland's mind swept over the shoals of letters he had written to the families of his fallen pilots. He thought about all the letters he had still to write. He saw their faces as surely as he knew their sacrifices. For Goering to accuse such valiant men of cowardice was monstrous.

With the bomber crews claiming that they were not being closely enough escorted, an adversary relationship had developed between fighter pilots and bomber pilots. Goering sided unreservedly with the bomber pilots. He returned now to the necessity for close escort, in view of the imminent use of hundreds of bombers in the London assault. Galland choked down his anger and tried again to explain to Goering some of the fighters' difficulties.

"*Herr Reich* Marshal, our Me-109 is superior to the Spitfire in the attack. That is the way we should use our fighters—hunting down the RAF and attacking them. We have a clear advantage in such operations."

"Galland, the size of your personal bag of enemy fighters is unimportant, compared with the protection of my bombers. I am telling you what is important."

"Sir, the Spitfire is an excellent defensive fighter, because it is more maneuverable than our Me-109, even if a little slower—especially in acceleration. Such a fighter is much better suited to close escort than our Me-109, which is handicapped in that role."

"I reject your arguments categorically, Major Galland. The bombers must be protected at all costs. You've got to get some fighting spirit into these pilots, instead of giving me reasons why you cannot protect my bombers."

Goering followed with more scathing criticisms, but, when he glanced at his wrist watch and realized his time was short, his mood changed abruptly. From reproachful abuse, he turned suddenly amiable, like the sun coming from behind a cloud.

"Now then, Moelders" he said, "what can I help you get for your *Geschwader?*"

Moelders asked for a new series of Me-109s, fitted with the more powerful DB 605 N engines. Goering said he would get them, and turned to Galland.

"And you? What do you want?"

"*I'd like an outfit of Spitfires for my* Geschwader!" Galland heard his impudent request go blurting out of himself as though coming from a third party. The words rushed out, propelled by his rage over Goering's vilifications of his pilots. Goering's amiable facade disappeared. The second greatest orator in Germany, he stood speechless at the insolence of the young *Kommodore* he had just promoted. Scowling and growling, he went stomping off to his train.

Galland's request would survive down through the decades as one of his most famous and oft-quoted remarks. In social gatherings and lectures all over the world, his request for Spitfires always surfaces. The full background to the remark is rarely understood, and it should be recorded that Galland definitely preferred the Me-109 to the Spitfire, not only in September 1940 but also later after he had personally flown the British thoroughbred.

He was seeking to emphasize with Goering that it was a disadvantage to fly the Me-109 and use the tactics suited to the Spitfire in escort missions. The advantage of the Me-109 became a disadvantage under these conditions. When Galland and Moelders put their heads together and adopted hit-and-run tactics with their speedy Me-109s—avoiding the turning dogfight where the Spitfire was superior—both their units did much better against the RAF fighters.

By 7 September 1940, the Battle of London had begun, as 625 bombers escorted by 648 single and twin-engine fighters were despatched to the attack. Goering and Kesselring watched from Cap Blanc Nez as the armada thundered

With his Mickey Mouse logo proudly displayed on his Me-109, the Kommodore of "Schlageter" JG26 dismounts from his trusty steed. Crew chief Meyer stands ready to help Galland to the ground.

Galland in the cockpit and crew chief Meyer on the wing make last-minute checks before take-off during the Battle of Britain.

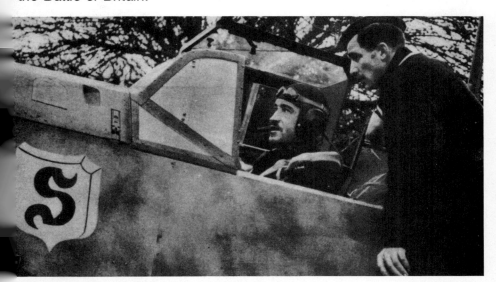

towards England. With them was General Bruno Loerzer, who had started Goering as an airman in World War I. In the history of the world, no such large force of aircraft had ever been seen. Supreme Commander of all these aircraft, Goering had come a long way since his days as the Flying Trapezist on the Western Front, but he still had a long way to go to win the present battle.

Throughout this fourth phase of the Battle of Britain, Galland found all his operations, plans, and tactical ideas overshadowed by the fuel problem. Everything was affected by the fighters going to the absolute limit of their fuel endurance, and not only the operations themselves but also pilot psychology and morale. The bomber men had no fuel problem, and their importunings for close protection took insufficient account of what this meant to fighter fuel consumption.

When the London flak punished the bombers with its accuracy and volume, the bomber pilots flew at 21,000 to 23,000 feet. This altitude was too great for their power and loading, slowing them down considerably. Escorting fighters had to make huge wide weaves to maintain station. Weaving chewed up fuel and often carried the fighters out of sight of the bomber crews, who complained once more that the fighters were not protecting them.

Pushing Me-109 fuel endurance to its limits resulted in a large number of Channel swimmers in the Fighter Arm. Galland was mortified on one mission, when seven of his JG-26 fighters went into the English Channel after surviving combat over England. He all but joined them. Bringing up the rear after staying too long in battle with the Spitfires, Galland's fuel gauge showed empty as he roared over Manston on the coast. He was about to land and surrender on the ground to the RAF, an ignominious fate for a high-scoring holder of the Knight's Cross. On the verge of turning, he reconsidered. Saying to hell with it, he headed out over the hated grey waters. Staggering across towards France, his engine began blurting in bursts as his fuel ran out. Then came silence save for the rush of the wind. The lessons of the Borkenberge came in handy. The former sailplane pilot bellied in with a dead engine on a beach near Cap Gris Nez.

Luftwaffe attacking forces in the Battle of London varied usually between 400 and 500 bombers, plus about 200 Stuka dive bombers. The latter were making a last return to English skies at the time of this supreme German effort; 500 single-engine fighters and 200 Me-110s were the escort. For operational purposes, the attackers proceeded in *Geschwader* strength, each bomber *Geschwader* (60–90 aircraft) with a fighter *Geschwader* as escort. Since not more than ten minutes could be allowed for linking bomber formations with their assigned fighter escorts, these assemblies proved almost as taxing as the raids. Once the whole mass of 1,000 or more aircraft was airborne, the spectacle was terrifying, but only the pilots knew the nerve-clanking strain that had gone into assembling each armada.

Returning the Stuka to the main battle was a disastrous error, a repetition of their earlier debacle. British fighters pounced on the Stukas just as they began their dives, one after another, in the classic Stuka pattern. Galland and his pilots could not protect the Stukas in their dives, since the latter were fitted with air brakes to help their aim. The Me-109 was far too fast to stay with any such aircraft as the Stuka, even if the latter was without air brakes. The RAF also slaughtered the dive bombers during their milling reassembly phase. Goering blamed these Stuka losses exclusively on his own fighters.

Galland kept a wary eye cocked at the weather. The September evenings were getting a nip of autumn, and the summer skies showed the early fingers of fall. On 10 September 1940, clouds and rain interrupted the daily thunder of bombs into London. The murk hung around for four days, with fighter activity continuing. Galland was well aware that the *Luftwaffe* had entered a race with the autumn weather of the English Channel, notorious for its inclement character.

Whenever weather curtailed fighter operations as fall advanced, Galland and the pilots of his staff and of nearby *Gruppen* switched to another kind of hunting and shooting. Hares, pheasants, and partridges were abundant. The non-hunters among the pilots participated gladly in the game meat. Evenings of any stand-down days saw the pilots patronizing the bars of Lille. Galland's preference was Paris and the famous Scheherezade nightclub, happily haunted also by U-boat and E-boat commanders. Late nights were incompatible with the possibility of morning operations, but the early evening outings were a priceless but brief respite from battle pressure.

15 September 1940 dawned with near-ideal flying weather, cloudy but with sufficient gaps for the *Luftwaffe* to find London. Goering again took personal command. By noon he was hurling everything into the battle. The invaluable *Ultra* decrypts kept Dowding aware of his opponent's plans and also of his plight. German morale was wearing down, along with aircraft strength. German losses had been heavy, especially in pilots and crews. When they survived from shot-up aircraft, they became POWs. RAF pilots who survived forced landings or who parachuted were able to return to battle.

Dowding knew through *Ultra* that 15 September was Goering's main punch. He also knew that *Luftwaffe* Intelligence had written down Fighter Command to 200 aircraft. His policy of committing limited numbers of fighters had the additional virtue of misleading his enemy. Dowding had considerably more than 200 fighters available. His pilots were near exhaustion, but Dowding judged that the day and time had come to wade into Goering's bombers with everything Fighter Command had available. Goering's big punch would be met with a counterpunch, packing the great imponderable of war—surprise.

Dowding passed the word to Air Vice-Marshal Park at No. 11 Fighter Group, and the able New Zealander alerted his 24 squadrons. Radar was following the assembly of huge enemy gaggles over the Channel and the French coast. Park began sending his squadrons in two at a time. They went right into the German bombers in line abreast, dispensing with the usual climb to "the perch" for a diving attack. More and more squadrons kept coming up. This was not the pattern of the past.

Churchill was watching in Park's operations room at Uxbridge, as the last six squadrons of No. 11 Group rose to battle. Five more squadrons from No.

12 Group north of London joined Park's final six. All 11 squadrons together slashed into the German bombers. By 1:30 PM, the RAF had over 300 fighters airborne. The effects were devastating, not only to the bombers but to the morale of the bomber crews. They had been assured by their higher commanders that the RAF was nearly finished. Their own recent experience at least partially supported this estimate. Now out of the blue came immense, terrifying swarms of Hurricanes and Spitfires.

Every German bomber formation was attacked. Galland and his pilots now had their arch foes up to do massed battle. Their restrictive close-escort orders were a continuing handicap, but both the circumstances and the balance of combat were drastically altered on 15 September 1940. RAF roundels seemed to be everywhere. Aircraft twisted and dove, smoked and exploded, tumbled and rolled in the skies all over southeastern England. Vapor trails laced the heavens and black smokestreams poured from aircraft screaming down to final impact. Somber palls rose from the funeral pyres of brave pilots and crews on both sides.

German bombers bored through, but not in the numbers sent out from France. RAF fighters and clouds over the target scattered the German bombing attacks and limited damage. Withdrawal by the German forces turned into a nightmare. Shoals of British fighters chased them out over the Channel, damaging and downing more of them far from the main battle scene. The counterpunch of Dowding had been far more effective than the big punch of Goering.

The German High Command immediately denied British press and radio claims of more than 180 *Luftwaffe* aircraft destroyed. For morale purposes, it was essential to minimize the serious reversal of German fortunes on 15 September 1940; 56 German aircraft did not return to base. Many that staggered back across the Channel did so only by the grace of God and the skill of their pilots and crews. These aircraft were often so badly damaged that they were scrapped. Dozens more were heavily shot up, and these buried the already overloaded repair depots under an avalanche of wrecks.

In the final reckoning, about one quarter of the bomber force assigned to the Battle of Britain had been put out of action. Personnel losses had been severe numerically, and the missing pilots and crews were an irreplaceable peacetime-trained elite. The British would ever afterward celebrate 15 September each year as Battle of Britain Day. They would always believe that they won the battle on that climactic September afternoon.

Galland believed for many years that, with different tactics and proper exploitation of its resources, the *Luftwaffe* could have done far better. Certainly Goering's presence and style in command was an encumbrance. His gross tactical and political error in bombing London instead of the RAF sector airfields and radar stations was high command at its worst. Goering's misuse of the Fighter Arm was tantamount to reducing its strength in what was essentially a fighter battle.

The *Luftwaffe* Fighter Arm was the most successful element on the German side in the entire battle. Despite the crippling effect of rigid close-escort orders

One of the JG26 "black men" (mechanics) is ready to paint three more victory stripes on Galland's Me-109 on 15 April 1941. This brought Galland's skein to sixty.

Galland protege. Captain Joachim Müncheberg was one of Galland's best friends. An expert at shooting at a moving target from a moving platform, he scored 135 aerial victories before losing his life when he collided with his victim over the African desert. He was Kommodore of JG77 at the time.

by their High Command, they pushed the RAF to the brink. Mistakes in the battle itself, and derelictions from the past on the part of the German leadership, had a detrimental effect on the efforts of the Fighter Arm. That they had no other single-engined fighter than the short-winded Me-109 was not the fault of the pilots. That chance was cast away years before. The absence of fighter control integrated with radar on the German side was not the fault of the young fighter pilots, nor were their inadequate communications.

British preparations for air defense paid off handsomely in the battle. The RAF's well-coordinated communications and its control and position-fixing facilities were coupled to the scientific triumph of their radar. British top leadership was of high quality, especially Dowding and Park, who were both privy to the *Ultra* secret. Crowning the British effort was the skill and devotion of the RAF fighter pilots.

Adolf Galland's respected standing among his former foes allowed him to meet in the postwar decades many of his adversaries in the Battle of Britain. Wing Commander Robert Stanford-Tuck became a close personal friend. Galland and Sir Douglas Bader shared many a distinguished podium in several countries and were mutual admirers. Twenty-seven years after the Battle of Britain, Galland finally met his main foe in that struggle, Sir Keith Park, retired to Auckland, New Zealand. In February of 1967 they had a lively meeting and discussion Down Under. Galland was mightily impressed by Park. In their reminiscences of the 1940 battle, Park did not mention the *Ultra* secret and its role in his handling of No. 11 Group's fighters. Like all others party to the greatest secret of the war, Park kept the faith.

The Battle of Britain did not terminate on 15 September 1940 but continued into the autumn. After that date, nevertheless, the *Luftwaffe* made no concerted effort to defeat the RAF. Goering's dream of wiping the British Air Force from the sky—the aerial conquest of Britain—dissipated with the forceful awakening of 15 September 1940. Although Goering was himself more to blame than anyone for the trend of events, he began a search for culprits. Galland continued to do his duty like the good soldier he had proved himself to be.

CHAPTER ELEVEN

Worse than the heavy material damage to the *Luftwaffe* on 15 September 1940 was the blow dealt to morale. Sudden RAF resurgence sent a demoralizing shock wave through the Bomber Arm, which loudly blamed the Fighter Arm for its failure to provide protection. Psychological impacts were felt in the *Luftwaffe* High Command. The RAF's dramatic rebound was irreconcilable with German intelligence estimates. When Goering suffered a defeat instead of an anticipated and badly needed victory, he was thunderstruck and angry. He blamed the Fighter Arm.

Hastily convening a meeting at Air Fleet 2 HQ in Brussels the following day, Goering delivered a recriminatory diatribe against the fighter pilots. His abuse went too far. Lt. General Theo Osterkamp sprang to his feet. *Jafü* 2 at Le Touquet and fully in touch with both the young combat commanders and the Air Fleet hierarchy, Osterkamp could endure Goering's insults no longer.

Osterkamp was well qualified to defend the fighter pilots. He had won the Blue Max in World War I and had downed 32 Allied aircraft. He added six more in World War II, while flying as *Kommodore* of JG-51, which formation he had raised and trained in 1939. He was one of the grand old eagles around whom the new Fighter Arm had been built, and the young pilots nicknamed him "Uncle Theo." He had been in aerial combat as recently as July of 1940. As *Jafü* 2, he was direct liaison between the combat fighter units and Air Fleet HQ. He knew the problems at first hand.

The slender Uncle Theo faced the bulky Goering unflinchingly. The *Reich* Marshal was livid with rage, but Osterkamp's bearing and expression made Goering fall silent. Osterkamp vehemently emphasized how the rigid direct-escort orders tied his fighter pilots' hands. He stressed how the recommendations of the best combat leaders to improve efficiency and inflict losses on the RAF were consistently ignored. The fixed close-escort orders resulted in heavy bomber losses and the High Command blamed the fighter pilots.

Strategy meeting at Le Touquet. On a bright and sunny day in 1940, Luftwaffe fighter leaders met to review operations against the RAF. Left to right, Adolf Galland, Günther Lützow, Werner Mölders, Cark Viek, General Theo Osterkamp, Günther Maltzahn and General Teichmann.

Galland would never make a victory "roll" after a combat because the airplane may have been hit or damaged by enemy bullets. Here, in June, 1941, he waggles his wings signifying he has scored his 60th aerial victory.

Unteroffizier Meyer, Galland's crew chief, directs Galland to his proper parking place after Galland had scored his 60th aerial victory. Meyer and the armament specialist, Olemotz, were the only persons authorized to be the first to congratulate Galland after each sortie. After they had done so, and after Galland had reported the condition of the Me-109 to them, others were allowed to crowd around and offer their felicitations.

Goering reddened at this rebuke, ready to explode. Osterkamp adopted a cooler tone.

"Yesterday the English used new tactics. They started using much larger formations to attack our bombers in force. They took us by surprise with this change in tactics."

Osterkamp's competent summation did not get through to Goering. His reaction was that, if the RAF were finally committing fighters in large numbers, *Luftwaffe* fighters should be downing them in large numbers. He refused to see that he was binding down the majority of his own fighters. Goering saw highly technical and tactical matters in a simplistic way. Professional counsel could not change his mind. The *Reich* Marshal's need for victory was personally and politically urgent. Technical problems obstructing victory were an irritation.

With air superiority over the invasion beaches now impossible before the onset of adverse weather, Operation Sealion could not go forward. Goering also knew that the planned invasion of Russia would require him to move most of his Air Fleets to the East before the favorable English Channel weather in the summer of 1941. His Douhet-style aerial conquest of England had failed. Goering knew he would have to make a humiliating change, and that his numerous detractors in the Army General Staff and high political spheres would enjoy his discomfort.

Worst of all, he had bungled his grandiose gamble to please Hitler. Although the *Fuehrer* had no real intention of invading England, Goering had hoped to score a major personal triumph by presenting him with the prize—exclusively by aerial action. Goering took out his frustration on the Fighter Arm. He now insisted that, since his fighters could not protect his bombers, the fighters would carry the bombs to England themselves.

As mass daylight raids were phased out in the latter half of September, fighter-bomber attacks were phased in, using both Me-109s and Me-110s. Galland maintained a high level of combat activity. By 25 September 1940 he had confirmed his 40th aerial victory.

His HQ teleprinter at Audembert hammered out a telex from Hitler. Galland's combat achievement of 40 aerial victories was being recognized with the newly created Oak Leaves to the Knight's Cross. This highest class of the decoration had thus far only been awarded twice. One of the recipients was Werner Moelders. Their rivalry was continuing, as emphasis passed to the fighter-bombers.

Experimental *Gruppe* 210, in which the first fighter-bomber conversions had been made earlier in 1940, moved into the Pas de Calais. Soon this unit was joined by Galland's old formation from the Polish campaign, II/SLG-2, now equipped with bomb-carrying Me-109s. To the chagrin of the fighter pilots, Willi Messerschmitt's slender, streamlined brainchild was loaded with a 250-Kg bomb that bulged down below its belly. Performance was seriously degraded by this protuberance.

The Me-110 was more suited to the fighter-bomber role, at least as far as bomb load was concerned. The heavy twin-engined aircraft could carry 1,400 pounds of bombs—two 500-pounders and four 100-pounders. Each *Gruppe* in every fighter *Geschwader* assigned to the Channel area was required to convert one squadron to fighter-bombers.

In what Galland regarded as the craziest High Command order yet, the remaining fighters escorted the fighter-bombers until they dropped their loads. They could marginally defend themselves then, because the drag of the bomb rack was still a handicap. More important, fighter-bomber operations became far too defensive in character to suit the fighter pilots or to get significant results. Most of the fighter pilots assigned to the new fighter-bombers hated this duty. They got rid of their bombs as soon as was decently possible, in order to join combat with the RAF.

The newly decorated young *Kommodore* of JG-26 was not opposed to fighter-bombers as such. He had proved in Spain what they could do in suitable situations. The task of suppressing the RAF fighter force was not a rational assignment for the limited numbers of fighter-bombers available. Maintenance of such an ineffective offensive, furthermore, required the *Luftwaffe* Fighter Arm on the Channel to give up one third of its strength. RAF Fighter Command meanwhile grew notably stronger as the weeks passed.

The only means of gaining air superiority was the fighter. Now that the long-coveted drop tanks were available for the Me-109, the same external rack was being used for bombs. The extra range advantage that had come too late for the biggest battles was thereby nullified. Confidence in high leadership is not born of such expedient processes.

When the RAF maintained its policy of jumping the bombers and avoiding the fighters, the fighter-bombers were taken out of formation and distributed among the escort. This made them harder to single out and made their escort to targets reasonably certain, but it slowed down the whole formation. When Galland from his cockpit thought about the organization, labor, casualties, and material losses that were required to drop each bomb from an Me-109, he was both disgusted and disquieted. This fifth phase of the Battle of Britain plainly had no more than nuisance value for all involved. The *Luftwaffe* fighter pilots were still being handicapped by their own High Command in doing what they did best.

Ordered to Berlin to receive the Oak Leaves to his Knight's Cross from Hitler personally, Galland had some guilt feelings on leaving the combat zone. He hated to leave his pilots fighting while he went off to Berlin. There was nevertheless a deep feeling of bodily relief at the removal of daily combat strain. He was physically and mentally exhausted, and he knew it in his bones.

When Galland had been introduced to the *Fuehrer* for the first time in 1939, he had been just one of the highly decorated pilots officially welcomed home from Spain. This time, things were different. After receiving the Oak Leaves and Hitler's congratulations, they sat down facing each other. He was alone with Germany's most powerful man, whose authority was unquestioned within the German state. They were sitting in the *Reich* Chancellery, center of Hitler's world.

Hitler had been commonly depicted in films as constantly raving like a maniac, but the Hitler now confronting Galland was the able politician, fully in command of himself. A former front-line soldier of World War I, Hitler admired the new generation of combat heroes, which Galland exemplified. The *Fuehrer* quietly questioned the young pilot about the battle over England and the fighting qualities of the Royal Air Force. Galland reported to Hitler the resentment that he and his pilots felt towards the German press and radio, because of their condescending comments on the RAF. The British were the toughest aerial fighters the *Luftwaffe* had ever faced.

When the young major further enlarged upon the fighting spirit of the RAF, which persisted despite heavy losses, Hitler continued listening and nodding. The *Fuehrer* said that Galland's experience in this new war confirmed his own view on the high quality of the Anglo-Saxon race. The war with them now was a world historical tragedy, which Hitler said he had struggled in vain to avert.

Hitler spoke admiringly of Britain's political development and regretted his inability to bring Britain and Germany together. He showed quick comprehension of Galland's views. The *Fuehrer* marshaled and presented his own facts with impressive lucidity. His reasonable reactions surprised Galland, who had expected to be interrupted, corrected, and silenced. The *Fuehrer* actually sided with him over the patronizing treatment of the RAF by Germany's news media. Galland left the Chancellery after this lengthy interview impressed by the *Fuehrer* and without any of the resentments that Goering always seemed to provoke.

The young ace was scheduled to give an interview to the foreign press corps in Berlin. At the Ministry of Propaganda in the Wilhelmsplatz, he found himself facing a large group of reporters in the Theatersaal. Initially resentful of this limelight, Galland's mood improved when the reporters asked him questions about the RAF. This gave him an opportunity to offset the German propaganda about which he had just complained to Hitler. (Years later, Galland would listen to a recording of this interview that was presented to him by the Ministry of Propaganda and find his opinions unchanged from 1940 on these matters.)

Goering now summoned him from Berlin for a congratulatory hunting trip at the legendary Reichsjägerhof, situated on Rominten Heath in East Prussia. Every German hunter dreamed of a sporting visit to the famous lodge, built of mighty tree trunks, with its thatched roof extending far out over the eaves. As Galland reached the gate, out came his rival Werner Moelders, now on his way back to the Channel Front. Moelders was in a hurry.

"The *Fuehrer* and the Fat One have been keeping me on these social visits as though the war is over," said Moelders. "I'm on my way back now, and I just got the Fat One's promise to keep you here for three days. Good luck with the stag. I missed him. *Auf Wiedersehen*"

As Moelders disappeared from view, Goering came in sight from the Reichsjägerhof, traditionally attired. High hunting boots, silk blouse with puffed sleeves, and green suede jacket made him a figure of which his godfather would have been proud. Goering was beaming with pleasure. Galland's request for a

Galland's crew check over the Me-109. Olemotz was the armament specialist and Meyer, right, the engine and airplane specialist for Galland while he was Kommodore of JG26, and throughout the war.

Perfectionist Olemotz. Galland's armament specialist inspected every machine gun belt and bullet used in Galland's fighter. A highly sensitive person, Olemotz, top, would suffer emotionally if anything went wrong with any part of the armament system on Galland's flights.

Geschwader of Spitfires, and the war itself, had been forgotten amid the joys of the hunt.

Galland had the same feeling now of the unreality that had bothered him during the Karinhall conference in August. While he and Goering talked about stags, the *Luftwaffe* on the coast was attacking the Supermarine works at Southampton, home of the Spitfire. Goering's numerous offices and titles included Master of the Hunt. A privilege of that office was the exclusive right to hunt in the magnificent royal preserve at Rominten.

With his love of animal life, in such contrast to his political ruthlessness, Goering even had pet names for the special strong stags at Rominten. As a congratulatory gesture for his 40 aerial victories, Goering invited Major Galland to shoot one of these strong royal stags.

"You have three days to do it," said Goering. "I promised Moelders to keep you here at least that long."

On the next morning, 27 September 1940, Galland's hunter's nose had led him to one of the superb beasts. By 10:05 AM, he had a trophy of unforgettable magnificence. Galland was ecstatic. His early triumph meant that he could now return to the front. The stag was also the one missed by Moelders the previous day. His eagerness to get back to the front was to minimize Moelders's extra scoring days while he was at Rominten. Goering forbade his return to the front. The *Reich* Marshal was going to keep his promise to Moelders. All this, thought Galland, while the war burns on every day, and my pilots are dying in combat.

Goering's resolution lasted until the evening casualty reports came in from Kesselring and Sperrle on the coast. Initially bad, the news grew steadily worse. By final tally, 55 *Luftwaffe* aircraft were missing, including 21 bombers and several fighters from Galland's JG-26. Goering took the bad tidings to heart.

In this essentially social setting, Galland saw how Goering reacted to the deaths of good men under his command. The *Reich* Marshal was now totally unlike his public image. There was no bluster. Shattered and shaken, Goering was unable to put it all together in his mind. The continuing inability of the fighters to protect his bombers was incomprehensible. With his frame of reference in World War I, Goering simply could not come to grips with the realities of this dynamic modern battle over England. He was nevertheless Supreme Commander of this powerful yet sensitive weapon called the *Luftwaffe*.

Galland understood the *Reich* Marshal's distress. The JG-26 pilots who had been posted missing or killed in action this day were men he knew and had led in combat. That hurt. Once more the young *Kommodore* tried to explain to Goering how the close-escort orders were largely responsible for the high casualties. Gently but clearly, he emphasized the price that was being paid for robbing most of the fighters of their offensive and aggressive role.

Little of what he said penetrated even this Goering, who was grief-stricken and far removed from the forceful public figure. Galland found himself bemused by the inability of this highly intelligent and cultivated man—a trained Army officer and a former ace fighter pilot and leader—to grasp the core of the problem.

Galland finally turned this awkward interview to good account. "Sir, I would like to return to my *Geschwader* on the Channel immediately." Goering nodded, his promise to Moelders forgotten. Shortly afterwards, Galland was out of the Reichsjägerhof, stag head and all, and on his way back to JG-26. When he was compelled to make part of his journey by rail, after a forced landing on farmland, his fellow passengers gawked at the stag head. Then they blanched at its odor. Their comments were appropriately pungent. Even the Knight's Cross with Oak Leaves at Galland's throat did not mollify his traveling companions. Heroes were not expected to smell bad.

The *Luftwaffe* High Command made a brief attempt to improve striking power against London by using small formations of Ju-88s, the fastest bombers. Fighter escort for these missions was in the ratio of seven fighters to each bomber. This proved unsuccessful, and the RAF continued taking a toll of the raiders despite its own severe shortage of pilots. On 30 September 1940, the Bomber Arm lost 47 aircraft, and that was the end of daylight formation bombing. The RAF inflicted this reverse at a cost of eight pilots and 20 aircraft.

The Bomber Arm now went over to night attacks. Daylight bombing was left to the fighter-bombers. Despite the obvious scaling down of daylight operations, none of the fighter *Kommodores* on the Channel Front could shake the feeling of being hampered. Their fighting power was not being fully utilized. Losses of the Me-110 fighter-bombers and crews were high, but losses remained within reason in the fighter units. Galland, Moelders, Trautloft, von Maltzahn, and the other *Kommodores* all discussed the problems with Osterkamp, who was their advocate with Kesselring, Sperrle, and Goering.

No significant changes were made. Air war against England continued easing down through October, when *Luftwaffe* losses dropped to 325 machines of all types, against more than 500 lost in the bloody September clashes. RAF losses fell to 251 machines in the same period, and RAF pilots killed in action totaled 100 for October against 148 and 159 for August and September, respectively. Already dramatically outproducing Germany in fighter aircraft, the RAF got substantial relief in its most critical deficiency—available fighter pilots. By October's end, the worst was over for the RAF.

To Major Galland of JG-26, events in October of 1940 did not appear in quite that perspective. *Luftwaffe* fighter pilots had no consciousness of having been defeated. As attackers, they expected losses. Galland and his pilots recognized from events crashing around them only that a peak had occurred in the struggle during September. The *Luftwaffe* was clearly not able to master Britain exclusively from the air. Autumn weather was upon them, and soon embraced all the combatants with clammy impartiality. As the weeks wore on, more and longer stand-downs were forced on JG-26 by the weather.

Animated conversations took place around the mess table during these stand-downs and between operations. Galland told his pilots that, in the spring, they would be forced to hurl themselves again in large numbers at the RAF. Together they had made JG-26 the most celebrated and sought-after German fighter unit

Happy Birthday, Onkel Theo! Galland, with polka-dot scarf and cigar, starts from Brest with a basket of lobsters and champagne stashed behind him in his Me-109. He was headed for Le Touquet to attend General Osterkamp's birthday on 15 April 1941. Taking a slight detour out over the Channel, he shot down three spitfires before landing at Le Touquet.

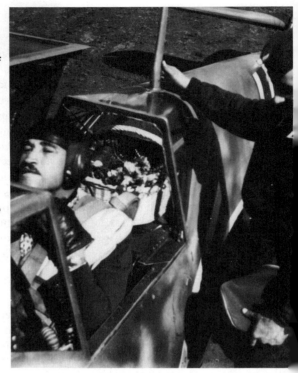

Strategy meeting, 1940. Theo Osterkamp (right) called his fighter leaders together at Le Touquet. From left, they are Günther Lützow (back to camera) of JG3, Major Dr. Wenzel (Mölders' aide and only survivor of the He-111 crash in which Mölders was killed), Adolf Galland of JG-26 and Werner Mölders of JG-51.

of the battle. They had traditions to uphold. Galland promised to do everything in his power to bring about the necessary tactical changes. In JG-26, they saw themselves in a draw, rather than as a defeated, formation. There was no lack of stomach for further battle amongst any of the fighter pilots in all the *Geschwader* on the Channel Front.

Unfortunately for Germany, not all her leaders were as honest and open as Adolf Galland. He knew absolutely nothing in the autumn of 1940 about the coming attack on Russia. Nor did the young men flying under his command. The observable decline of attacks on England took place against a subtle backdrop not evident to combat pilots. This backdrop was the mental pressure exerted on high *Luftwaffe* leaders by the demands of the colossal task looming in the East. These leaders had been blocked and frustrated by the RAF. In the presence of this uncompleted venture, the forthcoming plunge into Russia could only have generated anxiety. From this stemmed the steady shift of English Channel operations over to the defensive.

By the end of November 1940, something had to be done to refresh the human element in the fighter units. Galland and his fellow *Kommodores* on the Channel petitioned the High Command for a rest. They asked that each *Geschwader* be taken out of combat for three to four weeks, in rotation. Personnel were to recuperate, and their hard-driven aircraft would be refitted and brought up to full efficiency. This request was granted, though not immediately executed, and the forthcoming vacation became the main subject of pilot conversation.

By 5 December 1940, Galland had raised his victory tally to 58, despite bad weather and reduced opportunities. Christmas rolled around, by which time JG-26 had moved its HQ to Abbeville. In a season of surprise gifts, Galland and JG-26 got one that they had not remotely expected—a personal visit from the *Fuehrer*.

Hitler spoke to the JG-26 pilots in terms of the renewed assault on England that would take place in the spring of 1941. Operations would then be on a bigger scale and force the English to surrender. The Fighter Arm on the Channel would be strengthened. (Nothing was said about the second front that Hitler was planning to open against the Soviet Union in 1941.) The *Fuehrer* wished Galland and his pilots a Happy New Year. (For many of them, it would be their last.)

As the *Luftwaffe* Fighter Arm on the Channel Front passed over to defense, Galland mulled over and over the lessons of the 1940 summer battle. Bad communications had cost them dearly in their operations. They badly needed, before any new major assault on Britain, a fighter control system similar to the one that had served the RAF so well.

There had been no fighter control for the *Luftwaffe* in the worst of its struggle with the RAF. The only serviceable substitute had been provided by the foresight and abilities of Specialist (*Sonderführer*) Horst Barth, a linguist and radio operator of outstanding skill. Most of the combat leaders, including Galland, were skeptical of any ground-based control system that encroached on their airborne direction of operations. Barth's radio listening unit was particularly hard to accept, because it did not seem feasible to get timely information by listening to enemy radio traffic.

Barth's elite group of linguist-radio operators were sited at Wissant in the Cap Gris Nez area, and it completely mastered the jargon of the RAF fighter controllers directing their aircraft on interceptions. All slang, code, and nickname terms were penetrated, and individual RAF controllers became known by their voices as if they were actors.

Using a 1:50,000 scale map of southern England, Barth could listen to this jumble of language and put RAF fighters "on the plot" just about as well as it was done across the Channel at Bentley Priory. As he put the British operations together from the cacophony of RAF slang and jargon in English, he would pass the distilled data in German down the telephone line to Osterkamp's HQ.

When Galland learned of this work he was highly skeptical and resistant to the idea that perhaps someone might be trying to tell him where to fly and fight. Uncle Theo Osterkamp was convinced of the value of Barth's unit, which had provided data on British operations not otherwise available. Barth's unit also monitored *Luftwaffe* fighters, thereby earning the soubriquet "*Jafü* Police." Barth continued feeding data into Osterkamp's HQ, until Goering discovered this listening service.

Barth's specialist group was immediately enlarged and, in its inflated form, was placed under a high-ranking officer. Barth's pioneer linguist-radio operators were promoted and posted away. (Barth himself would later become Chief of the Fighter Interrogation Section at Auswertestelle West, where captured Allied pilots were interrogated by the *Luftwaffe*.)

Galland hoped at New Year of 1941 that the big new attacks on England promised by Hitler would be carried out with better-developed radar facilities. Improved knowledge of British intentions and better communications were also necessary. Radar, added to his hunter's nose, would make finding his opponents easier. (In the unfoldment of 1941, Galland was to have no difficulty finding the RAF. They came right at him—continuously and in force.)

Gallant leader on the western front. Johannes (Pips or Fips) Priller got his baptism by enemy fire over France and on the Channel front with JG51. On 20 November 1941 he was transferred to JG26. On 11 January 1943 Priller replaced Gerhard Schöpfel as Kommodore of JG26. Schöpfel had taken over command from Galland on 6 December 1941. Priller had a total of 101 aerial victories, all on the western front. On 31 January 1945 Priller became Inspector of Fighters-West.

Japanese General at the western front. Lt. General Oshima Hiroshi shakes hands with Adolf Galland. Japan's ambassador to Germany from 1940 to the end of the war, Oshima was convicted as a war criminal in the Tokyo trials and was paroled from his life sentence in 1955.

CHAPTER TWELVE

Promotion to Lt. Colonel on 1 November 1940 was a bright note for Galland amid the autumn drizzle. New Year 1941 brought even better tidings for JG-26. The long-awaited vacation granted by Goering was finally being organized. "The Abbeville Boys," as the RAF had come to know JG-26, looked forward to this break as small children long for Christmas. While JG-51 under the command of Werner Moelders moved into Abbeville to replace them, JG-26 personnel spoke and thought of little else but the Austrian Tirol.

Vacation for the technical staff took place in shifts. Pilots were sent for a short home leave, after which they met at St. Anton and Zuers on the Arlberg. Goering in a generous gesture arranged a pay bonus to cover expenses on an unforgettable skiing vacation. Every pilot present had earned this break, and all of them needed the therapeutic effects of a complete change of venue and action.

Stimulating exercise in mountain sunshine, combined with the exhilaration of the ski slopes, soon turned the pale pilots back into tanned and vigorous youngsters. Completely absent from these heights was that characteristic reek of an Me-109 cockpit. Evenings spent around roaring logs crowned each invigorating day. Good drinks, wine, and beer eased nervous tautness. Strain and tremblings from the hard months against the RAF gradually disappeared.

Staying in the best hotels, the Abbeville Boys were surrounded by pretty and friendly girls, some of them famous actresses. All of them knew how to treat tired combat pilots, deflecting their memories from lost comrades and recent battles. Many of these young women were strongly drawn to the dark-haired, moustachioed Galland. His many nicknames now included Mufti, Red Knight, and Dolfo, added to Capitano of the Condor Legion. He was already famous throughout Germany.

Galland's photographs had appeared in countless magazines and newspapers. Along with Werner Moelders, he was already in the company of von Richthofen, Boelcke, and Udet, according to the writers who were publicizing the new generation of air heroes. Dashing in appearance, and especially arresting in uniform with his decorations, Galland certainly was good copy.

Vacationing on the Arlberg, he was not in uniform. To the casual glance he was just another middle-sized guy who looked as though someone had slammed a door on his nose. Still, he drew women to himself as though he were a giant magnet. There has always been more to this than his fame, rank, and status.

Call it a powerful aura, a strong bioplasmic field, animal magnetism, or call it what you will. Scientists investigating the force that animates human beings are hard on the trail of what Galland has always exuded. He pulls people to him. Women have always reacted to this magnetism without any intellectual idea of why it is so.

In 1983, the authors attended an aerospace industry barbecue with Galland in Bonn. As he walked across the grounds, the authors were astonished to see numerous ladies of all ages pivot around on their heels and follow him with fascinated and entranced expressions. Asked about this, Galland merely shrugged. "You get used to it," he said laconically. He was in his 72nd year when this incident occurred. Back on that ski vacation in 1941, when Dolfo had plenty of flux in his magnet, the lovelies reacted by being attracted. Galland got all the attention he could handle.

From among these adoring ladies, the Red Knight selected Monica, a stunning divorcée who was taking the mountain air after shedding her elderly husband. With her was Michael, her four-year-old son. On the social scene, Galland liked things organized. Arrangements were soon made for Monica to help him forget the RAF for a while. (They would remain close friends until 1945. Monica would reside near him in Berlin, and she would eventually help save his life. His relationship with her caused him many difficulties, because her friends in the film industry and other circles were anti-Nazi and anti-war.)

Galland's attractiveness to women, which many more-handsome men could never understand, had already proved to be a little problem in France. Again it was a question getting organized socially. The dashing young *Kommodore* could not possibly deal with all the young women who sought him out by various ruses. Galland set up what he called a "filter," in the person of "Papi" Causin, a reserve officer from World War I assigned to JG-26 for administrative tasks.

Genial, tactful, and with plenty of worldly experience, Papi Causin was interposed between Galland and his female admirers. In private life, Papi was director of a brewery. On Galland's staff, he directed the diplomatic defense of his C.O. against excessive romantic entanglement. (Papi continued to act as a filter on Galland's staff throughout the war. Galland admitted at age 72 that there were "occasionally some holes in the filter.") He punched some of those holes himself, by commissioning Papi to organize dates for him with chosen ladies. This occurred when the circumstances—or the ladies—were exceptional.

Papi proved as adroit at inviting the desired ladies in as he was at filtering the others out.

Entertainment troupes visited JG-26 and other service units in France, and they were the counterpart of the USO entertainment teams for the American forces. The German groups invariably featured dazzling actresses, dancers, and entertainers from the Berlin scene. Dolfo did not believe that their talent had to be spread around quite so widely, and so Papi arranged for that. An exceptionally gorgeous actress named Joshy shared her talents exclusively with the famous *Kommodore* of JG-26.

Papi in Paris lined up a beautiful Belgian named Monique. Galland found excuses, thereafter, to visit Air Fleet 2 HQ from time to time. At the luxury night club Scheherezade in Paris there was yet another stunning female that Papi dated for his C.O. in advance. All this followed the pattern of Galland's early life, when he discovered his passion for good-looking girls. Unable to conquer this passion, he indulged it, instead. (There were plenty of women in his life, but Monica of the celebrated 1941 Arlberg vacation was undoubtedly closest to him until he married long after the war.)

Just how memorable this particular vacation was for the premier fighter *Geschwader* of the *Luftwaffe* can be judged from Galland's 70th birthday party in Cologne. In March of 1982, the heads were grey and bald, but the somewhat aged survivors of JG-26 present were still talking about the Arlberg vacation— 41 years later! While they rebuilt their stamina in the Alps, their aircraft, vehicles, and equipment were overhauled at the home bases of JG-26 at Düsseldorf, Mönchengladbach, and Krefeld. The *Gruppen* had not seen these places since the beginning of the Battle of France.

Ready for operations again by 1 March 1941, the three *Gruppen* of JG-26 were ordered to Brest, Morlaix, and Lannion in Britanny. They were assigned to protect the German battleships in Brest and the major new U-boat bases being established there and at Lorient. Galland disliked the posture of defense, and they were too far from action. A fighter pilot becomes like a fire horse. He wants to rush full speed to the action. He is restless pulling a milk cart.

Right at this time, Galland's youngest brother Paul finished his training as a fighter pilot. The *Kommodore* of JG-26 arranged for his brother's assignment to III/JG-26, where he could keep an eye on him. Off duty, they could be Keffer and Paulinchen, sharing memories of Westerholt and home, a human touch amid war's turmoil.

His next-youngest brother Wilhelm-Ferdinand, called Wutz, had met with him often on the Channel coast during the Battle of Britain. Wutz was adjutant of an elite flak training battalion but wanted to get into the Fighter Arm. He asked for his famous brother's help. In a short time, Wutz was transferred to an accelerated pilot training course. He would soon join the Fighter Arm in JG-26.

Completing the family scene, Keffer even did a favor for his eldest brother Fritz. Although he still did not care too much for Fritz, always recalling the time in his teens when Fritz tried to steal his girl, Galland made some arrangements. Fritz was duly transferred to a similar course to Wutz. (He served out the war as a reconnaissance and fighter pilot.)

As Galland took off for transfer to the Brittany bases, he realized that it was an incredible three months since he had last downed an enemy aircraft. Morose over his new defensive assignment, Galland decided to take the offensive personally, however briefly. After refueling at Le Touquet, Galland took off with Master Sergeant Menge for a provocative two-plane sweep over southern England.

"Find the enemy and shoot him down," said the Red Baron in 1917. The black-haired Galland, with his big black cigar parked in its special cockpit ashtray, stooged around over England to find the enemy so he could shoot him down. Pilot shortages of the Battle of Britain were long gone. Up came a whole squadron of Spitfires to clean Galland's clock.

Spotting the Spits on their way up, Galland plunged down on the climbing fighters for an unexpected bounce at 3,000 feet. Surprise was decisive. In short order, Galland and Menge each shot down a Spitfire and were barreling like hell for the Brittany coast. When they touched down at Brest, they had added two aerial victories to the JG-26 tally. Their gaping fellow pilots were astonished. They had not even sighted an enemy aircraft.

There was little action for a fighter *Geschwader* where they were stationed. Up in the Pas de Calais, things were lively. Werner Moelders was piling up more victories. The scoring race was now between Moelders and Galland. The two other leading scorers of the Battle of Britain period were out of the running. Major Helmut Wieck of JG-2 had been killed off the south coast of England. Captain Wilhelm Balthasar had been wounded and was now well behind Galland in the scoring. As Moelders steadily increased his score, Galland's envy grew. He wished he were in Moelders's place (and soon he would be, but not in the way that he wanted).

Galland pulled another unauthorized two-plane sweep over southern England on General Osterkamp's birthday on 15 April 1941. Uncle Theo was *Jafü* 2 at Le Touquet, and, since nobody knew in those days how many more birthdays anyone might have—due to all the lead in the air—he invited Galland over to help him celebrate. The young *Kommodore* had just turned 29 himself three weeks earlier.

Galland's staff packed a huge basketful of fresh lobsters and champagne, stuffing this cargo into the small space behind the pilot's seat in the Me-109F-2. Taking off from Brest with 1st Lieutenant Westphal as his wingman, Galland's sense of mischief took charge. Despite the insignia of a lieutenant colonel on his uniform, and despite the lobsters and champagne behind him, he led the way to England. They would go again and tweak the British lion's tail.

His luck held. Near the narrowest part of the Channel he spotted a lone

Butcher-Bird. The Focke-Wulf 190A-1 was delivered to II/JG26 in July and August, 1941 (Kommander Hauptmann Adolph) and based at Maldeghem. The first combat against the RAF took place on 27 September 1941. The FW 190 was slightly superior to RAF fighters and maintained this lead in performance until the Spitfire IX arrived.

Galland his men took every opportunity to go hunting and to ha~ a barbecue. This is in 1940 on the Channel front. Left to right, Lützow (profile), Schöpfel, Wieck, Galland, von Maltzahn and Ebersberger.

Stab / J.G.26

(Dienststelle)

Einsatzort, den   **08.11.1941**

Oberstlt. Galland   94. Abschuß

Stab J.G.26   91. "

ABSCHUSSMELDUNG

J. G. 26   **903. Abschuß**

1. Zeit (Tag, Stunde, Minute) und Gegend des Absturzes :   **18.11.41**   **12.32 Uhr**

   Höhe : **4000**   Meter :   **20 km westl. Boulogne**

2. Durch wen ist der Abschuss/Zerstörung erfolgt ? _   **Obstlt. Galland**
3. Flugzeugtyp des abgeschossenen Flugzeuges :   **Spitfire**
4. Staatsangehörigkeit des Gegners :   **engl.**
   Werk-Nr bzw. Kennzeichen :   **Kokarde**
5. Art der Vernichtung :

    a.) Flammen mit dunkler Fahne, Flammen mit heller Fahne,
    b.) Einzelteile weggeflogen, <u>abmontiert</u> (Art der Teile erläutern), **rechtes Querruder**
      auseinandergeplatzt   **abgeschossen**
    c.) zur Landung gezwungen (diesseits oder jenseits der Front,
      glatt bzw. mit Bruch)
    d.) jenseits der Front am Bodem im Brand geschossen

6. Art des Aufschlages (nur wenn dieser beobachtet werden konnte

    a.) diesseits oder <u>jenseits der Front</u>
    b.) senkrecht, <u>flachen Winkel</u>, Aufschlagbrand, Staubwolke   **in See abgestürzt**
    c.) nicht beobachtet, warum nicht ?

7. Schicksal der Insassen   (<u>tot</u>, mit Fallschirm abgesprungen, nicht beobachtet
8. Gefechtsbericht des Schützen ist in der Anlage beigefügt.
9. Zeugen;

    a.) Luft   **Lt. Hilgendorff**
    b.) Erde
10. Anzahl der Angriffe, die auf das feindliche Flugzeug gemacht wurden ;   **1**
11. Richtung, aus der die einzelnen Angriffe erfolgten ;   **in scharfer Rechtskurve**
12. Entfernung, aus der der Abschuss erfolgte ;   **50 m**
13. Takt. Position aus der der Abschuss angesetzt wurde ;   **Kurvenkampf**
14. Ist einer der feindl. Bordschützen kampfunfähig gemacht worden ?
15. Verwandte Munitionsart ; **S.m.K.v.,P.m.K.v.,M.H 1,Br.Spr.FF,Panzer Spr.151/20**
                                                            M 151/20,Br.Spr.151/
16. Munitionsverbrauch ; **62 MG 17/22 MG FF/2 cm** **14 MG 151/20 m**
17. Art und Anzahl der waffen, die bei dem Abschuss gebraucht wurden ?   **1 MG 151/20**
                                                                    2 MG FF/2 cm
18. Typ der eigene Maschine ; **F 6 U .**   **2 MG 17**
19. Weiteres taktisch oder technisch Bemerkenswertes ;
20. Treffer in der eigenen Maschine;   **./.**
21. Beteiligung weiterer Einheiten (auch Flak) ;

(Unterschrift)

Combat Report, 1941. Typical combat report required from pilots. This report by Galland was to record a victory over a Spitfire on 18 November 1941. It was his 94th aerial victory and JG26's 903rd victory. German victory claims were detailed and required a witness to the victory.

Spitfire, probably a returning reconnaissance aircraft. A wild chase immediately ensued. The champagne was subjected to more G-force than its bottler ever intended, but the corks held. Caught with a burst, the Spitfire crashed into a village west of Dover.

Turning for Le Touquet, Galland was astonished to see a squadron of Spitfires climbing ahead of him—probably scrambled on intercept. One British fighter was lagging badly. Galland came up on him unseen and shot him down with a short burst from astern. The high likelihood was that the two German planes had merged on radar with the echoes from their opponents. Keeping his cool, Galland closed in on a third Spitfire, hitting him immediately from short range. Losing speed instantly upon taking the burst, the stricken Spitfire nearly collided with Galland. Westphal was about to nail another Spitfire when his guns jammed. The British pilots now realized that German fighters were in their midst. They turned to wade into the invaders.

Firewalling his throttle, Galland put the nose of his fighter down and went racing across the Channel, tracers criss-crossing around his Me-109F-2. Tearing across the hostile grey sea, engines snarling and with tracers and Spitfires streaming after them, Galland saw Westphal pulling ahead of him. Some part of his own plane must have been hit. His mind turned oddly to the champagne behind him. What would an impact do to Uncle Theo's birthday present?

Outrunning the Spitfires by the barest margin, they went roaring in over Le Touquet. Starting to let down, Galland saw red flares arc up in front of him. Ground staff on the field below were giving him a frenzied wave-off. Puzzled and cursing, he went around the field again, wondering what was amiss. Finally he tumbled to the problem. He had been about to land with his gear up. What a birthday present for Uncle Theo. Lt. Colonel Galland, second-ranking ace of the *Luftwaffe,* landing gear up on the doorstep of his *Jafü:* one Me-109F-2 wiped out, plus the lobsters and champagne.

In action with the Spitfires, his knee had probably hit the landing gear button, dropping the gear while he was in combat. He had flown home across the Channel with gear down. No wonder he had to retrim his aircraft, or that Westphal had outstripped him. When he hit the landing gear button on final approach to Le Touquet, his landing gear had retracted. Just in time he had spotted the warning flares. Galland and Uncle Theo Osterkamp had more than one reason to say ''good luck'' when they raised their champagne glasses.

In April of 1941, the *Luftwaffe* Bomber Arm was building up its night attacks on Britain. This effort was to divert attention from the movement of most air units eastward for the assault on Russia. Multiple missions were flown by Bomber Arm units remaining in the West, to maintain an illusion of continuing strength. This was an exhausting ordeal for the bomber crews, but they managed to fly over 5,400 sorties in April 1941, more than they flew in August 1940. London suffered its two heaviest raids of the war in this period. On the nights of 16 and 19 April 1941, approximately 700 bombers struck each time at the British capital. Despite a diminishing number of available bombers, Goering

Galland on Channel Front wearing wool-lined flying suit taken from captured RAF bomber crew.

Galland's Me-109E4 lies bellied-in on the beach at Cap Griz Nez after running out of fuel. Escorting bombers to the London area during the Battle of Britain exceeded the range of the 109 in many cases and the Luftwaffe suffered heavy losses getting back across the English Channel to its bases in France.

was keeping alive the idea of another round to the Battle of Britain. German propaganda further emphasized this prospect.

Goering's deception efforts included calling an ostentatious April conference of air commanders and combat leaders in Paris. Galland and Moelders were present. Goering regaled his audience with a list of measures to be taken against the RAF. Galland's spirits rose as orator Goering carried the throng along with his fighting words. Moelders nodded approvingly when Galland shot him a sidelong glance.

The two young combat leaders were afterwards ordered to meet privately with the *Reich* Marshal.

"How did you like my speech?" said Goering. "Was it convincing?"

Their approval caused Goering to rub his nose with glee, a characteristic gesture of the *Reich* Marshal.

"Good. Very good. You believed it, and that is good. Now I will tell you that there isn't a word of truth in it."

Goering then launched into a description of the new glories his *Luftwaffe* would win in the *forthcoming invasion of Russia!* Galland was dumbfounded. Moelders's face was a mask as Goering laid out the plan. A short, violent campaign with about six weeks' actual fighting. Perhaps two or three months with all the cleaning up. Most of the Fighter Arm was being transferred eastward forthwith, including Moelders and his JG-51. The Channel Front would be defended by JG-2 and JG-26 alone.

Other fighter units would return to the West when Russia was conquered. Reinforced by the vast material resources of Russia, Goering's *Luftwaffe* would then bring Britain to her knees—unless the British came to their senses in the meantime. The Soviet Air Force? Nothing to worry about. "Shoot down the leaders and the illiterates won't even be able to find their way home."

While Goering was dismissing Soviet air power in this irresponsible fashion, Germany's air attaché in Moscow had formed a different impression. Lt. Colonel Aschenbrenner, who later rose to lieutenant general, arranged for a German engineering team to tour the Soviet aircraft industry. An immense flood of machines was being produced. Factories were employing 30,000 workers per shift, three shifts a day, seven days a week. Soviet aircraft designer Artemis Mikoyan told Aschenbrenner at the end of the conducted tour that the Soviet Union would destroy any attacker. This full-blast activity in the Russian aircraft industry contrasted starkly with the *Luftwaffe*, where Battle of Britain losses had barely been replaced.

Goering had initially opposed the invasion of Russia, directly to Hitler. The *Reich* Marshal cited the exhaustion of his *Luftwaffe* and the need for rest, refit, and expansion. When Hitler remained adamant in his plan to smash the Bolshevist colossus, Goering knuckled under. He fell again to the task of pleasing his hero. Hence his ridiculous minimization of the Soviet Air Force in discussing the invasion of Russia with Galland and Moelders. Goering's relentless overworking of bomber crews to fool the British was a completely wasted effort.

Priceless *Ultra* decrypts, combined with more orthodox intelligence from Germany, Poland, and the Balkans, clearly foretold Hitler's invasion of Russia. A copy of the actual code-name "Barbarossa" directive of 18 December 1940 was supplied to Moscow by Washington, the United States still being neutral. An anonymous anti-Hitler official in Berlin passed the document to the U.S. commercial attaché in a movie theater. Careful planning and stealth availed the Germans nothing. Through *Ultra* decrypts, the British gained encyclopedic knowledge of German movements, operational plans, and commanders.

Ultra and RAF intelligence were familiar with personalities like Galland's old boss in Spain and Poland, General Wolfram von Richthofen. When this capable commander and his 8th Air Corps were moved from the Channel coast to Rumania and Bulgaria, as part of an aerial build-up to support 20 Army divisions, the British certainly knew that the Germans were not on maneuvers. Russia's ambassador in London, Ivan Maisky, was summoned to the Foreign Office. He was given a comprehensive and forceful review of these vast German movements towards Soviet frontiers.

Goering made the invasion of Russia sound easy to his two leading fighter pilots. Galland was not persuaded. The *Reich* Marshal's Eagle Day telex kept echoing in his mind: *"Soon you will wipe the British Air Force from the sky."* That was also supposed to be an easy assignment. A desperate, bloody, nerve-draining ordeal had ensued, which had still not been forced to a final decision. In the light of this situation, Galland's shock over the coming invasion of Russia was considerable, and it did not readily subside.

His logic, common sense, and acumen for aerial warfare saw attacking Russia as an immense gamble. Even blacker were the prospects on the Channel Front. Just two *Geschwader* were to face the mounting power of the RAF, a skeleton defense by any measure.

Galland's apprehensions are justified by the now known historical facts. By 1 April 1941, RAF Fighter Command had over 1,200 aircraft on strength and 1,700 available pilots. The massive Empire Air Training Scheme was beginning its large-scale production of pilots, while training remained the *Luftwaffe's* ragged stepchild.

RAF Bomber Command was also rapidly expanding. An alarming production of four-engined strategic bombers was scheduled. Against this uncoiling strike power, the *Luftwaffe* was setting JG-2 and JG-26—one fifth of the fighter strength deployed for the Battle of Britain. Kesselring was posted to the eastern theater, Air Fleet 2 and all. Hugo Sperrle was left in solitary splendor on the Channel with his rump command, JG-2 plus JG-26, and 4 bomber *Gruppen* where once there had been 44.

From besiegers in 1940, the *Luftwaffe* on the Channel became the besieged of 1941. Numerical ascendancy by the British was backed with an aggressive spirit. The Brits were out to even the score for 1940. Now it was the *Luftwaffe's* turn to wait for raiders from across the Channel. Blenheims, Bostons, and Stirlings started crossing the Channel in gaggles of about two dozen, with about three times their own number in fighter escort. The Spitfires were new marques, better armed and well flown.

Railroad terminals, airfields, and strategic industrial targets in France as far as Paris and Lille were now subjected to steady RAF attack. Appearance of the British in a daylight attacking role caused a sensation at *Luftwaffe* HQs in Paris and Berlin. The tables had been turned, and again the *Luftwaffe* became dependent upon its Fighter Arm.

Colonel Joachim Huth, as Osterkamp's successor as *Jafü* 2 at Le Touquet, now had radar. This was a large benefit to the defenders. *Luftwaffe* fighters on the Channel began operating on the alarm-start system—scrambling against British raids as warning, weather, and time permitted. The numerical odds were against the *Luftwaffe* and continued to lengthen.

When Germany invaded Russia in June of 1941, the RAF bombing operations against targets in northern France were intensified. From operations in *Gruppe* strength, Galland was forced to begin leading his entire *Geschwader* against British incursions, as the RAF increased the number of escorting fighters. The British took their losses and made them up. Galland took his losses and felt them steadily. Sufficient replacement pilots and planes were simply not available. JG-2 and JG-26 both markedly declined in strength. Instead of the normal 80 fighters apiece, the two *Geschwader* defending the Channel coast were lucky to have 50 aircraft each in a serviceable state.

Part of Adolf Galland's lifelong respect for the RAF stems from this period, when he was living the life of a defending fighter pilot. RAF raids coming in daily, often twice daily and sometimes thrice daily, created a siege existence for JG-26. British bombers and fighters were being shot down, but their raiding strength never diminished. Losses were obviously made up immediately. For Galland and his pilots, the strain was again intense on bodies, minds, and machines, just as it had been in the Battle of Britain.

Attrition of the defenders was exemplified by a couple of successive orders from the High Command. First the German pilots were forbidden to fly over England. Then they were forbidden to pursue the enemy beyond mid-Channel. There would be no more "champagne flights" for Lt. Colonel Galland under these restrictions. Things had changed radically since August of 1940.

21 June 1941 saw Galland in a noontime battle with a formation of Blenheim bombers near St. Omer. Leaving his formation to its task of tackling the escort fighters, Galland led his wingman, Sergeant Hegenauer, into an attack on the bombers. Two firing passes resulted in two Blenheims downed, victories 68 and 69, but the Spitfires quickly intervened. Galland felt hits slamming into his fighter, and he went lunging for some low haze. Tracers laced around him and black smoke trailed behind his aircraft.

Whizzing into the haze, he was grateful for the white veil between him and his pursuers. His Me-109 still flew, but his temperature gauge was up in the red. His engine soon seized. Again he was drawing on knowledge gained in his soaring days at the Borkenberge. Emerging into clear air as he descended, he was over the Calais-Marck airfield—luck indeed. Bellying in and climbing out of the fighter safely, he was picked up within the hour by an Me-108 Taifun and flown back to his HQ at Audembert.

Over in England, he thought to himself, some RAF pilots would be carving up the credit for his downing. Hegenauer had been also shot down, but his trusty wingman from Battle of Britain days was unwounded. The ever-aggressive RAF were soon back. More bombers droned over, with another horde of escort fighters.

Taking off alone, Galland went climbing up on intercept. He intended to rendezvous with I/JG-26 during the climb. Southeast of Boulougne he could see the German fighters and a Spitfire formation to their left. There were British stragglers Hunter Galland forgot the axiom that "a fighter pilot without a wingman has less than half his strength." He went racing for his quarry.

Hitting what he thought was the tail-end Spitfire straggler, he suddenly realized that he had no wingman to confirm this victory. The British machine was spinning downward. This was his 70th victory. Important to get confirmation of this one.

BANG!

A merged chain of rapid explosions ended in a big blast, right in his Me-109. Heavy blows to his head and arm brought rushes of pain. Holes appeared in his wings, jagged and gaping. Cannon fire ripped away part of the fuselage, leaving the wounded *Kommodore* sitting half in the open at 18,000 feet. The stench of gasoline rose through the cockpit, and coolant went streaming away from the now engineless fighter.

He had learned anew the lesson he impressed continually on the young pilots he commanded: never seek combat without your wingman. That 70th victory he had just shot down was not the last Spitfire straggler. He had been blasted by another unseen Spit approaching from the distant rear.

His soaring skills came in handy for the second time of the day as he banked around to the north and found his shattered Me-109 still under control in the gliding mode. Blood was running down from his head. More blood was dripping from his torn sleeve. He could glide to a friendly field, maybe even get back to Audembert, if he could stay conscious. Without an engine, the aircraft seemed strangely quiet, despite the wind whining through the many holes in its fuselage and wings. . . . he could make it, he could make it.

BOOM!

Igniting gasoline fumes sent a muffled explosion woofing through the fuselage. Blazing gasoline came running into the cockpit. Flames leaped around him. Frantically he tore at the cockpit roof release. Stuck. Stuck. Stuck. More flames now, clawing, searing, scorching. Tearing open his safety belt, he thrust upwards at the hinged canopy. Air pressure was pinning it shut.

Terrified, choking, and verging on panic, he thrust upwards at the canopy with his back, putting all his strength into a do-or-die upward shove. Bursting off its mounting, the canopy went flashing away in the slipstream. Momentum from his upward thrust carried Galland halfway out of the cockpit, but again he was stuck. His parachute was jammed in the cockpit canopy support. Roaring earthward, his fighter was an inferno, dragging him to his doom.

Wrapping one arm around the aerial mast, he shoved and pushed with his booted feet against anything that would give traction. Pull, haul, twist, turn, pull more, twist again, and all the while the infernal earth was coming up at him like an avenger. Miraculously he burst free, tumbling like an acrobat. In his shaken state, he went to pull his ripcord, noticing just in time that he was fumbling inadvertently with his parachute harness quick-release—a passport to the next world. Making very sure he had the ripcord, he pulled. A plumping noise and a bone-straining jerk told him he would survive.

Squelching down in a boggy meadow, Galland now paid the price for the surge of adrenalin that had powered him through his ordeal. He went instantly to the fringe of complete collapse. Pain pulsed from his gunshot wounds and burns. Blood was all over him. A wrenched ankle sustained in his final landing ballooned up inside his boot. He could not even stand.

French farmers, who had seen him descend, nervously carried him into a nearby farmhouse. A Todt organization car soon afterwards whisked him back to Audembert. His fate was unknown at his own HQ. Fears had been expressed of his death. Papi Causin was again the sterling aide, providing a hefty jolt of cognac and a big black cigar to the wounded *Kommodore*.

At Hardinghem hospital, Dr. Heim of the German Navy sewed up his wounds. Heim was a good friend that Galland appreciated even more in his present extremity. Not every doctor could be responsible surgeon and friend simultaneously. Fighter pilot survival from such a brink was known as a "birthday." Luftwaffe pilots held that the fortunate flyer had been "born again" after a brush with death.

Galland staged the required birthday party at Audembert, celebrating his 70th victory at the same time. Congratulations came from Hitler via telex. The *Fuehrer* also announced the award to Galland, as the first officer of the *Wehrmacht* so honored, of a newly instituted order of the Knight's Cross. To his Oak Leaves were now added the Swords (*Schwerter*). The Swords were celebrated with high consumption of champagne. The bubbly wine helped drown for a while the pains of his wounds, but it could not wash away a Hitler order contained in the same telex: Lt. Colonel Galland was to cease operational flying on the express orders of the *Fuehrer*.

The grounding order was initially unnecessary. Galland wasn't fit to fly. He needed two weeks even to begin walking properly again. The RAF meanwhile just kept coming in day after day. Galland nearly died of frustration. He began edging his way back into the air with "test flights" and similar ruses.

Galland was unable to restrain himself from going back to regular missions. On the first such operation, he sprang into the cockpit of the new Me-109 prepared for his exclusive use by his crew chief, Sergeant Meyer. Upset by his *Kommodore's* near-fatal head wound, Meyer had thoughtfully fitted an extra piece of armor plate on top of the canopy—but he neglected to inform Galland. The *Kommodore* got a thump on his already tender head from the changed geometry of the cockpit roof. He bawled something like *"Dummkopf!"* as he roared away, leaving Meyer aghast.

In the ensuing wild battle with Blenheim bombers and their Spitfire escort, Galland sustained further head damage. A Spitfire shot his cockpit to bits and got him in the head. Blood running down his face, he landed at Audembert and got out of the aircraft before the horrified gaze of Meyer. Galland was lucky. Meyer's custom-fitted armor plate had absorbed a cannon hit, which would have ended Galland's life and terminated the worries he was now having over violating Hitler's personal grounding order.

Meyer got 100 marks and special leave as a token of his *Kommodore*'s gratitude. The tolerant Dr. Heim again sewed up Galland's head, while shaking his own with incredulity. Ordered to the Wolf's Redoubt to receive his Swords award, Galland arrived in East Prussia highly apprehensive over his violation of Hitler's order grounding him.

The *Fuehrer* showed appreciation of JG-26 and JG-2 in defending the Channel coast. He recognized the higher burden they were carrying. Hitler promised that he would soon relieve 50 Army divisions in the East, and more fighter *Geschwader* would be available to fight the RAF. Hitler made no reference to his grounding order. Galland had the eerie feeling nevertheless that Hitler knew he was worried about the *Fuehrer*'s adverse reaction.

As he dismissed the young ace, Hitler descended for a fleeting moment from his *Fuehrer*'s pedestal.

"We like your bravery," he said, "but please look after yourself."

On the Channel coast in 1941, any *Luftwaffe* fighter pilot who didn't look after himself had a short life expectancy. Galland loved life too much to throw his away.

CHAPTER THIRTEEN

Constant operational activity in 1941, with numerous targets provided by the RAF on every day suitable for flying, made this the most successful period in Galland's career as a fighter pilot. His expertise and acumen continued to increase, despite fatigue. His victory tally rose steadily. His boyhood dream of excellence was being lived daily in this world at war.

Warriors have always followed the exemplar-leader, and the pilots of JG-26 would have followed Adolf Galland anywhere. Among them in 1941 were his brothers Paul and Wutz. Hardly an operational day passed that did not involve one of the three brothers in action, and often all three were in combat simultaneously. Paul required a lengthy running-in period, during which success in aerial combat eluded him. For the 21-year-old youngster this time was especially frustrating. His brother was not only the famous ace-leader but also the *Kommodore*.

Paul therefore felt obliged to do well. Pressure on him became even greater when Wutz joined JG-26 as a fledgling fighter pilot and was quickly successful. Wutz had a marked talent for air-to-air shooting. Paul in the beginning thus had his moments of envy and regret. In due course, the youngster's patient persistence was rewarded, and he became an ace along with his brothers Wutz and Keffer.

Galland's leadership style as *Kommodore* was to always be first into the air. Any pilot quick enough to get airborne ahead of him would find his *Kommodore* hard behind. Tactics had to be devised to inflict maximum casualties on the RAF, with minimum attrition on his own numerically inferior forces. Aggressive defense keynoted his tactics, which always sought to keep the battle initiative for JG-26.

With sardonic joy he noticed how the British fighters were tied to the bombers, just as most of his fighters had been in the Battle of Britain. He could readily imagine the frustrations of the British fighter pilots. They would be cursing their damned orders, just as he had done when tied down to close-escort flying. They would be longing to lunge after JG-26 in the free chase.

Galland's usual tactic was to lead his fighters above and behind the bomber formation, up in the sun if possible. Diving down through the escorting fighters, they would attack the bombers and then dive away at full throttle. Initially ordered to attack the bombers only, Galland was able to get this restriction modified. This prevented his needless loss of part of the initiative.

After these diving attacks, the Spitfires would go after the JG-26 fighters, furiously chasing them right down to the deck. Quickly the Germans learned respect for the cannon fire from these new Spitfire variants. (German numerical inferiority at this time foreshadowed the coming years, in which Allied numerical ascendancy would be extended into Germany's own airspace.)

Galland developed tactics with his own staff, flight that demanded the top performance in his entire *Geschwader*. (Later on, the same excellence would be demanded from the squadron that was ordered to fly with him.) His tactics were dangerous, but effective. When cloudy conditions prevailed, he would cunningly inch his formation right in among the Spitfire escort.

Unless the enemy were supersharp and perceptive, the similarity between Spitfire and Me-109 silhouettes made this tactic feasible. Colors and markings were also difficult to distinguish at this speed in the diffuse glare of cloudy conditions. Easing along amid the escort, Galland would reach a position of advantage for readily attacking a bomber. Diving down suddenly, the German formation would clobber the bombers and be away into the distance, sometimes before the Spitfires knew what had happened. These tactics called for a cool head and nerves of steel. Pilot quality in Galland's formations was excellent, and they pulled off this ploy repeatedly.

Another Galland attack stratagem exposed him to the danger of flying alone, but it was also repeatedly successful. Directing the other JG-26 fighters to position themselves "on the perch" above and behind the bombers, Galland would make his stealthy solo approach from below. Cloud was also needed for this tactic, but it depended mainly upon the ostentatious assembly of the other German aircraft, capturing the attention of the escorting Spitfires.

If he was able to climb up to the bombers unseen, he would fire a lethal burst into one of the lower British aircraft, then whip away into the clouds before the escort reacted. Risk was high with this tactic. He was vulnerable to diving Spitfires after his attack and also during the approach. Galland never allowed his tactics to settle into a routine. Variations and innovations kept the enemy fighter escorts off balance.

The strain of leadership in an overworked fighter *Geschwader* was intensified by the daily combats of his brothers. No one has ever said of Galland that he was inhuman, but the presence of his beloved brothers exposed him to inhuman pressure. One or the other of them was always bailing out, bellying in, or being reported going down somewhere trailing smoke. The nervous strain of having his own blood in jeopardy, under his own orders, led him to suggest that transfers to other units or fronts were desirable. Wutz and Paul both adamantly declined. They were under no illusions about the risks. None of them expected to be an old grey-haired fighter pilot describing the war to his grandchildren.

Their evenings and leisure times together became the most precious interludes. The large and comfortable house at Audembert where Galland and the other pilots were quartered became their second home. Over the good French wine, they would recapture their loving yesteryears in Westerholt. Boyhood came even closer in the luxury bunker with its open fire. Galland had laid out a huge electric train set for relaxation and diversion, and they played with it for hours. Shut out briefly was the harsh reality that on the morrow one of them—or perhaps all three—might be meeting other fallen pilots in the airmen's heaven.

Not every evening brought relaxation and joy. One such evening was 10 May 1941, when Galland's telephone rang during the last minutes of daylight. An agitated *Reich* Marshal Goering was calling, his voice nearly babbling.

"Galland, you are to take off immediately with your whole *Geschwader.* With your whole Geschwader, *understand?*"

"*Herr Reich* Marshal, we have no reports of any aircraft flying in."

"Flying in? Flying in?" Goering's voice now was nearly hysterical. "What do you mean, flying in? An aircraft is flying *out!* The Deputy of the *Fuehrer* has gone mad and is flying to England in an Me-110. He must be shot down. And Galland, call me personally when you get back."

Getting the anticipated course and approximate 6:00 PM departure time of Rudolf Hess from Augsburg-Haunstetten, Galland put down the telephone with some of Goering's agitation roiling in his own mind. Ordered to shoot down the Deputy *Fuehrer* on the personal orders of the *Reich* Marshal? Galland was accustomed to occasional crazy orders, but this was absolutely cuckoo.

Night was falling fast. About ten minutes flying time remained. If he took off now with his whole *Geschwader* and went hunting for the Me-110 that Hess was supposed to be flying, how could it be distinguished from other Me-110s of the night fighter force? They would already be up on test flights and other missions around dusk. Even if they found and shot down Hess—a million-to-one chance—how would they get down themselves without wrecking half of JG-26's fighters? In unaccustomed night landings with no guidance, the carnage would be terrible. The whole thing was insane.

Galland accordingly ordered each *Gruppe* to scramble one or two planes, to make a couple of local circuits and land again. He did not tell his subordinates the reason for his order. They would already regard him as slightly crazy for ordering such dusk hops, without his adding orders to shoot down the Deputy *Fuehrer.*

After a suitable interval, Galland telephoned back to Goering, reporting that he had failed to find the missing Me-110. Goering was still agitated. Galland emphasized the slight chance Hess had of making it to Scotland, or of avoiding the Spitfires if he got that far. The *Reich* Marshal was not placated.

Hess did successfully cross the North Sea, landing near the estate of the Duke of Hamilton. According to some British historians, a British Secret Service party awaited Hess that night at a prearranged landing field. Officialdom brought down a security curtain on the whole affair. The truth remains concealed. Hess had been silenced by imprisonment in Spandau until he died.

Official deceit and obscurantism provoked much speculation about the Hess affair. Writers have asserted that Galland knows more than he is telling. All questions posed by various writers about Galland's alleged role in the affair have been asked him by the authors personally and bluntly. The truth of Galland's involvement is that Goering gave him crazy orders in a bizarre situation. These orders could not be carried out literally, without high hazard to the pilots and fighters of his command. They were therefore obeyed only in token fashion.

After the invasion of Russia, conversations among the three Galland brothers and their comrades centered on news from the Eastern Front. The *Luftwaffe* had covered itself with new glories, as Goering had predicted. In the history of aerial warfare, the greatest one-day victory is the *Luftwaffe* triumph over the Soviet Air Force on 22 June 1941. Over 2,000 Russian machines were destroyed in the "surprise" assault. Warnings to the Soviet government through diplomatic channels of the imminent blow, as well as Churchill's direct personal warning to Stalin, had resulted in no special vigilance.

Dr. Goebbels knew what to do with such victory tidings. Splashed through the German media with spreads of photographs, and with newsreels graphically depicting the shambles, *Luftwaffe* triumphs in Russia were difficult for Galland and his pilots to comprehend. Pinned down and outnumbered on the Channel coast, battling a foe who was capable, aggressive, and growing in strength, they were fighting a totally different war.

Soon came the reports of Eastern Front fighter pilot victories, many dozens of victories. In the big HQ house at Audembert, they would wonder about the incredible strings of downings in Russia. Moelders quickly reached 100 victories, unprecedented in the history of aerial warfare. Hitler awarded him the Diamonds to his Knight's Cross, the highest order of the decoration.

Other pilots were downing four and five Soviet planes a day; 20 victories in a month contrasted sharply with the creeping pace of their own victories against the RAF. In May of 1941, Field Marshal Sperrle had congratulated Galland and JG-26 for reaching the all-time *Geschwader* total of 500 victories. That had seemed like a major achievement then. At the Eastern Front scoring rate, a *Geschwader* there would register 500 victories in a couple of months. Were the pilots in Russia shooting down aircraft or ducks?

Galland and JG-26 had a chance to see at first hand the quality of their own opposition on 9 August 1941. Wing Commander Douglas Bader of the RAF literally "dropped in" on them, by parachute, after combat over the Pas de Calais.

First to know of Bader's imminent arrival was the wily specialist and master

"We've caught a big eagle!" August 1941. With these words, Galland was told that Douglas Bader, famed RAF legless ace, had been shot down and captured. Gesticulating Horst Barth, English-speaking chief of the radio listening post at Wissant, translates Bader's English into German for the benefit of Galland and his men. Left to right, Johannes Siefert, Schmitt, Galland, Meinardus, Pappi Causin, Douglas Bader.

On Christmas Day, 1940, the Fuehrer made a surprise visit to JG26 at Abbeville. Here, Adolf Galland, Kommodore of JG26, replies to Hitler's speech.

Major Walter "Gulle" Oesau, left, and Captain Josef "Fips" Priller seem to be silently appraising each other after their decoration ceremony on 1 July 1941. Oesau received the Swords to the Oakleaf and Ritterkreuz while Priller received the Oakleaves to the Ritterkreuz.

linguist, Horst Barth, at his listening post in an old farmhouse. He had followed Bader's unit in action, knowing well Bader's voice and nickname—the "Stationmaster" of Tangmere RAF Station. As soon as he heard that Bader was bailing out, Barth contacted HQ immediately, urging them to search for the famous RAF ace. Barth was unaware at this time that Bader had lost both his legs in a 1931 crash.

Bader believed he had collided in midair with an Me-109, or even perhaps with one of his own squadron's Spitfires, when he suddenly lost the empennage of his fighter. (Many years after the war, he was told that a *Luftwaffe* fighter pilot had caught him unawares at close range.) He bailed out. The Germans were astonished when they located Bader and found that he only had one leg, and that this one leg was artificial. His other leg was jammed in his stricken Spitfire. Impacting on the one artificial leg, Bader was painfully injured when it was rammed up into his chest. He was taken to hospital in St. Omer.

Galland's mechanics retrieved Bader's other leg from his crashed Spitfire, made it serviceable again, and returned the leg to Bader in the hospital. The British ace was gratified. Horst Barth had meanwhile been assigned to watch over Bader until he was taken to formal POW internment. Bravery and courage are much admired by German soldiers, and the pilots of JG-26 were intrigued to learn that the English ace was legless. That won respect.

Once Bader was able to move about a little, Galland invited him to Audembert to see their base and to meet his staff and some of the JG-26 pilots. A magnificent Horch sedan was provided by the *Luftwaffe* to Galland as the normal privilege of a *Kommodore*. Too grand and conspicuous for Galland's pleasure excursions, the Horch was seldom used. Here was a chance to employ the big car appropriately. Bader was collected at the hospital by an escort officer, a sergeant-major, and a driver from JG-26 HQ. The Stationmaster arrived at Audembert in style.

Squeaking along on his damaged tin legs as though needing oil, Bader stumped into a lavish reception that would have held its own with anything thrown at the London Dorchester. Colonel Joachim Huth had come over from Le Touquet where he was *Jafü*, and, with Barth as a rapid-fire interpreter, Bader's initial suspicions quickly disappeared. He realized that Galland was extending a soldierly courtesy and not trying to trap him into giving information. One of Galland's big cigars helped further.

Bader was shown the base facilities. He talked fighter planes and piloting with Galland in detail. Galland even allowed his English visitor to sit in the *Kommodore*'s personal Me-109. Bader was photographed in the cockpit, with the Abbeville Boys' C.O. explaining the layout. Bader's renowned gumption had not been affected by his injuries, or by his POW status. He actually asked Galland if he could take off in the Me-109 and "make a couple of circuits of the field."

Part of Galland wanted to let this admirable foe fly the Me-109, but of course such a request had to be denied. Galland did ask Goering, in Bader's behalf, if arrangements could be made to have his spare legs, his pipe, and his favorite tobacco sent over from England. Full of Old World chivalry, Goering agreed to safe conduct for an aircraft carrying this special cargo. The RAF was notified on a special rescue frequency but didn't emulate Goering's chivalrous spirit.

The legs duly came in a specially labeled crate during an air raid targeted on JG-26 airfields. The British did not want any local armistices or social matters to slow down their nonstop offensive. Bader got his legs and his pipe, but in the interim he had tried to escape on his old legs. The dauntless Briton lowered himself on knotted sheets from the top floor of the St. Omer hospital. Free for one night, he was recaptured by Horst Barth, who found him under a haystack.

Galland took considerable flak from the High Command over the escape incident. His reception for Bader was investigated and regarded stonily. The *Luftwaffe* High Command was as unbending as the RAF. (The two great fighter aces both eventually became legends. They did not regret the humanity of their first wartime encounter, which launched an enduring friendship. Bader enters our story again later, but it was a saddened Galland in California in September of 1982 who learned of Bader's passing. Enemies for a short time because of the decisions and actions of others, they were of their own volition friends for the rest of their lives.)

Four months prior to the Bader incident, an aircraft took off from the Heinkel factory that demonstrated Germany's vast technical lead in fighter development. The He-280 was a sleek twin-jet with tricycle landing gear, capable of over 500 mph even on primitive turbojets. Intended armament was initially three 20mm cannons. A proposed variant, the He-280B, was to carry six 20mm cannons and over 1,000 pounds of bombs. The Air Ministry was not interested in developing this revolutionary fighter.

The He-280 was flying and available for development to production when Bader dropped in on Galland. Eight of these fighters were actually built. Early in 1942, mock combat with the redoubtable FW-190 showed the clear superiority of the jet. (This digression is made here in the proper time context, because much has to be related in due course about the Messerschmitt jet, the Me-262, with which Galland was to be intimately concerned. The He-280 flew as a pure twin-jet aircraft more than 15 months before the Me-262. The Germans thus had within their grasp, during the RAF's first nonstop offensive, the weapon needed to abort the ruin that would later descend on them from the daylight skies.)

As 1941 wore on, the grinding struggle on the Channel coast never diminished. Amid the strain and stress, Galland never lost his ability to find humor even in irritating things. Witness this report to HQ from the *Kommodore* of JG-26, concerning certain *Luftwaffe* personnel who were seemingly unaware that Germany was at war.

To *Jafü* 2
From *Kommodore*, JG-26:

During several duty flights to the home territory of Germany, conditions were encountered at air bases, not to mention any names, which should be brought to the attention of higher authority. For reasons of military discipline, correction of these conditions seems urgently necessary. The following observations have been made:

1. In general, every landing of an outside aircraft for refuelling is perceived as a disturbance of the peace, and as a burden to base personnel.

2. Personnel for start support and especially the refuelling personnel are surpassed for their laziness and unmilitary slackness only by the air-control personnel.

3. Oil is basically never available at the fuel pump but in the most remote hangar, which is closed after 5:00 PM.

4. Air-control personnel give a most unmilitary impression. Saluting and other military customs are considered completely out of fashion. They also work as slowly as possible and invariably with a cigaret sticking out of their mouths.

5. Weather service stations are occupied almost entirely by officials on crutches, for war period only, who have to be supported by many girls. The impression is like entering a "Strength through Joy" tourist office. Weather for the route is exclusively couched in pessimistic terms, with much fussing and indecision. In the meantime, when the ladies present ask for autographs, the assistant meteorologists who are not involved loudly crumple sandwich paper wrapping.

6. At some bases, flight orders are controlled by civilian refuelling personnel. They say: "I have to see your flight order, or I cannot give you any fuel."

7. When landing after 5:00 PM, the impression given is that the base has been evacuated for several days. The possibilities for sabotage at the fuel pump, or at the hangars, are wide open for action.

Because of these circumstances, pilots at the front have an antipathy towards flights into the home territory. The difficulties are not the lack of manpower but the attitude and appearance of the soldiers and the posts themselves that are causing the trouble.

Signed: Galland

Lt. Col. and *Kommodore*

On a flight to the home territory about the time he wrote the foregoing complaint, Galland had gone hunting at Elchwald in East Prussia, another of the lodges Goering had assigned to himself as Germany's Master of the Hunt. Galland's companion had been Ernst Udet, Chief of Luftwaffe Procurement and Supply, with whom he enjoyed a warm personal friendship. They had first become friends when Galland was a successful new member of the *Luftwaffe* trap shooting team, founded by Udet in early *Luftwaffe* days.

Udet was idolized by the young fighter pilots. He exemplified those qualities that were expected of dashing, early aviators. A humorous, charming, and carefree man who loved aeroplanes, women, champagne, and fun, Udet's checkered interwar career included barnstorming, stunt piloting, test flying, and movie making. He even had a brief fling as an aircraft manufacturer as *Udet Flugzeugbau* in Munich. He was the top-scoring living ace of the German Air Corps, with 62 victories, and was the most famous active pilot in Germany. His personality and happy temperament made him a charming companion.

As the young aces of the new generation pressed towards his tally of 62 victories, Udet would chide and josh them that they were under no circumstances to pass his score. In his bachelor pad in Berlin, he would host the young aces with champagne and challenge them to target pistol shooting matches on his indoor range. Udet would ply them with cognac until their aim deteriorated and then outscore them. (His cartooning skill is illustrated in this book, with the victory "bags" of aerial hunters Galland and Moelders the subject of his art.)

A man of his sunny temperament did not belong in the intrigue-ridden maelstrom of *Luftwaffe* production. He was unfitted to be either an executive or a high military officer. He was incapable of the ruthlessness essential to any military procurement program, German or otherwise. Goering as his old C.O. from the Richthofen Circus nevertheless insisted that Udet join the *Luftwaffe* for public relations and political reasons. Udet's peace of mind essentially ceased as he sought to discharge duties for which he was not fitted.

As *Generalluftzeugmeister* he was out of his element. He had subordinates who were deceitful and disloyal. (Goering's counterproductive organizational arrangements, involving State Secretary Milch, the *Luftwaffe* General Staff, and Udet have already been recounted. Udet got all the blame for the material consequences of the *Luftwaffe*'s divided hierarchy. Adolf Galland would shortly have to deal with many of those consequences in a position of high responsibility.)

The Stuka disaster in the Battle of Britain had hit Udet hard. He was blamed for the Stuka and criticized for failing to expand aircraft production during and following the Battle of Britain. He caught hell for not bringing improved aircraft types quickly into service. By October of 1941, with the German Army in a critical race with the Russian winter, Udet was under heavy pressure from Goering and other high officials. Most of them were responsible in some degree for the things now going awry. Udet was essentially being blamed for being Ernst Udet and for not magically transforming himself into a production wizard. He got all the blame.

When Galland met the normally genial little dynamo at Elchwald, Udet was gloomy. Gone were the smiling charm and warm humor. Depression and guilt were in their place. Over and over, he told Galland that Germany needed many thousands of fighters. He blamed himself for not even being able to make up the battle losses of existing units. Galland left Elchwald with his own spirits markedly lowered by Udet's despondency.

When a radio broadcast on 17 November 1941 announced Udet's death,

Galland and his wingman flying Me-109F aircraft over France.

Göring, on his visit to Galland on the Channel Coast, has just informed Galland that he is now the General of the Fighters.

Lt. Col. Galland by Leo Poeten. Commissioned by Hitler, artist Poeten painted this official portrait of Galland in 1941. Poeten had painted another portrait showing Galland holding one of his famous cigars, but Hitler demanded the cigar be removed. Both canvases are now in the possession of Galland.

Leo Poeten paints the official canvas of Lt. Col. Adolf Galland in 1940 shortly after Galland had been awarded the oak leaves to the Ritterkreuz.

"while testing a new type of weapon," Galland felt sharp pangs of grief. Such a friend, a historical personality to boot, could never be replaced. Shortly afterward, Galland was ordered to Berlin for Udet's state funeral on 21 November 1941.

Six of Germany's leading fighter pilots, all holders of the Knight's Cross or its higher orders, formed Udet's honor guard. They wore steel helmets and carried the massive *Luftwaffe* swords. Word was now out that Udet's death was a suicide. Galland found himself recalling Udet's recent litany of failure, desperation, and guilt. Goering walked all the way to the cemetery behind the coffin, in a phony show of respect for his old comrade. (Udet knew better. On the head of his bed before taking his life he had scrawled: "Iron Man, why have you forsaken me?" Udet was right. Goering started a posthumous investigation to support a court martial of the dead Udet. Political dynamite turned up, and Goering dropped the idea.)

Werner Moelders should have been present at the funeral. He had looked up to Udet. Promoted to colonel and appointed General of the Fighter Arm by Goering, Moelders had recently flown to the Crimea for first-hand evaluation of urgent fighter and *Luftwaffe* problems in that sector. Despite a strict grounding order, he had shot down some more aircraft. He missed Udet's funeral because vile Crimean weather prevented his takeoff that day. The day after Udet's funeral, Moelders insisted on returning to Berlin to report on conditions in the Crimea. Loss of one engine in atrocious weather resulted in the mortal crash of his He-111 at Breslau-Schoengarten. Moelders had been about to achieve his ambition to be the *Luftwaffe's* Boelcke. He had risen to General of the Fighter Arm, only to be lost in a flying accident.

Galland was returning by train to the Channel coast with Walter Oesau, *Kommodore* of JG-2, who had also been in the honor guard for Udet. The train suddenly stopped at a small station in the Lippe district, and the local stationmaster ran the length of the train calling Galland's name. There was a telephone call awaiting him from Berlin. General Karl Bodenschatz, Goering's adjutant, gave him the ghastly news that Moelders was dead. Goering's orders were for Galland to return to Berlin immediately. A train passing the opposite way would pick him up in less than an hour.

In a depressing replay of the Udet funeral, Galland was again in the honor guard. This time he was saying his final farewell to his rival and friend, the man who had first shown him how to shoot down aircraft. Now Moelders was being buried in Invaliden cemetery, not far from Udet and von Richthofen. When the salvoes and tributes ended, Galland stood with five other aces at graveside, in steel helmets and with drawn swords, their heads bowed.

Memories of the departed comrade poured through Galland's mind: his great skill as a teacher, his leadership qualities, his incomparable combat gifts, and his moral stature. From classification as medically unfit for pilot training, Moelders had risen in the short years since the Condor Legion to the highest post in the Fighter Arm. He had not had time to fill the office fully with his talents. . . .

"Galland! Galland!"

Goering was calling, interrupting his sad reverie. Galland looked up and there was the *Reich* Marshal, urgently beckoning with his gold marshal's baton. Embarrassed at leaving the honor guard, and feeling clumsy and awkward with the unaccustomed sword, Galland made his way to Goering.

"Now it's your turn" said the *Reich* Marshal. "I name you herewith as Moelders's successor, to be General of the Fighter Arm."

In the most terrible fashion imaginable, Galland had finally caught up to his rival. Destiny had thrust upon him the Boelckean challenge.

CHAPTER FOURTEEN

Conflicting thoughts whirled through Galland's head as the significance of his new appointment dawned on him. Reluctance to leave his beloved JG-26 was his main reaction. Commanding his elite *Geschwader* had been the pride and joy of his life. General of the Fighter Arm? That meant desks, paper work, telephones, staff officers—and no combat action.

When he mentioned this to Goering, the *Reich* Marshal brushed it all aside. The *Fuehrer* had approved his appointment. A man of his ability had to be given wider scope. The death of Moelders was a tragedy for the Fighter Arm, but Galland had to carry on. Already the post had been given new and more comprehensive responsibilities, according to Goering.

The *Reich* Marshal mollified Galland's pangs at leaving JG-26 by promising to convey the ex-*Kommodore's* farewell wishes to his men personally. Goering was to visit his dead nephew's grave in Abbeville in a few days, and JG-26 HQ at Audembert was nearby. Peter Goering had died in combat under Galland's command and flying as his wingman.

Goering duly delivered Galland's farewell, his last Special *Geschwader* Report:

For 15 months I led JG-26 during the hardest combats as your *Kommodore*. The Commander-in-Chief of the *Luftwaffe* has appointed me as General of the Fighter Arm, to his HQ, which became effective immediately. The death of Colonel Moelders has hit us all very hard.

With a broken heart, I leave this *Geschwader*. The proud memory of having mastered every mission with you great fighter pilots, and the obligation we have towards the war heroes killed in action, give me the strength for a new and great task.

You will fight on with your new *Kommodore,* and you will be victorious. My thoughts will always be with you. The name of our wing must be covered with glory to enter the history of war."*

Galland's promotion to colonel was also celebrated at the farewell gathering. Amid the toasting and reminiscing, the departing *Kommodore* realized how well he had been served by his able *Gruppenkommandeure* in JG-26. Pingel had been downed pursuing Stirlings over England and was now a POW. Adolph had been killed in action. Muencheberg had been transferred to the Mediterranean. Here in the room now were Seifert and the diminutive "Fips" Priller. The swarthy, dark-haired, and dependable Gerhard Schoepfel had been named as his successor in command of JG-26. No *Kommodore* had ever been better served than by men like these.

Galland smiled and smoked his endless cigars, and downed his share of the champagne, but inwardly he was in turmoil. The honor of commanding JG-26 had been torn from him, when he was at his peak as a combat leader and ace pilot. In exchange, what was he getting? A brass hat, a desk in Berlin, and mountains of paperwork. General of the Fighter Arm was the highest post a fighter pilot could reach and still be wholly involved with fighters. The magnitude of the responsibility still had him stunned. A quantum jump upwards, the new job exacted a high price: relinquishment of the *Kommodore's* tasks that he had tackled with passionate interest.

Through the haze of cigar smoke, and over the top of the ambient chatter in the room, several times Galland heard what others were thinking. "Mufti will know how to get things done in Berlin, and he will help us here," and "If Mufti has to leave us, thank God it is for a job where he can really help the fighters." He wondered how he would fare, the hunter and fighter, in that Berlin anthill. His memory of its oppressive atmosphere when he had returned from Spain was still clear.

Galland's apprehensions about his new job were enhanced by his hazy ideas relative to its scope and nature. Goering had not discussed this with him. The *Reich* Marshal had been more concerned with crushing Galland's objections to leaving the front. The office assigned to the General of the Fighters on the Lindenstrasse in Berlin caused Galland to groan inwardly. A typical Air Ministry paper mill, it was manned by lethargic old-fashioned bureaucrats in the classic governmental pattern.

When Moelders had been appointed General of the Fighters on 7 July 1941, he spent little time in the office before going out on a full-scale inspection of fighter units. He wanted an accurate perspective on front line conditions. That was typical of the analytical Moelders. Galland knew his late rival well enough to know that there would have been sweeping changes in this part of the Air Ministry once Moelders got settled in the job. Now Galland would have to build up a modern, forward-looking staff.

---

* Galland was a Lieutenant Colonel when he was given the job of "General of the Fighter Arm." He was promoted to Colonel, and later to General Major.

The *Luftwaffe* from its inception had always had an Inspector of the Fighters, the department being originally known as the Office for the Inspection of Fighter and Bomber Aircraft. Udet was first to occupy the post, followed by Robert Ritter von Greim and Bruno Loerzer, both of whom had also been fighter aces in World War I. Raithel, Werner Junck, and von Massow—all belonging to the infant days of fighter aviation—were next in succession. Major General Kurt von Doering had immediately preceded Moelders. At the time of von Doering's appointment early in 1941, Goering retitled the office as General of the Fighter Arm (*General der Jagdflieger*).

Functions of inspection that had previously occupied the office were now augmented with new powers of command, advice, and consultation in technical development, operations, personnel selection, and planning. These were steps that should have been taken before the war. The scope of the office was thus made nominally extensive; but, as a new assignment within the *Luftwaffe* hierarchy, it would be largely shaped by the personality that discharged its responsibilities.

Moelders had vision, but had been killed before he could set his stamp on the office. All Galland's other predecessors were not men of either vision or strong inspiration. This fitted in well with the secondary and limited role originally assigned to fighters in the *Luftwaffe*. Goering's flair for administration may be seen in the way he extended the responsibilities of the General of the Fighter Arm, compared with the largely ceremonial Inspector's post. He was late in making the changes, which had been largely forced by events.

Goering did not shrink from the ultimate application of his 1940 policy of promoting successful young fighter leaders to significant commands. Moelders and Galland were both on the sunny side of 30 when named General of the Fighter Arm. Such promotions were unimaginable in the prewar *Luftwaffe*. Goering added another touch: Galland was made responsible to the Chief of the *Luftwaffe* General Staff in operational matters, and to the Commander-in-Chief of the *Luftwaffe* in disciplinary matters. This meant in effect that Adolf Galland, not yet 30 years of age, had only two superiors—Goering and Hitler.

Such arrangements raised eyebrows and temperatures among Air Ministry bureaucrats and high *Luftwaffe* personages. The currents of distrust and suspicion that run through all governmental organizations when innovations are proposed were now strongly stimulated. Everyone was mindful that this young colonel had Hitler's support, as well as being Goering's choice. An officer of 29 years with enormous responsibilities, *and minus any staff training whatever,* was looked upon as a phenomenon. His direct access to the two most powerful men in Germany excited considerable high-level disquiet.

These reactions of distrust communicated themselves to Galland as he began phasing himself into the Berlin scene. He made courtesy visits to the various bureaus and inspectorates. Although he had the advantages of his fame, outstanding combat record, and the Swords to his Knight's Cross, he had also been preceded by his reputation for outspoken frankness. A few high officials found it memorable to meet Germany's most successful fighter ace. Coolness elsewhere was marked, and he was greeted with bland official correctitude.

His charisma with the ladies was still in full function and reached with its usual power into the Air Ministry secretarial pools. His appearance in offices with female secretaries and clerks generated the same excitement as a visit from a movie star. This made the bureaucrats all the more suspicious, and envious, of the black-haired, moustachioed General of the Fighter Arm.

His black cigars had acquired similar symbolic status for his image as those of Winston Churchill across the Channel. Galland's promotion to General of the Fighter Arm was a golden business opportunity for Germany's cigar makers. Here was a charismatic cigar smoker, who was being prodigiously publicized throughout Germany. His picture was everywhere. Five companies wrote Galland, begging for the honor of being his exclusive cigar supplier for the duration. His personal cigars would be free. Galland magnanimously accepted all five offers, "so nobody would feel slighted." (At the surrender in 1945, he still had a stock of 60 boxes.)

Cigars remained a bone of contention with Hitler. Galland was never permitted to smoke them in the *Fuehrer's* presence. Hitler declared pointedly time and again how undesirable the cigar habit was for both health and educational reasons. Seeing a hero of Galland's stature with a cigar in his hand, or sticking out of his mouth, was a bad example to German youth, according to the *Fuehrer*. Despite these admonishments, Galland could not bring himself to throw away good cigars every time a photographer approached, even if they were free cigars. He was inevitably caught in photographs with the cigars. (Hitler eventually forbade him to have his photograph taken smoking, holding, or flourishing a cigar.)

As soon as he had made his Berlin rounds in December 1941, Galland flew to Goldap in East Prussia. *Luftwaffe* HQ was set up here in a specially equipped train carrying the good old English name of "Robinson." A suitably furnished additional car was coupled to "Robinson" for the exclusive use of the General of the Fighters. He would thenceforth always have accommodation, communications, and a staff available at Goldap, immediately adjacent to the Chief of the *Luftwaffe* General Staff. He was also handy to Goering at Rominten Heath and to Hitler at the Wolf's Lair, east of nearby Rastenburg.

His first official call at Goldap was to General der Flieger Hans Jeschonnek, Chief of the *Luftwaffe* General Staff. One of the architects of the *Luftwaffe*, Jeschonnek was occupying his high post at the age of only 42. His brilliant career was emblematic of both the strengths and weaknesses of the *Luftwaffe*.

While Galland had no conception of it at the time he met with Jeschonnek, he had inherited a complex legacy as General of the Fighter Arm, which was due in many ways to Jeschonnek's past actions.

The Chief of the *Luftwaffe* General Staff had devoted his entire life to military service. He was commissioned out of the Prussian Cadet Corps into the infantry in 1915, not yet age 16. Like Goering and many others, he volunteered for the German Flying Corps, became a pilot at age 17, and was able to shoot down two Allied aircraft before the 1918 armistice. He was selected for permanent

General of the Fighters Galland shortly after flying a Focke-Wulf FW 190. With him are Major Hein and 1st Lt. Behrens.

Lechfeld—Galland minus decorations. Field Marshal Erhard Milch is briefed by Galland on the Me-262 jet as a fighter. Galland is not wearing his decorations in protest to Göring's recriminations against the Fighter Arm.

duty with the 100,000-man *Reichswehr* that was permitted Germany after World War I. Assignment as adjutant to State Secretary of Aviation Erhard Milch was an important career step. He helped organize the Air Ministry and participated in the secret preparations for the new *Luftwaffe*.

Jeschonnek's intellectual capacity and energy marked him early for a significant role in the *Luftwaffe*. Appointed *Kommodore* of the training *Geschwader* after the *Luftwaffe* was officially announced, he was frequently consulted on operationa., technical, and training requirements. Air power conceptions were largely theoretical at this time. Operational requirements and goals for the massive air fleets that were planned were ill-defined. In this developmental period, Jeschonnek's abilities became widely respected, and on 1 October 1937 he was made chief of Branch I, the Operational Branch of the *Luftwaffe* General Staff.

As a rising star with access to the remarkable General Walter Wever, the first Chief of the *Luftwaffe* General Staff, Jeschonnek was regarded as a potential successor to Wever, despite his youth. Rapid promotions through significant posts saw him reach colonel at the age of 38, at a time when virtually all other colonels were past 50. On 1 February 1939, Colonel Hans Jeschonnek was appointed Chief of the *Luftwaffe* General Staff.

The string of early *Luftwaffe* victories in which Galland had participated as a combat pilot further boosted Jeschonneks's prestige. He was promoted to colonel general at age 42, the youngest officer in that rank in the *Wehrmacht*. Like Galland, his rise had been meteoric. Jeschonnek had risen as rapidly as the *Luftwaffe* itself. He had been close to, or directly involved in, all major decisions since the termination of Wever's strategic bomber program.

After Wever's death, Jeschonnek had advocated a strictly tactical air force. He backed the dive bomber concept with missionary zeal. Jeschonnek poured his energies into giving Germany the most effective striking air force in the shortest possible time. He translated Hitler's wishes into hardware. The efficient tactical *Luftwaffe* of 1939 owed much to Jeschonnek's dedication and ability.

Where all this impinged on the career of Galland was in Jeschonnek's indifference to anything that did not serve the goal of the largest possible force in being. Only the immediately foreseeable tomorrows of the *Luftwaffe* counted. Training programs were not set up as comprehensively as Hitler had demanded in October of 1938. Incredibly, there was no reserve of pilots at all when the *Luftwaffe* went to war in 1939. Jeschonnek had made neither provision nor effort to expand training. There was only one fighter pilot school when war broke out in 1939, epitomizing this cardinal prewar failure.

Organization of training in the *Luftwaffe*, furthermore, put pilot training commanders under the authority of the Air Fleets. The consequences were disastrous. Training units were relentlessly raided by Air Fleet commanders for both pilots and aircraft. Ju-52s widely used for training were snapped up by Air Fleet orders for transport duty. Air transport had similarly been neglected, in the single-minded drive to maximize the striking force in being. Germany therefore never ceased being short of air transport. Skilled flying instructors were used as replacements for the Bomber Arm in the Battle of Britain, and they were drained away into such ventures as the airlift supporting the Battle for Crete.

Jeschonnek's achievements were thus offset by many errors and deficiencies, concealed initially by the great opening victories of the *Luftwaffe*. Disaster nevertheless resided in Jeschonnek's mistakes in key areas, as Galland would progressively discover. Although a man of integrity, Jeschonnek was a loner, minus close personal friends. He was not spiritually strong enough to deal with a juggernaut C.-in-C. like Goering. Hitler left Jeschonnek awestruck.

Jeschonnek's vantage point near the heart of the *Luftwaffe* made him aware that Hitler's prewar triumphs had been accomplished with the *Luftwaffe* as his trump card. He saw Hitler as Germany's savior and regarded him as a genius of infallible insight. Despite this infatuation with the *Fuehrer,* the intelligent Jeschonnek was professionally realistic. *He knew that Germany had to win quickly.* The substance of the *Luftwaffe* was being consumed from the war's first day. His professional life thus became one gigantic roll of the dice. Jeschonnek was gambling on the *Fuehrer*—all or nothing.

As Adolf Galland sat across from this ill-fated man in the HQ train at Goldap, Jeschonnek's world was beginning to disintegrate. America had come into the war. The conflict was now a full-scale world struggle. Even without American participation, the *Luftwaffe* was already pinned down on the Channel and battling a determined RAF in the Mediterranean. Operations in Russia were chewing up the *Luftwaffe* in ceaseless close-support operations. A fierce winter was proving itself a savage ally of the Soviet Union.

Galland was received courteously by Jeschonnek, whose attitude was helpful. Unfortunately, the Chief of the *Luftwaffe* General Staff had no guidance whatever to offer the distinguished newcomer from the air war. Jeschonnek was obviously under heavy pressure. His worst fears were beginning to be realized. Although nothing to this effect emerged in their correct and professional conversation, a certain disquiet communicated itself to Galland from within Jeschonnek. The man obviously had bigger things to worry about than the Fighter Arm.

Feeling again completely out of place, just as he had in his Berlin HQ office, Galland left Goldap sick at heart. He needed the upright comradeship of JG-26. Using his new independence as General of the Fighter Arm, he flew straight to Audembert. He wanted to spend Christmas 1941 with the men he knew. In the atmosphere of his beloved JG-26 he renewed his perspective. His new job gave him the chance to help such men as these, with whom he had so often flown into battle. His New Year resolution was to press forward into his new job and give it his best.

The Byzantine world of the Air Ministry, with its intrigues, bureaucracies, politics, and ambitious climbers of all kinds was a world totally alien to Colonel Galland. Often he wondered in his first weeks if he had been teleported to some bizarre hidden world, so radically different was his new role from that of a fighter *Kommodore*. He had no staff training. According to the whispered judgments of the bureaucracy, that would result in his failure. Those whispers duly reached him and hardened his resolve. He had more experience of modern fighter aviation than anyone in the *Luftwaffe*. His logic and common sense, combined with his experience, would compensate for his lack of staff training. His old drive to excel was taking a new direction.

Certain inspection functions in the Fighter Arm had to be promptly delegated to lighten his own load. He brought in Lt. Colonel Guenther Luetzow, his comrade from the Condor Legion, as Inspector of the Fighter Units. Since the Ground Attack Arm (*Schlachtflieger*) also came under his office, Galland appointed Lt. Colonel Weiss, a Battle of Britain veteran, as their Inspector. From this beginning came the staff that would develop deep loyalty to him and to the Fighter Arm that was his passion.

Galland was often criticized for some of the men he appointed to his staff. Not all the officers he chose worked out in their jobs. Those that did became an elite group (and those who survived the war would cherish into their evening the memory of having served on Galland's staff). This elite included Luetzow, Trautloft, Brüstellin, Seitz, Schmoller-Haldy, von Maltzahn, and Andres, the latter doing a giant's work in training. Contributing mightily to the good spirit at Fighter Arm HQ was the tireless Chief Secretary, Anneliese Stiller. She had served in the office since 1936. (After the war, she became a secretary in the office of Economics Minister Ludwig Erhard.)

Galland was now moving in high councils, where three or four fighter *Geschwader* were moved about as flags on a map. Until now, he had understood moving a *Geschwader* only in terms of the turmoil involved in shifting 80-odd fighters in three *Gruppen* from one set of bases to another. A big undertaking when you were supervising it as a *Kommodore,* it was easy when you pulled some pins out of a map and pressed them in somewhere else.

The decisive spring push against the Soviet Union involved a heavy demand for combat fighters. Another raid was staged on the training schools. Conferences with Jeschonnek, in which Galland objected to these actions, gave the General of the Fighters insight into the High Command concept of the war.

Jeschonnek was sympathetic to Galland's desire to protect the Fighter Arm's future, since the young colonel's viewpoint was rooted in facts and logic. Jeschonnek nevertheless gave primacy to the *Fuehrer's* view, which was that the war against Russia was almost won. A massive spring push would favorably decide the campaign. Victory over Russia would secure the East, make Russia's resources available to Germany, and allow the war in the West to be similarly fought through to victory.

Jeschonnek was accordingly pouring all available *Luftwaffe* resources into winning the spring victory. Quick defeat of Russia was vital. Galland readily comprehended the consequences of a protracted struggle against the Soviets. Jeschonnek spoke of it all in laconic, professional terms and heard Galland's views with attention and courtesy.

The General of the Fighter Arm had no option but to acquiesce in the training school raids and in other emergency measures to reinforce the East. Goering backed Jeschonnek, closing any appeal in that direction. Galland's growing grasp of the true state of the Fighter Arm began to illuminate the errors, oversights, and omissions he had inherited from the past.

Recognizing the urgent situation in the East did not blind Galland to the threat from the West. As a Channel Front combat commander, he had seen and felt the mounting power of the RAF. American airpower would inevitably flow into the fight, increasing the weight from the West. East and West, prospects were gloomy. One fundamental towered above all murky imponderables: fighters would be needed on a scale never previously envisioned. No matter what direction the war might take, the *Luftwaffe* needed thousands upon thousands of fighters.

Galland went to see the man most concerned with fighter production, Field Marshal Milch. As Germany's aircraft production czar at that time, Milch had taken over Udet's functions as *Generalluftzeugmeister*. Cordial relations were immediately established between Galland and Milch. Although highly egocentric, when it came to the war Milch was a total realist. He had been to America and seen its mass-production feats. He had also visited England before the war and talked at length with Churchill, Viscount Swinton, and the RAF's great progenitor, "Boom" Trenchard. Milch was sharply aware of the aerial threat from the West and knew that fighters were needed in hordes. He also knew Jeschonnek well, having been his squadron commander in World War I and his chief in Black *Luftwaffe* days. Milch now regarded Jeschonnek with contempt.

Galland and Milch planned a fighter production increase from the current 250 per month to more than 1,000 per month by mid-1943. Milch had the know-how and drive to achieve this goal. He arranged for Galland to attend the *Generalluftzeugmeister* conferences and provide direct input from the Fighter Arm. These regular conferences were to bring Milch and his staff together with manufacturers, engineers, and designers. Galland was amazed in some of these meetings, at the way Professors Heinkel and Messerschmitt went at each other like a couple of strange bulldogs. Milch's realism was refreshing to Galland, and Milch had trust and confidence in the young fighter general. Their relationship aided the Fighter Arm.

Galland was now able to see how Goering operated in high *Luftwaffe* circles. Previous contacts with the *Reich* Marshal in brief meetings at the front, at HQ, or in the social setting of hunting did not provide such insight. Goering's lack of technical knowledge was appalling. This lack of technical expertise was shamelessly exploited by a circle of sycophants around him. Galland experienced a certain disgust at the way these officers fawned over and toadied to the *Reich* Marshal. They brought him gifts. They filled his insatiable ego with ceaseless flattery.

Galland had to make an early decision about Goering and his personal weaknesses. If he flattered Goering a little, the Fighter Arm might benefit. Strictly as a means to an end, it might be worthwhile. Galland's own character would not allow him to take this approach. He therefore decided to deal with Goering entirely on a factual and logical basis in any given situation. Galland never departed from this resolution. (In the twilight of his own life, he was without regrets over taking this stand.)

Weeks passed quickly after his appointment, and, as the scope and dimensions of his responsibilities became clearer, he was awed by what was expected of him as an officer not yet 30 years of age. The various powers and functions of the General of the Fighter Arm were as follows:

1. Inspection of operational units, training units, and schools, especially the Operational Training Units.
2. Direct liaison between operational units and Goering, Hitler, Jeschonnek, and other figures, avoiding all ordinary channels.
3. Evaluation of tactical and technical experience of operational units and dissemination of results.
4. Preparation of Tactical Regulations for all phases of fighter operations.
5. Continuous evaluation of all material and armament under development.
6. Provision for combat testing of all equipment, either in regular fighter units or in special test commandos.
7. Technical recommendations to industry for improvement of equipment, based on combat experience.
8. Expediting of equipment not forthcoming through normal supply channels or otherwise held up.
9. Proposals for new organization or reorganization of fighter-control systems and operational administration.
10. Proposals for setting up of operational units.
11. Recommendations for personnel in operational fighter posts from squadron leader upwards. [The Personnel Branch in practice always accepted Galland's recommendations.]
12. Maintenance of a card index of all aircrews under Fighter Arm jurisdiction.
13. Recommendations for the award of the Knight's Cross and its higher orders for Fighter Arm personnel.
14. Supply of the Fighter Arm with all new regulations and instructional material. [Galland disseminated this material direct to operational units.]
15. Control of training in Operational Training Units. Advisory supervision of other flying training as related to the supply of fighter pilots.
16. Absolute control over personnel assignment from Operational Training Units to operational units.
17. Suggestions, recommendations, and demands for development of organization and equipment for the reporting services, radar service, and other signals units.
18. Evaluation of operational experience with signals equipment, in cooperation with the Chief of *Luftwaffe* Signals, General Wolfgang Martini.
19. Advising the *Luftwaffe* Operations Staff, the *Luftwaffe* High Command, and Goering on Fighter Arm matters.

20. Cooperation and liaison with other offices, such as those of Milch, Speer, and, later, Saur.

21. Special duties assigned from time to time, such as preparations for the Channel dash by the battleships *Scharnhorst* and *Gneisenau,* and control of fighters in Sicily.

A fair assessment of these responsibilities nearly 50 years later is that no other officer 30 years of age in either the *Wehrmacht* or the Allied forces was charged with such burdens. The certainty of the old bureaucrats in the Air Ministry that he would fail is easy to understand. A successful fighter *Kommodore* had little of the background necessary to get things done in Berlin, where the inept and the inexperienced were "shot down" in an altogether different way.

Galland was awarded the Diamonds to his Knight's Cross on 28 January 1942. He was the second member of the *Wehrmacht* to receive the decoration, being preceded only by Moelders. Earlier on the Channel Front, Galland noted that, when Moelders was awarded the Diamonds, the *Fuehrer* also prohibited him from further combat flying. Moelders had reached 100 victories. Since Galland had 94 victories at the time of Moelders's award, he discreetly ceased counting his victories to avoid being taken off operations. In this way he was able to fly combat until his promotion to colonel and to General of the Fighter Arm.

Through his many informants, Hitler nevertheless knew what was happening. The *Fuehrer* appreciated that a grounding order that went with Galland's appointment as General of the Fighters would prevent his reaching 100 victories. Hitler also rated victories in the West more highly than those won in Russia. Therefore, he bestowed Germany's highest decoration on his new General of the Fighter Arm. (The Diamonds would become the subject of an inimitable Galland after-dinner story, which he would tell into his eighth decade in many different countries. At the end of January 1942, he was Germany's most highly decorated living ace. An appropriately important assignment was given him at this time: twisting the British lion's tail in a way that had not been equalled in two centuries.)

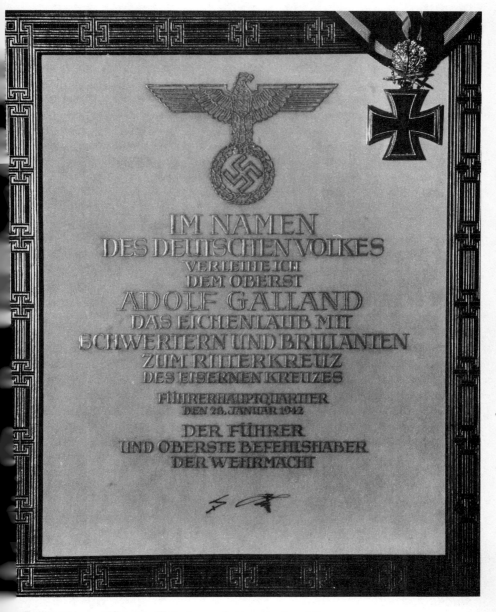

Brillant's certificate. This is a photograph of the certificate which accompanied the award of the Knight's Cross with Diamonds to Adolf Galland. Hitler's signature is at the lower center of the certificate.

Adolf Galland's two younger brothers, Wilhelm-Ferdinand "Wutz" and Paul. Both were excellent fighter pilots with JG26.

Star of Africa. One of Galland's favorite Luftwaffe "characters," Captain Hans-Joachim Marseille was the top ace on the Western Front with 158 victories. He died 30 September 1942 when the engine on his Me-109 failed and the cockpit filled with smoke causing him to have to parachute, but he hit the horizontal stabilizer and fell to his death. Galland said he "was the unequalled virtuoso among the fighter pilots." Eduard Newmann collection.

CHAPTER FIFTEEN

Operational authority was denied to the General of the Fighter Arm, under Goering's arrangements. Galland disliked intensely this particular limitation. The appointment to his high post had been thrust upon him because of his success as an operational fighter pilot and *Kommodore,* and yet in the Fighter Arm's highest appointment he was unable to order even a single squadron into the air. Exceptions to this were made only in specific assignments given to Galland by the *Reich* Marshal, whose personal intoxication with command has already been described. An important exception was made early in Galland's high command career. Goering assigned him to command *Luftwaffe* forces giving air cover to the planned breakout of the heavy ships *Gneisenau, Scharnhorst,* and *Prinz Eugen* from Brest.

British Intelligence had subtly continued with strategic deception over British intentions towards Norway. A Scandinavian invasion actually presented insuperable logistical problems, and the British had no operational plan for such an undertaking. They nevertheless kept this pot quietly boiling with a multitude of deceptive stratagems, drawing off substantial German forces that would otherwise face them on active fronts. Hitler was the main dupe of this intelligence ploy. He was the one who counted. The *Fuehrer* wanted the big ships to return to Norway, where they would discourage an invasion and intercept Allied convoys to Russia from secure bases.

The German heavy ships were a constant threat to Britain's Atlantic lifeline as long as they were in Brest. They drew off the Royal Navy's Force H from vital duty in the Mediterranean and thus weakened Britain's ability to reinforce the Middle East. *Scharnhorst* and *Gneisenau* therefore had high naval value even if they never left port. Alongside the dock in Brest, they were nevertheless a routine Bomber Command target and were subject to continual damage. These damage reports and Hitler's fears of an invasion of Norway prompted his decision at the end of 1941 to move the ships out of Brest as soon as possible.

Galland was summoned to the Wolf's Lair with Jeschonnek on 12 January 1942. Hitler had called a conference of naval and air leaders to plan the breakout. Goering shunted responsibility for *Luftwaffe* participation to Jeschonnek. This put some distance between the *Reich* Marshal and any potential disaster that might arise. Goering instructed Jeschonnek to propose Galland as commander of the Operational Fighter Protection. The famous young fighter general's popularity would thus provide additional insulation for Goering in the event of a catastrophic outcome. Goering's view that the *Luftwaffe* would be blamed by the Navy in the event of failure was substantiated by the tenor of the conference.

Goering was able to stay away from these proceedings but Grand Admiral Erich Raeder, Commander-in-Chief of the Navy, did not have Goering's political influence and had to attend. Loss of the *Bismarck* had placed Raeder low in Hitler's esteem, and he shared Goering's wish to be remote from a risky venture. Raeder emphasized to the conference that he was not proposing or recommending the breakout. Vice Admiral Otto Ciliax, O.C. battleships, and Commodore Ruge, O.C. minesweepers, were delegated to outline operational plans. In Raeder's words, this was "to make your decision easier, *mein Führer*."

In just such ways did Germany's highest commanders facilitate Hitler's meddling in their affairs. If they took a polite "hands off" attitude towards important operations, Hitler would take over. He had taken over Germany politically. Any high officer leaving a void in operational planning would soon find Hitler filling that void. What began as meddling by Hitler developed eventually into control of the entire war effort by one man. Galland saw this baleful trend at an early stage in the Channel dash conference.

Air cover for the ships passing through the English Channel in daylight was tactically essential. The Navy's main fear was that a sufficiently strong fighter screen could not be provided. General Jeschonnek stated that the 250 fighters available on the Channel Front were barely adequate for dawn-to-dusk air cover—considering the manifold problems of range, refueling, rearmament, and potential losses. Eastern Front demands made reinforcement impossible. Night fighters could give supplementary protection around dawn and dusk, but that was the extent of the forces available. Numerical inferiority of the German fighters to their RAF foes could not be redressed. Continuous protection of the ships could not be guaranteed.

Hitler decided to proceed with the operation. Breakout from Brest would be in darkness. Transit of Dover Strait would occur in daylight. The best possible fighter cover was to be given with the available forces. The *Fuehrer* decreed absolute secrecy from that moment. Hitler circulated a secrecy pledge, and all present were required to sign this document.

Galland listened closely to the give and take of the conference, conducted by high-ranking officers many years his senior. He gave opinions at appropriate points. His knowledge of fighter operations and flying conditions on the Channel was unrivaled and current. This more than compensated for his lack of seniority, and it quickly communicated itself to Hitler. The *Fuehrer* took his young general aside afterwards and asked him what the chances of success were—given the dependency of the operation on the air umbrella. Galland had already weighed the involved factors in his own mind.

"Everything depends on how much time the English have to mobilize the RAF against the ships," he told Hitler. "We need complete surprise and a bit of luck into the bargain. My fighter pilots will give their very best when they know what is at stake." (This was to prove a prescient estimate.)

Galland chose the code name "Thunderbolt" for the operation, while Navy planning went forward as "Cerberus." The secrecy ordered by Hitler was strictly observed. The fighter pilots were told that Thunderbolt was a new bomber offensive against Britain. Spies in the Brest docks reported to the British as activity began intensifying. The long electronic ears of *Ultra* overheard the German radioteletype traffic, which left no doubt about German intentions.

Ronald Lewin describes the unfolding situation of the British cryptanalysts in his *Ultra Goes to War:*

Ultra converted speculation into reality. All those small preliminaries necessary for the secret move of a considerable naval force were identified by Denning and his colleagues in the Operational Intelligence Center—the particular arrangements for U-boats and the *Luftwaffe's* fighters, the increased and clandestine activity of minesweepers along significant channels, the assembly of extra destroyers as escorts in the dash. A full appreciation was laid before Admiral Pound, and as early as 2 February the Admiralty issued its detailed conclusions which ended: "Taking all factors into consideration, it appears that the Germans can pass east up the Channel with much less risk than they will incur if they attempt an ocean passage." Coastal Command [of the RAF] took the same view.

The British Admiralty thus unwittingly endorsed the Channel dash that Hitler had thrust on his reluctant naval chiefs. The British cryptanalysts at Bletchley Park continued to break the unsecure *Luftwaffe* ciphers and the *Hydra* ciphers of the German Navy. The Admiralty's Operational Intelligence Center distilled all this into coherent hard information upon which commanders based their plans for turning the breakout into a German disaster.

Codebreakers provide information. How that information is used in making dispositions and conducting operations is the province of those in command of the forces involved. The information is thus mute and impotent until translated into action and orders. The battle is the payoff, and, in dealing with the breakout, the British command made poor use of the superior cryptanalytic intelligence that was abundantly available.

The British already had their Channel Stop Force in operation. Consisting of a squadron of Blenheim bombers based at Manston in Kent, and torpedo boats operating out of Dover, the Stop Force was charged with interdicting German surface traffic in the Dover Strait. Stop Force operations were eventually extended to include daily air reconnaissance of Brest by RAF Bomber Command and nightly reconnaissance flights over the German heavy ships by Coastal Command.

Bomber Command was to make daylight attacks only, because at full speed the German ships could only make half the distance from Brest to a German port by night. Departure from Brest had to be by 1300 in order to transit the Dover Strait before daylight the following morning. RAF bombers would thus have about three hours to attack the ships after their escape from Brest was discovered. This entire operation was code-named "Fuller." Preparations were code-named "Executive Fuller." Many important officers involved in the coming action did not know this code name. Arrangements were in place for eight months prior to the accelerated naval activity around Brest in January of 1942.

Short trial runs by the German heavy ships in the Gulf of Brest foretold the approaching breakout. RAF and *Luftwaffe* fighters clashed above these trials. Weather and tides were in favorable combination. A new moon was due 15 February. The British were able to calculate all these key elements as easily as the Germans. Knowing that a breakout was imminent, the Admiralty put Executive Fuller on alert on 4 February 1942. While unwilling to bring the Home Fleet heavy ships within reach of German bombers, the Admiralty ordered six additional old destroyers into Harwich and six additional torpedo boats into Ramsgate. Six Swordfish torpedo planes of No. 825 Squadron of the Fleet Air Arm were based at Manston. The S-Class submarine *Sealion* was sent to reinforce two older submarines already patrolling outside Brest. The Royal Navy was ready for the Germans, whether they took the Channel or the ocean route for their breakout.

Even more massive British forces were poised at the same time, in addition to the naval units. RAF Coastal Command had No.86 Squadron opposite Brest at St. Eval in Cornwall. Twelve Beaufort torpedo carriers were there, reinforced by three additional aircraft from No. 217 Squadron, the latter being stationed with its other seven torpedo carriers on Torney Island near Portsmouth. Coastal Command also transferred No.14 Squadron from Scotland to Manston in Kent, to operate with 14 more Beauforts.

These three Beaufort squadrons were therefore spread over the entire length of the breakout route. A joint attack could be mounted by all three in combination if the situation so dictated. Normal vigilance would see them sweeping hundreds of square miles of the English Channel and adjacent waters.

The RAF assigned 300 bombers to Fuller. Only daylight attacks were possible, but mass strikes on the German ships in the crucial waters between Brest and Dover could easily seal their doom. On 6 February 1942, the RAF reduced its commitment to 100 bombers, despite the high likelihood that the breakout would come between 10 and 15 February. This was a clear failure to use correctly the available intelligence on enemy intentions, even if 100 bombers was still an adequate force to sink the ships.

RAF Fighter Command had available at this time approximately 600 fighters. The well-tested No. 11 Fighter Group, Galland's adversary in the Battle of Britain, would protect RAF bombers against the anticipated *Luftwaffe* fighter umbrella. From bases at Kenley, Hornchurch, Debden, Biggin Hill, and Tangmere, No. 11 Fighter Group would deploy its squadrons against its old foes across the Channel.

German preparations for the breakout went forward in January with all speed. Secrecy and security seemed irrelevant as the ships and docks, the Brest approaches, and the adjacent Channel waters swarmed with activity. Camouflaging such massive preparations was impossible. The Germans attempted deception by circulating rumors of a breakout to the Pacific and by loading slings of tropical uniforms and pith helmets aboard the ships in full view of Brest's dockside spies.

Installation of additional 20mm quad mounts, jury structures that obviously would not survive a high seas voyage, virtually nullified the Pacific yarn. Rumors were deliberately circulated in the dockyard and conflicted with other rumors passed to the crews. Sea lawyers and hammock strategists were thoroughly confused about the intentions of their own side. A dash through the Channel ranked as the least likely possibility among the battleship crews.

Eighty minesweepers toiled through each icy night to clear three minefields astride the best escape route. The heavy ships required a minimum water depth of 80 feet for safety. A channel was laid out and marked. The vice admiral had, as ship commanders reporting to him, Captain Kurt Hoffman in *Scharnhorst,* Captain Otto Fein in *Gneisenau,* and Captain Helmuth Brinkmann in *Prinz Eugen.*

Complex planning for the fighter umbrella went forward under Galland. Thunderbolt was made to order for a general in search of a challenging operational command. Control of fighter units, communications, and ground operations for both Air Fleet 3 and Air Fleet *Reich* was centralized under Galland's personal command. These were considerable encroachments on the domains of Field Marshall Sperrle and General Weise, the two Air Fleet commanders, but neither of them seemed to mind. Probably sharing Goering's apprehensions and seeing failure inherent in the Channel dash, they watched Galland pile into his task with enthusiasm and energy. (Galland would say whimsically, in later years, that Sperrle and Weise took "malicious pleasure" in seeing him stick his neck out.)

Three fighter command centers were organized to cover the escape route progressively. The sector Abbeville–Lille–Calais had its HQ at Le Touquet in France. The Schelde–Rhine–Zuider Zee sector had its command center at Schiphol in the Netherlands. For the final stretch between Jever and Wilhelmshaven in Germany, HQ was set up at Jever. Good planning allows for contingencies. Galland held that a delay early in the breakout was the most likely modification of the plan. He prepared for this by setting up an emergency sector of bases in the area of Le Havre–Caen–Cherbourg, with HQ at Caen.

Since success depended upon communications, an elaborate series of radio links was established. VHF radiotelephone communication, with its line-of-sight range limitation, was supplemented by lower-frequency contact direct to the flotilla commander. Differences between Navy and *Luftwaffe* radio procedure, practices, and jargon had to be reconciled. Galland considered a fighter controller aboard the ships to be essential. He put his old C.O. from the French campaign, Colonel Max Ibel, aboard *Scharnhorst* with a small staff. Ibel had direct radio contact with the fighters overhead, as well as with Galland ashore. Ibel was designated Fighter Controller on Board. *Luftwaffe* liaison officers who were qualified pilots, with assisting *Luftwaffe* radio operators, were placed aboard both *Gneisenau* and *Prinz Eugen*.

A continuous fighter umbrella over the ships involved complex planning. Galland and his staff calculated that no more than 16 fighters could be maintained in the air cover. Each wave of 16 fighters would have 35 minutes on station. Time over the ships could be extended to 45 minutes if there was no combat. Each relief flight would have a ten-minute overlap with the fighters it was replacing. For 20 minutes of each hour, therefore, there would be 32 fighters in the umbrella.

All this called for top leadership, good navigation, tremendous pilot endurance, and a maximum effort from the ground crews. Galland was forced to limit turnaround times on the ground. Refueling, rearming, and minor servicing were held to a scant 30 minutes. Even with everything going to plan, there still were not enough fighters available to give the Navy all the cover the admirals would have liked.

Galland's limited resources consisted mainly of JG-2 and JG-26, veteran formations on the Channel Front, each with 90 fighters. An additional 60 fighters could be allotted from JG-1 for the morning of the breakout day. These aircraft would not be available for breakout afternoon operations, since they were responsible for protecting the ships the following morning as they crossed the German Bight.

Galland scraped up an additional dozen ME-109s from an operational training unit at Paris, posting them to Le Havre. From the Night Fighter Arm he assigned 30 twin-engined Me-110s to the half-light periods at dawn and sunset. They were too vulnerable to Spitfires by day, but they bridged the dawn and dusk gaps. Galland's grand aircraft total was 252 fighters maximum, with less than 200 available for the afternoon following the breakout.

Galland ordered total radio silence. German fighter pilots were notoriously talkative aloft. Their flow of chatter, slang, warnings, and commands was almost continuous on normal operations. Absolute radio silence was essential until Galland was certain that the British had discovered the breakout. The order "Open visor" would cancel radio silence. Pilots were ordered to fly low, for a minimal return on British radar, upon which some electronic deception was being practiced.

General Martini, as Head of the *Luftwaffe* Signal Corps, possessed jamming devices and other electronic countermeasures (ECM), to disturb British radar. These technical advances had been kept under security and ready for just such an introduction to operations. At dawn each day in January of 1942, British radars were subtly exposed to Martini's ECM for just a few minutes.

British radar displays appeared to lose considerable returns. Gradually lengthening the duration of the ECM, the Germans accustomed the British radar operators to its presence. Since these effects were not continuous, the British attributed it to atmospheric conditions or to enemy action, and the interference gradually seemed to become unimportant. The British had a few K-radars operating on 7–8 centimetres that Martini could not corrupt, but most of their radar stations on the south coast were set up by the Germans for jamming on breakout day.

Galland issued operational orders to *Geschwader, Gruppe,* and *Staffel* commanders in sealed envelopes, to be opened only upon receipt of the code-word Thunderbolt. The fighter pilots had been told that another big bombing offensive was about to open against England. Ranging them along the French coast in full available strength was consistent with another blitz.

Despite a bleak weather forecast, Admiral Alfreid Saalwaechter of High Command West ordered the operation to commence at 2000 on 11 February 1942. Cerberus/Thunderbolt was on. Galland flew directly from Paris to the Pas de Calais to confer with command personnel of the flying units—all men who knew, trusted, and respected him.

Opening and studying their orders, these veteran fighter leaders found their warrior hearts quickening. Immediate attacks on hostile aircraft from any position were demanded, the "aggressive defense" credo of Galland. *"Attack"* was the keynote. Any British machine penetrating the fighter screen was to be destroyed at all costs—even by ramming. Enemy aircraft leaving the combat area with no further offensive power were to be ignored. Downed enemy aircraft would not measure the success of Thunderbolt. Their objective was the safety and protection of the heavy ships.

The fighter officers who would lead Thunderbolt in the air were elated by their clear aggressive orders from a trusted commander. An historic task awaited with the dawn. In high anticipation, they sprawled on their beds for a restless night. Galland went sleepless, his mind racing with excitement. His whole life had been a preparation for this moment. All his experience, skill, and keenness had been poured into planning Thunderbolt, the biggest operation of his career thus far, and the most important. His mettle in handling operational high command was about to be tested.

CHAPTER SIXTEEN

By midnight on 12 February 1942, the German heavy ships were rounding Ushant with their escort and heading into the English Channel. Despite a two-hour delay in their Brest departure due to an RAF raid, they were in luck. The submarine *Sealion,* guardian of the Brest approaches, was 30 miles away on the surface, charging its batteries. The German force went racing up into the Channel at nearly 30 knots, with Admiral Ciliax and all hands alert for British warships and aircraft.

Along and over the Channel, an incredible chain of British misadventures and mismanagement was beginning. In all three zones into which RAF Coastal Command had divided the Channel for interlocking radar search patterns, British aircraft had difficulties. Mechanical, electronic, and meteorological problems disrupted normal patrol schedules. The German heavy ships slipped through the resultant gaps. By 7:30AM they were off Cherbourg, making rendezvous with an escorting E-boat flotilla, and the British were unaware that they had left Brest.

Radar deception measures by General Martini's experts, meanwhile, had begun well before dawn with the dispatch of two He-111 radar decoy aircraft from a base north of Paris. Each aircraft electronically simulated 25 circling aircraft. They flew parallel with the English coast, diverting the electronic attention of British radar operators from the Brest force. The German heavy ships thus reached the mouth of the Seine without any major reaction from the British. Royal Navy channel forces went through a routine alert in routine fashion at 0500, from which they were stood down at 0835—unaware that the German Navy was steaming up the Channel.

At 0750 the first Me-110 night fighters arrived over the German ships in the first hint of dawn, thundering under a 1,500-foot ceiling. These aircraft were flying higher than required by their orders. Across the Channel at Beachy Head, they were detected by one of the 7-cm wavelength K-radars that the

Me-110s circle over destroyers which were part of the German fleet making the dash up the English Channel from Brest.

Churning through the Channel. Part of the German Navy fleet is seen here in this dramatic photograph during the breakout of the German Battleships in February, 1942. The General of the Fighters, Galland, had the responsibility for the aerial defense of the maneuver, which caught the British by surprise.

Germans were unable to jam. Beachy Head radar reported aircraft circling over ships moving on the surface at 25 knots. Both the Royal Navy and the RAF were advised, but neither acted.

A second British K-radar at Swingate also detected the circling fighters at 0824 and evaluated the radar information similarly to Beachy Head. Repeated plots were made. Other radars reported interference, as the decoy He-111s moved down the Channel. Fighter Command at Stanmore received all this crucial radar data. In consultation with No. 11 Fighter Group's duty controller at Hornchurch, it was decided that a German air-sea rescue operation was in progress. The German battleships continued forging unmolested through hostile waters.

Galland had watched the progress of the German battleships up the Channel during the night, as German coastal radars periodically reported their position. His excitement mounted as, by 0900, the big ships had almost made up the time lost in their late breakout from Brest. Daylight had now eliminated the hazard of British night attack. The young colonel was further encouraged because the timing of the day's dismal weather forecast proved wrong. His fighter bases along the east side of the Channel continued to have good weather, while the English coast had low cloud and poor visibility.

Squadron Leader William Igoe was the senior RAF fighter controller at Biggin Hill, the most important fighter station in southern England. Radar blips and their evaluation were important parts of his job. Igoe tracked a string of aircraft returns from Contentin to the Channel and calculated a speed in advance of 25 knots—consistent with a fighter escort for battleships. At 0905, Igoe telephoned No. 11 Fighter Group HQ at Uxbridge and said: "I believe it is Fuller!" The crucial code word seemed to make no impression on personnel at Uxbridge, where Fuller orders were locked in a safe for security. RAF secrecy on Fuller was so tight that many people about to be critically involved were not even apprised of the code word.

Igoe's counterpart at Stanmore, Wing-Commander Davies, became convinced also by 1000 that the German heavy ships were out of Brest and coming up the Channel. Like Igoe, he was unable to get his signal conclusion across to No. 11 Fighter Group HQ. By this time, Galland's first relay of Me-109s arrived over the battleships, and British radar detected their entry into the drama.

Each day at dawn and dusk, No. 91 Squadron based at Hawkinge, under Squadron Leader Robert Oxspring, sent out two "Jim Crow" patrol Spitfires. Reconnaissance of French offport and offshore areas was their assignment. On 13 February 1942, the Spitfire covering the Gris Nez to Le Havre sector spotted an E-boat flotilla moving out of Boulogne. These German units were assigned as part of the Dover Strait escort for the heavy ships. Their presence and movement was duly reported and added to the mosaic.

When Squadron Leader Igoe at Biggin Hill found that comprehension of Fuller was lacking at No. 11 Fighter Group HQ at Uxbridge, he telephoned Oxspring at Hawkinge and asked him to make a special second sweep. Oxspring agreed to go personally. Warned by Igoe of the intense German air activity,

Oxspring took along a wingman. Sergeant Beaumont had formerly been with the RAF Marine Section in high-speed launches and knew his ships. They took off shortly after 1000, heading out into the Channel murk.

A few minutes later, another and entirely unofficial Spitfire element took off from Kenley. Group Captain Victor Beamish and Wing Commander Finlay Boyd were two of Fighter Command's bright lights. As operations officer of No. 11 Fighter Group, Beamish seized any excuse to get back into a fighter cockpit. With the weather too unfavorable for less-experienced pilots, this was a "Special Beamish Mission," and the Battle of Britain ace headed his Spitfire into the mist. Strict radio silence was required over the Channel, so Beamish and Boyd vanished from human ken, unaware that Oxspring and Beaumont were buzzing around in the same soup as themselves.

By 1020, the German heavy ships had been undetected at sea for almost 11 hours. They were bearing down rapidly on Dover Strait. In his control center at Le Touquet, Galland tensely followed the unfolding drama. The radio loudspeaker for communication with the aircraft carried the only sound, and for now it was still silent. Weather information, radar data, and monitoring of British communications were registered via switching lights. Galland did not speak aloud but wrote down his orders on paper and passed them to a staff officer for broadcast as appropriate.

Both of the two Spitfire elements discovered the German heavy ships within a few minutes of each other, 15 miles west of Le Touquet. Both pairs of Spitfires were bounced by German fighters and taken under fire by the shipboard flak. In the getaway, Oxspring and Beaumont almost pressed an attack on Beamish and Boyd, mistaking them for Me-109s in the poor visibility.

Despite the vital significance of the sighting, Group Captain Victor Beamish followed orders to maintain radio silence and flew back to Kenley with Boyd. Squadron Leader Oxspring had initiative enough to know when to disobey orders. At 1035, Oxspring broke radio silence. He reported battle cruisers and escort off Le Touquet heading for Dover.

The German listening service intercepted his report, and it was almost instantly in front of Adolf Galland. The battleships had been discovered and identified. Galland had now to decide whether to continue radio silence and low-level flying or cancel these orders. Maintaining radio silence cut him off from direct contact with Ibel aboard *Scharnhorst* for a situation report. *Luftwaffe* fighters would be vulnerable to Spitfires bouncing the battleships from out of the clouds. Every man in high command eventually reaches such a juncture, where men's lives hang in the balance along with the outcome of great events. Galland decided to keep the lid on.

The British did not act on Squadron Leader Oxspring's dramatic sighting report but waited, instead, for him to land. After he repeated his sighting report in person, buttressed by Beaumont who had seen the *Scharnhorst* close-up in peacetime, he was still not fully believed. A book of warship silhouettes was sent for, and, after an additional delay while its bearer stopped for tea, Oxspring and Beaumont made a firm identification of the big ships. All this went on as Galland, on the other side of the Channel, won more miles of safety for the German battleships. He kept both his nerve and radio silence.

Squadron Leader Oxspring tried personally to contact Air Vice-Marshal Leigh-Mallory, AOC No. 11 Fighter Group, and was rebuffed. Leigh-Mallory's staff refused to interrupt his inspection of Belgian RAF units at Northolt. Operations officers simply did not get excited over Oxspring's report. They promised only to enlarge an attack on the E-boats exiting Boulogne, which was already in preparation.

Oxspring telephoned back to fighter controller Igoe at Biggin Hill. He confirmed for him that the German heavy ships were moving up the Channel. Group Captain Victor Beamish landed at Kenley at 1110 and confirmed Oxspring's sighting. Both Beamish and Oxspring now continued independently to try and contact Leigh-Mallory, without whose orders No. 11 Fighter Group continued to decline decisive action.

While the Spitfire sightings were in progress, RAF radar at Swingate had picked up the large blips of the heavy ships at 56 miles at 1016. Galland's circling fighter escort was detected by other coastal radars and interpreted as E-boat activity. When the C.O. of Swingate radar tried to notify Royal Navy HQ at Dover Castle, defective communications blocked him for nearly half an hour.

The Swingate report and other radar information convinced Admiral Ramsay's air liaison officer at Dover that *Scharnhorst* and *Gneisenau* were forcing the Channel. Wing-Commander Constable-Roberts was responsible for liaison with No. 11 Fighter Group, but he fared no better than Oxspring, Beamish, and Igoe in convincing the staff at Uxbridge that the battleships were out. Alarmed and determined to act to the limit of his authority, Constable-Roberts telephoned Manston and requested Lt.-Commander Esmonde to put his six Fairey Swordfish torpedo bombers in ready condition. He requested similar status from Coastal Command for the Beauforts at St. Eval and for the Beauforts of No. 42 Squadron then belatedly en route to Coltishall in Norwich from Scotland.

These actions by Constable-Roberts were the first decisive steps taken against *Scharnhorst* and *Gneisenau* by the British armed forces. Constable-Roberts initiated action without even being aware that Oxspring, Beaumont, Beamish, and Boyd had all physically sighted the battleships. Galland's maintenance of radio silence continued to prolong British uncertainty during the most critical time of the Channel dash for the Germans.

By 1130, Group Captain Beamish had forced reluctant aides and adjutants to bring Air Vice-Marshal Leigh-Mallory to the telephone, interrupting his inspection of the Belgians. Leigh-Mallory quickly grasped the importance of what his own No. 11 Fighter Group operations officer was reporting. The British now began to move, both RAF and Royal Navy. Operation Fuller was on. More than three hours had uselessly drained away since Squadron Leader Igoe had first called Fuller to No. 11 Fighter Group's duty officer. Those three hours translated into at least 75 nautical miles of unhampered steaming for the German battleships. Near noon, the German force was already in the narrowest part of the Channel.

British countermeasures were mainly planned against a night passage through the narrows by any major German force. Conceived to meet the highest probabilities, British plans envisaged the brilliantly illuminated German ships being attacked by coast artillery, torpedo and bomber aircraft, and motor torpedo-boats and destroyers. Remnants of this nocturnal assault would be finished off at first light by Bomber Command. As the Germans now began forcing the narrows at high noon, surprise, confusion, and operational clumsiness hampered British reaction.

At 1225, the six Fairey Swordfish biplanes lumbered across the snow-covered Manston airfield and into the air. They were the only striking force available and ready to tackle the battleships. Five fighter squadrons were assigned as their escort, but only one squadron made the rendezvous over Manston with the old torpedo planes. Diving down to 50 feet, his attack altitude, Esmonde led his six wood and canvas relics out over the Channel to certain death.

Torpedo boats were already lancing towards the Germans. Coastal Command Beauforts that were supposed to attack with the Swordfish were not in position for a combined strike. British shelling by coastal guns was ineffective, and thus the obsolete Swordfish were the first main British attack. The storm of fire from the German ships would inevitably bring them down, even though their fabric wings and fuselages might allow the harmless passage of many bullets and cannon shells. At 90 knots, they would be little more than target drogues for Galland's fighters, who would not be deterred by a fighter escort of only ten Spitfires.

At Le Touquet in his Fighter Control Center, Galland received word of shelling shortly after noon by British coastal guns around Dover. The battleships were not hit, but it meant that the British knew about the escaping heavy ships and were going into action. He wrote down the order "Open visor" on his message pad, and it was immediately transmitted to Colonel Ibel on *Scharnhorst,* to all fighter units, and to other fighter control centers. Galland and the *Luftwaffe* officers around him were elated by the inertia of the British.

The entire German fighter force was still in readiness and without losses. Fighter escort for the convoy's passage through the narrows could therefore be doubled. As the weather deteriorated, the cloud base hung at about 1,000 feet, and vertical separation of the fighters reduced the danger of a surprise British bounce out of the clouds.

The circling German fighters over the ships began seriously their task of beating off attackers. Five motor-torpedo boats made the first thrust. German E-boats went into counterattack, and fighters swooped down to strafe the British small craft. The British MTBs nevertheless launched their torpedoes, forcing *Scharnhorst* and *Prinz Eugen* into evasive maneuvers. More MTBs broke through astern but were unable to close the racing German fleet, due to engine malfunctions.

No sooner had the MTBs receded into the murk than the ghostly forms of the Swordfish materialized to the astonished gaze of the Germans. Galland's pilots seemed as though they had flown into a time warp, as they fell upon the gaunt old canvas phantoms pressing their torpedo attack a few feet above the sea. The Swordfish flew into a fiery hell.

All six Swordfish were consumed by the hail of fire from the ships and escort fighters. They scored no hits on the German ships, and Esmonde's aircraft was blown to pieces in midair by a direct flak hit; 18 British crew members had flown the Swordfish out of Manston, and only 5 survived. This extraordinary bravery deeply impressed the German officers who witnessed it (and left Galland in awe even 40 years later).

In Le Touquet, Galland could now hear the progress of the constantly moving air-sea battle on his loudspeaker. Shouts and barked commands, fighter pilot jargon, cursing and slang, the lingo and tumult he knew so well, told of aerial battle joined. He yearned to be aloft amid the fray. His wings clipped, he lit cigar after cigar and listened intently.

By 1400, the battleships were through Dover Strait, but an RAF bombing onslaught was continuously expected. All eyes scanned the sky in search of hostile silhouettes amid the mist, cloud, and rain. From the ships, little of the aerial combat could actually be observed, but occasionally dogfights took place close to the ships and aircraft were seen plummeting into the sea in flames.

Scharnhorst hit a mine at 1432, losing all electric power as her boiler room was flooded. Belching black smoke and oozing oil behind her, she wallowed to a halt. Without waiting for full assessment of the damage, Admiral Ciliax transferred himself, Ibel, and some of their staffs to destroyer Z-29. In accordance with operational orders, *Scharnhorst* was hit and therefore was to be left behind. Two destroyers and two E-boats were left as protection, but most of Galland's fighters continued to follow and protect the main convoy.

The RAF made only one ineffective attack on *Scharnhorst,* but by 1500 had the main force under heavy aerial pressure. Waves of Whirlwinds, Blenheims, Beauforts, Hudsons, Wellingtons, and Hampdens successively pressed through the mist with bombing strikes. Under a 1,000-foot ceiling in low visibility, the convoy made an elusive target. Each RAF strike was greeted with retaliatory flak and was bounced by German fighters.

By 1540, the ceiling was down to 450 feet, rain lashed the scene, and visibility was no more than a mile and a half. Galland listened in his Fighter Control Center to his fighter pilots seeking the British bombers in the murk. Time after time they overshot in low visibility. Near-collisions abounded, between friend and foe and between friend and friend on both sides. British bombers shot often at their own Spitfire escort. About 100 aircraft were milling in the mist, while the ships sped towards Germany under the grey veil below.

The desperate maelstrom in the sky, where almost any moving form was fair game, had its counterpart down on the surface. *Gneisenau* and *Prinz Eugen* both took British destroyers under fire. When they sent *HMS Worcester* reeling out of the battle ablaze, two other British destroyers sped to her aid. British bombers hammered this trio of British ships, and the *Luftwaffe* joined in with strafing. The German destroyer *Hermann Schömann* was also strafed by *Luftwaffe* fighters. Far back in the gloom, engine room personnel had miraculously breathed life back into *Scharnhorst*. She began steaming hard after the main fleet.

Command decision was again thrust on Galland, as operational difficulties for his fighters increased. Diminishing daylight after 1500, plus the 450-foot ceiling, rain, and visibility sometimes less than a mile all united to reduce the effectiveness of the fighter escort. Takeoff and landing from French airfields remained undisturbed, but the distance between these bases and ships was continually increasing.

Galland had to land his fighters in Holland, where low clouds were beginning to sock in large tracts of countryside. To keep sending in waves of fighters without being able to assign safe landing areas put plenty of pressure on Galland. Continuous British air attacks on the ships left him no choice. He kept his fighters in action, wave after wave, determined not to squander the success already won.

Galland knew his pilots well. He had personally led many of the pilots who were now over the battleships and whose voices he recognized. Despite this familiarity with their capabilities, they still surprised him with their skill and ingenuity in making emergency landings. When they ran out of fuel or failed to find assigned landing grounds, they landed wherever they could. Losses remained far below Galland's estimates when he had planned the operation.

Final British bombing attacks went in around 1800 in near darkness, a tenacious strike by Wellingtons that cost them several aircraft. Fifteen minutes later, the last RAF aircraft had departed and German day fighters were groping their way down onto Dutch landing grounds in dim twilight. Night fighters took over the protective vigil. Galland transferred himself to his Fighter Control Center in Jever. His first high command task had been successful. The air umbrella had protected the Navy.

Later that night, while steaming in relative safety down the Dutch coast, both *Scharnhorst* and *Gneisenau* struck mines off Terschelling. They both made port under their own power despite this final ill fortune. (The British knew that both ships had hit these mines through *Ultra* decrypts, but the angry Churchill, humiliated by the Channel dash, could not release the information publicly. The greatest secret of the war had to be protected even when the British were smarting from a comprehensive tactical defeat.)

Both sides in their official communiques played down Thunderbolt. The Germans did not want to emphasize that it was an *escape* from Brest, which would automatically infer that Germany did not control the air and sea off the French Atlantic coast. The British had suffered a colossal shock and a national humiliation. No such naval force had been allowed to pass through the English Channel in two and a half centuries.

Official Britain handled Thunderbolt by casting it all in a somewhat specious strategic light, barely comprehensible to the outraged British public. Getting the ships out of Brest was depicted as being of "extreme advantage" to Britain.

The British public stoically choked down the whole thing and went on with the war, while an official British inquiry was launched.

Seen with 40 years of perspective, the air Operation Thunderbolt was a masterpiece of operational planning and execution by Adolf Galland. Major Hans-Heinrich Brustellin, who helped him plan Thunderbolt and served on his staff right through the war, described it to the authors as Galland's best moment in high command. In his own evening, Galland numbers Thunderbolt among the greatest moments of his life, ranking it equally with the birth of his son and daughter.

Exemplary cooperation between the German Navy and *Luftwaffe* can also be largely attributed to Galland's qualities as a leader and planner. Everything was subordinated to operational success. Competent professional skill and his long experience of modern combat went into the operational planning. His background allowed Galland to foresee and plan for virtually every eventuality. Thunderbolt was essentially flawless.

Galland won his Thunderbolt victory with a total of 252 fighters of all types. This inferiority of force, compared with the RAF, was overcome by excellent planning and a stellar performance by the German fighter pilots. Galland's decisions from inception to end showed a cool command brain and the firmness of mind essential to high command. The *Luftwaffe* lost 17 aircraft and 11 pilots in Thunderbolt, and the British lost more than 60 aircraft of all types.

Gneisenau never went to sea again. RAF Bomber Command blasted her in the Kiel drydock within two weeks. She was eventually filled with concrete and used as a flak fort at Gdynia in the bay of Danzig. *Scharnhorst* underwent extensive repairs for months and duly reached Altenfjord in Norway early in 1943. When she was ordered to sea by Admiral Doenitz on Christmas Day 1943, to attack convoy JW55B, *Ultra* overheard all the preparatory phases and final orders. Admiral Fraser in HMS *Duke of York* was promptly informed and *Scharnhorst* went down under Royal Navy guns on 26 December 1943.

Although the Channel dash was a tactical triumph and a strategic defeat, the operation strengthened Hitler's status with his admirals. The *Fuehrer* had correctly assessed British inertia and inability to improvise in the face of surprise. Galland's personal estimate of Thunderbolt's likelihood of success, given to Hitler at the initial conference, had proved remarkably accurate. Galland's stock rose with Hitler, and, for a relatively short time thereafter, he was one of the *Fuehrer's* military favorites. With Thunderbolt successfully concluded, Colonel Galland turned his attention to pressing problems afflicting the far-flung Fighter Arm.

CHAPTER SEVENTEEN

Hitler vowed during his drive to power, and later, that Germany would never again be exposed to the fatal strain of war on two fronts. Galland's new vantage point in early 1942 let him see how comprehensively Hitler had violated his vow—as far as the Fighter Arm was concerned. German fighters were in combat on six distinct fronts.

JG-5 operated over Scandinavia and the Arctic, mainly from Norwegian bases. Being fighter cover for the Navy and assisting in attacks on Allied convoys to Russia were JG-5's main missions. Four more *Geschwader* were strung thinly from the Baltic to the Caucasus. They were providing local air superiority and close support for a battlefront of unprecedented length.

JG-2 and JG-26 struggled far below full strength on the Channel Front, battling the RAF's nonstop offensive. JG-27 and JG-53, the latter with one *Gruppe* from JG-3 *Udet* added, fought on yet another two-front war. In the central Mediterranean against Malta, and over the deserts of North Africa, they had been successful—for the moment.

The sixth fighter front was over the homeland itself at night. The RAF had bombed Germany at night from the time of the Battle of Britain onwards, stepping up this effort in 1942. The *Luftwaffe* High Command had been forced to set up a completely new organization of fighters and ground-control facilities. Night fighting required specially developed tactics and new electronic techniques for detection and control. Night fighting had not been taken seriously in the short peacetime life of the *Luftwaffe*. This sixth fighter front was now consuming immense resources in dealing with British night attacks.

Each of these six fronts had its own special needs, but they were commonly dominated by four problems: numerical inferiority, replacement aircraft, pilots to fly them, and the manifold needs of service and supply. The night fighters were not under Galland at this time, but the rest of his fighter empire sprawled from the Arctic to the Middle East and from the English Channel to the Caucasus.

"Franzl" Lützow, Inspector of the Fighters in Sicily, meets Galland on Sicilian territory.

As General der Jagdflieger, Adolf Garland visited all his fighter units, this one to JG5 at Petsamo, Finland.

Josef "Fips" Priller. "Fips," which translates into "agile little man," was exactly that. He was Kommodore of JG26 from January 11, 1943, until January 27, 1945. After the war he owned the Riegele Brewery in Augsburg until his death in 1961. Beloved by everybody who knew him, Priller and his wife Johanna produced an outstanding family of two boys and a girl: Sebastian, Markis and Maria-Luise "Schnucki."

Salute to a fallen comrade—his own brother. In August, 1943, the General of the Fighters, Adolf Galland, bids a final farewell to his beloved brother, Wilhelm Ferdinand "Wutz" Galland. Wutz was shot down by a Thunderbolt pilot on 17 August 1943.

The responsibility was sobering to a man just turned 30. War dynamics had proved decisively that *no major military operation could be sustained without fighter aircraft.*

The successful umbrella provided by the Fighter Arm for the geographically compact and brief Polish, Norwegian, French, and Balkan campaigns had now been stretched in all directions like elastic. JG-5 and JG-27 were thousands of miles apart. The protective capabilities of this umbrella were thus sharply reduced. This stretched umbrella was also relatively delicate and fragile. Heavy and concentrated blows against it at any point could bring about its local collapse, from which disaster could be transmitted to the whole military structure. The most important single action in Galland's effort to keep the umbrella intact was, somehow, to increase the number of fighters and pilots available for combat.

Galland had already taken action through Milch to substantially increase fighter production. To obtain more pilots, Galland surveyed and then radically reorganized his own creation—the Operational Training Units (*Ergänzungsgruppen*). The system he initiated as *Kommodore* of JG-26, where freshly trained pilots were taken under the care of active fighter units and familiarized with current experience, had spread through the Fighter Arm. The merits of these OTUs were well-established.

In JG-26 Galland had kept his pioneer OTU administratively lean. His resources there were limited and he did not want the OTU to generate paper work. Analyzing the OTUs now in early 1942, he could see that a large and cumbersome bureaucracy had developed around the units. Vast resources were being absorbed. Efficiency was low. Standards and methods of OTU training differed widely.

Galland consolidated the OTUs into three OTU *Gruppen,* assigned to the East, West, and South. Five full *Gruppen* of fighters were made available for the front by this reorganization. Part of this new-found power was used to form JG-1, which was assigned to Holland and the German Bight, easing the strain on JG-2 and JG-26. Other personnel and aircraft "wrung out" of the reorganization helped to form two new twin-engined fighter units and a fighter-bomber unit for the Eastern Front. Galland had begun his struggle to increase the size of the Fighter Arm.

In the forefront of his mind even at this time was the production power of the Allies. Interested in aircraft since boyhood, he had a profound respect for the American aircraft industry. Americans had invented the aeroplane. They were a competitive people who liked to be the world's best at everything. In the light of his own desire always to be the best, Galland knew what might be expected from this facet of the American national character.

Galland's recent experience combating the rising power of the RAF on the Channel Front made him apprehensive about the aerial threat from the West. Intelligence reports he was now routinely receiving as General of the Fighter Arm dealt frequently with American aircraft production goals. With their superior resources, the Americans would soon eclipse British aircraft production. The combined production of these two powerful Allies would then come winging across the Channel. This specter of enemy air power never left him, because experience had proved that only a large fighter force could stop such an assault.

Japan had inflicted a series of defeats on the United States at this time, but it had failed to deliver a finishing blow. In Galland's military estimation, Japan's lack of a final victory could only mean that the Americans would recover and strike back. The continental United States was untouched and contained colossal human and material resources. Parts of Roosevelt's "fireside chats" that appeared in German newspapers promised massive bombing fleets. The four-engined B-17 Fortress and the B-24 Liberator were already in production and tested and ready for combat. British four-engined production was also going full blast. These were the strategic bombers, the master offensive air weapon advocated by Douhet.

The German media ridiculed the American production figures, but the intelligence reports crossing Galland's desk told a sobering factual story, divested of all political rhetoric and wishful thinking. With his own logic and professional experience, Galland could readily draw the outline of tomorrow in the air: a veritable blizzard of aircraft attacking Germany from British bases. The storm would probably come before he could build up an air defense with the Fighter Arm to protect his homeland.

German fighters were holding their own in Russia, and they had temporary ascendancy in the central Mediterranean; but on the Channel Front they were already beleaguered. A potential catastrophe loomed. Galland was appalled to find that even some responsible high-ranking members of the High Command looked on the American threat as bluff.

The more he learned of the true state of the Fighter Arm, the more Galland was convinced that only a Herculean effort would suffice. That effort would also have to be timely. He was confident that current marques of the Me-109, with the new DB 605 engine, and the FW-190 would be able to handle the daylight threat in the West—if there were enough of them available with well-trained replacement pilots. The measures he was now taking would have to be greatly magnified to meet the USAAF–RAF threat. Maintenance of the elastic fighter umbrella was meanwhile devouring everything that he could find.

When Galland took up with Goering the impact that USAAF reinforcement of the RAF offensive would have on the Fighter Arm in the West, the *Reich* Marshal waved it all aside with his gold baton.

"The Americans?" said Goering blandly, "They are being badly beaten by the Japanese. Besides, Galland, you should remember that the Americans are good at making fancy cars and refrigerators, but that doesn't mean that they are any good at making aircraft. They are bluffing. They are excellent at bluffing."

This interview was in March or April. As late as Harvest Thanksgiving, in October of 1942, Goering repeated these trite notions in a public speech. This was three months after the USAAF had dropped its first bombs on continental targets. With juvenile words did the *Luftwaffe*'s Supreme Commander thus dispose of both the U.S. aviation industry and the USAAF. Galland was shocked by this irresponsibility towards an urgent national danger.

After several months as General of the Fighters, Galland had seen plenty of Goering's reactions to weighty technical matters. They did not inspire confidence. USAAF daylight bombing of Germany could be foreseen—technically, tactically, and strategically—but Goering could not accept such a development politically. When Goering made a fatuous response to such serious questions, often a member of his personal circle would chime in with supportive comments.

Anything the *Reich* Marshal said that was derogatory to the Fighter Arm was endorsed within his circle. Galland found this highly irritating. Young Bomber Arm personalities around Goering used his favor to produce a destructive polarization of the *Luftwaffe*. Bomber Arm was pitted against Fighter Arm in an internecine contest for Goering's approval. Galland's basic emotional cleanliness put Germany first, although he unfailingly defended the Fighter Arm. He saw Bomber Arm and Fighter Arm as sword and flail, commonly fighting a powerful alliance in mortal combat. Goering's sycophants preferred divisive, counterproductive rivalry.

Goering's personal idleness, egotism, vanity, and incompetence promoted this internal schism and all its destructive consequences. His own best leaders were induced to struggle with each other. As these crazy rivalries began spoiling the best impulses and ideas, Galland's mind went back to the smooth-working Condor Legion. All then had worked as one. Those were becoming the "good old days" for him as 1942 wore on.

Galland had problems now that he had never encountered or contemplated as a combat *Kommodore*. How was he to get his ideas through to such a man as Goering? The *Reich* Marshal was an overpowering personality oblivious to his own command shortcomings and supported always by his brain trust of "yes men," not one of whom was a fighter pilot. The employment, technical performance, and training of the Fighter Arm required practical, realistic, wide-ranging knowledge that could give due weight to the crucial human element.

Goering liked to preface his views by emphasizing that he was himself "a former successful fighter ace." By this device he assumed contemporary expertise. The Western Front of World War I was light-years behind this present aerial struggle. Goering's fawning circle gave the *Reich* Marshal no useful technical help and played, instead, upon his rampant vanity. These officers were interested solely in expanding their personal influence and in having a good life—to which Goering held their passports.

The smallness of these officers was galling to Galland. Their influence was one more deplorable and needless problem that he had to contend with in running the Fighter Arm. What hit him hardest, as the weeks passed, was the substantial number of high-level *Luftwaffe* people who were opposing any strong enlargement of the Fighter Arm. Goering's circle, and many others as well, were resisting the Fighter Arm expansion that Galland regarded as vital for Germany's survival. He had his own personal two-front war as a result.

While the highly secret operation "Thunderbolt" preparations had been in progress, Galland had been occupied as well with the Malta situation. After Thunderbolt, the island came to the center of his attention, reaching out to dominate his thoughts, even as it dominated the Axis supply lines to Rommel. Many echoes of the Battle of Britain appeared in the new air assault on Malta. Among them was the presence of Galland's Battle of Britain Air Fleet Commander, Field Marshal Kesselring. He was to orchestrate the aerial campaign.

Kesselring had urged Goering and Hitler to seize Malta from 1941 onward. Capturing the island was essential to a successful Axis North African campaign. (Only 153 square miles in area, Malta lies 56 miles south of Sicily, a distance not significantly greater than France to Britain in terms of air assault. Malta is also 225 miles from the African coast at Tunis. This unique and isolated position allowed British aircraft and submarines to control the shipping of Axis logistics from Italy and Sicily to North Africa.)

By cutting off Rommel's vital supplies, Malta was more effective against the *Afrika Korps* than many divisions in the field. Interdiction operations from Malta in October of 1941 sank over 60 percent of the supplies shipped to Rommel. The tally rose by more than 15 percent in November. Field Marshal Kesselring was thereupon sent to Sicily from Russia, with part of his Air Fleet 2, to mount countermeasures.

German intelligence did not report large air, naval, or army forces on Malta. Galland wondered at the time how such modest forces were able to inflict such heavy losses on Axis convoys. He therefore tended to discount the intelligence reports. (*Ultra* decrypts were again responsible for Malta's efficiency. Kesselring's detailed reports to Berlin and to Rommel on convoy loadings, routes, and estimated arrival times were decoded promptly and were probably read in London before Rommel received his copy.)

In possession of comprehensive information on convoy composition, routes, and departure times, the RAF readily intercepted and sank Rommel's supplies. To protect *Ultra*, RAF reconnaissance pilots were instructed to deliberately allow themselves to be sighted by the convoys. British pilots were mystified by these orders, but they must have guessed that British intelligence was good when they were repeatedly vectored to areas where the convoys appeared.

Substantial economy of effort was thereby made possible out of Malta. The small Malta-based RAF contingent was concentrated on its targets through *Ultra*. Within individual convoys, specific ships were singled out for concentrated attacks if they carried such critical cargoes as gasoline, tanks, or spare parts. Kesselring had unwittingly supplied such detail. The Germans wrongly blamed Italian Navy Intelligence and British spies for the security leaks.

The fighter component of Air Fleet 2 that had been withdrawn from Russia was commanded by the tireless Major Guenther von Maltzahn of JG-53. Galland knew him well from Battle of Britain days. "Henri" von Maltzahn's leadership had made JG-53 the *Luftwaffe*'s top-scoring *Geschwader*. He now had available four under-strength Me-109F *Gruppen,* plus one *Gruppe* of Me-110s. This day fighter force consisted of no more than 80 serviceable fighters. Von Maltzahn was to escort and protect the bombers that would blast Malta into impotence. The main bombing force was five *Gruppen* of the fast Ju-88 A 4s, with one *Gruppe* of Stukas in support. Early in 1942, the Malta attacks did not go well, despite many downings credited to JG-53. Dive bombing was still being employed, in accordance with High Command obsessions and directives. The proficient Malta flak and British fighters were chewing up too many German aircraft. Goering blamed Galland and the fighters for these losses.

Kesselring and his chief of staff, Colonel Paul Deichmann, were able to convince the High Command by March of 1942 about the costly ineffectiveness of dive bombing at Malta. Successive concentrated attacks were approved on the RAF fighter base at Ta Kali, on the torpedo-plane and bomber bases at Hal Far, and on the docks at Valetta harbor. Level bombardment was authorized instead of dive bombing. Galland followed reports from this theater with limited satisfaction.

The combination of concentrated carpet bombing and aggressive action by JG-53 virtually suppressed British fighter activity. By the end of March 1942, the *Luftwaffe* held air superiority over Malta, and, by mid-April, had virtually driven out the Royal Navy. British bomber and torpedo-bomber action was also suppressed. British supply convoys to Malta were now heavily attacked from the air, and thousands of tons of food, ammunition, and fuel were sunk by the *Luftwaffe*.

By the end of April, von Maltzahn's fighters had flown well over 5,000 sorties. German bombers had been successfully escorted, and they dropped almost as much explosive on Malta as the entire Bomber Arm dropped on England in September of 1940. Malta was toothless. Rommel again received his supplies. The Fighter Arm had won a hard victory over its old RAF adversaries.

Both Hitler and Mussolini had been dithering over a Malta invasion for months. Now the *Luftwaffe* had provided air superiority over the island and its lengthy coastline. Germany's elite XI Air Corps was ready with its experienced paratroops and was waiting to drop on the island. In support were German-trained Italian paratroops, who outnumbered Malta's defenders; 70,000 more Italian troops were earmarked for the invasion force.

Hitler was suspicious of Italian ability to carry out its end of the proposed Operation ''Hercules'' for Malta's capture. Shadows of the Pyrrhic paratroop victory in Crete the previous year still loomed in the *Fuehrer's* mind. A prize had been won then that events had since proved was not worth its high cost. Goering fanned Hitler's fears, being himself opposed to the Malta invasion.

After two days of conferences with their military chiefs at the Obersalzberg, Hitler and Mussolini decided on 30 April 1942 to postpone the Malta assault for three months. This was to prove a fateful decision for Axis fortunes in the Mediterranean. Rommel wanted to strike at the British immediately, before the Brits could mount a desert offensive to take pressure off Malta. The Axis leaders let Rommel have his way. After his successful attack on Tobruk, Rommel would wait at Halfaya Pass on the Egyptian border while Operation ''Hercules'' seized

Malta. Supplies then secure, the Desert Fox would immediately press on to take Alexandria and topple Allied power in the Middle East.

Postponement of Hercules lost the Germans their golden chance. The dynamic Mediterranean war once again showed its sensitivity to air superiority, the pivot upon which everything turned. On 9 May 1942, on a second attempt, 61 RAF Spitfires were flown off the U.S. aircraft carrier *Wasp* to provide mass fighter reinforcement to Malta. A finely orchestrated reception had them refueled and back in the air in a few minutes. They waded into an incoming *Luftwaffe* force, which had expected them to be on the ground, when they struck. Fighters again demonstrated their ability to reverse a military situation.

When the *Luftwaffe* renewed its bombing offensive on 10 May 1942, the new Spitfires began hacking its formations to pieces. At their best defending close to their bases, the Spitfires inflicted more losses in the ensuing three days than Kesselring had suffered in his entire five-week offensive. Having advised his superiors that Malta had been eliminated, Kesselring suddenly found his fighter force halved as three *Gruppen* were ordered away from his Malta operations—two to Russia and one to North Africa. The elastic umbrella was under too much strain to provide fighters for the continuing operations against targets that the C.-in-C. South had reported as "eliminated." Bombers were similarly taken from Kesselring and reassigned to Russia, Greece, and Africa.

Drastic reversal of *Luftwaffe* fortunes over Malta had its impact at *Luftwaffe* HQ in Goldap, East Prussia. From triumph and victory, with air superiority hard won over the troublesome island, the *Luftwaffe* descended again into grinding weeks of struggle and losses. Galland was dismayed by the increasing fighter attrition, but he did not regard this as disproportionate to the task of neutralizing Malta, the key to North African success.

Amid the decline of *Luftwaffe* fortunes over Malta, the first great hammer blows against German cities and the civil population were being driven home at night by RAF Bomber Command. Air Marshal A. T. "Bomber" Harris launched a series of area attacks, culminating with history's first thousand-bomber raid at Cologne on the night of 30/31 May 1942. The center of the city was burned out, and the swamped German night fighters were only able to claw down 41 of the 1,046 raiding bombers.

The night fighters were obviously facing serious difficulties. Massed formations of bombers called for new tactics and control techniques. Here was the very situation against which Galland had already warned Goering—the blizzard from the West. Holes were appearing in the umbrella.

Dismayed by the sarcastic, unforgiving comments of Hitler after Cologne, and incensed by bomber losses over Malta, Goering ordered a conference in Naples. The *Reich* Marshal was visiting there with his wife, Emmy. Every *Kommodore* and *Gruppenkommandeur* from every fighter unit on the Southern Front was summoned. Galland flew down in his personal He-111. Here in another way and place, the phantoms of the Battle of Britain rose again.

In the warm Italian weather, Goering turned the heat on the Fighter Arm.

He launched an abusive tirade that had Galland seething. Galland could see von Maltzahn, Neumann, Luetzow, and others sitting white-faced with anger as Goering lashed at them with allegations of cowardice. Galland contained himself until it was his turn to speak. He sprang to his feet. Countering every Goering charge with logic, facts, and the competence born of leading fighter formations personally, the young General of the Fighters spoke for all the leaders in the room. A noisy and bitter argument with Goering ensued. The *Reich* Marshal ended proceedings by ordering Galland to fly over to Sicily, inspect the fighter units and "put some spine into them."

Taking "Franzl" Luetzow with him, Galland went to the dusty and scorching airstrips on Sicily to investigate the fighter situation. Hard flying on escort missions had taken some toll of the pilots and aircraft, and so had the unaccustomed heat. Morale was good. A negative factor was open resentment of Goering's telexed allegations of cowardice.

At Taormina, Galland found Kesselring to be his usual optimistic self. He had been the first high *Luftwaffe* officer to urge on Hitler the invasion of Malta. He had in recent days laid the groundwork in vain for Malta's capture. Yet here at this time he knew that it could not be done with air power alone, and certainly not with the reduced *Luftwaffe* forces he now commanded.

Galland was concerned by a practical gulf that existed between Kesselring and current realities of fighter operations on this front. Optimist Kesselring was expecting too much of his fighters. Kesselring overestimated the possibilities of fighter units that were geographically scattered and below strength. His part of the umbrella was too thin. Instead of concentrating his fighter forces on reduced main operations, Kesselring split them up and still wanted them to fulfill all requirements despite their weakness.

Kesselring touched on some of his differences with Rommel. From JG-27 leaders at Naples, Galland already knew that Rommel was asking more of the fighters than they could possibly deliver. Rommel's genius, his sense of mobility, did not extend to appreciating the limits of fighter power. He saw fighters in World War I terms—as boys playing in the air. These reports, and Kesselring's seeming inability to find a center of gravity for his operations, boded ill for the *Luftwaffe* on the Southern Front.

Galland flew back to Berlin to write new tactical regulations for escorting bomber missions and for other pressing tasks. The consequences of unleashing Rommel and postponing the Malta invasion were soon apparent. Seizing a vast hoard of supplies in Tobruk on 21 June 1942, Rommel had sufficient logistics, in his own opinion, to reach Alexandria. On 26 June 1942, the (now famous) "Field Marshals' Conference" took place at Sidi Barrani. Against Kesselring's strongest opposition, Rommel persuaded the two Italian marshals, Bastico and Cavallero, that he could be in Cairo in ten days.

Although Kesselring was a hard driver, ready to push his *Luftwaffe* units to their absolute limits, he balked at the Alexandria thrust. Supply problems were basically unsolved. The fighter umbrella was at its breaking point. Enemy

Galland's choice, Günther Lützow, who had 108 aerial victories, was called "the finest leader in the Luftwaffe" by Galland. Flying an Me-262 jet from Galland's JV44 squadron, Lützow was shot down and killed on 24 April 1945. USAAF records credit 9th Air Force pilots led by Major James E. Hill with the victory.

Major LÜTZOW

"One of the best we had . . ." Major Walter Nowotny was chosen by Galland as commander of Kommando Nowotny, to test operationally the Me-262 jets against Allied bombers. With 258 credited victories behind him, Nowotny was killed in an Me-262 before Galland's eyes.

power was not only growing but also being compressed by the Axis advance closer and closer to its main base. Kesselring called Rommel's plans to advance "madness," but the Italians were convinced by Rommel. Hitler ordered Kesselring to cease his objections.

Rommel was subsequently blocked at Alam El Halfa and at El Alamein, with *Ultra* decrypts playing a major role in frustrating his thrust. Rommel's dream of the Nile was replaced by an imminent nightmare. When Galland flew down to Africa to evaluate the situation, Colonel Hoffman von Waldau was awaiting him at Fuka. As *Fliegerführer Afrika,* von Waldau had wrung the last ounce out of the *Luftwaffe* in aiding Rommel. One of the most capable officers in the *Luftwaffe,* von Waldau was under no illusions about the current predicament of the German forces. Galland's old Condor Legion friend, Major Eduard Neumann, was *Kommodore* of JG-27 and added further detail to von Waldau's grim summary.

The greatest German ace of the North African campaign, Captain Hans-Joachim Marseille, had died in a crash on 30 September 1942. He was credited with 158 victories and had been awarded the Diamonds to his Knight's Cross. His death had shocked and saddened the JG-27 fighter pilots. Marseille's loss was highly symbolic.

Worn-out men and materiel were only one aspect of the desert crisis. Aerial reconnaissance and photographs showed massive enemy air fleets deployed close to the front. Studying the aerial photographs, Galland's apprehensions turned to alarm. An attack by this armada of nearly 800 aircraft would rapidly obliterate Rommel's exhausted air power.

Impelled by the need for urgent action, Galland wrote a realistic and bitterly pessimistic report to Goering and the High Command. He warned of the debacle that total Allied air supremacy would inflict. With thousands of German and Italian soldiers about to feel this aerial lash, Goering and the High Command directed their concern to the tone in which Galland's report had been written.

Kesselring was also resentful of Galland's "unwarranted intrusion" on his sphere of authority. When Galland flew back to Germany and showed Goering the aerial reconnaissance photos, the *Reich* Marshal demonstrated how to handle such problems. Riffling the photographs in his pudgy hands, Goering smiled triumphantly. "Dummies," he said. "Dummy aircraft. Nothing but dummy aircraft."

Without operational power of command, Galland could not change any disposition in Africa. Other events pressed in on him. He had to begin organizing the Fighter Divisions (*Jagddivisionen*), a step he had recommended and which the High Command had approved. The Fighter Divisions consolidated Day Fighter, Night Fighter, Signals, and Observer Corps control into one organization for each region. Substantial manpower economies, greater efficiency, and improved control were thereby achieved. (These consolidations continued into 1943.)

Considerable staff work was required for this reorganization, and the lack of Fighter Arm officers with General Staff training was severely felt. Due to the primacy given to the Bomber Arm in the *Luftwaffe*'s infancy, Fighter Arm officers had in general not done well at the War Academy, nor been there in appropriate numbers.

Galland's reaction to this had been similar to that of most Fighter Arm officers—hurt pride. In his new post with its heavy responsibilities, he could see the need for General Staff training. Organic, systematic, detailed military management would have facilitated the formation of the Fighter Divisions. He was nevertheless convinced that an experienced combat leader's eye could see many things to which the General Staff types seemed oblivious. Both were clearly needed for a successful Fighter Arm. Rapprochement with the War Academy was indicated, but he procrastinated over its initiation.

USAAF bombers were meanwhile being flown across the Atlantic to England by their own combat crews. Thousands of USAAF personnel were arriving in England by air and sea. On 18 June 1942, the British published a list of 87 British airfields being made available to the USAAF. By the end of August, the USAAF had put in a bombing strike against the Potez aircraft works at Meaulte, which were being used as a repair depot for *Luftwaffe* aircraft. This was closer than it seemed. Fighters of Galland's own former JG-26 were repaired at Meaulte.

The Battle of El Alamein on 23 October 1942 launched the end of the *Afrika Korps,* and the disaster that Galland had warned against was soon in horrifying progress. JG-27 was overwhelmed and hounded relentlessly by Allied fighters that swarmed in the desert air. They ate up every German aircraft in sight. Roaring down to strafe everything that moved on the single coast road, or across the desert floor, they drove home the true meaning of air supremacy.

On 8 November 1942, as Rommel's remnants retreated across Egypt and into Libya, the Americans struck with Operation "Torch" at the western end of the Mediterranean. A fresh horde of aircraft entered the fray there. Another front to fight on, while JG-27 struggled for its existence, struck at *Luftwaffe* morale. The elastic umbrella began its collapse in North Africa.

As Galland had feared, and as he had forecast, too much had been asked, expected, and demanded of a Fighter Arm stretched beyond its capacities. Neither verbal nor military abuse of the fighter units had served the German cause. The gloomy tidings from Africa brought Galland no joy in having been proved right. He knew personally far too many of the brave pilots who were now statistics.

Another brave fighter pilot close to Galland's heart had fallen on 31 October 1942. His youngest brother Paul, a developing ace with 17 victories, was shot down and killed over the Channel Front. Pangs in the heart came with that particular telex. The beloved Paulinchen and Wutz had often joked with him in JG-26 that "there'll be no 'after the war' for us." Nothing dulled the pain of such a deep personal blow.

On 19 November 1942, a telephone call from the *Reich* Marshal advised him of his promotion to general (*Generalmajor*). Goering proudly pointed out that the youngest general in the German Armed Forces was in "his" *Luftwaffe*.

November was otherwise noteworthy as USAAF heavy bombers began battering U-boat pens on the French coast and struck at airfields and repair depots.

North Africa provided an unbroken chain of disasters. The elastic umbrella had given way at its southern extremity. Galland hated to contemplate the further consequences. Massive and diverse problems pressed in on him from all quarters. By Christmas of 1942, he was ready again to seek brief sanctuary with JG-26 on the Channel, his second home.

Christmas 1942 was much more serious than the previous Yule season. Nobody was as lighthearted as they were a year ago. Galland was also now a general officer. That changed slightly the relationship he had previously enjoyed with the pilots and leaders he knew so well. This change had nothing to do with standing on ceremony, and they drank wine together as always.

The change was most evident when they told him of their difficulties and problems. These ranged from the number and quality of the enemy to materiel and supply difficulties, by way of tactics, of weapons, and of training. This was the terminal point for all the mistakes that were made higher up. This was where the suffering and bleeding were done.

Subtly, respectfully, and sincerely, these brave men were expecting that Galland would help them—that he had the power now to do so. He had left them and gone to dwell among the great gods of the *Luftwaffe*. Ethics and good discipline precluded his telling these warriors how things really were in the pantheon. He made a New Year resolution to himself, instead. He would throw himself into his tasks with all his strength in 1943. The fighting pilots deserved no less.

CHAPTER EIGHTEEN

Galland carried his New Year resolution into effect in January 1943 by summoning every *Kommodore* in the Fighter Arm to a Berlin conference. These men were the cream of Fighter Arm leadership, and all of them were also successful aces. They carried within themselves a vast store of current knowledge about fighter operations. The conference was to pool this knowledge and experience, with cross-fertilization of ideas. New tactical insights and initiatives were expected to result.

For eight days the cadre of top-flight pilot-leaders conferred on weapons and tactics, further developments, results from test units, logistics, training, personnel, and the enemy. Each *Kommodore* gave a one-hour speech on the experiences and most important requirements of his *Geschwader*. With solidified morale, each left the gathering in a renewed understanding of his task, and with a grasp of the challenges faced by the Fighter Arm as a whole. Shorthand transcripts were made, and Galland had these typed and distributed to each *Geschwader* at the front.

On 21 January 1943, Allied leaders at the Casablanca Conference set up round-the-clock bombing of Germany. The Casablanca Directive issued by the Allied Combined Chiefs of Staff was to have a profound influence on the life and career of Adolf Galland. The objectives of British and American airpower based in Britain were broadly defined as:

1. Destruction of the German military, economic, and industrial systems.
2. Undermining the morale of the German people.

Primary target priorities were listed as U-boat building yards, aircraft plants, transportation, petroleum facilities, and other war industries. General Ira Eaker, the able commander of the 8th USAAF, made the main case for daylight bombing at the conference. Eaker converted Churchill to his views. RAF Bomber Command would henceforth raze German cities by night. Eaker's daylight heavies would wage the strategic bombing offensive. Galland's fighters were the main opposition.

Galland at his work in his headquarters in 1943. His staff was extremely loyal to him. Says one surviving member: "Three-quarters drunk, the Boss was still more efficient than anyone else!"

Serious discussion. General der Jagdflieger Adolf Galland, night fighter Werner Streib, aircraft designer and manufacturer Kurt Tank, and Colonel Hannes Trautloft, Galland's inspector of fighters on the Russian front. Kurt Tank's Focke-Wulf 190 was considered the best all-around fighter in WWII. 20,001 were produced.

German fighter wastage on the Southern Front by early 1943 far exceeded losses on the Channel Front or on the huge Eastern Front. In North Africa, Tunisia, and Sicily, JG-27, JG-53, and JG-77 struggled not only against overwhelming Allied air power but against the disintegration of the Axis African effort. Allied airpower grew continually in weight and expertise. Luftwaffe casualties rose proportionately. Galland regarded this wastage as futile. He favored saving irreplaceable pilots and crews for battles looming ahead.

Hitler persisted with his "victory-or-death" edicts. Every position was either lost or abandoned only at the last possible moment. Ground support equipment, spare parts, fuel, and other stores, as well as unserviceable aircraft, had to be blown up as the Germans fell back before Allied power. Their formations were therefore equipped over and over with new aircraft from Germany. The ⸝ilots fought to exhaustion. This high wastage gave no useful return.

On the Eastern Front, five *Geschwader* were strung out thinly from Norway and Finland to the Caucasus. With unimpaired morale and excellent leadership, they were able to provide local and temporary air superiority for the Army, like a fire brigade. They were less worrisome to Galland than the other fronts. Mediterranean demands had slowed the development of Eaker's 8th USAAF, but their experimentation with escorted daylight raids over France continued. Similar daylight raids on Germany were an inevitable extension of this beginning, unless it could be stopped. Galland's concerns grew as the American effort developed.

Sixty-eight American heavy bombers struck at the St. Nazaire U-boat pens on 3 January 1943. German fighters met them in force. Seven bombers were downed and 47 damaged. The Americans returned to their British bases with 70 men missing and killed. The *Luftwaffe* had inflicted 10 percent losses.

American leaders were bedeviled at this time by complex operational problems and decisions. General Eaker remained certain that B-17 Fortresses could fly unescorted in daylight in large formations. Eaker's boss and personal friend, General Carl "Tooey" Spaatz, was not so sure but he remained optimistic that American heavies could repel German fighter attack without relying on a fighter escort. The Battle of Britain had written the lesson in blood: *Daylight bombing operations require a fighter escort in the presence of an enemy fighter force.* General Jimmy Doolittle in North Africa had abundantly proved the value of his P-38 escort fighters in daylight bombing missions. Insufficient attention was paid to this experience, as ETO commanders grappled with their problems.

In January of 1943, the undetermined factor in the B-17 escort question was the self-defensive power of these aircraft. Never before had there been such strongly armed bombers. Operational experience gained with lightly armed British and German bombers in prior battles might not be valid for American B-17 formations carrying many hundreds of guns. (War's crucible would soon boil away any theoretical falsehoods.)

Galland's brother Wutz was among the German pilots notably successful in downing the B-17 with a head-on attack. The forward-firing hemisphere of the B-17 was a relatively weak spot, but attacking fighters had to face a daunting hail of tracers on every pass. Skill, daring, and success in such attacks won for Wutz Galland the command of II/JG-26. His famous brother sent him written counsel on 17 January 1943, along with his congratulations.

Dear Wutz,

I was very pleased with your letter and your attitude towards your new task. My congratulations on your promotion and appointment.

. . . . here are a few more hints. At the beginning, everybody will now look more or less critically at your efficiency as a *Gruppenkommandeur*. I urge you to work like a lion for your *Gruppe*. The last man must feel that there is a leader in charge, and then they will go through the fire for you.

Regard nothing as self-evident or as running by itself. Everything has to be checked and rechecked. You must work for every success. How much a man can endure you cannot foresee, but let there not be a failure that could have been prevented by better planning, clearer orders, or more accurate execution.

It is not advisable to be on intimate terms with your squadron commanders or other officers. By avoiding such intimacy you can be their best comrade. This does not mean you cease caring. The NCOs and ground crews show full gratitude for the presence of a gulf. The highest principle to seek is for them to say among themselves, "Our C.O. knows the worries and needs of the last man. He is accessible to everybody. What he demands is necessary and he never demands more than he is willing to do himself at any time."

Now one more word about your new *Kommodore*. There is only one acceptable attitude, and that is to be a faithful and sincere follower of your *Kommodore*, as nothing will work without this. He is responsible for everything. He can lead efficiently only when he can count on every *Gruppenkommandeur*. The alternative is that the whole *Geschwader* will fail.

The parliamentary system of leadership, with its free and wild criticism, is a thing of the past. There is only one conception—that of the *Kommodore*. Then the entire *Geschwader* acts in unity. JG-26 fought for its reputation under my leadership, and my wish is that its reputation would continue to grow.

Now you know clearly what I expect from you. Any time, you can count on my advice and help. I wish you complete success in your new military position, and I know that you will make it. Good luck.

A. G.

The USAAF took its losses in the feeling-out period of 1942 and early 1943. Faith in its heavy bombers was resolute. On 27 January 1943, it finally struck at Germany by day. At Wilhelmshaven in an unescorted raid, 53 USAAF heavies raided U-boat facilities and lost only 3 aircraft. This opened a new phase of the air war.

Hitler promptly summoned Galland to the Wolf's Lair. Heavy pressure was on the *Fuehrer* at this time. A near-rout in North Africa and a national tragedy at Stalingrad were happening simultaneously. American unescorted bombers over the *Reich* in daylight made everything even worse. Galland was asked what it would take to stop these raids completely. He replied that the *Luftwaffe* Day Fighter Force would have to be substantially enlarged.

"Enlarged how much?" the *Fuehrer* demanded. "How many? Must you outnumber the enemy?"

Galland had already studied the problem, convinced that the Western air offensive was the major threat to Germany's war potential.

"For each unescorted enemy bomber, sir, I will need three or four single-engined fighters airborne."

"And if you had such a number of machines available, what results can I expect?"

"The daylight raids will be stopped, based upon losses unbearable to the enemy."

Galland threw another factor into the equation without being invited.

"When the American bombers come escorted by fighters, sir, I will need in addition one single-engined fighter airborne for each enemy fighter."

Hitler's face darkened. "The question of enemy fighter escort over the *Reich* does not arise," said the *Fuehrer* harshly. "*Reich* Marshal Goering has assured me that it is not technically possible to build such fighter planes."

Galland was thereupon dismissed.

Events in the next two years would verify the general validity of Galland's estimates in this conversation with Hitler. Galland's evaluations took no account of the later advent of radar bombing, which he did not foresee. He did not allow, furthermore, for the significant deterioration of *Luftwaffe* pilot training or for the fuel shortage that was later consequent to U.S. strategic bombing.

Had such forces as Galland specified to Hitler in February of 1943 been available to him even by mid-year, there is the highest probability that daylight bombing of Germany would have been made too expensive for the Americans to sustain. The 8th USAAF command was deeply concerned about casualties and aircraft losses, in what was a highly uncertain time for them. In the spring of 1943, proper defensive and escort tactics had not yet been developed by 8th USAAF Fighter Command. Large-scale *Luftwaffe* fighter defense of the *Reich* might well have changed Allied minds about daylight strategic bombing.

Goering's assurance to Hitler that no long-range fighter could be built to penetrate German airspace was a serious error. The *Reich* Marshal made many other mistakes in this period through incompetence. As Milch boosted fighter production, Goering dispersed hundreds of these vital new aircraft to units outside the Fighter Arm. Fighters were issued to *Jabo* units for long-range but inconsequential operations against shipping on the Channel Front, and into the Bay of Biscay. More fighters went to reconnaissance units in Russia. Still more were issued to the Ground Attack Arm. All these operations were essential in their own way, but they consumed FW-190s and Me-109s crucially required for the air superiority task over Germany.

Despite Milch's feat of 7,600 fighters produced in the first eight months of 1943, Galland therefore found himself minus the forces necessary to counter the daylight threat at its inception. Goering had created these numerical deficiencies through his own misassignment of aircraft. He tried now to compensate through greater utilization of existing fighter aircraft in Germany.

Drop tanks for Me-109s and FW-190s on the Channel Front increased their flying time to two hours. They still had difficulty climbing to combat altitude after scrambling, in time to intercept the enemy. Goering devised a way of further increasing endurance, against Galland's strongest opposition.

The *Reich* Marshal ordered that no fighter was to jettison its drop tanks until actually hit by enemy fire. Goering's anxieties over the political consequences for him of daylight raids over Germany were considerable. This induced him to issue such an inhuman and stupid order. Mistrust between the fighting pilots and their Supreme Commander resulted from this and other erroneous decisions. When reports came in that fine young pilots had been blown to bits or incinerated in mid-air when their drop tanks exploded, a shaken Goering withdrew his order.

Galland discharged fully his responsibility to warn about the daylight aerial menace from the West with Goering and others in high posts. When Armaments and War Production Minister Albert Speer asked him about possible daylight bombing of the Ruhr, Galland told him the truth. Such strikes could be expected, and soon. When Speer later voiced his concern about such attacks on war production, Goering was furious. Sending for Galland, he ordered him not to further discuss the matter with Speer or anyone else. Daylight bombing was a political nightmare for Goering. He tried to order this nightmare to vanish.

In a further effort to increase the fighters available in daytime, German night fighters were pressed into daylight service. Equipped mostly with heavier armament, and with longer endurance, these night fighters provided a supplement for the single-engined day fighters—in theory. Normal night fighter operations saw them working singly, directed by their radar controller on the ground. Assignment of these crews to the daytime melees proved disastrous.

Night fighter crews were not used to operating in formation or to launching concentrated attacks. Out of their element, they suffered heavy losses from the American defensive fire. They were no match for the nimbler U.S. fighter escorts, wherever such fighters appeared. This abortive effort by the High Command to boost Germany's day fighter defense destroyed many well-trained and successful night fighter crews. Each such crew had required many hours on night operations together to become effective.

The night fighter force viewed daytime operations with disfavor. Although such operations were an official order, night fighter units were instructed by their own command not to send top-flight crews to day operations. The High Command began backing down by ordering day-employed night fighters to attack only those bombers that were separated from their formations. (The costly misuse of the night fighters in daytime was eventually halted.)

March of 1943 saw the enactment of the final scenes in the Stalingrad disaster. Despite the pressure of events in his own sphere, Galland experienced personal depression at the catastrophic loss of the German Sixth Army. Goering's precipitate undertaking to supply the Sixth Army by air had been a key factor in the disaster. Hard on the heels of Stalingrad came the moment of truth in Tunisia. Again Galland went winging southward for a personal evaluation of the growing shambles.

JG-27 and JG-53 had been ground down in Tunisia to impotency. They were hard pressed just to stay alive. Even local and temporary air superiority for Axis rearguard actions was beyond their power. Like any army without air cover, the *Afrika Korps* was doomed—pushed, rolled, and bludgeoned back by swarms of Allied aircraft and the armies they protected.

Right before Galland's eyes now was the disaster scenario he had drawn for Goering and the High Command from Fuka, a bare six months previously. Skinny, half-starved, nervous pilots tried to recount their haunted existence aloft, their words drowned out by the roar of Allied bombers overhead. Worried, driven, fighter leaders, with worn-out and battered aircraft, harassed by lack of fuel and supplies, told him of air superiority gone with the wind and enemy air supremacy in its place. For his prediction of these conditions, Galland had been castigated for the sharp and pessimistic tone of his report.

Galland was pained and embarrassed, as a general standing before old comrades, not to have the power to order them out of North Africa immediately. Sicily would provide at least temporary sanctuary. Orders had to come from Berlin to save these men. No retreats were permitted.

Evacuation orders finally came at the absolute end in Tunisia. Surviving German pilots ferried out their own ground crews, somehow stuffing two men into the slender tail sections of their Me-109s and three men into the FW-190s. Pilots made repeated ferry flights to get the ground crews out, exemplifying the bond between pilots and crews in the Fighter Arm. Taking off in the face of such enemy air supremacy was in itself a gamble.

General von Arnim surrendered what was left of the *Afrika Korps* on 7 May 1943, after Hitler had again tried to supply a beleaguered army by air. Allied aircraft shot down scores of German transports like ducks in a gallery. Through *Ultra* decrypts, Allied air forces were supplied with the German air transport operating schedules, with fearful subsequent carnage.

After the Tunisian surrender, Galland was given his second operational command as a general. Goering put him in personal charge of the remaining German fighters based in Sicily. This proved to be a hectic high-pressure assignment, as Allied aircraft bombed and strafed German airfields in Sicily relentlessly.

With their best ground equipment lost in Africa and not replaced, the *Luftwaffe* fighters in Sicily had their backs to the wall. Commanding successively from Trapani, Comiso, and Catania, Galland used every ounce of his experience to keep his small force operating and inflicting losses on the Allies. More aircraft might well have been available to him had Hitler not been hoaxed by British deception teams into reinforcing Sardinia and Greece at the expense of Sicily.

The story of "Major Martin," the celebrated "Man Who Never Was" has become well-known since the war. The British planted fake high-level dispatches on a corpse dressed as a Royal Marine major. They dropped the body in known ocean currents so it would wash ashore near Huelva in Spain. Fake dispatches to General Alexander and to Admiral Cunningham identified Sardinia and Greece as Allied invasion sites.

When this was buttressed by other deception stratagems, Hitler was convinced. His directive of 12 May 1943 deemphasized Sicily and ordered that measures for Sardinia and the Peloponese Islands take top priority. *Panzer* divisions were switched from France to Greece and even from Russia to Greece. Sardinia was reinforced. The 400-odd *Luftwaffe* aircraft in Sicily after the African surrender were in the right strategic and tactical place. Only 125 *Luftwaffe* aircraft were in Greece and Crete. When Hitler finished his changes, there were fewer than 300 aircraft in Sicily and more than 300 in Greece and Crete. That is one reason why Galland found himself with such slender resources in Sicily.

A graphic account of *Luftwaffe* fighter travails in Sicily appears in Johannes Steinhoff's *Straits of Messina,* published by Andre Deutsch of London in 1971. Steinhoff gives sensitive insight into the pressures on Galland at this time. Steinhoff recounts how the young general's burdens are increased by an irrational telex from Goering. Referring to a recent unsuccessful fighter attack on bombers in the Straits of Messina, Goering orders that one pilot from each participating *Gruppe* is to be tried by court martial for cowardice in the face of the enemy.

This notorious order was never carried out, but it was devastating to the morale of the spent young pilots who had just escaped the African collapse. Galland had to maintain the appearance of loyalty to his commander-in-chief, despite deep personal revulsion at the order. He sought to mollify the angry young Steinhoff by assuring him that the *Reich* Marshal "didn't really mean" the order. While Galland's personal sympathies were with the pilots, he made it clear to Steinhoff that he was first of all a general with a job to do. He laid down the law to Steinhoff about the need to tackle the B-17s head on, and to get in close before firing.

"As he spoke," says Steinhoff, "he transferred his black cigar from one corner of his mouth to the other, and looked at me in an unfriendly manner."

No generalship on the spot, or spiteful reprisals from Berlin, could change the facts in Sicily. Overwhelming Allied air power was concentrated on the island with the inevitable result. Once more the remnants of the Fighter Arm crammed their ground crews into the tail sections of their fighters. Leaving everything behind, they withdrew to Viterbo, in Italy. Permission to leave came only at the last hour.

Within 24 hours of this desperate withdrawal, the German command was ordering the exhausted fighters from Sicily back into the air from their new Italian base. The USAAF intervened. A massive American bombing strike targeted on the fugitive *Luftwaffe* units sent their aircraft up in smoke at Viterbo. (The Mediterranean thereafter declined steadily in importance as a sphere of Fighter Arm engagement.)

As Goering in 1943 began taking more and more pressure from Hitler, he steadily sought to shift the blame for *Luftwaffe* failures onto ordinary combat fighter pilots. (The court martial order to Sicily is a case in point.) Goering's response to Hitler's increasingly bitter reproaches about the *Luftwaffe* was, essentially, "I am not responsible. Failures are due to the pussyfoot fighter pilots."

At a 1943 conference of Fighter Division and Air District (*Luftgau*) leaders in Schleissheim, the *Reich* Marshal decided to pass on some of the heat that Hitler had been turning on him. Galland was present. Goering's opening speech referred to the Battle of Britain, but he did not deal with the consequences of his own command meddling. He warmed to the theme of fighter pilots' failings— and their frauds.

"Then there are those Battle of Britain heroes in the Fighter Arm," said Goering, "who lied in mutual support of each other's victories—false victories— so that they could get the Knight's Cross."

Galland saw red. He wanted to hurl himself at Goering, to grab him by the throat, but instead his hands went to his own. Tearing off his Knight's Cross with its Oak Leaves, Swords, and Diamonds—Germany's highest award for valor—he slammed it down resoundingly on the table in front of Goering. Galland said nothing. His action said everything. His hunter's eyes bored into Goering's eyes. Total silence reigned in the room.

Rarely at a loss for words, the *Reich* Marshal was clearly flustered by Galland's action. He resumed haltingly, his criticisms markedly toned down. Many other fighter pilots present wanted to take off their decorations in protest and in solidarity with Galland. He would not allow this. More fighter pilots volunteered this same protest when word of the incident spread to the combat units. Galland denied them permission.

He made his own removal of the Knight's Cross an enduring symbol. Even though Goering later apologized for his remarks, the General of the Fighter Arm did not wear his Knight's Cross again for at least six months. (Photographs in this book taken during this period show that the decoration is missing from his throat. Hitler eventually noticed its absence and inquired through his *Luftwaffe* aide why General Galland was not wearing his decorations. Galland was not known as the *enfant terrible* of the *Luftwaffe* for nothing.)

His presence as an operational commander in Sicily could not make a difference to the outcome. No commander with a gross inferiority of force ever prevailed in a battle of attrition. As crisis piled upon crisis in the air war, the young General of the Fighter Arm still felt that he knew what must be done to protect his country. His homeland and his people had to be shielded somehow from the kind of aerial flail he had seen wielded in North Africa and Sicily. Everything possible had to be done to diminish their coming ordeal by fire. He returned to Germany with hardened resolve. A bloody summer lay ahead.

CHAPTER NINETEEN

Galland kept pressing in 1943 for timely and vigorous fighter action against the menace of American daylight bombing. Goering and the *Luftwaffe* High Command, including Jeschonnek, continued to discount the danger. High officers cited the *Luftwaffe*'s daylight bombing failure over Britain and asserted that the Americans would fare no better in attacking Germany. Galland, by contrast, saw the center of gravity of the entire air war inexorably moving towards German skies. If this process were not checked, measureless ruin lay ahead for Germany.

Galland's untiring theme in 1943 was strong and rapid reinforcement of the Western Front fighter forces. Only by this means could unacceptable losses be inflicted on the Americans at the outset of their strategic offensive. Aborting the U.S. effort was preferable to tackling it when fully developed. Such a Frankenstein should be strangled at birth.

Galland's analysis appears strikingly prescient from the perspective of more than four decades, especially considering that the travails of his American foes in the spring of 1943 were unknown to him. Nobody in the USAAF then knew with certainty the practical methods of successfully operating strategic bombers in daylight. War games and doctrine were one thing. Real war was something else. Massive and immediate fighter opposition by the *Luftwaffe* could well have decided the issue against daylight bombing.

Pressure remained strong at the highest Allied political and command levels against the strategic daylight bombing program. Skepticism and resistance continued despite the temporary agreements reached at Casablanca in January of 1943. Breaking-in was therefore not confined to bomber crews gaining combat experience but extended to the highest levels of leadership. At stake was a doctrinal principle dear to the hearts of American high commanders: B-17s and B-24s could penetrate German skies in daylight unescorted.

Study of correspondence and official reports of this period, containing the contemporary thinking of such famous generals as Eaker, Spaatz, Arnold, Stratemeyer, Anderson, and Hunter, conveys dramatically the numerous imponderables that haunted the American command. Chief among these unknowns, and the factor involving the greatest apprehension, was the potential power of *Luftwaffe* fighters to make daylight bombing too expensive. Galland thus was right at the heart of the problem with his recommendations for urgent Western Front fighter reinforcement.

Had the early operations of USAAF heavies encountered opposition from four or five *Geschwader* of Galland's fighters, instead of half that number, there can be little doubt that their losses would have been severe. This was the program being urged on his superiors by Galland. Given the circumstances and the psychological climate, a fair supposition is that the Allied air offensive would have become exclusively a night operation. Fortunately for the Allies, Galland's recommendations were not followed. Hundreds of German fighters were instead consumed in the maw of the Mediterranean war, where overwhelming Allied air power was already decisive. Only after the Hamburg fire raids in late July did Goering and the High Command recognize fully the aerial threat from the West.

American air leaders clung strongly to the hope that their heavy bombers could fly missions into Germany minus escort, and with bearable losses. These hopes still were held as late as May of 1943. No official requirement or specifications for a long-range escort fighter had yet been developed by the USAAF. The confrontation between *Luftwaffe* fighters and U.S. heavy bombers on their first unescorted strikes into Germany became known in the 8th USAAF as "The Bloody Summer."

The shape of things to come was emergent in the first week of May. On 4 May 1943, a force of 65 American heavies attacked Antwerp in Belgium, with Ford and General Motors plants as their targets. P-47 Thunderbolt fighters, minus belly tanks, could accompany the bombers for only 175 miles. Aided by a diversionary USAAF thrust at the French coast, which drew more than 100 German fighters onto itself, the Antwerp mission was a success. Fighter escort and diversionary tactics resulted in a mission without a single aircraft missing. The Americans were elated.

Three days later the battle pendulum swung to the *Luftwaffe*. German fighters shot down 7 of a force of 31 U.S. heavies that were raiding St. Nazaire. Unescorted Fortresses and Liberators began more frequent sallies into Germany itself. Raids on Kiel by 126 heavies on 14 May and by 102 heavies on 19 May saw the USAAF lose a total of only 14 bombers in both operations. Yet when the Americans returned to Kiel on 13 June with an even heavier force of 182 bombers, the *Luftwaffe* clawed down 26 American aircraft—a U.S. loss rate that could not be consistently borne.

On 18 May 1943, the Allied Combined Bomber Offensive plan for *round-the-clock bombing* of Germany was approved by the Combined Chiefs of Staff. Eaker's 8th USAAF was now formally authorized to proceed with the strategic

Party officials at Rechlin. Galland, center, with Minister of Armaments and Production Albert Speer at his elbow, conducts a visit of Nazi Party officials at the Rechlin Test Center.

The airplane that changed the art of flying! This is the Messerschmitt Me-262, one of Galland's JV44 jet fighters, in 1945.

Serious discussion about the Me-262 jets. Colonel Edgar Petersen, Commander of the test center at Rechlin, and Generalmajor Galland ponder Hitler's decision and order that the Me-262 would be used only as a bomber.

Serious times. Col. Nicolaus von Below, General Adolf Galland and Col. Hannes Trautloft stop by Göring's famed Karinhall enroute to a command appearance with Hitler. The facial expressions tell the whole story.

offensive against key targets. Galland may well have gained some grim satisfaction from the projected program had he been able to study its detail. Listed as the top priority objective: destruction of the *Luftwaffe* Fighter Arm.

On 29 May 1943, the Americans put their first YB-40s—converted B-17s—into battle, in an interim effort to solve the escort problem. The YB-40s—heavily armored B-17s with increased firepower and loaded with additional ammunition instead of bombs—were an operational failure. Too heavy and too slow to keep up with a B-17 formation, their local increase in firepower did not compensate for their drawbacks. B-17s in formation did better without them. At about the time of the YB-40 experiments, some of the intercepting FW-190 fighters began mounting 30mm cannons. Their attacks were devastating.

By mid-June, the Allies were convinced that the *Luftwaffe* Fighter Arm had to be conquered or the strategic bombing program would not succeed. Since most major strategic targets lay beyond the reach of fighter escort, even with belly tanks, past mistakes and oversights caught up with the American High Command. A long-range escort fighter became absolutely essential. A technical miracle was needed.

General Henry "Hap" Arnold had initiated an all-out program by 28 June 1943 to produce escort fighters for all U.S. bombers operating from England over Germany, and later from Italy. Industry was to "start from scratch" if need be. Arnold cared not how the job was done, as long as he got the aircraft. President Roosevelt backed him. (The evidence is historically clear that the *Luftwaffe* fighter defense forced a massive technical development program on the USAAF. This requirement had not been foreseen, and this was understandable. Most aeronautical engineers regarded such a long-range fighter as beyond existing technical capabilities. Goering had reported in this vein to Hitler. The superb P-51 Mustang resulted from this crash development program.)

Germany was still technologically ahead of the United States in mid-1943. Amid the intensifying battles with the American heavy bombers, Galland got a clear look at what the *Luftwaffe* Fighter Arm's future might hold. On 22 May 1943, he was invited to fly a prototype of Willy Messerschmitt's Me-262 twin-jet fighter. This was an unforgettable moment for the General of the Fighter Arm, militarily, technically, and emotionally.

Galland had advocated jet fighter development from the time he was first apprised of this new propulsion method in December of 1941. A jet-propelled "speed bomber" was discussed at the first procurement and supply conference he had attended, at the invitation of Erhard Milch, early in 1942. The young leader immediately recommended that fighter aircraft should be included in jet development. Emphasizing the vast resources of the Americans, he pointed out the existing urgent need for a superior fighter to offset expected Allied progress in both performance and numbers.

Messerschmitt agreed with these views. He sought permission to build some jet fighters as well as speed bombers. Galland henceforth hung on to his vision of operational jet fighters like a bulldog. He was willing to risk his career for the sake of getting his pilots a superior weapon. (Hard-driving Karl-Otto Saur, Albert Speer's deputy, would later call Galland "the father of the Me-262." There may well never have been an Me-262 jet fighter in combat had it not been for Galland's relentless determination.)

At Lechfeld on 22 May 1943, Galland lowered himself into the unfamiliar cockpit of the sleek propellerless aircraft. He watched with intense interest as the ground crew started one turbine. When they tried the other turbine, it burst into flames, a typical reaction with the immature Jumo 004 jet engines. Like any good combat pilot, Galland was out of the aircraft instantly, and heading for the second prototype. This machine was being held in readiness against technical failure in the first aircraft.

Taking off in the prototype Me-262 was a hair-raising experience. With no tricycle landing gear, Galland found himself tilted back at a fairly alarming angle, almost like a man awaiting a shave in a barber's chair. He had no forward vision. Whizzing down the 150-foot wide Lechfeld runway, he kept the strange aircraft on the concrete with feather-touches on the brakes, all the while turning his head from side to side. As he came up to 80 mph, the tail of the jet had not lifted. How much more runway was left? Touching the brakes with hardly enough pressure to break an egg, he brought the tail up. (Forty years later he would tell lecture audiences in America: "I think it is a good thing that we don't have to do this with our commercial airliners today.")

Once the tail came up, the speed of the jet rose rapidly. At 120 mph the former Gelsenkirchen Soaring Club pilot was not only airborne but entering a new epoch. Thrust from the jet engines gave the sensation of being pushed, with a smoothness and quiet that were incredible after the racket, vibration, and torque of a piston-engined fighter. The Me-262 whistled through the air. ("It felt as though angels were pushing" was how he later described the sensation of his first jet flight.)

Since the flight was not a joyride but an evaluation of a prototype by the General of the Fighters, Galland probed the Me-262's flying characteristics with his veteran's skill. With a level-flight speed of 520 mph, the aircraft handled smoothly and the controls were well-harmonized. Professor Messerschmitt had also come a long way since sailplane days on the Wasserkuppe. His design skills had been carried into a new era. The Me-262 was sensational.

During this test flight with the Me-262 V 4, the Me-264 *Amerika-Bomber* ultra-long-range prototype happened to pass over Lechfeld. Mentally substituting a B-17 for the friendly four-engined bomber, Galland made a mock attack. The speed and flying qualities of the Me-262, combined with the heavy armament that it had the power to carry, clearly would make it a formidable opponent for four-engined bomber and piston-powered fighter alike. Knowing how the Fighter Arm was having its back pressed to the wall, Galland rejoiced at the new tactical possibilities opened by the jet. Here in his hands was the sorely needed technical quantum jump.

When the sounds of the turbines died away back on the apron at Lechfeld,

Galland hoisted himself out of the Me-262 in high excitement. Enthusiasm largely purged out of him by the Fighter Arm's many reverses and his own battles with Goering had returned with a rush. The Me-262 could give back air superiority to his pilots, if it were mass produced without delay.

Three days later, Galland reported on the Me-262 to Field Marshal Milch, head of development and procurement:

1. This model is a tremendous stroke of luck for us; it puts us way out in front, provided the enemy continues to use piston engines.
2. As far as I could tell, the fuselage appears to be entirely satisfactory.
3. The engines are everything that has been claimed for them, except for their performance during take-off and landing.
4. The aircraft opens up entirely new possibilities as far as tactics are concerned.

Galland further recommended that production of the Me-209, a projected successor to the Me-109, be dropped. Professor Messerschmitt was nevertheless determined to make his Me-209 a success, despite predicted inferior performance to allied fighters, and since he had not yet been ordered to give the Me-262 priority. The jet had long languished in the background. Galland recommended limiting single-engined fighter production to the FW-190D and turning the productive capacity thereby released to mass production of the Me-262. Galland also insisted on some important design changes, including a tricycle landing gear for the Me-262.

A proposal was developed to reduce drastically the time needed to get the Me-262 into mass production: 100 Me-262s would be put into series production immediately. These aircraft would be put through tactical and technical tests simultaneously. This unorthodox approach would allow test results to be incorporated into the aircraft as engineering change proposals, before mass production. Goering and Milch both approved, carried along by Galland's enthusiasm—and prodded as well by the American daylight offensive.

Galland's enthusiasm increased. Suddenly all significant persons for once were in accord. Goering had only to get Hitler's approval and the two sleek silver arrows at Lechfeld would soon be joined by 100 more. Hitler crushed this bold idea immediately.

Claiming numerous disappointments at the hands of the *Luftwaffe*, Hitler cited the still unavailable He-177 four-engined bomber as an example of Goering's unfulfilled promises. Due to the He-177 and other *Luftwaffe* derelictions, Hitler was adamant that the Me-262 was not going to be rushed. Calling a conference with Messerschmitt and the responsible officials who had assembled the all-out Me-262 proposal, Hitler overruled everyone. Talking them all down, Hitler climaxed the conference with an order expressly forbidding mass production. Only tests with a few prototypes were permitted.

Galland was not invited to this conference. The only *Luftwaffe* officer present was Goering. Hitler's mistrust of the *Reich* Marshal was now well-known to all who moved in high circles.

All this transpired just as the Americans were driven by events and experience to develop their long-range escort fighter. They had made their mistakes and errors just like the Germans. The Americans recognized their mistakes in timely fashion and took action. What a contrast appears between the reactions to crisis by the German and American leaderships. Hitler's exaggerated caution again wasted six crucial months in the final development of the Me-262. During those same months, the P-51 learned to fly all the way into German skies. The Me-262 was not aloft to deny air superiority to the Anglo-American fighter. This was a bitter cup for Galland and the Fighter Arm to drain.

Milch agreed personally with Galland's urgent desire to mass produce the Me-262 as rapidly as possible. Milch's position unfortunately was deteriorating. He was often another Goering scapegoat. Milch could not afford a major rift with the *Fuehrer*. He therefore followed Hitler's orders for limited Me-262 development. Milch's 17 August 1943 announcement of 4,000 fighters per month as the new production target accordingly specified only existing piston-powered types.

Galland demanded that 1,000 of these fighters be Me-262s. Milch turned him down, emphasizing that other developments could not be halted or postponed for the sake of the Me-262. Milch also said that he was obeying Hitler's order for caution on the Me-262 as one a soldier should obey. Galland could not influence Milch's stance but hoped that the *Generalluftzeugmeister* might throw his weight behind the Me-262 later on.

The young general felt that the wonder weapon was slipping from his grasp, even as airborne terror and torment of the civil population increased. Many weeks had passed since his first jet flight, and the project was virtually paralyzed. Galland found himself thinking that refusal to force through the Me-262 bordered on criminal negligence by Germany's leaders.

Galland's forecast of daylight bombing strikes against Ruhr industry came true on 22 June 1943—182 USAAF heavies ran the *Luftwaffe* fighter gauntlet to bomb chemical and synthetic rubber plants at Hüls. By early July, the Americans were able to launch over 200 four-engined bombers in daylight operations, despite significant losses to German fighter action.

Galland foresaw that shortly 300, 500, and 700 heavies would be launched on daylight strikes against Germany. He pressed for strong and centralized fighter defense, for concentration, as opposed to the dispersal of fighter units ordered by Goering and the Operations Staff. Centralized defense meant maximized attacking power for the Fighter Arm, with superior ground control and improved logistics. Goering clung to the politically desirable idea of stopping bombers before they reached German territory. Such peripheral defense could not be other than weak, since available fighters were geographically dispersed.

The first three weeks of July 1943 were marked by only a few daylight strikes by the USAAF into northwestern Germany. This lull portended a storm, the fiercest in military history up to that time. On the night of 24/25 July 1943, Air Marshal Arthur Harris of Bomber Command launched Operation "Gomorrah" against Hamburg. Four tremendous RAF blows were struck at night, ending on 4 August 1943, which destroyed half the city and killed more than 50,000 civilians. Over 9,000 tons of bombs were dropped. USAAF heavies provided daylight counterpoint with raids on 25 and 26 July as part of the operation.

On the night of 24/25 July, 728 RAF bombers reached Hamburg, after blinding both ground and airborne German radar by dropping "chaff" at intervals during their approach. Chaff was the British counterpart of German *Düppel*, strips of tinfoil cut to the wavelengths of enemy radar. These foil strips returned radar echoes out of all proportion to their physical size. Fighter control data were totally corrupted. Since the same data were used by the German flak, Hamburg's hundreds of antiaircraft guns lost their electronic guidance.

As a consequence, the first raid on Hamburg resulted in heavy destruction and in minimal losses for the RAF. The second raid two nights later ignited a firestorm in the city that was to eclipse every prior entry in the index of man's inhumanity to man. Scores of adjacent fires united into a mighty, roaring holocaust that became self-sustaining. Rising superheated air triggered volcanic updrafts, and, as surrounding ground-level air rushed into the void, the flames were stoked to blowtorch intensity—and beyond.

Thousands of human beings were instantaneously incinerated in the firestorm, many of them sucked bodily into the fire. Everything combustible in the firestorm area was ashed and everything noncombustible was melted. Entire blocks of houses and apartments were swallowed into the inferno, which seemed to take on a hideous life of its own. Temperatures far exceeding a thousand degrees Fahrenheit literally snuffed out the living. Hundreds of unfortunates who had sought sanctuary in Hamburg's underground air raid shelters were roasted to ash in these chambers. No such devastation, misery, and disaster had ever been inflicted on a city in the history of the world.

Hamburg's soul-searing horror spread to every corner of Germany, as refugees streamed out of the shambles. (Books have already been written detailing this nightmare catastrophe, and there is no place for that here. However, Hamburg was a national tragedy for Germany, and it had as an immediate consequence a galvanizing, unifying effect on the entire *Luftwaffe*.)

The fires of Hamburg melted the differences large and small between *Luftwaffe* leaders high and low. Borne in upon all of them, from Goering downward, was the *unthinkable yet undeniable probability of more such blows*. Action had to be taken, lest every large city in Germany be similarly laid in smouldering ruins.

Aside from surrender, only one rational response was possible: an aggressive defense of the *Reich* by a much more powerful Fighter Arm. Events had placed Galland at center stage in the *Luftwaffe* hierarchy. Dreams of vengeance raids on Britain, hopes for superweapons, ambitions for a massive Bomber Arm, all seemed to evaporate in the Hamburg holocaust. Goering called a conference of *Luftwaffe* leaders in his office at Hitler's HQ at Rastenburg.

Almost the entire *Luftwaffe* pantheon was assembled. A chastened Jeschonnek was present with his many staff officers, convinced finally of the four-engined bombing threat from the West. Erhard Milch had been summoned. He and Galland had agreed all along for a strong homeland fighter defense. Colonel Dietrich Peltz, General of the Bomber Arm and a Goering favorite, sat with others of the *Reich* Marshal's "brain trust," all of them now serious and silent. Generals Weise, von Axthelm, Kammhuber, and Martini and numerous other important commanders attended this post-Hamburg conference.

Turning the *Luftwaffe* to the defense of the German homeland became the unanimous spirit of the conference. Goering summarized by stressing that there must never be another Hamburg in the life of the German people. A defensive role for the *Luftwaffe* was now essential to maintain the national war potential. Goering for once had united the entire *Luftwaffe* hierarchy, aided by the Hamburg holocaust. Galland's hopes soared as Goering strode buoyantly away to the nearby *Führerbunker* for Hitler's approval of the new priorities. Top priority was regaining air superiority over the *Reich*.

When Goering returned from the *Fuehrer*, he walked wordlessly right through the room, staring straight ahead like a zombie. Entering an adjacent room, Goering closed the door, symbolizing what had happened. Hitler had closed the door on any new priorities.

Summoned to Goering soon afterwards, Galland and Peltz found the *Reich* Marshal sobbing uncontrollably. Head down on his arms on the desk top, Goering was an embarrassing and pitiful figure. Hitler had reacted with rage to his proposal to switch the *Luftwaffe* to a defensive role. The *Fuehrer* would allow no defense except attack. British terror would be met by *Luftwaffe* terror. A new bombing force was to be assembled and sent against England in retaliation—a deterrent to future Hamburgs. Emerging from his tears, Goering appointed Peltz as "Assault Leader against England," and terminated the interview.

Galland's brain reeled. His personal options swam through his head amid the bizarre unreality of it all. Should he quit? He told himself he ought to get out. Nothing useful could be accomplished without air superiority. That was the only sane strategy. The Fighter Arm had become the key to survival. He decided to keep his job, believing that Hitler could not make such a decision irrevocably. His duty in the meantime was to give his all to the defense of Germany.

A timely counterblow against the night bombing was struck by Major Hajo Herrmann, who had advocated for some time the use of single-engined fighters at night in flak-free zones over German cities. These aircraft could be guided to their targets visually, since RAF bombers could be held in searchlight crossbeams for long periods. Herrmann's "Wild Boar" night fighter tactics bridged a serious gap in Germany's night defenses, until German radar experts could counter Allied use of chaff. Favorable weather conditions were necessary for the Wild Boar, but it was summer and many nights were clear enough for Herrmann's operations.

Bomber expert Colonel Viktor von Lossberg also convinced the High Command at this time that night fighters could infiltrate British bomber streams, both coming and going, and inflict serious losses. Like the Wild Boar tactics over lighted cities, von Lossberg's infiltration attacks would depend upon direct visual sightings by night fighter crews. Wild Boar and infiltration tactics permitted partial recovery of the night defenses, pending development of radar countermeasures.

General Kammhuber's night fighter empire was centered on the so-called Himmelbett tactics, in which a night fighter was directed by an individual radar controller in a given area. British bomber stream tactics and chaff had overrun Kammhuber's facilities. The night fighter boss nevertheless disagreed with both the Wild Boar and the infiltration tactics. Galland was grateful that he had not yet been charged with responsibility for the night fighters. He and Kammhuber did not get along.

German civilians by the 1943 summer had become resigned to night bombing attacks. They showed resilience similar to the Londoners of 1940. The sight of American bombers overhead in daylight exceeded civilian tolerance. This was an important morale factor added to the strategic impact of daylight pinpoint bombing.

Combating the USAAF in daylight remained Galland's major concern. The Americans kept pressing unescorted attacks into Germany. Goering's constant importunings to have German fighter pilots fly three missions a day bore fruit on 17 August 1943. A two-pronged assault was made by 315 Fortresses deep into the *Reich*. Schweinfurt's ball-bearing factories and the Messerschmitt factories at Regensburg were the targets. Schweinfurt I was about to enter the war's history as the scene of one of its most bloody and significant battles.

The Messerschmitt complex was heavily hit. More than 400 aircraft workers perished. Aerial photographs showed more than 80 hits on the Schweinfurt targets, but the Fighter Arm subjected the U.S. bombers to heavy punishment; 60 American bombers went down, with the loss of most of the 600 men in their crews. Over 100 other bombers suffered extensive battle damage and crew casualties; 17 Fortresses that made it back to England were damaged to the point of salvage.

Galland's reaction to Schweinfurt I had both personal and professional aspects. Downing 60 heavies in one day proved that strong persistent attacks by large fighter forces could inflict unbearable losses on the Americans. The numerical increase in fighters had been achieved at Schweinfurt by multiple missions, with fighter pilots operating to the limits of their endurance. Equivalent steady strength would require the provision of many more aircraft and pilots.

Across the Channel the Americans were licking their wounds. General Eaker was already hard pressed for trained crews. Schweinfurt put a large crimp in the expansion of 8th USAAF Bomber Command. (The record of these times in Eaker's correspondence and elsewhere testifies to the adverse effect of Schweinfurt I on American commanders: 60 heavies down in one day certainly impressed the surviving American crews. Galland's early advocacy of such heavy fighter attacks on the Americans stands historically vindicated.)

On a personal basis, Schweinfurt I on 17 August 1943 was to inject into Galland's life one of the worst personal tragedies he would suffer. His brother Wutz led II/JG-26 against the bombers on their way back from Schweinfurt. Having downed a B-17, Wutz was shot down by P-47s near St. Trond. The death of young Paul had been a bitter blow, but to lose Wutz as well was a tremendous hammer blow in the heart. Smiling, charming, happy Wutz would grace this world no more. Thunder in the air drowned out the agony in Adolf Galland's heart. He had to go on.

After the Regensburg strike, the 4th Bombardment Wing did not return to England but flew on in diminished strength to North Africa. This was another baleful development of the bloody summer—shuttle bombing. On 13 August 1943, four days prior to Schweinfurt I, the 9th USAAF in the Mediterranean sent 61 Liberators against the Messerschmitt factory at Wiener-Neustadt, attacking the *Reich* from the southeast. Surviving bombers from the Regensburg strike later flew from Italy back to their British bases, attacking U-boat facilities at Bordeaux en route. The Fighter Arm had now to contend with another extension of home defense.

Schweinfurt became the *bête noir* of the 8th USAAF. Even after the heavy crew and aircraft losses of the bloody summer, which sorely taxed Eaker's resources, the idea of unescorted deep penetrations into Germany did not die. On into the fall, the Americans clung to an idea whose time had gone. After further heavy losses in the first half of October, in attacking Bremen, Marienburg, Danzig, and Münster, Schweinfurt II taught the Americans their final bloody lesson.

On 14 October 1943, 229 heavies with nearly 200 escort fighters winged out of England for Schweinfurt. The fighters took the big bombers 240 miles and then turned back to the fuel pump. Shadowing the formation, the *Luftwaffe* had waited for this moment.

Before the target was reached, the *Luftwaffe* was driving home fighter attacks, initially in javelin formation, from both front and rear. Gaggles of 7 to 15 German fighters hacked away at the heavy bombers with rockets, cannons, and machine guns. Plunging down from near-vertical angles, other German fighters sought to eliminate the forward turrets of the Fortresses.

The Americans pressed on through the fighters and the flak to their targets at Schweinfurt, before heading back through more fiery harassment on the return route. As with Schweinfurt I, this raid saw 60 Fortresses downed, with the loss of 600 trained airmen.

In American war lore, the day would live forever as "Black Thursday." Black was appropriate, for it was also the death of unescorted daylight bombing over Germany. Galland's fighters had won that particular round, but on the Allied side there were positive effects. More energy than ever went into increasing the range of P-47 and P-38 fighters. Even more vigor was put behind the P-51 project. By December of 1943, P-51s were flying all the way to German targets with the American heavies.

From May of 1943, when he first flew the Me-262 jet, until Schweinfurt II in October, Galland had seen Germany's aerial fortunes drastically decline. The Me-262 had meanwhile languished—the proper technical counter to daylight bombing. Even while living through these events, the whole scenario had seemed to Galland like a nightmare from which he could not awaken. Forty years later, when all the involved and hidden aspects of Me-262 development could be examined in the cool of his evening, it would still seem no less of a nightmare. The real world had been more incredible than any dream.

CHAPTER TWENTY

While the Me-262 jet was by far the most promising fighter under development, there were other machines in the official program as improvements on the Me-109 and FW-190. These aircraft should have approached production about the time that the USAAF strategic bombing offensive gained momentum. A prime objective of the USAAF was to stop all German fighter production. Galland had these new fighters dangled in front of him for his hard-pressed pilots. Always they stayed just out of reach.

Dornier's Do-335 Arrow (*Pfeil*) was scheduled for production in the 1943 autumn. Galland intended to reequip the badly outclassed heavy fighter units with this promising 413 mph aircraft. Equipped with twin engines in "push-pull," one driving a tractor propellor in the nose and the other a pusher propeller in the tail, the Do-335 ran into delays. Complex technical problems arose from mutual interference between the propellers. All hope of prompt deliveries soon faded.

Similarly planned for assignment to the heavy fighter units was Professor Kurt Tank's twin-engined Focke-Wulf Ta-154 *Moskito,* a fast heavily armed response to the RAF Mosquito. Like the Mosquito, Tank's machine made extensive use of wood construction. Based on a German Air Ministry specification issued in September of 1942, the prototype was flying by July of 1943 but without likelihood of production before mid-1944. Planned as armament were 30mm MK 103 cannons, weapons with long range and flat trajectory, for downing American heavies from greater distances.

Development problems with engines and aircraft were endless. Deprived of performance improvements that could underpin new tactics, Galland had to soldier on with existing aircraft. The technical race with the Allies was lost before his eyes. The Me-262 jet therefore became a tantalizing vision of reasserted *Luftwaffe* air superiority. Failures, deficiencies, intrigue, and boondoggles abounded in the German aircraft industry. All this was made worse by round-the-clock bombing.

Professor Tank's Ta-152, the long-nosed variant of the FW-190, was another eagerly awaited fighter subject to frequent postponement. Professor Messerschmitt kept struggling to make his Me-209 into a worthwhile successor to the Me-109. He was unsuccessful, despite the commitment of huge resources. Messerschmitt's twin-engined Me-210 and Me-410 were descendants of the Me-110 heavy fighter concept. They were not successful combat aircraft. In daylight attacks against U.S. bomber formations, they had to be provided with a single-engined fighter escort.

Numerous variants of the main fighter types in service created operational problems that arrived frequently in Galland's office. During one period, the Me-109 was in squadron service with four variants and the FW-190 with five. Significant performance differences were thereby injected into each *Geschwader* nominally operating the same type of fighter. Combat regulations issued by Galland required that the fighters stay together. Performance gains in the superior fighter variants were thus virtually nullified, speed being held down to that of the poorest-performance aircraft. Logistical requirements increased with each fighter variant that entered operations.

When new fighter types failed to get into production, Galland began expediting armament improvements to increase combat performance. Downing bombers was the main task. Armament experts and innovators in the fighter units concentrated on improving firing power. Centrally mounted heavy-caliber weapons were favored. Wing-mounted heavy weapons degraded maneuverability. As U.S. fighters began penetrating deeper into Germany, maneuverability was vital in coping with the American escort.

Fuseless incendiary ammunition was copied by the Germans from captured American .50 caliber shells. Installation of the MG 151 20mm cannon on the Me-109 and FW-190, as standard armament from 1942 onward, had proved itself a sound step. The MG 151 was dependable, with higher muzzle velocity and rate of fire than the Oerlikon MG-FF 20mm cannon it replaced.

Neglect of airfield development in Germany in 1940–42 had serious consequences in 1943 as daylight bombing of the homeland intensified. Two operational missions a day, and pursuit of U.S. heavies, were scattering fighters far and wide. They were often landing far from their home bases and frequently came down on remote airstrips and improvised fields.

Fighters landing on isolated and unequipped airfields were completely out of the fight. When landing on the last of their fuel, such fighters were immobilized, unable to take off to the nearest fueling point. Galland tackled this problem with Air Fleet *Reich* and Fighter Corps I.

Concentrating on western Germany, Holland, Belgium, and northern France, the critical areas for fighters pursuing homebound U.S. heavies, Galland organized minibases. Facilities for rearming and refueling were established, along with an aerial situation room, refreshments, medical, and meteorological facilities. A telephone to the nearest Fighter Division HQ completed the arrangements. Galland issued regulations for the use of these minibases. Slowly the chaos and uncertainty that had surrounded these semiemergency landings were overcome.

Pilots from different units landing on the same field were placed under the command of the senior pilot present. This officer or NCO was required to lead his conglomerate formation back into the air against the bombers. Once aloft, their instructions were to tune in the *Reich* Fighter Frequency (*Reichsjägerwelle*), which broadcast a running commentary on aerial action over Germany.

The conglomerate formation would direct itself back into combat with the invaders by following the reported position, course, speed, and altitude of enemy formations. Second missions like this were successful as long as the pickup formations did not encounter strong American fighter opposition. In the ensuing battles, the unfamiliarity of the German pilots with their pickup leaders and wingmen was a handicap against the ordered opposition of the Americans. Cohesion and operating efficiency in a fighter unit stem from joint experience, mutual knowledge, and mutual confidence of the pilots.

As soon as the strength and range of the U.S. fighter escort increased, high losses resulted from second missions by conglomerate units. Galland knew why. He had personally built up efficiency as a leader from squadron to *Geschwader* level. He was not surprised when the Fighter Divisions began rebelling against High Command insistence on second missions in all circumstances. The Fighter Divisions ordered that second missions were only to be mounted when a worthwhile force of at least 20 fighters could be assembled.

Tactical development in 1943 required a lively mobility of mind, as well as experience, for the proper deployment of such tactics. Although forbidden to fly on operations, Galland had the trust and confidence of every significant combat leader in the Fighter Arm. They became his hands, feet, and eyes in the air, as various stratagems were devised and tested. They all knew also that their boss was making occasional clandestine missions to test his own regulations for attacking heavy bomber formations. Galland maintained touch with battle conditions by downing three Fortresses in 1943.

Shadowing aircraft were recommended by the young general for assignment to each incoming U.S. raid. The High Command approved. Twin-engined fighters with good fuel endurance were used. Reporting on the status of each bomber box, the shadowing aircraft detailed the bombers shot down or separated from the box. Running commentaries were provided by these *Fühlungshalter* on the effects of German fighter attacks, actions of the U.S. fighter escorts, and also on the state of the weather. Shadowing aircraft were effective until larger U.S. fighter formations started sweeps far ahead of and around the bombers. Heavy losses reduced the shadowing aircraft to a weather observation role by mid-1944.

This typified the tactical ebb and flow of the air war. A stratagem that worked well in the spring could be useless by mid-summer. An open mind was essential. Tactical rigidity quickly produced casualties and operational failures. In this spirit, Galland opposed High Command orders that German fighters were to attack bombers only. American fighters were to be ignored, unless the German fighters were themselves jumped by the escort.

German pilots were initially wary of the P-47s. When the Thunderbolts did not attack and clung close to the bombers, German fighters became more aggressive. Galland stated that attacks exclusively on the bombers would inevitably draw the P-47s out of their passive defense of the heavies. He emphasized that, once the Thunderbolts broke out of their defensive posture, they would develop a highly aggressive defense. As the high priest of aggressive defense himself, Galland implored the High Command not to provoke this change in American escort tactics. The High Command was not persuaded. The "bombers only" order stood.

As Galland had forecast, the American fighter pilots soon tumbled to the significance of their situation, when they found themselves ignored by the attackers. They began breaking out of their defensive posture and discarding their defensive frame of mind—the latter having been imposed on them by their orders. Protection of the bombers was paramount. In the USAAF in 1943, as in the *Luftwaffe* in 1940, bomber crews were reassured to see a "little friend" off their wingtip.

American fighters began tearing into the attacking Germans, who were hell-bent for the bombers in obedience to *their* orders. The Americans began taking the battle initiative away from the *Luftwaffe*. As Galland's warnings to the High Command had predicted, U.S. fighters were soon departing from close escort to hunt and pursue their foes. These actions frequently took German formations by surprise. *Luftwaffe* fighters often resorted to bolting when jumped.

Psychological ascendancy rapidly passed to the Americans, who were fresh and well trained. To Galland's mortification, German fighters went into the era of "split-S and dive away," as it was called. Friendly terrain was below. Many German pilots began diving for it as though it truly were Mother Earth, warm and safe. American fighters made it the reverse. All American fighters dived faster than German types, especially the Me-109, which, for structural reasons, was red-lined at about 375 mph in the dive. The Americans overhauled their diving opponents from astern and shot them to pieces.

This psychological malady among some German fighter pilots was called *Jägerschreck*—fear of fighters. Battle-hardened formations like JG-26 and JG-2 were not afflicted. Other units with large complements of young and inexperienced pilots became infected. In such formations, even some veteran leaders were temporary victims. Until the Fighter Arm snapped out of this embarrassing lapse, Goering had some justification for his vilification of the fighter pilots as cowards.

Jägerschreck was rooted in wrong tactics and showed how dangerous it was to have operational orders issued by officers who had never flown in modern fighter combat. A crisis of morale and severe losses resulted. Although the entire train of events was due to ignoring the tactical advice of the General of the Fighter Arm, he was blamed by Goering for the debacle. The *Reich* Marshal acted as though Galland had issued the orders instead of the Operations Staff.

Galland never relinquished his basic conviction that only an aggressive defense could succeed. He again implored Goering and the High Command to assign part of each *Geschwader* to attack U.S. fighter escorts. Goering stuck stubbornly to the bombers-only edict. Most of the battle initiative was thereby handed to the Americans.

Failing in this corrective action, Galland then proposed that JG-26 and JG-2 on the Channel coast attack the fighter escorts as the U.S. bombers passed over their territory. Galland held that such attacks would force the American fighters to drop their belly tanks to join combat. They could then not fly into German territory with the bombers, which would then be much more vulnerable to German fighter attacks.

This stratagem was approved by the High Command on a one-time basis. The plan was successful. The USAAF bombers arrived over Germany without most of their fighter escort. Refusing nevertheless to persist with this effective stratagem, the High Command claimed that its steady employment would expose France and the Low Countries to bombing and strafing in the absence of JG-2 and JG-26. The High Command would not allow this. Galland's credulity was strained by this response. The RAF had been attacking these targets steadily since 1941. He had shot down dozens of them himself.

Galland went ahead and issued tactical regulations designed to foster aggressive defense. These regulations conflicted with High Command operational orders for bombers-only attacks. Other conflicting orders emanated from Fighter Division HQ and Fighter Corps HQ. Combat leaders clearly perceived the high-level policy quarrels reflected in these conflicting orders. High-level disunity disturbed men who were daily dodging lead and tracers aloft. Morale was damaged by the obvious schism between Galland and the High Command. Each *Kommodore* therefore chose the course that he felt to be most effective. Many ignored all orders from higher up and simply did what they wanted with the *Geschwader* they commanded.

Galland's tactical expertise was thus largely ignored by the *Luftwaffe* High Command. Officers without any experience of modern fighter combat had the authority to issue operational orders. Galland would have preferred to demonstrate personally, from a fighter cockpit, the value of his tactical recommendations. Since this was prohibited, he had to live with his frustrations. He felt deeply his responsibility to make tactical knowledge that was won with blood—paid for with the lives of many pilots—serve other comrades facing the challenges aloft.

He sought a change in arrangements from Goering. He asked specifically for more operational authority over the Fighter Arm. He particularly wanted this authority for dealing with the American heavy bombers.

Goering's gold baton immediately rose, just as though Galland had actuated a mechanism. The baton waved from side to side, denoting negation.

"That is absolutely unnecessary," said Goering emphatically. "If a paper clip falls to the floor anywhere in the Fighter Arm, you know about it immediately. All your excellent advice is taken into account. Therefore, there is *no need* for you to have increased operational authority.''

The bizarre and unrealistic command arrangements of the Fighter Arm were thus allowed to continue contributing to its destruction. (Goering would never budge on this issue.)

Galland knew the Fighter Arm's technical limitations. He therefore declined to try and combat the incursions by RAF Mosquito aircraft, which were faster than any German fighter then operating. Goering became incensed by these nuisance strikes into Germany, by day and by night, especially when Mosquitos arrived over Berlin during one of his fighting speeches. The *Reich* Marshal became the butt of many jokes and jibes circulating among the German public.

The Germans had been astounded to learn that the wooden Mosquito could carry a larger bomb load than the B-17 and carry it faster and with a crew of only two. The Mosquito could fly at 38,000 feet, but was equally at home roaming Germany at treetop height, harassing *Luftwaffe* bases and making precision bombing attacks on small important targets. The Mosquito to Goering was both a technical riddle and a political embarrassment.

Goering was not content with Galland's explanation that the intruders' high speed would prevent interceptions. The wooden Mosquito returned a small radar echo, or none at all if it came in low. This meant insufficient radar warning to scramble German fighters. Fuel shortages precluded standing patrols to await the next Mosquito raid. At high altitude, the Mosquito outpaced existing German fighters.

The angry Goering set up JGr-25 and JGr-50 as special anti-Mosquito units. Two prominent fighter aces, Major Herbert Ihlefeld and Major Hermann Graf, were chosen as commanders of these units, which were based at Neubiberg and Wiesbaden. For five months the two highly decorated leaders struggled with the Mosquito problem. Engine-boosting experiments with their Me-109G6 fighters and other stratagems failed. Amid pressing demands for fighter aircraft and leaders, JGr-25 and JGr-50 were disbanded without downing a single Mosquito.

Technical difficulties had proved to be exactly as Galland had described. Goering was not satisfied until inordinate manpower, materiel, technical effort, and fuel had been dissipated in the useless project. A more graphic example of the consequences of technical illiteracy in high command would be hard to find.

Galland set up Experimental Unit 25 (*Erprobungskommando* 25) as a special technical tactical force operating directly under his own staff. Experimental and inventive activity flourished in the fighter units as combat pilots devised new and additional weapons mounts, modified gunsights, and fabricated what they wanted within their own units. Experimental Unit 25 with its two combat squadrons winnowed out useful innovations. Initially under Me-110 ace Captain Eduard Tratt, and shortly afterwards under Captain Horst Geyer, Experimental Unit 25 took inventions and innovations into combat, attacking bombers just like other *Luftwaffe* fighters. Air-to-air bombing, cable bombing, and photocell detonators were just a few of the proposed weapons tested.

Development of wing mountings for the 21-cm Army rocket was successfully carried out and tested in combat by the *Kommando*. The same large rocket, to be fired backwards and downwards from the FW-190 fuselage and timed to burst amid the H-17s, was called *"Krebs."* The *Kommando* developed and tested this weapon. The R4M rocket finally used in salvoes from the Me-262 was also put through its trials by the Unit 25. All results of tests were funneled directly into Galland's office and thence made available to appropriate Fighter Arm formations.

Galland could not divorce himself from a principle he had helped establish in the Fighter Arm: a fighter leader must be a successful ace pilot, and he must fly with those he leads and orders into combat. Galland therefore continued to sneak off on combat missions, swearing his staff to secrecy when it was necessary for any of them to know his whereabouts. He flew about 10 missions in 1943, taking off with different pilots from Berlin-Staaken.

Galland set up a travelling circus (*Wanderzirkus*) of Allied aircraft that were in flying condition. He remembered how helpful it had been when he had patched up one of the first downed B-17s so fighter pilots could board and fly in the American bombers, simulating U.S. gunners as *Luftwaffe* fighters made mock firing passes. That helped morale. The travelling circus expanded this idea.

Commanded by Captain Rosarius, the strange circus of patched-up Allied aircraft of all types toured fighter training schools, operational training units, and active fighter bases. German pilots flew in these aircraft. In the bombers, they were placed in different crew stations and got first-hand experience of the aircraft they were trying to down. Rosarius's Traveling Circus broadened their experience and lessened their apprehensions about the enemy.

For years Galland had been aware that gunnery instruction for fighter pilots was inadequate. Hunting parties in France during 1940–41, furthermore, had clearly demonstrated that far too many otherwise good fighter pilots were poor marksmen. Galland's predecessors had not addressed this problem. Available fuel did not now permit aerial gunnery practise with drogues or permit mock combat with Robot cameras actuated by gun buttons.

Six instructional firing staffs were organized. These *Schiesslehrstäbe* toured fighter facilities like the Traveling Circus. Weapons experts demonstrated new armament, taught weapons maintenance, and, with special sights, aids, and instructional tools, hammered home the principles of air-to-air shooting. An improvement in marksmanship resulted.

The human element for the Fighter Arm was a continuing Galland concern. Getting the right kind of men to be pilots and securing them in sufficient numbers was the essence of the problem. Experience had shown a significant temperamental difference between the successful fighter pilot and the ordinary fighter pilot. Those who became aces were tremendously effective. Perhaps 45 percent of all aerial victories were scored by 5 percent of the pilots. Galland reasoned that there must be a way to increase the percentage of successful pilots by preselective analyses of some kind.

He proposed psychological tests in 1943 for all pilot trainees, whether officers or NCOs. Prior to any flight training, these tests would determine a recruit's assignment to bombers, fighters, reconnaissance, or other duties. Training for fighter pilots would be specialized from the first flight. Galland backed his proposal with an offer to supply expert instructional personnel. Twelve general flying training schools would be converted to preliminary fighter schools. Three new fighter air war schools would be organized for officers.

Galland's proposal simply died in the *Luftwaffe*'s higher echelons. (Worth recording here is that a study of pilot selection was made 34 years later, by the U.S. Defense Advanced Research Projects Agency. The American research team, in its 1977 report, concluded that ineffective fighter pilots could be eliminated early by psychological testing and other techniques. Combat effectiveness and ace potential could in some degree be predicted. That was the essence of Galland's proposals to his superiors in the war year 1943.)

Fuel shortages seriously curtailed training. As a counter, Galland proposed the transfer of surplus pilots from other branches to the Fighter Arm. He organized a conversion facility at his HQ, where the conversion needs of such pilots could be assessed. Suitable pilots were retrained. Experienced officers were acquired in this way. Even if they were not capable of becoming successful fighter pilots, they could help lead fighter units.

The piloting reactions of these otherwise able officers were, in most cases, not fast enough for the flashing speed of fighter combat. By the end of 1943, Galland was glad to have leaders of any kind for his embattled formations. By the end of 1944, some 12,000 pilots had been through the program; 8,000 were accepted for conversion training as day fighter, night fighter, or ground attack pilots. The program provided pilots and leaders and saved training fuel.

Tardy in taking measures to ensure a supply of formation leaders, Galland found this a particularly awkward problem. His own combat experience led him to expect that leaders would arise through merit and experience, directly from the ranks of active fighter pilots. Losses of experienced formation leaders in 1942–43 were severe and outran this process of natural selection for replacements.

Galland failed to perceive the problem early enough to prevent its becoming critical. He met the crisis by establishing a formation leaders' course (*Verbandsführer-Lehrgang*) at Koenigsberg-Neumark in the 1943 autumn. His experience in setting up the first OTUs in JG-26 gave valuable guidance. Three courses were established. One was designed for the future *Kommodores* and *Gruppenkommandeure*. A second course was tailored to the aspiring *Staffelkapitäne*, the squadron commanders. A third course was given to all officers leaving the operational training *Gruppen* so all new officer pilots joining units would have basic training in leading formations. They formed a sort of ready-reserve of squadron commanders in each fighter *Geschwader*.

The shortage of leaders was further countered by increasing the establishment of each *Geschwader*. Normal strength of 124 aircraft, around which the prewar fighter *Geschwader* had been built, was boosted to 160 by adding four aircraft to each squadron. At the end of 1943, a fourth squadron was added to every *Gruppe*. By November of 1944, *Geschwader* establishment had risen to 288 aircraft. These increases accommodated the mixed formations of light and heavy fighters set up to combat the American heavies and their escort fighters. Surviving top leaders therefore commanded ever-growing formations—a dilution that was the only way to meet the emergency.

Systematic pilot recruitment for the Fighter Arm was nonexistent, another legacy of Galland's unenterprising predecessors. He sought to organize direct recruitment of air-minded youths as soon as they were of age. The Navy and the *Waffen* SS both had such programs. Their expert recruiters haunted the paramilitary Labor Service (*Arbeitsdienst*) camps, which were compulsory for all German boys.

As a famous figure in Germany, Galland was deluged with enthusiastic letters from boys wanting to become fighter pilots. Upon investigating the situation, he was appalled by the divided and self-defeating arrangements that stood between such boys and the Fighter Arm—where their spirit and enthusiasm were sorely needed. The Hitler Flying Youth and the National Socialist Flying Corps (NSFK) were ostensible links between the *Luftwaffe* and aspiring youths, but they competed with each other. Both of them feuded in turn with the *Luftwaffe* bureaucracy. The NSFK did not follow up and ensure that its boys got into the *Luftwaffe*. Petty vanities and squabbles over fiefdoms diminished to a trickle the flow of premium youth to the Fighter Arm.

Luftwaffe recruiting was itself a shambles. All recruiting was lumped under the General for *Luftwaffe* Personnel Recruitment (*General der Nachwuchs Luftwaffe*). There was no recruiting agency exclusively for aircrew. Camps were organized to provide boys with physical and preflight training, in the expectation that this would be an acceptable substitute for Labor Service duty. Hitler killed this idea. The *Luftwaffe* youth camps faded out. Galland was left with a pilot recruiting problem he could not solve.

After seeing the political mess associated with youthful aspiration to the air, Galland shirked the problem. Goering could have done more to get the best boys for the Fighter Arm, but he stonewalled the issue to avoid Hitler's wrath. The *Reich* Marshal's extensive wiretapping system kept him abreast of all machinations. He was thereby able to block many stratagems of the SS that aimed at promoting Himmler's status as the expense of his own.

Himmler wanted to breed supermen, with cradle-to-grave saturation in SS dogmas. This came back to Galland by a strange avenue. He strongly disapproved of fighter pilot marriages and made this known throughout the Fighter Arm. He contended that fighter pilots had to be single-minded in their lethal work, with minimum distractions. His opposition to marriage for his fighter pilots was also born of the high probability that widows and fatherless children would be the outcome.

Human concern of this kind never complicated Himmler's views. Goering broached the whole matter to Galland on a hunting trip at Karinhall. Sitting in a horse-drawn landau in the woods, Goering was at his paternal best. Goering the man had appeared from inside the image of the *Reich* Marshal. He wondered out loud if Galland's antimarriage policies were not unwise in a broader context.

Goering dwelt with disdain and contempt on Himmler's stud-farm ideas for breeding the new Germans.

"We must not surrender the German youth of tomorrow to the likes of Himmler," said Goering. "We have to perpetuate our own kind in traditional ways."

The astonished Galland did think about Goering's counsel. He saw its merits. He nevertheless maintained his opposition to fighter pilot marriages as the best policy for both the Fighter Arm and the individual pilots. While preference was given to unmarried officers for nomination to such posts as *Geschwader Kommodore*—when married and unmarried pilots of equal merit were eligible—war needs were more important than Galland's policy. He knew this. No capable leader was ever held back in the Fighter Arm because he was married.

Steps and measures taken by others had an impact on Galland's responsibilities in 1943. The ground attack units (*Schlachtflieger*) were anomalously under his office. Ground attack units in direct support of the Army were a tactical world apart from regular fighter missions. As the war advanced, each phase become more demanding and more highly specialized. Galland was therefore gratified when a General of Close Support (*General Der Schlachtflieger*) was appointed in October of 1943.

Under Colonel Dr. Kupfer, their entire activity was removed from his responsibility. His relief at being divested of the ground attack arm was short-lived. The night fighters were placed under his authority in November of 1943, a vast and sophisticated defense empire created by General Josef Kammhuber. General Kammhuber controlled his night fighters through Air Corps XII.

Kammhuber was known for his organizational talents, his inflexible thinking, and his high demands for equipment. Goering described him to Galland as the most expensive general in the *Luftwaffe*. Kammhuber's *Himmelbett* system of guiding one night fighter within the radius of one radar was doomed when the British began employing bomber stream tactics. After the night fighters were blinded and swamped in the Hamburg disaster, Kammhuber was on his way out.

Galland's relations with Kammhuber had always been difficult and barely satisfactory. Goering made Kammhuber the Inspector of the Night Fighter Arm in an empty gesture, just prior to banishing him to command Air Fleet 5 in Norway. Galland's responsibilities now became round-the-clock, just like Allied bombing. Heavily overburdened despite his devoted staff, Galland did not want the night fighters. Like the ground attack arm, it was another world, technically and operationally. He nevertheless had to obey orders.

Adding a night fighter staff to his existing staff, Galland brought in Major Hajo Herrmann, originator of Wild Boar night fighting, as Inspector of the Night Fighters. Herrmann handled his responsibilities with capable skill. Later he was

Adolf Galland and Oberst von Beckh of JG51 during a visit to the Russian Front by Galland.

The hunter and his prey. Galland checks a Wisent (buffalo) shortly after his successful shot at Schorfheide in 1942–43.

Hajo Hermann, the "Wild Boar." Single-engine visually guided fighters were used against RAF night bombing attacks after the Hamburg fire raids of 1943. Progenitor of the idea was Colonel Hermann. Wild Boar was intended to bolster night defenses over Germany after the British introduced "chaff" which confused and often blinded German radars.

succeeded in the inspector's post by Lt. Colonel Werner Streib, the legendary "Father of Night Fighting." Appalling weather, serious electronic problems, and the RAF night offensive against Berlin taxed the night fighters in the fall and winter of 1943. The center of gravity in the air war had arrived over the *Reich* as Galland had earlier foreseen. German skies were a 24-hour battleground.

This chapter has provided a sketched overview of the main responsibilities that devolved on Galland as he grew into his job in 1943. Complete books could be written detailing and documenting each phase of Galland's inhumanly busy life at this time. The former sailplane pilot from Westerholt took every possible step and measure against the coming avalanche from aloft.

CHAPTER TWENTY-ONE

Bad weather hampered full implementation of the U.S. strategic bombing offensive from November 1943 and restricted daylight bombing on into early 1944. While this gave some daytime relief to the German civil populace, Galland watched fighter casualties mount. Goering's policy of meeting every Allied thrust with all available fighters caused the Fighter Arm serious bad-weather losses. No comparable losses were inflicted on the Americans. Galland was opposed to this steady wastage of pilots and aircraft.

The ordinary *Luftwaffe* fighter pilots of 1943–44 had no instrument flying skills or training. They had to learn "on the job." Neglect of training and time pressure in the *Luftwaffe*'s earlier days precluded the establishment of blind flying schools for fighters. When Galland organized some facilities, fuel shortages nullified his efforts. Numerous German fighters crashed in bad weather, untouched by Allied bullets. Fatal crashes into mountains and crackups due to icing and forced landings were numerous. Pilots in extreme situations, often disoriented, bailed out and left their aircraft to crash. Galland saw no return for this attrition. His proposals for husbanding, concentrating, and increasing effective fighter strength went unheeded.

Appalling weather in the 1943–44 winter was too much for all save the best and luckiest German fighter pilots. Even the talented pilots of the single-engined Wild Boar night fighters, some of them with commercial piloting experience and instrument flight capability, suffered in the winter attrition. The night fighters were locked in bitter combat with RAF Bomber Command, as Air Chief Marshal Harris sought to wreck Berlin with area raids, guided by the RAF's *Oboe* device.[*]

Luftwaffe night fighters met every thrust. They made the RAF pay dearly

---

[*] Oboe was a radar and blind-bombing system using two radio stations on the ground which measured the distance to a radar beacon carried by an aircraft.

in the night war, but themselves suffered heavy losses. That Harris did not win the Battle of Berlin was due to the sacrifices of the defenders. Wild Boar losses led eventually to the abandonment of single-engined night fighter operations. In the spring of 1944, Galland was able to have the Wild Boar transferred to the day fighter forces as bad-weather units. From inception to end, Galland estimated that the Wild Boar had cost the *Luftwaffe* over 1,000 aircraft and hundreds of skilled pilots.

By early December 1943, the combined bombing offensive against the German aircraft industry—code-named Operation "Pointblank"—was three months behind schedule. Pointblank's strategic purpose was the elimination of Galland's fighters prior to the invasion, which was then scheduled for 1 May 1944. General Eaker was under heavy pressure to smash the German aircraft industry. Only the weather and the *Luftwaffe* Fighter Arm stood in the way. With radar bombing to become available in the spring, even weather hazards would be reduced; but, at Christmas of 1943, the Allied timetable was far behind.

The Eighth Air Force by then had 26 groups of heavy bombers, each group consisting of four squadrons with 16 aircraft each. Eleven groups of fighters were under Eighth Air Force Fighter Command. The Americans could now put up 600–700 bombers for a massive and escorted attack on German targets. Galland was aware, from the intelligence reports he studied, that this daylight strength would be doubled and tripled in the next year. Emblematic of growing American strength was the 13,142 tons of bombs dropped by U.S. aircraft on European targets in December of 1943. The USAAF had exceeded the RAF's monthly load for the first time.

The winter months of 1943–44 were a brief breathing space for a Germany about to go under the flail. This pause was a last opportunity and a lost opportunity all in one. During these critical winter weeks, gross high-level mistakes by the Germans crucially delayed the Me-262 jet fighter.

Galland was pressing for action on the Me-262 far beyond the theoretical limits of his responsibilities. No opportunity to advocate top priority for the jet fighter was overlooked by the young general. This aircraft was, in his view, the last chance for the Fighter Arm against the impending avalanche. Only a technical quantum jump could change the balance of power in German skies.

Hitler actually saw the Me-262 for the first time on 26 November 1943, as part of a *Luftwaffe* weapons demonstration at Insterburg airbase in East Prussia, near his HQ. The *Fuehrer* was well aware of the jet fighter's existence. (His overcautious reaction to Galland's bold May proposal for accelerated Me-262 development and production has already been described. The dictator's later insistence that the revolutionary aircraft be produced as a Blitz Bomber is generally accepted as the ruination of Germany's last aerial chance.)

Less well known historically is the manner in which the Blitz Bomber entered the *Fuehrer*'s mind, there to become an obsession. Although ignorant of aeronautical engineering, he had long advocated a "speed bomber" for the *Luftwaffe*.

Without comprehending the technical problems involved, Hitler's speed bomber was to be faster than intercepting fighters. The RAF Mosquito bomber actually proved this Hitler concept to be feasible, through the anachronistic use of wooden construction. German engineers never came up with a comparable speed bomber, but such an aircraft was among Hitler's military visions.

The specific bomber idea for the Me-262 came directly from the fighter's own creator—Professor Messerschmitt. He planted this idea in a personal conference with Hitler on 7 September 1943. The professor was probably attempting by devious means to keep alive his Me-209 piston-engined fighter, which both Galland and Milch had rejected as insufficient in performance. Messerschmitt's draft for this fateful discussion with the *Fuehrer* survives as pages 102 and 103 among two bulging files of the professor's personal papers at the Imperial War Museum in London.

Under heading 5 in this draft, Messerschmitt notes for presentation to the *Fuehrer* that Colonel Peltz of the Bomber Arm, in a report from Rechlin, had "urgently demanded" the jet bomber for missions against England. "The quickest possibility for the job is the 262," says Messerschmitt's draft. Further searching for the origin of Hitler's "crazy" idea of converting jet fighters into bombers is superfluous. Messerschmitt himself initiated the debacle.

Messerschmitt always had the *Fuehrer*'s ear. Hitler trusted the professor. What Messerschmitt put into that trusting ear on 7 September 1943 kindled Hitler's fecund imagination. Already present therein was the *Fuehrer*'s unfulfilled speed bomber concept. With this phantom, the Me-262 of the real world was immediately synthesized, complete with Messerschmitt's own seal of feasibility. Thus arose Hitler's Blitz Bomber fantasies, with all their measureless impact on the air defense of Germany and on the hopes of General Galland to counter daylight bombing.

By 28 October 1943, Hitler was describing to Goering his vision of jet fighter bombers. Each carrying a pair of small bombs, these revolutionary machines would streak over the invasion beaches, strafing the landing enemy. Demoralization, death, and panic would ensue. (Hitler never relinquished this odd and limited vision of jet operations, until it was too late.)

On 2 November 1943, less than two months after Messerschmitt had touted the Me-262 to him as a fast bomber, Hitler sent Goering to the Messerschmitt plant at Augsburg. The *Reich* Marshal was charged with discussing the bomber version of the Me-262 with the professor. The question of bomb racks was taken up. Messerschmitt falsely assured Goering that bomb-release devices were incorporated in the original design. The jet fighter could carry either two 550-lb bombs or a single 1,100-lb bomb.

Hitler's requirement for a couple of small bombs was modest, in view of the bomb-carrying capabilities of every other fighter aircraft in the *Luftwaffe*. When Goering asked Messerschmitt when the first bomb-rack models would be ready, the professor was forced to admit that they had not yet been designed.

When pressed further by Goering—who expected to be grilled later about the whole matter by Hitler—Messerschmitt recklessly asserted that the bomb racks could be made ready in about two weeks. (These were deceptive assurances.)

On this same day, 2 November 1943, a special commission was established to oversee development of the Me-262. Colonel Edgar Petersen, Chief of the Research Establishments, headed this evaluation panel. As *Kommodore* of KG-40, he had flown long-range Atlantic reconnaissance missions in the four-engined FW-200 and later had evaluated captured Allied aircraft at Rechlin. Other commission members included engine builder Franz von Jumo, engine designer Dr. Anselm Franz of Junkers Motorenbau, Messerschmitt himself, Chief of Technical Development Lt. Colonel Knemeyer, and a group of top engineers and industrialists. Galland was not appointed to the panel, even though his troops would be receiving the new aircraft. *The Fighter Arm was unrepresented on the evaluation panel.*

The stage was thus set for the Insterburg demonstration. Most of the high-level attendees were ignorant of what had been planted in Hitler's mind by Messerschmitt in September. Galland had no inkling of what was brewing. Famous faces at Insterburg that day included Galland, Goering, Bodenschatz, Milch, Speer, Himmler, Peltz, Kurt Tank, Claudius Dornier, and Chief of the *Luftwaffe* General Staff Guenther Korten. Messerschmitt himself stood with Hitler, Goering, and Galland as the Me-262 stole the weapons show.

As the jet went whistling past, Galland heard Hitler ask Goering if this aircraft could carry bombs. Before Goering could reply, Messerschmitt interjected immediately that the aircraft had enough power to carry 1,000 pounds of bombs and "perhaps 2,000 pounds." This latter figure was more than 12 times the bomb weight the *Fuehrer* originally envisioned for his jet fighter bombers.

Hitler nodded knowingly, and turned on the assembled *Luftwaffe* gods.

"For years I have demanded from the *Luftwaffe* a speed bomber that can reach its target in spite of enemy fighter defense. In the aircraft you present to me as a fighter plane, I see the *Blitz Bomber,* with which I will repel the invasion in its first and weakest phase . . . it will strike the recently landed mass of material and troops, creating panic, death, and destruction."

There was a loaded pause while Hitler glared around at his shocked air chiefs.

"Of course, none of you thought of that!"

Galland's heart sank. An incredibly bizarre development was beginning before his eyes. Anything that now delayed the combat advent of the Me-262 fighter served the enemy. Only this weapon could deter masses of daylight bombers. Galland knew all too well how making fighters into bombers degraded performance. The complex factors additionally involved with the revolutionary Me-262 boggled the mind. There was no proper bomb sight. High fuel consumption at low altitude imposed severe range limits. Above 600 mph, the Me-262 became uncontrolable, which precluded dive bombing. Center of gravity problems in a bomber version were likely to be complicated.

Galland foresaw complex training problems with a bomber version. The defensive attitude of bomber pilots towards enemy fighters could not be eradicated. Only the best fighter pilots could be successful with the Me-262. All these thorny technical and human problems militated against an Me-262 Blitz Bomber, but unfortunately that mutant craft was already flying around in Hitler's imagination.

On 5 December 1943, Hitler had Colonel Nicolaus von Below, his *Luftwaffe* aide, send Goering a telegram in which he stressed the importance attached by the *Fuehrer* to jet fighter bombers. The von Below language was plain:

IT IS IMPERATIVE THAT THE LUFTWAFFE HAVE A NUMBER OF JET FIGHTER BOMBERS READY FOR FRONT COMMITMENT BY THE SPRING OF 1944. . . . THE FUEHRER FEELS THAT DELAY IN OUR JET FIGHTER PROGRAM WOULD BE TANTAMOUNT TO IRRESPONSIBLE NEGLIGENCE.

Goering was directed to submit bimonthly reports on the Me-262 directly to Hitler, plus reports on the Arado-234 reconnaissance jet bomber—a parallel project. Hitler thus clearly envisioned the fighter bomber role for the Me-262. Work at the Messerschmitt factory nevertheless remained concentrated on the fighter version, as the company struggled to complete the first series of prototypes. Only prototype V-10, scheduled for completion in May 1944, had experimental bomb racks.

The Germans at this point were already losing the race between jet fighter production and the Eighth Air Force. The Allied strategic bombing program had the Messerschmitt factories targeted for obliteration. By early 1944, P-51 groups were going into action with the Eighth Air Force, and production of P-51s in the United States was soaring under top priorities. Deep penetrations of German airspace would in 1944 be covered all the way by high-performance fighters that outnumbered the German defenders. Only the jet fighter could at this stage deter daylight bombing.

On 6 January 1944, the Eighth Air Force got a new commander, an aviator destined to enjoy a long relationship in peace and war with Adolf Galland. He was Major General James H. Doolittle, whose 1942 Tokyo raid had lifted American spirits. Doolittle had then made an outstanding record commanding the Twelfth Air Force in North Africa. His career as an aviation pioneer, Schneider Cup racing pilot, and businessman had endowed him with acumen, wide vision, and the ability to get things done. Doolittle had moral as well as physical courage, and he was to be the most sagacious Allied air leader, in Galland's estimation.

Eighth Air Force Intelligence presented Doolittle with a report when he took command that defined the essentials of the January 1944 air situation. The strategic bombing program, and its critical role in a successful Allied invasion, was threatened unless the German Fighter Arm could be suppressed. Increased fighter production, more fighter pilot trainees, improved German weaponry, and transfer of additional fighters to the defense of Germany from other fronts were all cited as adding to *Luftwaffe* strength. Issued on 5 January 1944, the report's message was driven home by the downing of 25 American heavy bombers.

Destroying the *Luftwaffe* Fighter Arm and its industrial infrastructure was code-named "Argument." There was disagreement in high Allied councils about the employment of the Eighth Air Force, for the overall goal was Allied air supremacy over the invasion beaches and immediate hinterland. Pressure was exerted to draw the Eighth into more direct support of tactical operations against French targets. Such a course would have helped Galland build his fighter reserve for the defense of Germany.

Doolittle saw the war on a broad canvas, as a mighty production struggle. The road to air supremacy in Normandy, in Doolittle's thinking, lay in the destruction of German fighter production centers and the synthetic fuel industry and to attack aggressively the existing German fighters. Had their positions been reversed, it is fair to say that Galland would have followed the same course.

Echoes of the Battle of Britain and Galland's hard experiences in that encounter appeared in the way that Doolittle tackled the challenge. Lt. General Eaker in building the Eighth into a massive war machine had defined the role of U.S. fighters: escort the heavies and protect them from fighter attack. In practical application, this led to the same close-escort orders under which Galland had chafed in the Battle of Britain and which aided the British defenders.

Doolittle analyzed the essentials in the same way as Galland had in 1940. Doolittle's position differed radically, however, inasmuch as he had the authority to make far-reaching operational changes. Doolittle ordered his fighter groups to destroy the *Luftwaffe* fighters—to find them and to shoot them down or strafe them on the ground. German fighters were to be intercepted and downed before they could find the heavies. Eighth Fighter Command leaders greeted these orders with enthusiasm, just as Galland and his pilots would have in the Battle of Britain had they been similarly unleashed.

Galland of the Luftwaffe fighters and Doolittle of the American Eighth Air Force seemed to be the visionaries of aerial warfare. Opposed on all sides by others who fancied themselves experts, these two generals realized that attack was the principal factor of a successful defense.

"Only the spirit of attack born in a brave heart will bring success to any fighter aircraft, no matter how highly developed it may be" is the way Galland expresses his conviction. There is little doubt that Doolittle was thinking the exact same philosophy when he ordered the Eighth Air Force fighters released from their close-formation leashes while escorting the bombers.

The U.S. bomber leaders did not like this reversal of established operational procedures. They were comforted by close-escort fighters. Setting his fighters free to hunt and destroy Galland's fighters earned the new Eighth Air Force boss the epithet "Killer Doolittle"—used directly to his face. Doolittle stood by his decision despite criticism, some of it from high-ranking officers. In the flaming war above Germany, his fighters proved that he was right. The classic success Doolittle enjoyed also proved that in 1940 Galland had urged the correct tactical employment of German fighters on Goering and the High Command—in vain.

Sweeping far ahead of the bomber boxes, usually out of their sight, searching far around to each side of the majestic formations, American fighters carried the battle to the *Luftwaffe*. Galland's fighter leaders were soon reporting grave difficulties in making proper assemblies, as hunting U.S. fighters slashed among them. Galland had long dreaded this tactic of the U.S. fighter escort.

German fighter formations were scattered and thrown into confusion before they could assemble. When they were able to form up, and lurked awaiting their chance to attack the heavies, the Mustangs jumped them. The inherent defensive power of the bomber box and escort had been projected by these tactics miles out from the bomber formation itself. Well-trained American pilots flying excellent aircraft struck at German morale as surely as they struck at the Messerschmitts and Focke-Wulfs. Another *Luftwaffe* era ensued of split-S and dive away. The American fighters were relentless, following their opponents down to the deck. If the Americans could not find the Germans aloft, they strafed *Luftwaffe* airfields.

In later years, General Doolittle would regard turning loose the American fighters as his best decision of the war. Adolf Galland agreed. The two generals often discussed Doolittle's masterstroke in their peacetime meetings. The American's classic employment of fighters on their classic mission was tactically excellent. More than anything else, this decisive change by Doolittle began the twilight of the Fighter Arm.

After a long spell of bad weather, Doolittle got 857 heavies airborne to attack the Frankfurt area on 27 January 1944. Poor visibility over their English bases hampered their assembly, and only about 450 bombers were actually dispatched. In bad weather over Germany, fewer than 60 attacked their targets. The weather was blocking the strategic bombing offensive, and there was high-level chagrin and impatience.

On 8 February 1944, General Spaatz ordered that "Argument"—the destruction of every factory producing fighters and fighter components—would have to be completed no later than 1 March. "Big Week" was accordingly organized to seal the doom of Galland's fighters, by obliterating the German aircraft industry. The weather was the controlling factor. As soon as the weather was good enough, a mighty maximum effort would roar into the sky. Thousands of Allied aircraft stood poised and wet in England.

Galland anticipated Big Week. He had marshaled his resources and overseen the formation of mixed *Geschwader* of light and heavy fighters. These units consisted of one *Gruppe* of heavily armored FW-190s, strongly armed and somewhat slower than regular single-engined fighters. Two *Gruppen* of the latter flew escort with the heavily armed fighters to make up the mixed *Geschwader*.

Galland hoped that such composite formations might be more effective if the greater hitting power of the special FW-190s could be used in close.

These units were moderately successful, but Goering and the High Command continued their bombers-only attack orders. The single-engined fighters were thus bound again to an escort role while the heavy fighters were attacking, so their aggressive potential was negated. Hordes of American fighters made assembly of the mixed German formations extremely difficult. The heavy fighters could not defend themselves against the much nimbler Mustangs. Galland reflected often and bitterly that the bombers-only attack regulations issued to the Fighter Arm were a certain way to give the American fighters a free hand.

Big Week actually began on the night of 19/20 February 1944. Over 700 RAF Lancasters and Halifaxes struck at Leipzig. These aircraft carried considerably more explosives than the B-17s, and the ancient city took a terrible beating. German night fighters fell on the RAF fiercely. They attacked the British over Leipzig and in pursuit across Germany after the raid, while a sleepless Galland followed the action; 78 British bombers were shot down during the night.

Doolittle opened Big Week by dispatching more than 1,000 American heavies for the first time in history, on 20 February; 940 of these aircraft reached their German targets, escorted by an incredible 700 fighters. The vast aerial armada, with its fighter escort hunting, sweeping, and hounding, plastered its targets and lost only 21 aircraft.

The RAF hit Stuttgart that same night with another force of 600 bombers, in an area raid intended to help stifle ball-bearing production. On 21 February, the Eighth Air Force put 764 B-17s and B-24s over Germany in daylight. General Twining's Fifteenth Air Force heavies winged in from Italy the next day, blasting the Messerschmitt plant at Regensburg, while more than 100 U.S. bombers from England struck at other aircraft industry targets. Galland's fighters contended hotly with the American bombing pincer. In combination with German flak, they shot down 54 American aircraft.

On 24 February, the Eighth returned to its nemesis target—Schweinfurt; 231 bombers attacked the ball-bearing plants. A further 238 Liberators hammered Gotha. Galland's fighters and the flak clawed down another 44 American bombers, but it was not enough: 700 Lancasters droned over Schweinfurt that same night and cast their awesome loads into the flames left by the Americans.

On 25 February 1944, as Allied weather experts were predicting further deterioration, 680 of Doolittle's bombers concentrated on the Me-109 centers at Augsburg and Regensburg, with blows also at Fürth. Fifteenth Air Force bombers from Italy joined in again at Regensburg, at a cost of 30 aircraft shot down. Total U.S. losses for the day were 64 bombers destroyed, with many others damaged. Major General Joachim Huth, Galland's old *Jafü* from JG-26 days, did an outstanding job in directing fighter operations from Schleissheim, as C.O. of the 7th Fighter Division. The *Luftwaffe*'s best was again insufficient. The numerical odds were against the Germans in their own skies.

As Big Week ended on the night of 25 February 1944, the RAF struck a final blow. It attacked the Messerschmitt factory at Augsburg, once again aiming into the fires started by the Americans during the day. Bad weather then terminated Big Week, but it looked as though Big Week had terminated the German aircraft industry.

The Allies lost nearly 300 aircraft. They could make up such losses rapidly. They dropped over 19,000 tons of bombs on the German aircraft industry, blasting or burying over 700 Me-109s that were either complete or in final production. More than a thousand German aircraft, mostly Me-109s and FW-190s, were lost in the factory attacks. Galland's own heavy losses in combat with the raiders had to be added to the tally, as well as numerous losses from flying accidents.

Here was the avalanche of aircraft and explosive that Galland had dreaded, had endlessly warned against, and had sought by every means in his power to abort. Usually imperturbable in his outward bearing, his inner turmoil was intense. The shambles, ruin, and suffering were indescribable in themselves, but were doubly painful because it was a body blow at the Fighter Arm. There were private, quiet moments when he put his head in his hands, but they were brief. He was always wanted or needed somewhere, so he put on his imperturbable expression and put in his cigar and went to work.

Hundreds of trained aircraft workers were among the civilians who perished in the Big Week raids. They were irreplaceable. Hundreds of others were injured. Many more bolted their jobs and homes in terror, disappearing in the confusion to seek refuge away from the targeted cities. Messerschmitt's factory at Regensburg had been leveled. Four months would be needed to make it operational again, Allied bombers permitting.

Other critical aircraft and component factories had been reduced to rubble. Allied commanders studying aerial reconnaissance photographs could hardly believe the extent of the destruction. They were justified in believing that Big Week had smashed German aircraft production.

Alarming reports of aircraft industry devastation and production losses came quickly to Galland's staff. The *Luftwaffe* High Command functioned feverishly now. These were the same officers, pale and confused, who had refused to believe intelligence reports from America about the fleets of bombers and fighters being produced. Goering had called these reports "bluff." The *Reich* Marshal was now appropriately on leave, insulated against bad tidings by the medieval splendor of Castle Veldenstein. When Galland had warned that this terrible scenario was coming, Goering and others on the High Command had told him he was a defeatist. Events had proved Galland's realism. Defeat came from unrealistic policies followed by his superiors.

Pulling the aircraft industry back into function was a Herculean task. Field Marshal Milch worked wonders in reestablishing the supply of fighters, despite his waning status with Hitler and with Goering's now open and abusive animosity. Due largely to Milch's energy, ideas, and optimism, blue sky was somehow found amid the gloom.

Large numbers of aircraft bombed and buried proved to be repairable. Precious machine tools exhumed from under rubble required only to be cleaned and checked before going back into use. All kinds of equipment were salvageable, except where fires had raged. Industry labored feverishly. Messerschmitt's at Augsburg was back in production a month later.

Armaments Minister Speer, with whom Galland had always enjoyed frank and cordial relations, decreed industrial dispersal as state policy. Aircraft production began rising again from new and dispersed facilities. Galland took grim satisfaction at the way fighters had finally come to center stage. He still found it incredible, nevertheless, that such enemy blows were necessary to drive home the importance of fighter production. Everyone now finally agreed, amid the ruin and wreckage, that only fighters could protect German war potential. Galland had urged top priority for fighter production virtually from the time he became General of the Fighter Arm.

The Fighter Staff was organized, as a new bureau within the Ministry of Armaments, charged with dispersing, expediting, and expanding fighter production. Milch was inspired with the Fighter Staff idea during Big Week: top priority for fighters, the best talent from his own and Speer's ministries, and authority to boost fighter production to record levels. Milch recommended Karl-Otto Saur, Speer's deputy, as head of the Fighter Staff. Milch's own star was setting. Saur in the past had frustrated many *Luftwaffe* requirements in favor of the Army, but now he was fighter production czar of Germany. Hitler promptly approved the Fighter Staff.

Galland had only the slightest inkling of the complex power, personalities, and political plays behind these events. He had no taste for any kind of machinations. His straightforward fighter pilot's approach to life was that merit ought to rule everything. Only the air defense of Germany and the welfare of the Fighter Arm mattered to him. On this account, he rejoiced that finally his beloved fighters were to have first priority.

Despite the bombing, Big Week, and all the ruin, there would henceforth be plenty of fighters, once Saur dragged production out of the February-March abyss. Rough, brutal, and relentless, Saur raised fighter production by June of 1944 to unprecedented levels. Fuel was by then an irremovable bottleneck, and fuel was the problem, rather than aircraft. Saur's fighter production feats did not include the Me-262, which Galland desperately needed—all the more so because jet fuel was relatively abundant. The Me-262 drama continued unfolding against the backdrop of imminent Allied invasion.

CHAPTER TWENTY-TWO

Miraculously, the series of Me-262 prototypes escaped the avalanche of Allied bombs targeted on Messerschmitt factories. So vast was the destruction at Augsburg that Galland could hardly believe that the precious jets had survived almost unscathed. Even at the eleventh hour, as he saw things, a chance remained. His optimism grew as he saw the aircraft industry being rapidly resurrected, but fuel was a limiting factor. Fighter pilot flying training was hamstrung by fuel shortages.

Plans were made by Saur to produce 1,000 Me-262 jet fighters per month, together with their engines, in a vast underground complex at Nordhausen. By April of 1944, Hitler was giving top priority to a fighter umbrella over the Fatherland. Accepting at last that he needed at least 2,000 fighters to defend the *Reich,* Hitler ordered the construction of new bombproof factories. These immense facilities were to be established under mushroom canopies of reinforced concrete.

Galland learned with relief of the *Fuehrer's* new priorities. The General of the Fighters reflected wryly on the recommendations he had made to Hitler when U.S. heavies first bombed German targets. Galland had waited vainly for appropriate action to be taken, while misery and death cascaded from the skies upon the civil population. The USAAF kept the problem in the forefront of Hitler's mind by bombing German industry one day out of two in April, despite adverse weather.

Galland's most urgent task early in 1944 was the refreshment, reinforcement, and rebuilding of existing fighter formations. Round-the-clock defense of Germany worked a heavy attrition on both pilots and units. The continuing High Command policy of sending all available fighters against every raid, regardless of weather, lowered combat effectiveness and undermined morale. Pilots and aircraft were scattered far and wide by this policy, posing a nearly insuperable problem.

Too many pilots were operating too often in pickup formations from strange airfields. Using the same aircraft for day and night operations intensified mechanical attrition. Fighter Arm battle losses were nominally less most of the time than the casualties inflicted on the raiders, but overall Fighter Arm losses were amounting to about 50 pilots and aircraft for each incursion by the American heavies. As the Fighter Arm declined in combat effectiveness and efficiency, the Americans kept improving.

General Doolittle concluded that a standard operational tour of 25 missions for his bomber crews was too short. He reasoned that they were being taken out of combat just as they reached peak team efficiency in manning a bomber. Doolittle increased their duty tour to 30 missions and raised efficiency by more than 30 percent. Later tours were extended to 35 missions. Doolittle made his bombers fly at the speed of the slowest aircraft, thereby using the firepower of the bomber box to protect the cripples. U.S. efficiency thus rose as that of the Fighter Arm declined, a tipping of the combat balance of which Galland was well aware.

The narrow prewar training base of the *Luftwaffe*, and its subsequent neglect and ruin after the war began, now seriously bedeviled Galland. Pilots simply could not be produced fast enough in Germany. Capable instructors were rare. Fuel allocations for training were progressively curtailed, necessitating constant reductions in flying training. Young boys were sent to the fighter squadrons with 65 hours total flying time, and sometimes less. The Allies meanwhile were producing thousands of pilots at modern facilities far from the war zone. Dissolution of the Fighter Arm was imminent in this single fact.

Galland was finally able to persuade Goering to create a reserve of fighters, instead of hurling every plane and pilot into the shambles. In his recommendations and proposals, as well as in his personal encounters with Goering, Galland kept stressing the need for such a reserve. His conviction was that only a "Big Blow"— a strike with perhaps 2,000 fighters in the daytime—could saturate the American fighter defense and inflict unacceptable losses on the bombers.

Galland also emphasized the coming invasion of Europe, a military certainty as soon as the weather permitted. Field Marshal Sperrle on the Channel coast had less than 200 fighters to face the combined might of the Ninth Tactical Air Force, the Second Tactical Air Force, and the RAF Fighter Command. A *Luftwaffe* fighter reserve was essential, unless air superiority was to be simply surrendered to the powerful Allied air fleets, especially the Eighth and Fifteenth Air Forces that were now hammering the homeland.

In finally assenting to Galland's program for building a fighter reserve in the *Reich*, Goering added a proviso: in addition to the reserve held ready for the Big Blow, *Reich* fighter defense was to be built to 2,000 fighters. Hitler was to cite this same figure in April. Galland considered such a force unattainable, since Hitler had earlier forbidden the withdrawal of any more *Geschwader* from other fronts for the defense of Germany.

Galland accordingly proposed, and Goering agreed, that they transfer one squadron from each *Gruppe* in the North and East and thus add a fourth squadron to each *Gruppe* defending the *Reich*. Each *Geschwader* would also receive an additional *Gruppe*. Galland had already used this stratagem in 1943 to increase the establishment of each home defense *Geschwader*. An additional operational squadron was to be formed with each fighter pilot school and also with each operational training unit. Full implementation of these measures could give Galland a reserve of 1,800 fighters. Their necessity was driven home by the Ninth Air Force on 23 April 1944. More than 1,000 American fighters and fighter bombers were sent to beat up French, Belgian, and Dutch targets. As Galland had emphasized in his proposals for the fighter reserve, such Allied air supremacy would make operations almost impossible for the German Army in France.

The invasion aborted Galland's goal of 1,800 fighters for *Reich* defense by mid-June 1944, exclusive of JG-2 and JG-26 on the Channel coast. Galland had intended to stretch the limited supply of experienced combat leaders over the larger establishments. The number of officers able to effectively lead a *Gruppe* or *Geschwader* was now dwindling dangerously. The 7 to 1 numerical edge in fighters held by the Allies proved lethal even to Germany's most habile aces and leaders. Dissolution of leadership in this way haunted the General of the Fighters.

The highly decorated, high-scoring ace-leaders who were lost in the spring of 1944 included the redoubtable Lt. Colonel Egon Mayer, *Kommodore* of JG-2. He was shot down over Montmedy on 2 March by pilots of the U.S. 365th Fighter Group. Colonel Wolf-Dietrich "Fürst" Wilcke died over Schoppenstadt on 23 March. The irreplaceable Colonel Walter "Gulle" Oesau was shot down over St. Vith in the Ardennes. Oesau was *Kommodore* of JG-1, with a splendid combat career extending back to the Condor Legion in Spain. All these *Kommodores* were personally well known by Galland. ("They belonged to the inestimable elite of our fighter leaders," said Galland. "They were irreplaceable, and their deaths shook me.")

Such crippling losses went far beyond the three lives. Galland well understood the damage done to operational effectiveness when great fighter leaders were killed. Their presence leading in the air was enormously reassuring to raw young pilots, and essential to keeping the youngsters alive long enough to gain experience and become effective. Their combat deaths struck harsh blows at morale.

Only the night fighters against the RAF provided encouragement in the winter and spring of 1944. "Bomber" Harris of the RAF had launched his Berlin wrecking program back in November of 1943. He kept the pressure on despite heavy losses inflicted by the *Luftwaffe* night fighters. On 24 March 1944, Harris sent 811 heavies to Berlin, and 72 of them were downed before dawn. The German night fighters were proving incredibly resilient and capable.

Deep penetration night raids climaxed on 30 March 1944, when Harris sent nearly 800 bombers to Nuremberg. Due to British meteorological miscalculation, the raiders found themselves over the Continent in unrestricted visibility and all-revealing moonlight. Their contrails etched their tracks across the frosty sky. German night fighters began attacking near Aachen. Repeated attacks were made under conditions requiring no radar or groping in the clouds.

The greatest fighter victory of all time, day or night, resulted from the German attacks: 94 RAF heavies were downed. After hours of wild pursuit across Germany, and savage hunting amid thunderheads over the North Sea, another 20 RAF heavies landed in England ready for the scrapheap. Losses had exceeded 11 percent. This severe defeat was the culmination of earlier losses and led to curtailment of RAF deep penetration night raids. ''Bomber'' Harris had not won his greatest battle, despite a swathe of destruction inflicted on Berlin.

Galland was gratified by this significant night fighter victory. A string of similar but even more effective triumphs by day was what he now planned against the Eighth Air Force. Swarming and aggressive U.S. fighters made daylight victories extremely difficult. Even days like 6 March 1944, when 69 American heavies went down in Berlin raids, exacted an insupportable price in life, aircraft, and leaders from the Fighter Arm. Only a Big Blow, with a blizzard of fighters, could bring down 200 or more heavy bombers in one big daylight attack. For this Galland continued his planning.

Many German minds focused on how to down more bombers in daylight. Proposals for ramming attacks were inevitable under the circumstances. Fighters would ram heavy bombers for a sure downing, and wherever possible German pilots would bail out after the impact. Ramming suggestions came from combat units, from individual combat pilots, and also from some officers who would not personally be involved in any ramming or bailing out.

One such ramming advocate was the creator of Wild Boar night fighting, Colonel Hajo Herrmann, who appeared before Galland to press for the immediate use of ram-and-bail-out tactics. Galland heard him out.

''And who will be leading such ramming attacks, Colonel? Hopefully you, perhaps?''

Herrmann explained that he was having trouble with his ears. Galland observed dryly that he did not think it would be necessary for the colonel to hear the ramming impact, thanked him for his proposal, and dismissed him. The General of the Fighter Arm would not relinquish his requirement that a leader be first in all combat matters. If ramming was to be used, then all the more the commanders should ram first. He was personally opposed to this suicidal approach to combat, suited as it was to oriental consciousness, rather than to the current German mentality. Galland believed inflexibly that a fighter pilot was owed the chance to survive his victory over a foe. Ramming at nearly 400 mph or perhaps at almost 700 mph in a head-on attack made that chance unacceptably slender.

Desperation was inherent in such tactics, and to Galland they were further signals of the proximity of dissolution. The ramming idea was nevertheless translated into the assault squadrons (*Sturmgruppen*). These elite units were to press home their attacks short of ramming. Going straight to the bombers on the shortest distance, they were to open fire with all armament at the last possible moment. The blast of close-range fire, with almost no projectiles missing the target, was expected to bring down the heavies. Nerves of steel and a dauntless heart were essential.

Pilots for the assault fighters were all volunteers, and they came forward in droves. The best of these brave men were given special training. Here was the answer of the fighting pilots to Goering's carping allegations of cowardice in the Fighter Arm. These men willingly sought the highest-risk assignment aloft for a chance to bring down more bombers.

Assault units were equipped with a specially armored marque of the FW-190 (FW-190A-8/R7) carrying four 20mm cannons and, later, two 20mm and two 30mm cannons MK-108. These aircraft had cockpit armor and carried a 66-gallon additional external fuel tank to increase their endurance and range. Under Major von Kornatzki, a leading advocate of these tactics, the first units did well. Kornatzki's force was enlarged to a *Gruppe*. Major Wilhelm Moritz and others distinguished themselves with the assault squadrons.

Galland proposed setting up one *Sturmgruppe* in each *Geschwader* for *Reich* defense. Special assault fighter training was organized with the OTU *Gruppen*, all this being put in hand late in the 1944 spring. The invasion then upset these preparations. Assault fighter successes were usually achieved by line-abreast attacks on the bombers from astern. The fighters went sweeping through the bomber boxes in three or more waves.

There were excellent and encouraging successes. The increasing vulnerability of the heavier assault fighters to the nimbler Mustangs soon nullified these early triumphs. Keeping the assault fighters competitive soon required the removal of their armor plate and long-range tanks. Loss of the armor was a physical and psychological drawback in point-blank attacks. The assault fighter pilots had to compensate with their fighting hearts for the lack of armor. (Outstanding gun camera films of attacks by these fighters on B-17s and B-24s are still in existence today.)

Early in May of 1944, General Doolittle's bombers were being diverted increasingly from strategic targets to support of invasion preparations. V-weapon sites in France received special attention. By 12 May, nevertheless, Doolittle was able to launch a strategic attack that he had long advocated—a major blow against the German synthetic fuel industry. Bad weather and invasion-support demands had held him up for three weeks after he received approval for these attacks.

Galland meanwhile had been anticipating precision daylight bombing of the synthetic fuel industry with trepidation. The Fighter Arm had serious fuel difficulties, most keenly felt in the training schools, but slowly extending to operational units. *Luftwaffe* fighter units defending Rumanian oil installations had for weeks reported consistent attacks by Fifteenth Air Force bombers. As Rumanian oil production fell, German synthetic fuel facilities became an especially critical target.

Gratified and amazed as Galland was by Saur's fighter production miracle, he had a grim intuition about fuel. Saur had produced 2,000 fighters in April and was improving on that tally for May. Galland was haunted by the strategic realities. Fighters without fuel did not need to be shot down by the enemy. They would already be useless, whatever their numbers.

On 12 May 1944, 800 American heavies struck at the synthetic oil plants and the Leuna facilities at Merseburg, Böhlau, Zwickau, Lutzendorf, Brüx, and Tröglitz. All targets were heavily hit. Over 400 *Luftwaffe* fighters milled in combat with the bombers and their escort, clawing down 46 heavies. Galland took only slight comfort from these downings. He knew that Doolittle had gone for the Fighter Arm's jugular.

Production of synthetic fuel dropped sharply. Consternation and alarm swept through the oil industry, the Ministry of Armaments, and Galland's office. Persistent similar strikes against synthetic fuels would clearly wither Germany's war potential. This stunning blow by Doolittle on 12 May was not immediately repeated. The Eighth Air Force was again mainly engaged in invasion area attacks. Synthetic fuel facilities were not battered again until 28 May 1944. During the intervening 16 days, the most fateful decisions of all were taken on the Me-262—Galland's last hope for a fighting chance against the Eighth Air Force.

Immense increases in fighter production had been achieved by Saur partly via diversions of manpower, materials, and manufacturing space from bomber construction. Less than 700 bombers were produced in April of 1944, as fighter production soared to more than 2,000 aircraft. Aiming at production of 1,000 fighters per week, an incredible figure by all prior *Luftwaffe* standards, Saur's projections showed an eventual drop in bomber production to around 300 machines a month. This was the price for a vast fleet of fighters.

This feat of deliverance, giving Germany the fighter umbrella that Hitler himself had latterly demanded, was evaluated negatively and narrowly by the *Luftwaffe* High Command. Chief of *Luftwaffe* General Staff Guenther Korten regarded the drop in bomber production, and Saur's goals for the coming months, as the death of the Bomber Arm. General Karl Koller, Korten's deputy (and later his successor) held a similar view. Failing to grasp fully that strategic bombing had to be stopped if Germany were to have any war potential at all, the High Command indulged in fantasies about the role of bombers in the year 1944.

The High Command failed to see that, in an improved aerial situation, where such steps made military sense, Saur would be able to deliver a flow of bombers comparable to the current fighter production miracle. Regardless of the aerial situation over the *Reich,* the top *Luftwaffe* leaders wanted more bombers immediately. Goering agreed.

General Koller prepared a memorandum on the need for increased bomber production and sent it to Hitler. Amid the relative respite provided by diminished bombing of Germany by day and night in May, Hitler's April resolve for a massive fighter umbrella began evaporating. Intoxicated by the opportunity for attack, Hitler developed fantastic notions about a revitalized Bomber Arm. Goering further stoked the *Fuehrer's* imagination with visions of more than 10,000 bombers on first-line strength, in a phantasmagoric future *Luftwaffe*.

The real-world ruin at the synthetic fuel facilities and its crippling consequences failed to disperse these aggressive fantasies. Hitler accordingly decided on 23 May 1944 that Saur's skeleton bomber production was unacceptable. With this in view, and under the impression that the Me-262 was coming shortly as a Blitz Bomber, Hitler met with his *Luftwaffe* chiefs on 23 May 1944 at the Berghof at Obersalzberg.

Galland was not asked to be present at this meeting. He was at his HQ in Berlin-Kladow. (The consequences of the discussions were nevertheless to affect him intimately.) Goering was present with his entourage. Speer, Milch, Saur, Colonel Petersen, and several members of the Me-262 commission also participated. As discussion moved to Saur's large production program for the Me-262 jet fighter, Hitler sat bolt upright and interrupted.

"Jet *fighter?*" he said. "I thought the Me-262 was coming out as a speed bomber."

Obviously agitated, the *Fuehrer* then asked the question that would wreck Galland's chances for a reversal of the aerial situation. *"How many of the Me-262s already produced can carry bombs?"*

Field Marshal Milch replied that none could carry bombs. The aircraft was being manufactured exclusively as a fighter. He emphasized the design revisions that would be required to convert the Me-262 into a fighter bomber. Hitler was turning purple. This was an almost poetic situation, for Milch had deliberately circumvented Hitler's orders to produce the Me-262 as a Blitz Bomber.

Milch had gambled. Basing his actions largely on Galland's evaluation of the Me-262 fighter, Milch believed that only this machine could salvage the situation. Now he had been compelled to personally drop this bomb of bad news on the *Fuehrer*.

Hitler passed into a violent rage. Since long before the Insterburg demonstration of the previous November, he had nurtured his vision of Blitz Bombers, immune to interception, racing over the invasion beaches and terrorizing Allied troops. The Allies would land any day. Now, at the last minute, he was being informed by his highest and most trusted officials that his orders on the Blitz Bomber had been disobeyed. Hitler raked the men before him unsparingly.

With maniacal determination, the *Fuehrer* began on the spot the conversion of the Me-262 to a Blitz Bomber. With armament and load statistics produced by the stunned Saur, Hitler stripped the aircraft of guns, ammunition, and armor-plate. In a few minutes he had shown them all how to modify a jet fighter plane. His rage was such that the gathering of high officials stood mute before it, except Milch, who urged Hitler to think over the matter. Having already completed the redesign of the Me-262 on the Berghof table top, the *Fuehrer* poured vituperation and abuse onto Milch.

Stung by Hitler's invective, Milch shouted that "the smallest child" could see that the Me-262 was a fighter aircraft. The Field Marshal thereby essentially ended his career. Hitler refused to address him again. The Me-262 was ordered into service exclusively as a high-speed bomber. Reference to the aircraft as a fighter was forbidden.

When word of these new edicts reached Galland from Milch and Colonel Petersen, he found them almost impossible to comprehend. Germany was being battered to pieces from the air. He felt rebellion rise inside himself. Even though he had heard Hitler regale the *Luftwaffe* chiefs at Insterburg with his vision of the Blitz Bomber, Galland never believed that such a technical travesty could be forced on the *Luftwaffe*. The small Me-262 commando operating at Lechfeld under his supervision had been proceeding well. Their work had received his special attention and interest. Saur's plans for 1,000 Me-262 fighters per month had given everyone hope. All this was now to be swept away by the Fuehrer's pique and Goering's acquiescence.

On 29 May 1944, as though nailing the coffin shut, Goering issued orders transferring the Me-262 from Galland's office to that of Colonel Dieter Peltz, General of the Bomber Arm. This stroke was intended to silence all talk of an Me-262 fighter. Relations with the Bomber Arm thereafter became increasingly strained, as Peltz took steps to prepare bomber *Geschwader* for Me-262 operations. There would be no more prototypes officially supplied to Galland's test commando at Lechfeld. The young general therefore began organizing additional aircraft via various sub rosa routes. The two major arms of the *Luftwaffe* struggled with each other, while the Allies blasted them both. Goering's appalling leadership had brought them to this.

The disheartening diversion of the Me-262 to the Bomber Arm came as Galland and his staff were already under multiple pressures. The master plan for countering the invasion had proceeded since February of 1944, while the defense of the homeland had to be simultaneously sustained. The central fighter reserve was being built up after Goering's belated approval. Galland's intention was to keep these new units in Germany, while they acquired strength, experience, and coordination.

The main *Reich* defense after the invasion would be carried out by JG-300 and JG-301, backed by the twin-engined fighters of ZG-26 and ZG-76. All other *Geschwader* were to be transferred under the master plan to France, as soon as the Allies were committed to their main landings. *Luftwaffe* airfields were being prepared and provisioned in France, in the face of constant Allied bombing and strafing.

Once again the Allied deception experts, basing their actions largely on *Ultra* intelligence intercepts, set about misleading the Germans. These experts created a phantom army in Kent. Purportedly commanded by Lt. General George S. Patton, Jr., this nonexistent army generated vast radio traffic, studded with clues that Patton would land in the Pas de Calais. These deception stratagems were designed to reinforce the personal conviction of Field Marshal von Rundstedt that the Pas de Calais would be the main Allied invasion area. German *Panzer* dispositions were made accordingly. Other deception tactics prepared the Germans for a feint landing.

This German combat film demonstrates how closely some Luftwaffe pilots would approach to assure a kill.

Caught in the sights of an FW-190, an American P-47 "Thunderbolt" long-range fighter takes wing-root hits.

All the careful planning done in Galland's office for rapid transfer of the Fighter Arm to France was virtually nullified by these successful Allied deceptions. Germany's High Command West initially evaluated the Normandy landing as a feint, predisposed as they were by Allied deception to focus on the Pas de Calais. Movement of Fighter Arm units was therefore not ordered for more than 24 hours. Transfer of fighters to invasion area airfields became a wild scramble, as the *Luftwaffe* finally issued its own orders for the move.

Galland's pilots flew barely 300 sorties on invasion day, against more than 10,000 sorties by the Allies. Only a handful of fighter bombers took off on missions against the beachheads. All save a few were forced to jettison their bombs to survive, while Allied fighters in swarms attacked relentlessly. Hardly a single *Geschwader* or *Gruppe* reached its French bases with its own squadrons attached. Every *Gruppe* became a mix of squadrons from other *Gruppen*.

Invasion zone airfields on which such effort had been expended were mostly bombed out and the installations wrecked by strafing. Other landing grounds were now chosen and prepared in feverish haste, with all the mistakes that stem from action under pressure. Fighter Arm signals broke down. Coordination became almost nonexistent. Pilots accustomed to the sophisticated fighter control of *Reich* defense proved to be sadly deficient in navigation when divested of such aids. They came down in dozens on the wrong airfields, miles from where they had been assigned.

Missions degenerated into miserable hedge-hopping sorties around the beachhead areas. The small *Luftwaffe* pickup formations were hounded relentlessly by hordes of Allied aircraft. When the Germans were lucky enough to get back down on a *Luftwaffe*-controlled airfield, they would find only skeleton ground crews present, flown in by Ju-52s that had braved the Allied air armadas. The full ground crew complement would be days or even weeks away, advancing over battered railways that were dominated by Allied fighter bombers. Supply problems became acute for fields that were too few and too poorly camouflaged to sustain successful fighter operations. Disorganization and disaster engulfed the *Luftwaffe* effort.

Galland set up a new supply system a week after the invasion. Ferry pilots minus combat or navigational skills were incapable of delivering new fighters to France. Galland organized a central supply base in Wiesbaden, with subdepots at Cologne and Mannheim, from which combat pilots could take aircraft on into France. Fighter Corps II, with General Werner Junck in command, allocated replacement fighters. Allied air dominance forced these German fighters to fly to their French fields late in the evening, when Allied air activity diminished.

Galland despatched Colonel Hannes Trautloft, the Inspector of Day Fighters, to evaluate the situation in France and to pull the Fighter Arm together. Although he was one of the most capable officers in the Fighter Arm, Trautloft's best efforts were needed just to keep the German fighters functioning at a minimum. He sought to keep his formations as large as possible, for mutual protection and increased striking power, and he did everything possible to effect rapid assemblies. This was a tall order in the shooting gallery of French airspace. Just getting back down safely after operations was a small victory.

In the lull before the Allied breakout from Avranches, Galland flew out for a personal tour of the invasion area airfields. His report to Goering was a catalog of deficiencies and errors, crowned by the technical performance inferiority of German fighters to the best Allied machines. Pilot skill and morale were at an all-time low. German fighter pilots soon had to keep their heads down even walking on their own airfields, since everything that moved on the ground was hosed with Allied fire from the air. (In Galland's words, "It was like a Wild West show.")

Touring the Fighter Arm units in this cauldron was a grim experience. Getting from airfield to airfield in one piece was a major feat. Galland's feelings of dismay and sadness, as once-proud *Gruppen* were reduced to sending up a handful of fighters each day, were intense. He had to conceal these feelings. Any kind of negative emotion was unthinkable. These embattled pilots and their commanders still looked on him with the greatest respect and trust. This touched him amid the shambles and made the dissolution all the harder to bear.

Across the Channel, the enciphered radio traffic of Speer's repair organization had been monitored and broken by the *Ultra* decrypters. This significant information, combined with other intelligence, made clear how drastically the German war effort had been hampered by the May attacks on synthetic fuel targets. On 8 June 1944, Strategic Bombing Chief General Spaatz assigned top priority to further attacks on the German oil industry. Misburg was struck on 15 June, and on 20 June more than 1,200 heavy bombers drove home devastating attacks on synthetic fuel facilities. These blows and those that followed aimed at the complete paralysis of German war potential.

Fighter Arm fortunes in Galland's eyes at this time held only one positive aspect—the *Reich* central fighter reserve. Events were proving the wisdom of organizing this force. Allied air power was grinding at the ragged *Luftwaffe* formations in France. The first four post-invasion weeks had cost the Fighter Arm more than 1,000 aircraft. Approximately 800 fighters were now in the central reserve. Strained fuel supplies were making it difficult for them to become battle-worthy, but their efficiency was slowly rising. The Fighter Staff had provided these 800 planes. Even if the pilots were inexperienced, Germany was not naked before the storm of renewed strategic bombing.

Resumption of massive daylight attacks on Germany, with fleets of more than 1,000 heavy bombers, compelled Hitler to forsake his fantasies of a renewed *Luftwaffe* Bomber Arm. The *Fuehrer* became disillusioned with the bombers. Renewed attacks on synthetic fuel facilities prompted Hitler to insist, on 29 June 1944, that only fighter aircraft were henceforth to be built. The Me-262 was to come as a Blitz Bomber. Anyone disobeying these orders was to be shot. The *Fuehrer* was dissuaded from these extreme measures, and limited bomber production continued, while the Fighter Arm fought for its existence in France.

Galland was able to extricate fighter units from the French maelstrom for rebuilding, but getting them back to Germany was hazardous and costly. He continued wangling Me-262s for his test commando. Sympathetic officers in high posts smuggled sufficient jets to the test commando to keep it functioning. Experience with these bootlegged jet fighters in test operations provided exciting evidence of their decisive performance edge. The Me-262 was an interceptor *par excellence*.

The attempt on Hitler's life on 20 July 1944 added to the atmosphere of dissolution. Details were lacking and rumors were rife; but when the dust settled, Hitler was still in charge. Heinrich Himmler rose in authority and status. Himmler's SS hunted down and executed the plotters. Galland would shortly find out that Himmler and the SS had a strong interest in the Me-262.

Early in August, the Allied breakout from Avranches sent armored spearheads racing across France. Rout threatened the German Army, battered at every turn by overwhelming Allied air power. Galland and Speer were summoned to a conference with Hitler. Present also were Saur and General Kreipe, the new Chief of the *Luftwaffe* General Staff. Kreipe had replaced Guenther Korten, who had died of wounds sustained in the Hitler assassination attempt.

Hitler demanded immediate commitment of the central fighter reserve against the Allied breakout from Avranches. Galland was not permitted to voice his objections, which were based on the chastening experience of the post-invasion disaster. Inexperienced reserve pilots could accomplish something in air defense under homeland conditions. Under current conditions in France, where the Allies enjoyed a superiority of 20 to 1, the raw pilots would be rapidly devoured.

The "conference" continued as a Hitler monologue. Even Speer was not permitted to speak. Hitler also objected to the wasting of the central fighter reserve, which would leave German industry naked. Factories, synthetic fuel plants, and railways had to be protected or the war effort would collapse. Speer had to remain silent about these crucial matters, as Hitler held the floor.

The *Fuehrer's* commitment of the fighter reserve began turning into a diatribe against the Fighter Arm. Standing with cotton wool in his damaged ears, trembling and shaking, the *Fuehrer* was becoming irritated by his own oratory. He was considering doing away with the Fighter Arm, or reducing it to a few *Geschwader* equipped with new-type aircraft—but not the Me-262. Hitler glared at Galland.

"The rest of them," he said harshly, "I am going to *scrap,* in favor of a tremendous production increase in flak."

The word "scrap" lashed Galland. He hardly heard Speer's desperate attempt to explain to Hitler that, reducing fighter production did not mean flak production could be automatically increased. Available explosives imposed a limit. General Kreipe cut the ground from under Galland and Speer by taking Hitler's side. Kreipe asserted that the 800 fighters of the reserve could easily fly 1,000 missions a day in the West. The Chief of the Luftwaffe General Staff had not recently been in France. Galland and Speer were not permitted to respond.

"I have no more time for you," said the *Fuehrer,* turning to his maps.

The General of the Fighter Arm and the Minister of Armaments were thrown out.

The central fighter reserve was hurled in. Conditions in France were now far worse than in the first invasion days. Paris had fallen. The situation was irretrievably lost, with a highly fluid ground war complicating the transfer of a large fighter force to France. Pilots in unfamiliar terrain, minus cross-country flight experience, landed on airfields that were deserted, wrecked, or behind the rapidly advancing Allied armor. Communications were a shambles. Many aircraft had to be destroyed by their pilots for lack of fuel upon landing in France.

Fighter units already caught up in the general retreat had to give part of their invaluable ground crews to the paratroops. Many were left behind to fight as infantry. The pilots who got out, ferrying ground crews in their fighters where possible, were lucky to survive. German Army and SS units seized *Luftwaffe* transport at gunpoint and drove off, leaving the *Luftwaffe* men to destroy their own installations and await capture.

These days of dissolution would be burned into Galland's soul forever. Behind his imperturbable expression and manner, and the jaunty cigar, churned a corrosive inner turmoil. His beloved Fighter Arm, the pride of his life, was being smashed before his eyes. This was happening less by the hands of the enemy than by the *Fuehrer's* crazy order to throw in everything. Telephone, radio, and teletype poured out ceaseless disasters.

The immense and dedicated labors of his staff in creating the reserve, all his hopes for the Big Blow and the production miracles of the workers who built the 800 fighters, were simply being flushed down the drain. The fate of the inexperienced young pilots did not bear thinking about. Most of them were killed, wounded, or captured—without having the slightest effect on the Allied breakthrough.

Galland searched desperately for a redeeming element in this mindless ruin. All he could find was that the 800 fighters of the reserve had shot down 12 Allied aircraft in France before disappearing into the void. A fighter force as large as that used in the Battle of Britain had vanished from the earth. Galland told himself that he should quit. He'd had more than enough of Hitler and Goering. He would be better off fighting—to the death—in the air, finding an honest soldier's end. Then he thought about the peerless leaders and pilots and crews in the Fighter Arm who trusted him. They were men whose advocate he had always been in high councils. He could not put from his mind the people in the cities. Fighters were still being built in droves.

He decided that he would stay until sacked. The Fighter Arm had to be rebuilt.

CHAPTER TWENTY-THREE

The Big Blow remained Galland's prime objective as he drove forward with another rebuilding of the Fighter Arm. Only the downing of 300–400 American heavy bombers in a day could possibly halt stratcgic bombing, through which Germany's war potential was now being systematically smashed. This final rebuilding of the Fighter Arm was a taxing and complex task.

Fighter units struggling back to Germany from their French ordeal had lost pilots, aircraft, unit cohesion, and much of their morale. Weeks of desperate operations, while they were hunted relentlessly in the air and on the ground, had taken a psychological toll to match the physical damage. Confused *Gruppe*—operated with at least one squadron mixed into it from a different *Gruppe*. Operational efficiency was at an all-time low, despite the leadership of outstanding *Kommodores* in most *Geschwader*.

Returning also to Germany were the battered remnants of the once-vaunted IX.*Fliegerkorps,* with which Hitler, Goering, and Peltz had intended to terrorize Britain. (The brave crews in this formation would be remembered mainly for their heavy losses.) Barely able even to find London, the vengeance mission of IX.*Fliegerkorps* turned out to be futile and wasteful, as Galland had predicted. Reduced now to fewer than 200 aircraft, IX.*Fliegerkorps* was finished as a striking force, and its remnants were immobilized by the fuel shortage. Peltz himself nevertheless remained active, under the patronage of the *Reich* Marshal. The unsuccessful Assault Leader against England was casting an ambitious eye on the Fighter Arm.

Galland persuaded Goering and the High Command to allow the Fighter Arm a brief respite, before again committing it in strength. Lowered morale was seriously lowering combat efficiency. The only remedy was a combination of rest, reequipment, reorganization, and improvement of pilot quality, the latter within the strict limits imposed by available fuel. Galland faced a monumental task in rebuilding the Fighter Arm's striking power.

Fighter aircraft now were abundant. Saur had pushed fighter production to record heights in June and July. More than 1,000 pilots came out of the training schools in August. They were not the pilots of 1940 in terms of skill, but they were able to bring down bombers if properly employed and rightly led. Galland shaped everything towards his goal of mighty and concentrated blows against the daylight raids. All pilots and units were trained, prepared, and directed toward this end. Goering put his full authority behind the effort to refurbish the Fighter Arm and to plan its tactical employment.

Galland stripped Austria and the Southern Front of fighters. The Italian Front henceforth would be weakly guarded by two *Gruppen* of Me-109s, manned by Italian pilots and commanded by his trusted friend and old comrade, Colonel Eduard Neumann. For additional protection of key Italian targets, Galland planned to set up an Me-163 rocket fighter unit in Italy. 20 Italian pilots were actually brought to Germany for Me-163 training. (Fuel shortages brought this idea to nothing.)

By early fall of 1944, the *Luftwaffe* had in the West JG-2, JG-26, JG-27, and JG-53. For the defense of the *Reich*, JG-3, JG-300, and JG-301 were assigned. In the South were the two Italian *Gruppen* already mentioned. Resting and refitting in Germany were JG-1, JG-6, JG-11, and JG-77. JG-4, JG-7 and JG-76 were newly-formed *Geschwader*. The Eastern Front was left intact.

Once more Galland raised *Gruppe* strength to stretch out the thinning supply of experienced leaders, whose numbers had been further reduced in France. *Gruppe* strength now became 68 aircraft, including reserves. In each *Gruppe,* pilots were given 15 hours of additional training, specialized to *Reich* defense operations. JG-27 was duly moved from the West to central Germany for rest and refurbishment.

The assault fighters (*Sturmgruppen*) were exchanged with those in stronger *Geschwader,* to increase overall efficiency. Squadrons mixed into strange *Gruppen* during the French debacle were left where they were to save fuel, which was now almost as precious as blood. The various *Geschwader* were simply reconstituted with their adopted squadrons. Graduates were now being turned out rapidly from the formation leaders' courses. Officers were in short supply. Galland broke this bottleneck by promoting 350 NCO pilots to war commissions, simultaneously and without ceremony.

By early November of 1944, the Fighter Arm had reached a strength of 3,000 aircraft, with about 2,500 operational. Creating this force out of the post-invasion chaos was probably Galland's major organizational achievement. Even his development of the central fighter reserve prior to D-day had been surpassed. This incredible resurrection brought into being a Fighter Arm nearly double the size of that available in 1943. The feat was accomplished despite U.S. strategic bombing attacks.

Correct tactical employment of this potential blizzard of fighters was absolutely vital. Tactical operations of this reborn force were accordingly well rehearsed. Preparations were made to meet several different types of American raids, with all unit officers participating in the drills and exercises. In overseeing all this planning and training for the Big Blow, Galland continuously marveled at the sterling efforts of his staff. Without their dedication, this 11th hour rebirth of the Fighter Arm would not have been possible.

The assault fighters again came to the fore, charged with carrying out massed attacks from the rear at close range. Development of these *Sturmgruppen* units had been largely aborted by the invasion and its aftermath. The fighter *Kommodores* had called for them again in the new buildup, with Goering's support. Galland was compelled to fall in with these developments, although personally he was opposed to the way in which the assault fighters were to be used.

Galland objected to the proposed repetition of a past costly mistake—fighters flying defensively. The combination of assault fighters (mostly heavily-armed FW-190s) with a lighter escort of Me-109s and regular FW-190s, was called a *Gefechtsverband*. Consisting of up to 300 aircraft in three or four *Gruppen,* these formations flew defensively, with the fighter escort to the sides and above the assault fighters.

Strict High Command orders required the assault fighters to attack straight to the bombers. Numerous and nimble American fighters were able to sweep in behind these assault fighter vics and shoot them down readily, since the German pilots refused to engage. They also would not flee. This brave adherence to orders was costly in German lives.

Galland's unimplemented recommendation to the High Command was to assign only half the light fighters as escorts, leaving the remainder free to tackle the American fighters. Such aggressive action would force the American fighters into defending themselves, instead of leaving them free to intercept and engage the German assault fighters. Despite the inherent drawbacks of the High Command's close-escort orders, considerable successes were scored by the assault fighters in September, October, and November. Success was dependent upon getting behind the American formations and making close-range firing sweeps through the bombers. Assembling these large *Luftwaffe* fighter formations nevertheless proved increasingly difficult. American fighter opposition continually grew stronger.

When *Luftwaffe* fighters became fewer after the withdrawal from France, the Americans went hunting for them. Strafing of *Luftwaffe* bases became commonplace. Any attempt to assemble a formation the size of a *Gefechtsverband* received immediate and aggressive attention from U.S. fighters. Since the majority of German pilots were not only inexperienced but also outnumbered in their own airspace, Fighter Arm morale continued to decline.

Galland analyzed the entire aerial situation as being determined by the impact of fighter on fighter. The Big Blow would be the *Luftwaffe*'s last chance. Beyond that, only the massive employment of Me-262 interceptors, with the most experienced and successful pilots, could possibly affect Allied ascendancy.

When Doolittle sent a mighty bombing force of more than 1,100 heavies to Germany on 2 November 1944, most of them were assigned to synthetic fuel targets. Most important of these were the Leuna plants. Seventeen groups of American fighters escorted the bombers. A force of about 500 German fighters bitterly contested the skies over the Merseburg area. Assault fighters from JG-300 and JG-3 claimed 30 U.S. bombers downed, and 28 American fighters were shot down that same day. There were still too many American fighters in the sky for a *Luftwaffe* force of up to 500 fighters to handle.

Galland's forces suffered the loss of 70 pilots killed and 28 wounded. The newly refreshed JG-27 was heavily stricken, with 25 pilots killed. The Leuna Company's synthetic fuel facilities around Merseburg were seriously damaged. As a large-scale interception, the Merseburg battle was not successful, but Galland's thinking was still directed towards a much larger scale of operations. He planned the mass commitment of 2,500 fighters, saturating the American defense and allowing the assault fighters through to the bombers. The essence of the Big Blow was tilting the all-important numerical advantage over to the Fighter Arm suddenly and decisively in a determined area and time.

Galland continued flying occasional combat missions, against strictest orders. This experience confirmed how vital it was to get Me-262 fighters for attacking the American heavies. None of the elaborate ploys and stratagems the Fighter Arm was now using to get assault fighters into contact with the bombers would be needed. The Me-262's great speed would allow it to simply break through the escort; and, with its heavy armament, the Me-262 was an assault fighter *par excellence*. Fire from four 30mm cannons could literally saw the wing off a B-17. The jet could outdistance its pursuers.

Reports from Test Commando 262 at Lechfeld, equipped with its own fighter control station and radar, continued to confirm the high promise of the Me-262 as an interceptor. Many Mosquito reconnaissance aircraft were downed. On the basis of these reports and results, and out of his own professional convictions, Galland continued his struggle for the Me-262 fighter. Not even the ruin on Germany from the air prevented the irrational misuse of the world's fastest fighter.

While Galland pressed for the establishment of jet fighter units manned by the most capable aces in the *Luftwaffe,* the limited Me-262 production was scandalously misassigned. From Galland's viewpoint, something almost diabolical was in supplying Me-262s to ground attack units, the Bomber Arm, and to research and testing stations unconnected with the Fighter Arm. Even Mistel composite pick-a-back experiments were authorized. All this went on while American bombers droned over Germany in their thousands.

Galland tackled Goering repeatedly about the Me-262. These interviews left Galland convinced that Goering knew deep inside himself that the Me-262 was a superlative interceptor. The *Reich* Marshal's personal political policy nevertheless remained firm. He would do nothing that would increase Hitler's disapproval or provoke his wrath. Goering had lost Hitler's confidence long ago. The *Reich* Marshal therefore deflected all of Galland's urgent requests to get the Me-262 into squadron service without delay.

Even Germany's foes knew what a threat the Me-262 fighter posed. Allied air intelligence had comprehensive knowledge of all Germany's jet and rocket developments, information largely provided through the *Ultra* decrypting teams. As Germany's internal communications were disrupted, radioteletype was used increasingly as a replacement for landline. This fed the data directly to the Allies. Far remote from this high secrecy level, American fighter pilots formed their own opinions of the Test Commando Me-262s that occasionally slashed among them. They were in awe of the German jet.

One American fighter pilot, interrogated by the masterful Hans Scharff at Auswertestelle West, ridiculed the misuse of the Me-262 as a bomber. He further asserted that the USAAF was living in fear of the day when the Me-262 would fly against them in the hands of top German aces. Galland fell on this report like a gold nugget and showed it to Goering. The *Reich* Marshal was impressed, but politics came first. He remained loyal to Hitler's edicts. The report was widely circulated. Eventually the American pilot's views were read by the only other man in Germany besides Hitler who could make Goering shake in his boots—Heinrich Himmler.

The gimlet-eyed SS chief nurtured the idea that the SS should take over the Fighter Arm. He welcomed any evidence of Goering's incompetence. Himmler's standing with Hitler was high, while that of Goering was barely hanging on. Through the SS and *Gestapo,* Himmler controlled the internal security of Germany, so he held all the cards in any poker game with Goering. When Himmler put pressure on Goering to set up Me-262 fighter units, the *Reich* Marshal had to comply. (Himmler would henceforth meddle continually in *Luftwaffe* business.)

Galland's surprise was total when ordered early in October by Goering to set up an operational jet fighter unit. The Lechfeld Test Commando was to serve as a nucleus. Galland's joy was lessened when Goering insisted that the new unit be set up in western Germany, so it could operate early against the Allied bomber streams and their escort. Galland recommended basing the jets in central Germany, where operations and tactics could be developed with less harassment from Allied air power. Goering rejected this recommendation. The new unit was based, accordingly, northwest of Osnabrück, at Achmer and Hesepe, with a nominal establishment of 40 aircraft, 12 officers, and 315 other ranks. Major Walter Nowotny, an Austrian and former *Gruppenkommandeur* of I/JG-54, was put in command.

Nowotny was only 24 years old but had already won the Diamonds, and he was credited with over 250 aerial victories. Galland considered him the best young ace in the *Luftwaffe*. Nowotny was entrusted now with a considerable and historic responsibility. The first operational jet fighter unit in the world was named *Kommando Nowotny* in his honor. Everything about the new unit was known instantly to the Allies through *Ultra* decrypts. Allied air intelligence ensured that Achmer and Hesepe were made hot.

Two squadrons of JG-54 were assigned to the specific operational task of the protecting the jet airfields. They were kept busy. Allied fighters haunted the area, awaiting the golden chance to catch an Me-262 landing or taking off—their most vulnerable moments. These harassments added a nasty aspect to technical problems in preparing, servicing, and maintaining the Me-262s that were especially complex. At peak initial strength, *Kommando Nowotny* had about 30 jets, but technical difficulties lowered this number rapidly, despite excellent combat successes. Galland followed Nowotny's activities with passionate interest. The tally of jet downings kept rising, despite the unit's low serviceability.

Combat successes with *Kommando Nowotny* crowned the efforts of Galland, Saur, Speer, Milch, and many others to get Hitler's approval for series production of the Me-262 fighter. The *Fuehrer* liked to hear of raiding aircraft being shot out of the sky by Nowotny's jets. On 4 November 1944, Hitler finally gave in. Even if he required that each fighter aircraft must be able to carry a 550-lb bomb in an emergency, his approval for jet fighter production was a landmark.

On 7 November 1944, as the refurbished fighter reserve approached final readiness, Goering summoned a conference at Air Fleet *Reich* HQ at Berlin-Wansee. All high officers of the Fighter Arm and all combat formation commanders down to squadron level were ordered to attend. The *Reich* Marshal delivered yet another abusive diatribe against the Fighter Arm that was monstrous both in content and in length. For an incredible three and a half hours, Goering laid all the blame for Germany's woes on the "pussy foot fighter pilots." There were aces in the room who had flown over 1,000 combat missions. Others had been shot down five and more times, returning always to the shambles aloft. Many had bodies under their uniforms that were laced with wound scars. The burned faces of others were special combat badges that they would wear for the rest of their lives.

This was Goering's way of inspiring the most important officers in the Fighter Arm: his top leadership who would direct operations and the officers who would lead the formations into battle. All of them were too war-weary to be uplifted by abuse from a superior, and least of all from one who had concentrated with such visible effects upon the joys of the table. The consequences were unpleasant and destructive.

Galland heard and saw the open grumbling, the protests, and the disillusionment. Goering had cast an appalling negativity over the assembly. Even that was not enough for the *Reich* Marshal. Recorded excerpts from his speech were distributed by his orders to all fighter units, with instructions that all pilots were to hear his speech. The incensed Galland left Berlin immediately. He flew to Achmer, where Nowotny and his commando were casting positive light, despite comprehensive technical difficulties.

Nowotny was full of enthusiasm for the Me-262. He described to Galland his tactical experience in closing with American bomber formations. Totally absorbed in the conversation, Galland did not notice how the hours flew. Hardly anything in life meant more to him now than proving this aircraft, and here was a top-quality fighter pilot who was doing the job. They retired late, fired with hope.

On the morning of the next day, 8 November 1944, air raid sirens and barking flak signaled American bombers approaching. Nowotny took off with other commando pilots. Galland prayed for him to get airborne before American fighters found the airfield. Nowotny disappeared safely into the overcast. Radio chatter soon reported that he had downed a bomber but had lost one engine to hits. He was trying to make it back but was jumped by fighters. Close to the airfield, but out of sight above the overcast, Galland heard the firing. Then Nowotny's Me-262 came straight down, to impact with a thunderous explosion.

Galland had seen many fighter pilots die, but this scene shook him. Nowotny was not only a splendid young man but in the vanguard of a new epoch. Standing beside Galland throughout the tragedy was his old boss from the commercial pilots' school at Brunswick, Colonel-General Alfred Keller—veteran of an earlier epoch. Galland telephoned immediately for permission to move the remaining jet fighters to Brandenburg.

As Nowotny had made clear in their discussions, more pilot and crew training and experience in the ground handling of the Me-262 were all needed. *Kommando Nowotny* was disbanded, and it provided a cadre around which III/JG-7 was formed into a successful jet fighter unit. Nowotny's few hectic weeks had been invaluable. Theoretical objections to the Me-262 fighter had been overcome. The allegedly poor maneuverability of the jet, the purported intolerable strain on the pilot, the anticipated difficulties in accurate shooting, and the claimed inability of the Me-262 to fly in formations had been proved to be nonsensical. Jet fighter operations had been moved forward—at last.

Immediately after Nowotny's death, Goering called yet another meeting, this time in Berlin-Gatow. The *Reich* Marshal's abusive speech of 7 November had been distributed on records to the fighter squadrons. Near-rebellion ensued as pilots listened to Goering berating them as cowards. Not content with this morale-eroding mischief, Goering now brought together 30 leading *Luftwaffe* figures in a symposium. They were to develop proposals for rapid renewal of *Luftwaffe* striking power. In all of the *Luftwaffe*'s colorful and sometimes bizarre history, there had been nothing quite like this event.

Goering opened the symposium, calling for proposals to refurbish the whole functioning of the *Luftwaffe*. Recommendations were to be made for the transfer or retention of various officers in highly responsible posts. Everything was up for wide-open discussion.

"Permission is hereby granted," said Goering, "for criticism of anything in the *Luftwaffe,* or anybody . . . *except me.* Since I have been appointed by the *Fuehrer,* there is no need to discuss or criticize me or my office."

Goering appointed Peltz as symposium leader. Despite the scope of the proposals being demanded, effectively a top-to-bottom revision of *Luftwaffe* organization and appointments, Goering had not invited the Chief of the *Luftwaffe* General Staff. Similarly omitted was the Chief of the Operations Staff. Goering's revision of the *Luftwaffe* was being undertaken mainly by a parliament of high-ranking young officers, who were mostly combat veterans. Rivalry between Fighter

Generalmajor Adolf Galland reflects upon his new responsibilities. Adolf Hitler had awarded him the Brillanten to the Eichenlaub and Schwertern to the Ritterkreuz on 28 January 1942.

Likeable Kommodore of JG52. Dietrich Krabak, popular commander of JG52 Fighter Wing on the Soviet front. He was considered a real professional by his subordinates, and his 125 aerial victories prove their trust was not misplaced.

Arm and Bomber Arm officers ran strongly.

Studying the assembly while Goering detailed its alleged purposes, Galland could conceive of nothing constructive developing from such a symposium, only friction and acrimony. Goering's kindergarten was there in force. Included were Peltz, Kraft von Delmensingen, the young von Brauchitsch, Diesing, Storp, and Knemeyer. The Fighter Arm was represented by Galland, Trautloft, Luetzow, von Maltzahn, Roedel, and Streib—all high-quality leaders.

A third group represented the Bomber Arm, with Baumbach, Harlinghausen, Schubert, and Mueller in attendance. A fourth group injected a political tone into the proceedings, because of its sympathies with the NSFO (*National-Sozialisticher-Führungs-Offizier*). NSFO personnel functioned as Nazi Party commissars, assigned to indoctrinate the troops. The NSFO sympathizers were fighter officers of lesser stature than those in Galland's group, and the most significant figure among them was Colonel Gordon Gollob. This officer was Galland's onetime protege, who had now chosen a political pathway for his own further advancement, because of personal and professional shortcomings of which Galland was well aware.

Bomber Arm officers immediately proposed a scheme of strategic bombing, so unrealistic as to be absurd. Galland faced each day the tactical and strategic crux of the air war: Allied air supremacy over Germany. Such air supremacy precluded any strategic bombing by the *Luftwaffe*. Fighter Arm officers advocated a realistic program: a greatly enlarged fighter force to regain air superiority over Germany as a fundamental first step. All other *Luftwaffe* activity was to be subordinated to this aim.

Gollob's group, with its political bias, proposed to redeem the situation by a massive infusion of Nazism into the *Luftwaffe*. All formation leaders should immediately attend a four-week political course. Gollob's group did not address problems of personnel, armament, or operations. Nazi indoctrination was deemed the correct palliative.

While stenographers frantically wrote down the proceedings in shorthand, for Goering's study and for historical purposes, chits were passed out for recommendations on dismissals, transfers, and appointments. Tempers boiled and nerves frayed as old grievances erupted. Galland readily perceived that Goering's minions were determined to have him removed. Colonel Gollob was obviously their opportunistic ally. His lust to be General of the Fighter Arm was beyond concealment. Not one of the purposes for which the meeting was allegedly convened was ever achieved. Discipline was undermined. The High Command was outraged and slighted, even though Generals Stumpff, Schmid, and Weise had been present at the symposium. Mistrust and confusion were rife. Galland emerged from the "*Luftwaffe* Parliament" convinced that his days as General of the Fighters were numbered. The Big Blow therefore became of supreme importance to him. He would end his tenure with a major victory.

On 12 November 1944, Galland notified Goering and the High Command that the reconstituted Fighter Arm was ready for action. Eleven massive *Gefe-*

chtsverbände were poised under the command of I.Fighter Corps. JG-2, JG-26, and JG-53 in the West, under II.Fighter Corps, would harry the heavies on the way in and on the way out, as weather permitted. Airfields in western Germany were ready to receive and support fighters flying multiple missions. And 80–100 night fighters would attack crippled heavy bombers staggering to Swiss or Swedish sanctuary.

Necessary now was for a major American formation to head for central Germany on a clear day. Galland estimated that the Big Blow would bring down between 400 and 500 heavy bombers, for the loss of about the same number of German fighters. Perhaps 150 German pilots would be lost. He expected that the material damage to the Eighth Air Force would be accompanied by an equally powerful blow at morale—a psychological shock: 4,000 to 5,000 aircrews lost in one mission would shake even the Americans. The weather remained maddeningly unfavorable, and the Fighter Arm waited.

Unknown to Galland, just two days before he pronounced the Fighter Arm ready for the Big Blow, Hitler had conceived a big blow of his own. The *Fuehrer* decided to make a massive surprise thrust through the Ardennes. Momentum would be sufficient to carry his armies to Antwerp. Hitler envisioned another Dunkirk.

To dupe the Allies into thinking that the German Army was preparing defensive operations along the Rhine near Cologne, the code name "Watch on the Rhine" was chosen. Everything was organized in deepest secrecy. Rigid security excluded even Galland from knowledge of the plan until early December. Two *Panzer* armies, with two more armies in support, were moved into position by night under total radio silence. Only top commanders and staff officers knew the secret. Motorcycle dispatch riders carried the most vital orders, to preclude Allied eavesdropping. The same weather that was delaying Galland's Big Blow also imposed an aerial reconnaissance blackout on German Army concentrations.

Sudden large demands were made for transfers of fighters to *Luftwaffenkommando-West,* the rump command left in the West after retreat from France. Galland and the others involved were told that the Allies were mounting a major offensive. Large fighter forces were therefore required for tactical support of the defending German armies; 1,200 of the Big Blow fighters were now moved to the Vechta–Arnheim sector in late November.

A controversial and unwelcome presence amid Ardennes preparations was Major General Dietrich Peltz, a brilliant bomber pilot and a Goering favorite. He emerged as C.O. of II.Fighter Corps in the West. This nepotistic appointment outraged the experienced Fighter Arm *Kommodores.* They deemed Peltz completely unqualified for fighter command. (Events would soon prove them correct.) Over 2,000 aircraft were eventually involved in the Ardennes thrust. Galland was stripped of his Big Blow forces, so arduously assembled.

Allied intelligence and the Allied commanders were this time completely deceived. The radio blackout had silenced *Ultra.* Attack by the German Army at dawn on 16 December 1944 took the Allies by surprise, confusing them.

Galland's realization that the force he had built was being committed to a nonsensical all-or-nothing gamble caused him to follow events with anger and fury.

Despite hundreds of ground attack and fighter sorties, the *Panzers* ran out of fuel after by-passing Bastogne. Their fuel never came. As soon as the weather cleared, Allied air power came instead, in all its awesome might. Air superiority was rapidly wrenched from the *Luftwaffe*. "Watch on the Rhine" was over (famous in history only as one of the war's greatest surprise attacks).

Painfully gone forever was Galland's vision of the Big Blow. Fighter losses in the West rose steeply, due largely to the inexperience and ineptitude of Peltz and his staff in commanding fighter operations. These losses were for no return. Crowning the Ardennes disaster was a climactic brainchild of Peltz and Hajo Herrmann, Operation "Groundplate" (*Bodenplatte*). This desperation strike was to be launched against a dozen Allied airfields in Holland and Belgium.

Over Galland's vigorous objections, low-level surprise attacks were planned. After two delays, the strike went in at 9:20 AM on New Year's Day of 1945. Most of the participating German pilots had been trained for Big Blow operations against bomber boxes. They were minus the special expertise required for ground attack. Results were accordingly erratic. Some Allied airfields suffered heavily and others escaped almost unscathed. RAF losses were 144 aircraft destroyed and 84 damaged. The USAAF lost 84 destroyed and 62 damaged. This one-time loss of aircraft could be easily absorbed by the Allies. Peltz gave the *Luftwaffe* a truly Pyrrhic victory, because the damage to the Fighter Arm was mortal.

Thus 237 German pilots were killed, missing, or captured. Many of them were downed by their own flak. Two *Kommodores,* 6 *Gruppenkommandeure,* and 10 squadron commanders were lost in Operation Groundplate—irreplaceable formation leaders. They all went in one day. For Galland, it was like seeing a fine rapier used to cut sugar cane, an appalling misuse. Fighters were a deadly yet delicate instrument of war, and Peltz had proved himself even more inept in their handling than his patron, the *Reich* Marshal, in 1940. (Galland would always regard Groundplate as the final stab in the back for the Fighter Arm.)

At New Year of 1945, Galland found himself significantly changed. All the heart to lead the Fighter Arm had gone out of him. Only his immense fortitude brought him through the mindless waste of the reconstituted fighter force. Small men in high rank who were now machinating for his dismissal hardly even bothered to conceal their scheming. The monumental damage to the Fighter Arm even seemed to bring them perverse pleasure. Galland had always stood firm for the Fighter Arm in the past, based on his own professional competence and combined with the loyalty of the fighting pilots and their leaders. Now he wanted out.

Ready to relinquish his heavy responsibilities, he wished to return to a fighter unit as an honorable soldier. He yearned for the primal simplicity of a fighter pilot's life, the black and white of battle aloft. Girding himself for his terminal struggles in the increasingly political ant hill of *Luftwaffe* command, Galland knew his dismissal was imminent.

CHAPTER TWENTY-FOUR

The slaughter of irreplaceable combat leaders in Peltz's New Year gamble climaxed for Galland a period of almost unbearable frustration. Command arrangements bordering on fantasy blocked his knowledge from application to the defense of Germany and denied him the power to prevent gross wastage of the Fighter Arm. Machinations against him by Bomber Arm leaders who sat at Goering's table became steadily more open. The bungling intrigues of Gordon Gollob came amid other strains as a wearying nuisance that Galland could not eliminate. Capping the whole scene was the imminence of his own dismissal, which precluded effective action.

The young general was like a man with his head locked in the stock of a guillotine—certain of his end, but uncertain of when the blade would fall. Laboring to speed that moment was the furtive Gollob, leaving no avenue unpursued that might discredit, smear, or professionally destroy Galland. A rational man could hardly have wished to preside over the disintegration everywhere evident at New Year of 1945, but Gollob coveted Galland's job with a consuming passion.

Gollob's unrealism was illustrated by his efforts to turn Galland's staff against their chief. Their loyalty proved to be like armor plate, forged in years of fire and shared stresses. The staff members were also aware that certain clerical workers had been infiltrated into Galland's office as spies. Seeming irregularities were reported to Gollob. The latter's influential friends could arrange for such infiltrations. Gollob consorted openly, furthermore, with bomber pilots Dieter Peltz and Hajo Herrmann, both of whom had been mentioned as replacements for Galland.

Gollob had long been allied with the NSFO, the Nazi Party commissars who were attempting the indoctrination of fighter pilots. Goering's entire kindergarten was eager to see Galland removed. They believed that he had "too much influence"—their perverse evaluation of the loyalty shown to him by the Fighter Arm.

Goering eventually asked Galland for a detailed, special report on Gollob. The *Reich* Marshal knew that Gollob was being politically pushed as Galland's successor. Goering disliked Gollob. Adverse reports on him had already reached the *Reich* Marshal. Any intriguer in Germany could count on his doings showing up in Goering's daily digest of tapped telephone conversations.

Galland was therefore required to prepare a comprehensive account of his experiences with the man who was advocating and plotting his dismissal as General of the Fighters. Galland had originally proposed Gollob, as a brave and capable fighter ace, to be *Kommodore* of JG-77. Gollob was a Galland protege at that time. Galland later proposed Gollob to be *Jafü* 5, an even more responsible post. That was as far as Gollob went without problems arising. His tenure at Deauville as *Jafü* 5 was terminated for disciplinary and operational reasons. Galland then brought him to his own staff, assigning him to work independently on the Me-262 and Me-163.

Gollob's services were unsatisfactory. He confined his interest to technical development. Training of pilots and technical staff, necessary improvements to communications, and the overall business of handling these complex and revolutionary aircraft were all seriously neglected. Despite his high rank, Gollob proved unreliable. (This same evaluation of him was made by his postwar Allied interrogators, who raked through his background and exhaustively questioned him face to face.)

Friction was created with Galland and his staff by Gollob's shortcomings. Galland was compelled to dictate to his subordinate exactly what he was to do, which Gollob resented and resisted. Galland's reaction was to transfer the troublesome officer to the Test Center Command. Gollob's desire for vengeance on his chief was thereby kindled. The most disgraceful vendetta in the *Luftwaffe* resulted, with Galland as the victim.

Galland omitted from his report to Goering the numerous repugnant incidents involving Gollob, some of which had occurred in his own office. The report stated, objectively and without rancor, that Gollob could not work in a responsible post without close supervision. Goering thus received reinforcement for his own personal aversion to Gollob.

Goering was adroit at setting subordinates upon each other like dogs. He had demonstrated this talent recently with the bitter "*Luftwaffe* Parliament," which unleashed needless acrimony between his own high officers. Further damage was thereby inflicted on the *Luftwaffe*, already reeling from battle losses. In this same pattern, Goering now handed to Gollob the report on him that he had asked the General of the Fighters to prepare.

Already seeking revenge on Galland for what he deemed to be past injustices, Gollob became incensed. (In a further effort to undermine his former C.O., Gollob took a step for which most surviving German fighter pilots would never forgive him.) He went to the SS. Audience was gained with Heinrich Himmler.

Into the receptive ear of the *Reichsführer* SS, Gollob poured his tales of Galland's mistakes, incompetence, and malfeasances. Galland was even accused of preventing the development of the Fighter Arm. Gollob urged the intervention of the SS, with a full-scale investigation. According to the ambitious colonel, the SS should take over the Fighter Arm and appoint him General of the Fighters.

Himmler's meddling in *Luftwaffe* business was an escalating irritation to Goering. Himmler was eager to give SS divisions their own jet fighter units. Gollob's ploy was welcome amid these ambitions. The *Reichsführer* SS repeated Gollob's tales to Hitler, with whom Himmler's standing was currently the highest. Hitler thereafter spoke often of Galland in derogatory terms at major war conferences. SS undercover operatives were planted on Galland's staff. His political past was comprehensively investigated—without significant results.

Peltz and Herrmann were also in line to be General of the Fighters, but Himmler planted Gollob's name repeatedly with Hitler. As soon as Hitler suggested Gollob to Goering, the *Reich* Marshal conveniently ignored all the negative reports he had accumulated on Gollob. Goering knew that Hitler wanted a new Supreme Commander for the *Luftwaffe*. The *Reich* Marshal was hanging on by his fingernails. Goering therefore decided to replace Galland with Gollob to placate Hitler, even if it meant further encroachment by Himmler into *Luftwaffe* affairs.

Goering ordered Galland to Karinhall and regaled him with another lengthy monologue, this one on the reasons for his dismissal. As the *Reich* Marshal droned on, silencing Galland's efforts to justify his actions, one thing emerged clearly: *Goering himself had no coherent idea of why he was axing Galland.*

Excuses, superficialities, notions, and fantasies were interwoven in a rambling discourse. Moderate in his tone for once, Goering stumbled to the end of his reasons for dismissing the young general. The *Reich* Marshal knew that he had been served with competence and dedication by Galland, for years and through terrible times. For a moment, Goering's facade fell away. The true man spoke.

"I am much obliged to you, General Galland, for all your good advice, and your services in your post. Thank you for all you have done. As soon as you have had a vacation, I will put you in an important, leading position."

"I am sorry, Herr *Reich* Marshal, but I cannot accept such a position."

Goering's blue eyes widened. "Why not?"

"Considering the influence of officers like Gollob, Peltz, and Herrmann, sir, and the imminent collapse of the Fighter Arm, I wish only to be an Me-262 fighter pilot."

"I could put you in command of . . ."

"Thank you, *Herr Reich* Marshal, *no!* I do not want to command anything. I just want to be a simple combat pilot doing my duty. That is what I request of you, sir."

Goering waved him out, insisting that a decision would be made after Galland's vacation. The young general felt considerably cleaner when he left Karinhall, but four gruelling years could not be waved away with the *Reich* Marshal's baton. The Fighter Arm was in his blood.

Galland feared in his heart for the brave fighting pilots whose fortunes and fate would pass now into the hands of Gordon Gollob, or of others like him.

He also knew that a storm was brewing in the Fighter Arm, with himself at its eye. His imminent dismissal was common knowledge down to the humblest NCO pilot and the ground crews. Goering's intention to pitchfork Peltz, Herrmann, or Gollob into his job was viewed by the pilots and combat leaders as the ultimate insult—eclipsing all the other Goering slurs through which they had suffered. Loyalty and allegiance to Galland were well-nigh universal. In any military force, anywhere in the world, this spirit was what competent commanders always sought to evoke.

Luftwaffe fighter pilots were now enraged by the Me-262 fiasco. Priority assignments of jet fighters as bombers, and to the hybrid formations designated KG (J) under Peltz, caused anger and frustration. The fighter pilots regarded the Me-262 as the weapon for which they had waited, while their comrades died in dozens attacking the enemy heavies.

Bad weather operations still were continually ordered, with heavy and needless losses to weather, rather than to enemy fire. These losses disgusted the experienced fighter *Kommodores*. They knew that these futile operations were urged by the Goering kindergarten, as part of the "advice" they gave the *Reich* Marshal. Goering's prestige within the Fighter Arm had sunk to an all-time low, but he continuously worsened the situation by harping on fighter pilot cowardice.

These massive currents of discontent and mistrust, washing away morale and efficiency, had brought some of the *Kommodores* and division commanders to Galland's office before he was dismissed. He was fully familiar with their grievances, but he was on a tightrope himself. All he could do was listen sympathetically. His responsibilities precluded his becoming directly involved with the highly decorated aces and old comrades who sought his ear and his aid in their extremity.

The *Kommodores* were seeking an audience with Hitler. They intended to ask the *Fuehrer* to make the drastic changes that they deemed essential to the restoration of morale and combat effectiveness. Removal of Goering as *Luftwaffe* Supreme Commander was at the top of their proposals.

Before going to Hitler, these disillusioned officers on 13 January 1945 sent Colonel Guenther Luetzow and Colonel Johannes Steinhoff to see *Generaloberst Ritter* Robert von Greim, the senior World War I fighter pilot. Von Greim was a Hitler favorite, and the *Fuehrer* was already considering him as a replacement for Goering. Von Greim's advice and influence were sought by the frustrated fighter leaders.

The World War I ace listened to Luetzow and Steinhoff. The next day, von Greim called General Karl Koller, Chief of the *Luftwaffe* General Staff, and reported on the interview. (According to Koller's diary, von Greim was sympathetic to the honest search of the *Kommodores* for a way out of their difficulties, but he calmed them down and advised them to see Koller first.)

Koller was already aware of what was afoot. He had received informally, on 13 January 1945, Major Gerd Müller-Trimbusch, who was Galland's operations officer and practically his chief of staff. Without Galland's knowledge or authorization, Müller-Trimbusch had asked to discuss Fighter Arm problems with Koller on a man-to-man basis, all rank being temporarily set aside.

As a result of Müller-Trimbusch's indiscretion, which the *Kommodores* would regard as treachery, Koller was aware that the combat leaders wanted to brief Hitler without going through Goering. The *Kommodores* all knew Goering's ways. The *Reich* Marshal would block them from seeing Hitler.

Koller understood the situation. Loud and bitter talk resounded through the Fighter Arm that Goering should retire. Koller nevertheless correctly emphasized that enforced retirement of Goering could only be regarded as mutiny, when he saw Steinhoff and Neumann on 17 January 1945.

Koller now informed Goering, in writing, of the potentially catastrophic foment in the Fighter Arm. He suggested that the *Reich* Marshal receive a *Kommodores'* delegation for frank discussion of their proposals and requests. Koller gently inferred that, if Goering could not straighten things out, then perhaps the *Reich* Marshal could secure an audience with the *Fuehrer* for the *Kommodores*.

Goering immediately saw Steinhoff and Neumann at Karinhall. Their visit and views convinced Goering that he had a major crisis on his hands. The *Reich* Marshal thereupon called a meeting of all available *Kommodores* at the House of Pilots (*Haus der Flieger*) in Berlin. Colonels Luetzow, Steinhoff, Roedel, Trautloft, and Neumann; Lt. Colonels Graf, Bennemann, and Priller; and Majors Michalski and Aufhammer were available to attend. Galland was not invited. Trautloft and Luetzow nevertheless kept him informed about events.

Luetzow had assembled all the *Kommodores'* requirements into a comprehensive proposal. He was appointed by the combat leaders as their spokesman. All the officers present were highly decorated aces, but Luetzow was something much more. A man of high intelligence, outstanding leadership gifts, and noble character, Luetzow was not overawed by the *Reich* Marshal's rank, reputation, or charisma. A tall man of distinguished lineage, the blood and iron in him contrasted starkly with Goering's decadence. The *Reich* Marshal may have been his superior officer, but Luetzow was the superior human being. Everyone present knew that.

Luetzow read aloud the proposals. All causes of friction and inefficiency in the Fighter Arm were covered, including Galland's dismissal. The *Kommodores* stated that Galland had the trust and confidence of the entire Fighter Arm. They requested that he be retained as General of the Fighters.

Vigorous arguments ensued for the next four hours. The Me-262 and its assignment to the Bomber Arm, new tactics, new operational controls, and the unacceptable presence of Bomber Arm officers in command of fighter units were all ventilated. Objections were voiced forthrightly to Goering's allegations of fighter pilot cowardice. Goering got the worst of these encounters. His main responses were to blame Galland. This further infused the arguments with heat. Goering became steadily angrier, as Luetzow in particular applied inexorable logic. Luetzow finally asked Goering to resign. The *Reich* Marshal blew up.

"This is *mutiny*" he bellowed. "There are going to be arrests!"

Flinging out of the room, Goering turned and glared at the honest and upright Luetzow. "I'll have *you* shot!"

The *Kommodores'* revolt was terminated, but bitter feelings were unabated. Arrest warrants were issued that evening for Galland and Luetzow. Goering had insisted all through the revolt that Galland was the instigator, despite the *Kommodores'* denials. Ordering Galland's arrest was a serious step. General Koller persuaded Goering not to proceed this way against his former fighter general or against Luetzow.

Luetzow was ordered to leave Germany within 48 hours. He was to take over Colonel Eduard Neumann's post as *Jafü* Italy. Luetzow was forbidden to have any visitors in Italy, or to communicate with Galland or any of the "mutineers." This was *Reichsverbannung*—banishment from Germany. The Swords to the Knight's Cross hung at his throat—Germany's second highest decoration for valor.

Galland reported next morning to General Meister, now Chief of *Luftwaffe* Personnel. From this officer he learned of Goering's rage against him for "masterminding" the *Kommodores'* revolt. Galland made it clear to Meister that he had neither initiated nor participated in the *Kommodores'* actions. Their wish to approach Hitler directly was also their own. Galland further emphasized that he had already been dismissed and was without any position or influence in the Fighter Arm.

Orders issued to Galland required him to leave Berlin within 12 hours, notify General Meister of his destination, and to stay under house arrest wherever he went. He chose the Giant Mountains and left Berlin for Oberwiesenthal. All fighter units received a Goering telex: General Galland had retired for health reasons.

With his former boss now under house arrest, Colonel Gordon Gollob took over the Fighter Arm. His first act was to stage a victory banquet. Outraged by this gross bad taste, Galland's staff wished to resign *en masse*. Their dismissed chief nevertheless pledged them to continue in their posts, for the good of the Fighter Arm, no matter how detestable the conduct of Gollob.

Friction between Galland's staff and Gollob left almost all work effectively paralyzed. The new General of the Fighter Arm was out for vengeance. His first two weeks in office were spent rummaging for evidence of Galland's "corruption." Files and records were ransacked for proof that Galland did the same sort of things in his high post as Gollob had pulled in France when he was *Jafü* 5. Alleged evidence of gambling and private use of *Luftwaffe* cars were uncovered. Such trivia were combined by Gollob with charges of disloyalty to the Nazi Party, of defeatism and of incompetence. This "evidence" was used as backing for Gollob's demand that official charges be pressed against Galland.

While Gollob was pouring his energies into this effort to disgrace Galland, his own official sphere of action was ignored. Slaking his hatred of his former chief, he was oblivious to the responsibilities he bore to the fighting pilots and to the German civil populace. General Doolittle was now sending over at least

1,000 heavy bombers every day that the weather permitted. Upwards of 300 more heavies winged in from the 15th Air Force in the south. Additional hundreds of 9th Air Force medium bombers roamed over western Germany with impunity. Gollob's main interest as Germany fell into final shambles was the destruction of Adolf Galland. The RAF and the USAAF received only his minimal attention.

Gollob's accusatory report on Galland fell into eager hands. Goering was seeking a scapegoat for the final disintegration of Germany's aerial defenses. The *Reich* Marshal quickly concluded that he could put the onus on Galland with all the blame for the Fighter Arm's imminent collapse. Goering could possibly even keep his own political hide intact, if he did a thorough enough job of blaming Galland.

Goering quickly appointed an investigating commission that he could control, consisting of Chief *Luftwaffe* Judge von Hammerstein and two other general officers. The SD, or *Sicherheitsdienst,*—the secret service of the SS—went into vigorous action. They arrested Major Rolf Meinardus, Galland's adjutant, and threw him into jail to await trial. Close surveillance was placed on Galland. The SD brutally grilled his trusty batman, Sergeant Benno Reiske, and forced him to spy on his chief in the mad scramble for evidence.

All of Galland's staff, from the decorated combat veterans down to the secretaries, were intensively questioned. Through his former staff and other sympathetic friends in high posts, Galland learned of Goering's plan to assemble an air-tight case against him. On top of defeatism, he would be charged with serious breaches of duty. Collapse of the Fighter Arm would be driven home to him in an ostentatious legal proceeding. General Galland would end in national disgrace.

When Galland returned to Berlin, his personally owned car was confiscated. His every move was watched. His telephone was tapped. The SD investigators turned up some people who had heard Galland say that the military situation was hopeless. Doubts were raised by the SD about his political views. Although he had avoided politics all his life, his relationship with Monica and the anti-Nazis in her circle came in for scrutiny. Tremendous energy was expended in digging out of Galland's past anything that could be used against him in his projected trial.

The general was operating almost completely in the dark. He had only snippets of information, sneaked to him by friends at risk of their own liberty. The entire apparatus of the SD and the Nazi Party was being used to frame him. The odds against him were long. He had no means of fighting back in the political arena, where he was a novice. Galland the fighter was at bay. He thought fast. He had not dodged hostile lead in hundreds of combats, nor suffered wounds, nor worn the Knight's Cross with Diamonds to end up being humiliated in a kangaroo court owned by Hermann Goering. There would obviously be no justice. He was driven into a corner.

Galland considered escaping to the Allied forces, but, after six years of war, he knew he could not live with that course of action. Goering would have him convicted *in absentia.* His parents and surviving brother would be called to account. He could not escape, nor could he stay.

His only option was the ultimate way out—suicide. Galland disclosed his intention to shoot himself that night to Monica and a small group of his friends. He even mused grimly that Goering might mouth lardy platitudes over his grave, as the *Reich* Marshal had done with Udet. His decision to kill himself left Monica appalled. She took action.

Risking her own personal freedom, and after many difficulties, she finally made contact with Albert Speer late in the night. She told him of Galland's intentions. Alarmed and concerned for the general, Speer went personally to Hitler despite the late hour. The *Fuehrer* knew nothing about Goering's legal vendetta against Galland, but he did know Goering. He took immediate action.

Hitler called in the SD in the middle of the night and demanded a briefing. He quickly saw through Goering's plan to make Galland into a scapegoat. Hitler would not tolerate such an action.

"This nonsense is to be canceled immediately," he ordered.

Before Galland could shoot himself in the small hours of the morning as planned, he received two highly improbable phone calls. One came from Ernst Kaltenbrunner, head of the dreaded *Reich* Security Service. The bulky and much-feared Kaltenbrunner, whose orders had snuffed out many lives, smoothly explained to Galland that there had been a mistake in his case. He was, please, not to kill himself.

Right afterwards came a second calming phone call. This time it was *Gestapo* Chief Heinrich Müller, no doubt rousted from bed at Hitler's orders. Again it was emphasized that there had been a mistake. Another plea was made that he not commit suicide. Galland counted himself lucky never to have had prior dealings with these two terrible personalities. He hung up the phone on Müller, incredulous that both of them were intent on saving his life. They even assigned a young *Luftwaffe* officer to watch over him until morning.

In the morning, a telephone call from Hitler's *Luftwaffe* aide, Colonel Nicolaus von Below, summoned Galland to see the *Fuehrer*. At the Chancellery, von Below in the name of the *Fuehrer* advised him that the pending trial and all attendant matters had been canceled. Galland was relieved. He was also irritated by the needless ordeal that Goering had forced him to endure.

"The *Fuehrer* is still fond of you, General Galland," said von Below. "He did not want a public scandal at this time such as your trial would create."

Goering's investigation promptly collapsed. Major Meindarus was released from prison, although Goering vindictively transferred him to the paratroops. Galland was summoned to Karinhall two days later. The *Reich* Marshal was flanked by stacks of thick files created by his investigation.

Goering made many accusations based on these data. Galland was forbidden to respond. The *Reich* Marshal was grasping at straws. With typical dishonesty and cant, he asserted that, because of Galland's past services to the *Luftwaffe,* he had ordered the investigation terminated.

Goering added magnanimously that he had also canceled the pending trial.

The *Reich* Marshal was unaware that Galland already knew, through von Below, that his trial and all other proceedings had been quashed by Hitler's personal order. Galland stood before his old adversary, imperturbably listening to one more Goering lie.

The *Reich* Marshal then told him that Hitler had withdrawn his prohibition on further combat flying for Galland. The *Fuehrer* had directed that Galland was to form a small unit of approximately squadron strength and prove that the Me-262 was a superior fighter aircraft. More was not to be expected of Hitler.

More? What more was there for a German fighter pilot doing his duty than to be given an Me-262? Galland's spirits rose. Even though he realized that his superiors expected him to be killed—with fate replacing legal judgment—he could not suppress his excitement. *He would lead a jet fighter unit!* His stony expression creased into a slight smile.

There was still more. Goering told him to select the pilots he wanted and to send him their names. The *Reich* Marshal glared at his onetime protege, the man he had himself promoted from *Kommodore* of JG-26 to General of the Fighter Arm.

"And if you want them, you can have that dismissed colonel, Steinhoff, and that mutiny leader, Luetzow. I certainly don't want them."

Galland could scarcely contain his elation. Jet fighters, and the best pilots in the *Luftwaffe* to fly them with him. His wild excitement resembled what he felt in combat, but, as in combat, he kept a cool head. He pointed out to Goering the intolerable situation with Gollob, and said that he could only form his jet unit if it were completely divorced from Gollob's authority. Goering agreed.

"Your unit will not be under Gollob. Nor will it be under the command of any air fleet, division, or fighter corps," said Goering. "You alone will decide where and how operations are conducted. You are also not to come into contact with any other fighter or jet fighter unit. I will issue orders to that effect."

In the dying days of the Fighter Arm, here at last was freedom to act as Galland judged fit. He could now implement personally what he had urged on his superiors since he first flew the jet in May of 1943. Hitler's action that had made this possible was not born of any benevolence, but rather of the certainty that he would die in combat—a clean end to the embarrassing "Galland affair." Combat hazards did not deter Galland. He would gladly take his chances aloft as always.

Rising from despair and the edge of self-destruction, he had soared in a few days to new hope. Never again would he see the doomed *Fuehrer,* but it was the strangest twist of his life that Hitler's intervention had taken him from suicide to salvation. Few indeed would there ever be who could make that claim.

CHAPTER TWENTY-FIVE

According to Newton, what goes up must come down, and this law applies to pilots as well as planes. The General of the Fighter Arm was back down to a squadron commander early in 1945—the same assignment he had held during his Spanish Civil War service eight years previous. A lieutenant at that time, he had risen to lieutenant general. His piston-powered biplanes of 1937 were replaced now by a squadron of the fastest fighters in the world—Me-262s, powered by twin turbojets. All in all, for Adolf Galland it had been a hell of a ride, a career having no counterpart in the armed forces of any other belligerent power.

He now was probably the most enthusiastic squadron commander in the *Luftwaffe,* for everything he had pleaded for during the bitter years was suddenly granted to him in miniature and under his personal control. A combat command after years of frustration was like a redemption. A hectic week followed his "appointment" as a squadron commander.

He went to officers he knew well on the Operations Staff and in the Quartermaster-General's office to begin organizing his unit. Aircraft, pilots, ground staff, spare parts, equipment, motor vehicles, and a massive list of other items had to be procured and assembled. *Jagdverband Galland* had to be created from zero.

Initially established at Brandenburg-Briest, the new unit drew upon the nearby resources of JG-7, also equipped with the Me-262. JG-7 was Steinhoff's last command before his dismissal. This connection resulted in Gollob's order to JG-7 not to assist Galland being completely ignored. Steinhoff's old comrades took an enthusiastic interest in the elite new squadron and provided everything they could to help.

Gollob continued his vendetta by blocking transfers of the pilots requested by Galland. Complaints by the new jet squadron commander to General Meister's personnel department went unheeded. At this stage of the war, Galland was not going to be denied through this kind of silent sabotage. He telephoned Colonel von Below at Hitler's HQ, and through the highest channels Goering quickly

Lt. General commands a squadron. The ex-General der Jagdflieger and Oberst Lützow stride towards their Me-262 jet aircraft at München/Riem early in 1945.

Blond knight of Germany. Erich Hartmann, 352-victory ace of JG52.

got the message—even as he had over Galland's trial.

Immediate orders were issued by Goering to fill Galland's unit with the requested pilots and material forthwith. Word of this elite "turbo" unit had swept through the Fighter Arm, igniting new enthusiasm. Successful aces vied to experience once more the half-forgotten thrill of air superiority. Sensing the historic nature of this jet squadron, they wanted the honor of such an assignment. Captains, majors, and colonels eagerly requested to fly as ordinary pilots.

Trautloft, at the 4th Division of Fighter Pilot Schools, had already sent Galland some of his best instructors, aces with extensive combat experience, when the Personnel Office was blocking other transfers. More pilots came to the new squadron on their own initiative, disdaining Gollob's authority. Most of them did not even bother to check with the Personnel Office. Some rode to Brandenburg-Briest on bicycles. Legendary pilots began gravitating to Galland's squadron.

From the Russian Front came Major Gerd Barkhorn, credited with 300 victories. Major Walter Krupinski, the fabled "Count Punski" with 197 victories, was coaxed out of the hospital, as were Erich Hohagen and "Bubi" Schnell. Guenther Luetzow returned from exile in Italy to find fellow "mutineer" Johannes Steinhoff, credited with more than 170 victories, in charge of conversion training and operations. Lesser-known aces from the war's first days added their experience and skill to Galland's roster of pilots.

Galland had also requested the transfer of Captain Erich Hartmann, the most successful fighter pilot in the *Luftwaffe*, with nearly 350 aerial victories. Hartmann made check flights with the Me-262, but he wanted desperately to return to his old comrades in JG-52 on the Eastern Front. Gollob was naturally happy to grant Hartmann's request to return to JG-52 (but it led to the personal tragedy of ten and a half years of Soviet captivity for Germany's greatest ace).

In the history of aerial warfare, there had never been such an elite fighter squadron. The Knight's Cross could have served as its badge. Almost all the pilots had won this decoration or its higher orders. Their commander was a lieutenant general. Steinhoff and Luetzow were both colonels. Heinz "Pritzl" Baer, a *Luftwaffe* legend with 220 victories since 1939, was a lieutenant colonel. Krupinski, Barkhorn and Hohagen were all majors. These aces and their illustrious squadron commander had almost 900 victories between them. When the numerous captains, lieutenants, and sergeants who were aces were included, the squadron became the only one in the world whose personnel had downed over 1,000 aircraft!

Ranks rapidly blurred into insignificance, as the most distinguished ace leaders in the *Luftwaffe* did the work of junior officers and NCOs in ordinary units. The designation JV-44 (*Jagdverband* 44) was chosen by Galland and approved by Goering. The *Reich* Marshal was not told that the double F in 44 was a play on words—a pilots' jibe at the *Fuehrer,* single F. The two Fs symbolized in their own circle that they were now going to try two *Fuehrers,* since 12 years with one *Fuehrer* had gotten them nowhere. The 44 designation also harked back to the highly successful Fighter Group 88 of the Condor Legion, when Galland had gone into combat for the first time. He hoped that JV-44 would be as good as Fighter Group 88, for that would be significant success.

Chief of the *Luftwaffe* General Staff Karl Koller asked Galland to transfer JV-44 to southern Germany, to provide at least some protection for the Me-262 factories. General Koller suggested Lechfeld. After a rapid check, which disclosed overcrowding at Lechfeld air base, Galland chose Munich-Riem. Plenty of room was essential for successful Me-262 operations, including dispersal space as an antistrafing measure. Transfer went forward against tremendous Allied opposition. Bombers were roaming in droves far into Germany every day. Hundreds of long-range American fighters hunted their adversaries and strafed airfields wherever they were found.

These realities stood starkly against high-level German charades that continued as though it were the spring of 1940. Highly placed people still thought in terms of promotions, organizations, and appointments. As JV-44 was coming to combat readiness despite incredible difficulties, General Kammhuber was ordered back from Norway and his command of Air Fleet 5. Goering appointed him as his Commissioner for Jet Fighter Operations. This was Goering's last attempt to counteract the SS, made in response to Hitler's appointment of SS General Hans Kammler as Commissioner for Jet Aircraft Operations. Goering saw this correctly as Himmler's takeover stratagem.

Galland the squadron commander was asked by Kammler and Kammhuber for his advice on what actions should be taken on the jet fighter situation. Galland's suggestions were:

1. Terminate "Blitz Bomber" missions by the hybrid KG (J)-51 using the Me-262, and concentrate on fighter missions.
2. Disarm KG (J)-6 and KG (J)-27 and give their Me-262s to KG (J)-54 and JG-7, which were already operational. At the same time, stiffen these *Geschwader* with the most successful fighter pilots from all fighter wings.
3. Provide immediate jet-conversion training for the most successful fighter pilots from all *Gruppen*.
4. Assign all available towing tractors, tank trucks, and ground support equipment to the jet fighter units.
5. Stop all other Me-262 operations and tests, in favor of fighter missions.

Galland held that these steps would keep almost three powerful Me-262 *Geschwader*, as well as JV-44, operational until the final days of the war. By concentrating this force geographically, possibly 150 jet fighters could have been put up daily against the daylight bombers. This would be a relatively formidable air defense, right to the last. Events would soon prove, furthermore, that the 5cm R4M rockets were especially effective against tight formations of U.S. heavies. (This was the last recommendation Galland made to higher authority in his military career. There is little doubt of its soundness, within the limits of conditions then prevailing.)

Past patterns were repeated. No action along the recommended lines was ever taken. Physically achievable despite difficulties, a final fierce stand by massed jet fighters required agreement among too many disintegrating commands. Such a final resistance was never mounted by the *Luftwaffe*. Already being described as the Squadron of Experts, JV-44 carried the torch.

The inspirational force that had previously emanated from Galland's HQ to the entire Fighter Arm was now concentrated on one squadron. Spirit and morale were unquenchable. Prodigious efforts by all personnel pushed the squadron through complex organizational difficulties. On 31 March 1944, JV-44 formations took off from Brandenburg-Briest on their first ferry operation. Led by Colonel Steinhoff, this dawn sweep covered 300 miles in 42 minutes. All landed safely at Munich. The Squadron of Experts was a reality.

Operational difficulties seemed endless. Jet fighters were revolutionary. With them came technical, tactical, and logistical problems of an entirely new character. These problems had to be studied and solved amid fighter strafings and frequent bombing attacks. Allied air intelligence knew, through *Ultra* intercepts, that Germany's downfallen fighter general was going back into battle. Life was accordingly made as hot as possible for the Squadron of Experts.

Highly decorated aces with their Knight's Crosses and jet fighters were also now armed with shovels. Each man was made responsible for preparing and maintaining his own foxhole. All of them made the breathless sprint from the cockpit of the world's fastest fighter into these shallow sanctuaries—including General Galland. No more *Reichs* Chancellery, *Luftwaffe* HQ, or the Fighter Control Centers with their glittering officers and luminous displays of enemy activity. Now it was a foxhole at Riem, with bomb splinters and bullets clanging and pinging on its improvised steel lid.

Luftwaffe radar and tracking facilities, as well as communications, were approaching their final breakdown. Galland therefore had to depend mainly on the limited-range radar installed at JV-44's own small command post at Feldkirchen for making interceptions. Pilots and dedicated crews toiled feverishly amid the shambles, and JV-44 slowly became airborne against the Allies. Usually despatching a *kette* of three jets, JV-44 pilots rarely returned without downing Allied aircraft.

Though seasoned combat pilots, JV-44s airmen found it difficult to transition from the prop-driven fighters to the jets. Takeoffs and landings were simple once the pilots had mastered the technique, but combat was another story. At speeds well over 800 kilometers per hour, the closing rate on enemy targets was so high that complete concentration was required during the few seconds the pilots had for aiming the guns and rockets. This caused many aborted passes at the targets, but the pilots soon learned to zoom or dive away and return for another pass, this time getting telling shots into the quarry.

Around 10 April 1945, Galland was ordered to meet with Goering at the *Reich* Marshal's Obersalzberg villa near Berchestgaden. The sorely harried commander of JV-44 half-expected another blast of blame, or more of Goering's dilettantism. To Galland's surprise, the *Reich* Marshal received him with an almost exaggerated courtesy. This paternal and civilized side of Goering had not appeared to the young general for a long time.

Goering questioned him with great civility about the first victories of JV-44. The *Reich* Marshal surprised Galland even more, pursuant to these questions and answers, by fully acknowledging the value of the Me-262 as a fighter. Goering's admission was hedged with politician's reservations; but, according to him, Galland had been correct in urging full-scale use of the Me-262 fighter against Allied bombers. The war seemed strangely far away amid the peaceful grandeur of the Obersalzberg.

Goering was too intelligent not to realize that he was personally doomed, and Galland guessed that, with his courtesy and civility, the *Reich* Marshal was trying to make amends. He seemed as though he wanted to apologize openly but could not quite bring himself to do so. This awkwardness was especially evident as Galland departed.

"Someday, Galland, you will realize what I have done for you by dismissing you as General of the Fighter Arm. Now you return to combat, as you always wanted. I envy you. I only wish that I could myself fly into combat beside you. *Auf Wiedersehen.*"

In his mind's eye, Galland remembered the massive Goering stuffing himself into the cockpit of an Me-262. Only in fantasy could such a thing happen. (Galland never saw Goering again.) Heading back to his embattled minicommand, Galland reflected on what a terrible antagonist the *Reich* Marshal had been. Goering would soon be telling his captors how fortunate he was to have had Galland's expert advice. He would omit from such confessions that he and Hitler had sent him to JV-44, in the expectation that "the Galland affair" would be closed by his death in combat.

JV-44 kept operating. Allied bombers kept going down from their attacks. JV-44 took heavy casualties of its own. When engine failures or Allied hits took out one of the Me-262's jet engines, performance fell below that of a P-51. Most of JV-44's casualties and losses came during landing, takeoff, and taxiing, when they were especially vulnerable to fighter attacks.

Pilot losses rose. On 18 April 1945, Galland led into the air what was probably the most elite formation in *Luftwaffe* history: himself, Gerd Barkhorn, Macky Steinhoff, Klaus Neumann, Lt. Faehrmann, and Sgt. Eduard Schallmoser. All aircraft were carrying a full load of 24 R4M rockets. Steinhoff's fighter dropped one wheel into a poorly patched airfield crater. With insufficient speed to become airborne, the stalling aircraft crashed in flames. Out of the inferno reeled the stricken Steinhoff, clothes smoldering, his face seared. (The burns would mark him for the rest of his life.) Galland had lost the services of his close friend and staunchest aide in organizing and operating JV-44.

Six days later, on 24 April 1945, "Franzl" Luetzow downed a Marauder bomber near Augsburg in the morning. That same afternoon, he flew his last mission and went missing west of Donauwoerth in Allied territory. (His actual

On 18 April 1945 at Munich-Riem, Johannes Steinhoff's Me-262 hit a soft spot on take-off and the airplane crashed and burned. Steinhoff was seriously burned but survived.

Hitler insisted the jet Me-262 be used as a dive bomber.

Edward Schallmoser, Me-262 pilot, is chastised by his boss for ramming an enemy aircraft for the second time, thereby losing two Me-262s. Standing at the left is Klaus Neumann, 37-victory ace including five with the Me-262. Seated center, dark hair, is Heinz Bär, 220 victories, top jet ace of WWII with 16 scores.

James Finnegan, the USAAF P-47 pilot who wounded Adolf Galland during aerial combat near the end of the war.

fate remains unknown to this day. Neither his aircraft nor his body were ever found.) In Galland's eyes, Luetzow was the quintessential fighter leader—brave, honest, and capable. He had become passionately devoted to proving the Me-262 fighter in the final weeks of his life.

Despite his long experience on every front, Luetzow had almost despaired in his efforts to close correctly with the bomber formations he was intercepting. The jet fighter's speed made all their past reactions and actions out of time in the new era. Virtually all the JV-44 aces experienced this difficulty to some degree, until they forced themselves to think and act faster. Late though all this had come, it was the fiery proving of all that Galland previously said about the unsuitability of bomber pilots to fight with the Me-262. Few bomber pilots ever became successful fighter pilots, even in piston-powered fighters. Jet fighters belonged in the hands of only the best aces.

The day after Luetzow's death, American and Russian forces met on the Elbe River. Galland called his pilots together for one last talk.

"Militarily speaking, the war is lost. Our action here cannot change anything, but I shall continue to fight because operating with the Me-262 has got hold of me. I am proud to belong to the last fighter pilots of the *Luftwaffe*. Only those who feel the same are to go on flying with me."

Two pilots asked to be excused from further flying duties for family reasons. They were allowed to remain with the unit. Everyone else wished to go on to the end. As long as Allied bombers came over to attack Germany, JV-44 would fight back.

Installation of wooden rails on the Me-262 permitted up to 12 R4M rockets to be carried under each wing. These 5cm projectiles were spin-stabilized and could be launched from beyond the effective range of defensive fire from the bombers. A hit with such a single rocket usually destroyed any heavy bomber.

Flying in a rapidly scrambled formation with Eduard Schallmoser, Walter Krupinski, and Klaus Neumann, Galland made his first interception with R4M-equipped jets near Landsberg. A tight formation of Martin Marauders opened fire on the jets. Their tracers could be seen curving downwards when Galland released a salvo of 24 R4M rockets. Two bombers were mortally hit, one exploding in midair, the other spinning down minus its tail. Galland's talent as a marksman had been carried into the rocket era. (Forty years later, Krupinski would describe his witnessing of Galland's first air-to-air rocket attack in one word: "Fantastic!")

All this vindication of technical viewpoints and tactical advice that had been expressed for years was occurring in the twilight of the *Luftwaffe*. Theory and argument became old history, as, in Steinhoff's words, "The rockets roared among the bombers like a shotgun into a flock of ducks." The Lord of Battles had not smiled on Adolf Galland for many moons, but his war ended with at least an amiable grimace. JV-44 won its way to aviation immortality.

Albert Speer had made Galland aware that it was his intention to capture

Germany's top leaders in April 1945. He asked the former fighter general to join him. Galland agreed. When the time came, his assignment was to capture Goering. Nothing came of this plan because of the unexpected rapidity of Germany's final collapse, which included Goering's abortive effort to take over from Hitler in the last week in April. This resulted in Goering's arrest by the SS in the villa where Galland had bid him farewell scarcely two weeks earlier. Speer therefore could only alert Galland to prevent any possible escape by air that Goering might attempt.

Galland's last aerial battle took place on 26 April 1945. Again it was a formation of Marauder bombers, with six Me-262s under Galland's command making an interception near Neuburg. Closing from astern with at least a 200 mph speed advantage over the bombers, the distance diminished like lightning. Galland armed his four 30mm cannons and took the safety catch off his rocket switch.

His tenseness over the interception and his high excitement made him forget the *second* safety catch fitted to the rocket switch. In firing position and with perfect aim, the great marksman pressed his rocket switch. Nothing. No whooshing sound, no 24 trails of fire and smoke, no hits. In a fraction of a second, he lined up a Marauder, and his four cannons flamed the rearmost bomber. Attacking another at the head of the formation as he raced rapidly through, Galland saw heavy hits on the bomber as American bullets began thudding into his jet. Passing closely above his target at high speed, he could not judge if the bomber was finished. Turning away from the bombers to the left, he was preparing to observe the final effects of his attack on the last bomber he had hit. Machine gun fire suddenly hailed down on his Me-262, shattering his instrument panel, cracking the canopy and slamming into his right knee. More hits smashed into his right turbine with mortal effect, and the faring swung open to trail in the wind. The fusillade hammered into his left turbine, which began running out of control, but at least it was running. (An American fighter pilot that he would identify and meet decades later, had caught him with a blast of fire.)

His stricken Me-262 was still flying, and he did not want to risk parachuting and landing as a corpse. Jet pilots were regarded as valuable targets by the Allied commanders, although most Allied fighter pilots disagreed with the principle of shooting at parachuting enemies. Galland took no chances and went diving in his soggy Me-262 through a cloud layer to evade his tormentors. Spotting the *autobahn* leading to Munich, with Riem airfield ahead to the left, he nursed his battered fighter back to base with his radio dead.

Seconds later he came whistling downwind to the field, his one damaged engine running wide open. Right at the field boundary he had to cut this single turbine completely. Pouring out smoke behind him, he began easing his stricken aircraft down. Intent on getting home in one piece, and minus radio, Galland had not seen that Riem was under attack by strafing Thunderbolt and Lightning fighters.

Excitedly intent on beating up JV-44's base at low altitude, the American fighter pilots did not see the incoming jet in their midst in time to fire on Galland while he was landing. Down he came on an already rough field, to land on a nosewheel whose tire had been shot out. Jarring, jolting, and rattling along at a too-fast 140 knots, Galland the hunter became the hunted, as around him rockets and bombs roared and thundered.

Wounded knee hurting abominably, he sprang out of his Me-262 like a jack-in-the-box. Hurling himself into a bomb crater, through his thoughts amid the hellish din ran his long struggle for the jet fighter. Moments before, he had been flying the world's fastest fighter. Now he crouched, bleeding, in a crater. The rise and fall of the Fighter Arm were contained in his plight, no less than in his person.

Galland's two victories in this final battle were supplemented by three more scored by his fellow pilots. They lost no pilots in the encounter. Galland's wrecked Me-262 might have been a serious loss a few weeks previously, when he had to scrounge for fighters. Now it could be replaced readily from dozens of jets that were donated to JV-44 by units that never should have been equipped with them in the first place.

Research units, test commandos for night fighters and ground attack, reconnaissance and bomber outfits landed almost daily at Riem and handed over their Me-262s. Soon the field and its environs were sheltering more than 70 of the revolutionary machines. The wounded Galland felt like a beggar suddenly admitted to a banquet.

For him, there would be no more war. Splinters in his knee could not be removed from its joint capsule, and his leg was put in plaster. With Luetzow gone and Steinhoff injured, Lt. Colonel Heinz Baer assumed direct operational command. The unit soon had to be moved to Salzburg airport, with a small detachment flown out to Innsbruck. Galland followed these moves from the *Luftwaffe* hospital at Bad Wiessee and then from a private villa at Tegernsee. From this latter makeshift HQ, he maintained contact with Baer and JV-44 at Salzburg by telephone, Fieseler Storch courier plane, and motorcycle dispatch riders.

Immobilized by his wound, Galland reflected upon the most constructive and purposeful means of concluding the war for JV-44 and its personnel. Strong rumors had circulated in Germany, originating with Hitler, that there were mortal differences between the Western Allies and the Soviet Union. The belief was widespread that it was only a matter of time before the West and the world revolution of Soviet Russia would be at loggerheads. Some said there would be armed conflict immediately, with prostrate Germany as the battlefield.

Galland had brought JV-44 to operational status from nothing and had created a functioning model of a modern jet fighter unit. All nations would inevitably acquire jet fighters. Why cast away, he reasoned, the decisive advantage of keeping intact an operational jet fighter unit in which all essentials had been worked out? These aircraft, pilots, and ground crews were not only formidable, despite the small size of JV-44, but formed a cadre around which larger units could be built rapidly.

Whatever jet combat might become in the future, JV-44 was a microcosm of that tomorrow. Galland reasoned that his squadron had a military value beyond price at the dawn of a new era. If the West and the world revolution were to clash militarily in the near future, JV-44 could play a role out of all proportion to its size.

At Tegernsee on 1 May, he accordingly prepared in secret his attempt at a special surrender of JV-44 intact, for such later use as the U.S. authorities might determine. Despite the imminent end of the war, Nazi fanatics still abounded. Such people would execute Galland immediately if they heard of his surrender offer to the Americans. Caution was also warranted, because even some decent *Luftwaffe* officers might not understand the scope and direction of his reasoning. May of 1945 was a chaotic and desperate time. (The full story of JV-44's end has not been told until now, with the perspective provided by four decades.)

In careful confidence, Galland commissioned Major Wilhelm Herget to fly by Storch from Tegernsee to Schleissheim. Herget was an outstanding night fighter ace who had transferred to JV-44 and was a fine officer. With Herget went Galland's personal aide, Captain Hugo Kessler. These officers made contact with HQ of XV Corps, U.S. Army.

Galland's special surrender effort came to nothing. The original documents in the Appendix tell the story. U.S. field commanders had no authority to make exceptions to the unconditional surrender orders issued by General Eisenhower's HQ. Those on the spot lacked the necessary insight into air power to appreciate the prize they were offered.

When it seemed that surrender in the air for JV-44 might eventuate, with the jets airborne without ammunition and their landing gear lowered, word of this possibility galvanized the 64th Fighter Wing of the USAAF. Every available P-47 was to be put into the air for this dramatic airborne surrender scenario. Galland rejected this course. Captain Dick Perley, meanwhile, was awaiting reassignment at 50th Fighter Group HQ when the electrifying teletype came through. He was immediately put in command of a pickup section of P-47s that had been operating in close support of the U.S. 7th Army.

Reading the teletype, Perley felt the hair rise on the back of his neck. A whole squadron of German jets was nothing to fool with, especially if they took off *with* ammunition. In appalling weather, Perley's section milled around in the soup, while a sort of blow-by-blow on the jet surrender rasped in his earphones. "They are getting ready to take off," came the word. "Be alert!" Perley strained his eyes through his streaming windshield. No Me-262s.

The attempt at intact surrender of JV-44 was to have a startling echo for Perley, 38 years later and half a world away in Los Angeles, California. Adolf Galland was the 1983 Thanksgiving dinner guest of North American Rockwell executive Ray Heman and his wife Lesley Lewis. The former Captain Dick Perley, now a greying and sixtyish electronics executive, was also invited by the Hemans. They knew he had been a WWII fighter pilot in Europe and might enjoy meeting the famous German general.

While Perley knew Galland's name well, he was unfamiliar with the details of his career. Perley casually opened conversation by harking back to May of 1945, when "there was some jet outfit in Salzburg that wanted to surrender." Now it was the hair on Galland's neck that stood up. "That was *my* unit," he said, eyes wide with astonishment. The two former foes ended their encounter marveling at the smallness of a world that had brought them face to face after nearly 40 years.

Perley had sought Galland in the "soup" near Salzburg in 1945, and found him in the sunshine of Los Angeles in 1983. In the spirit of Thanksgiving, they were both grateful that they had never been required to exchange fire. Exchanging reminiscences in peace was better.

Failure to accomplish the special surrender of his jet squadron was the war's last bowl of bitter rice for Galland. His attachment for JV-44 was intensely personal. He hated to let go of what had been created amid the *Luftwaffe*'s terminal ordeal by the individual sacrifices of JV-44 personnel. Inexorable and charged with emotion, the moment came when he was compelled to issue his last significant order as a *Luftwaffe* general.

"Blow up all JV-44 jet fighters on the ground."

Just as they had built JV-44, unit personnel placed the charges and destroyed the Me-262s for which they had been willing to give their lives. (A cause of gnawing regret at the time, destruction of JV-44 was actually Galland's definitive severance from a military era that was ending.)

Honest soldiers were on their way out all over the world. Political generals were on their way in, together with wars without victories. With his direct line of thought, tactical and strategic insight, and unrelenting defense of the basic rights of his soldiers, Adolf Galland was already at 33 an old-fashioned general— a Hot War general. The Cold War would soon start, and a different type of general was emergent in the Western world.

On 5 May 1945, *Generalleutnant* Adolf Galland of the *Luftwaffe* and of JV-44 presented himself as a prisoner of war. He had been defeated but not dishonored. Shame or guilt would never be on his face before history. His captors, furthermore, were eager to find out all about the meteoric rise and catastrophic fall of the *Luftwaffe,* especially its Fighter Arm. Galland knew more about the Fighter Arm than any man living.

CHAPTER TWENTY-SIX

An armed American sentry at his door in Haus Kathrein at Tegernsee was final proof that World War II was over. Galland had gone down fighting, consumed by his passion for the jet fighter. His realism had for years made him aware of looming defeat, and he had tried to prepare himself psychologically for this moment. Finally falling into enemy hands nevertheless was a smashing emotional punch.

All the sacrifices, hopes, battles, and labors of the terrible recent years had shrunk to nothing. He thought of the long parade of fighter pilots lost since 1939—expended like ammunition. Now they were only names in *Luftwaffe* records and phantoms in the memories of their devastated families. The tragedies of his own family, with the battle deaths of his brothers Wutz and Paul, were repeated a millionfold throughout the German nation.

Guarded by American soldiers, he had seldom felt more downcast. The encumbering plaster on his leg further contributed to his dejection. He was nevertheless aware of his rank and position and put the best possible face on his captivity. Outwardly his usual imperturbable self, he was inwardly consumed by wretched feelings inseparable from defeat.

Galland was taken to Bad Tölz in an ambulance for his first interrogation. Never again would he ride in the *Luftwaffe* staff cars that for years had whisked him from one important meeting to the next. Months of interrogations began. At Heidelberg he met his first capable interrogator, Major Max van Rossum-Daum, USAAF. Trained in his task and with fluent German, Van Rossum-Daum was C.O. of the Air Prisoner of War Interrogation Unit (APWIU). This able officer quickly established rapport with Galland and obtained for him, through the USAAF command, confirmation of his last two aerial victories over the Marauder bombers. (A friendship developed between Van Rossum-Daum and Galland that was to endure for the rest of their lives.)

As an important prisoner, detailed interrogation was scheduled for Galland.

Flown to England on 14 May 1945, he was taken to Camp 7 at Latimer, on the estate of Lord Chesham in Buckinghamshire. A leading Allied interrogation center, Latimer had Wing Commander King of the RAF as its C.O.

The chief American interrogator was "Major Emery," a pseudonym for Major Ernst Englander, USAAF. Among his assistants was "Captain Todd," the pseudonym of Captain John M. Whitten. (In this man, the former General of the Fighter Arm found one of the greatest friends he would ever know.) Difficult months lay ahead. The worst of it would be softened by Whitten's humanity. The two men were to examine, analyze, and set down all Galland's experiences. Rare personal accords developed during these labors.

Whitten was temperamentally and educationally well suited to the Galland interrogation. His work became an important contribution to air history. This book has also taken its main direction from Whitten's massive interrogation monograph, on which the two men worked for many months. The intelligent Whitten was much more than just an expert interrogator, with qualities that inspired Galland's confidence.

Jack Whitten is the particular kind of decent human being that springs so often from American service families. Born into a U.S. Navy family in 1920, with all-American lineage on both sides back to Puritan pioneers, he had a world-wide schooling. Finishing head of his class of 441 at the University of Maryland in 1941, his major was German. This put him on an interception course with Adolf Galland.

After drafting in 1942, basic training, and officer candidate school, he was sent to the Interrogation Training Center at Camp Ritchie. There he was turned into a POW interrogator and order-of-battle expert. His talents soon led his superiors to throw him in with the real POW "toughies" that nobody else could break. Shunning violence, he broke them all, in his own words, "by boring them to death."

Jack Whitten makes light of himself in this way, but like Galland, he is a man of wit and humor. Educated, cultured, and kind, and minus any rancor toward a beaten foe, he had everything he needed to persuade a prisoner. He also had character, something Galland valued in friend and foe. When the former fighter general arrived at Latimer, Whitten had already been interrogating *Luftwaffe* prisoners there since September of 1944. For nine months prior to that, Whitten had been interrogating German POWs in the United States.

Known as the Combined Services Detailed Interrogation Center (CSDIC), Camp Latimer authorities had already interrogated numerous *Luftwaffe* fighter pilots. Galland's reputation had preceded him. His new hosts received him with respect, for his pilots had all described him as a "very good man." When the Latimer C.O. reported this to Galland, it injected some warmth into his barren world. His worldly goods were now contained in two suitcases and a few cigar boxes, the latter the last of his free wartime stogies.

Since Allied interest in jet fighters remained high, Galland was first interrogated about the Me-262, as were other pilot POWs who had flown the jet. A special report on the Me-262 was compiled at Latimer. Famous American aces like Colonel David Schilling and Colonel John C. Meyer came to interview Galland and other Me-262 pilots. Whitten interpreted for these early meetings with senior USAAF officers and found that Galland always made an excellent impression, pilot-to-pilot and man-to-man. He was clearly an officer who knew his profession thoroughly.

"Galland was modest, confident and extremely well-spoken," Whitten recalled. "His answers to complicated questions were 'ready to be set in type'."

Whitten's interrogation experience made him adroit at gauging a POW's capacities. In Galland he knew quickly that he was dealing with a man of exceptional mentality. Only the sharpest mind can think through, and then speak out in perfect form, the answers to complex technical questions as Galland consistently did. Whitten's interest in Galland grew accordingly. Although Whitten was also interrogating dozens of *Luftwaffe* intelligence officers at this same time, to compile other major reports, he welcomed the order to prepare a major report on Galland.

Before all this, and towards the end of May, Galland was contemplating his fate in his small Latimer room, when the door suddenly swung open and admitted Field Marshal Erhard Milch. Both were astonished and momentarily speechless. Milch had been through hard times, including physical abuse by his British captors. Suddenly the Field Marshal found himself facing the young general he had always trusted without regret. Out of the man who had built the *Luftwaffe* for Goering came a verbal torrent.

Galland had assumed all along that his room had hidden microphones, which it did, and Milch was oblivious to his warnings that they were being overheard. While the Field Marshal rambled about their mutual experiences, Galland stepped around thumping the thin partition walls. (He was told later that this countermeasure defeated the eavesdroppers.)

Milch's presence had one serious drawback. He kept "borrowing" cigars. Without any means of paying back the cigars he borrowed, Milch's impact on Galland's meagre stock became dismaying. Field Marshal and fighter general came to a trade agreement. Milch had a new hunter's pipe, and both could get tobacco. Galland got the pipe, and Milch continued his inroads into the remaining cigars.

About two weeks later, Milch was transferred to another room. When he packed his kit, he reached over and took the hunter's pipe from beside Galland's bed without saying a word. As Milch closed the lid of his suitcase, the hunter's eyes were on him and the air became charged.

"That wasn't our agreement," said Galland.

Milch hesitated. (Galland's gaze in such circumstances acquires a searing quality.) Milch opened his suitcase and gave back the pipe. (That same hunter's pipe is displayed today in Galland's trophy hall at his home in Oberwinter, near Bonn.)

During his early confinement in England, Galland was held for a while at the Beaconsfield interrogation center. He was roommate there to General Franz Halder, former Chief of the Army General Staff. Sacked by Hitler in September of 1942, and in a concentration camp since the attempt on Hitler's life in July of 1944, Halder knew plenty about the excesses of the Nazis since 1933. He was now casting himself in the role of being a victim of Nazi politicians. Galland had experienced a chilling brush with Nazi methods during his dismissal ordeal.

The professorial Halder now detailed for him some of the high intrigues and ruthless policies of Germany's political leadership. The elderly general gave Galland a crash course in what the Nazis were really like. Such things as Hitler's intention to exterminate the Polish nation in 1939, in which Halder had acquiesced, left Galland stunned.

Halder's stories dragged Galland out of the clean blue sky. The airman's war that he had fought with honor had no correspondence with the revolting labyrinths that Halder described with firsthand knowledge. He began wondering what he had been fighting for—willing even to sacrifice his life. For Germany? The embittered Halder was not talking about the Germany of Westerholt, hospitality, decency, and goodwill.

When he next sat down with Jack Whitten to begin their joint account of his life, Galland first interrogated Whitten. From the American he received basic confirmation in outline of what Halder had told him. His devotion to the Fighter Arm, and the immense range of his responsibilities, had separated him from politics—which he disliked in any case. His capabilities alone had carried him through his military career. (Other young German generals at Latimer, who had not risen to the command hierarchy, had similar rude awakenings at this time, according to Jack Whitten. They learned for the first time, for example, about the unconscionable murder of Anglo-American POWs in the "grand escape" at Stalag III.)

Intensive work began on the Galland report, uniting the two men through their common wish to make the report as complete as possible. Whitten went through all the secret Air Ministry Intelligence Summaries circulated during the war. He selected material that could be included in the report after confirmation or amplification by Galland.

Detail in this material on *Luftwaffe* organization, tactics, developments, equipment, personnel, and all other aspects was incredibly comprehensive. Galland was dumbfounded. Why had the Allies wanted to know all these things? More was in these reports on the *Luftwaffe* than he had himself known. Whitten also thought it strange that the Allies had been able to obtain such detail on the *Luftwaffe*. He attributed it largely to expert espionage.

The Air Ministry material that Whitten and Galland were using was actually compiled from sanitized *Ultra* decrypts. All linkage to mastery of German war ciphers was eliminated from this material. Such carefully edited information could be circulated to levels below the exclusive upper circle that received pure *Ultra*—Churchill, Eisenhower, Doolittle, and other high commanders.

More than 30 years later, when the *Ultra* secret was made public, both Galland and Whitten realized whence came the comprehensive detail that had astounded them in 1945. *Ultra* material is still being released. Many years will pass before most of the material enters the public domain, and some of it will be hidden forever. Enough is available now to convince Galland that the Allies continuously looked over the shoulder of the General of the Fighter Arm.

Around 9 July 1945, Galland was taken by an RAF interrogator to visit the RAF station at Tangmere. In a two-day stay, he met many high Fighter Command officers and numerous British aces. All of them were anxious to talk to the *Luftwaffe*'s famous ace and general. Since Galland had held the *Luftwaffe* post most closely approximating their own AOC Fighter Command, he was especially intriguing to pilots who had flown against him.

At the gate of the Tangmere base, who should come stumping out of a group leaders' conference but the onetime Stationmaster of Tangmere himself, Wing Commander Douglas Bader. Here again was a full circle. Bader now had the cigars and Galland was the prisoner. Bader was spick and span and Galland was the rumpled one. Bader concerned himself for Galland's comfort, even though he had to make a fast departure next morning—just as he had done in France four years previously. (From this short second meeting, a warm friendship flowered that endured until Bader's passing in 1982.)

By mid-August the Galland report was completed, officially known as ADI (K) 373/45. As a rare privilege, Whitten was permitted to sign this report with his true name over the typed name of the Latimer C.O., Wing Commander King, RAF. The report ran in a series of instalments in Air Ministry and USAFE Intelligence Summaries. (Galland would later use material from this report for his memoirs, published a decade later.)

On 24 August 1945, a B-17 Fortress took off from Bovingdon loaded with the very people it had recently been trying to bomb. Field Marshal Milch sat in the bombardier's seat. General Galland sat with Colonel Werner Baumbach, the famous bomber pilot and one-time General of the Bomber Arm. Colonel Edgar Petersen, the last C.O. of the *Luftwaffe*'s Rechlin Test Center, was also aboard with another dozen German pilots and Jack Whitten.

Over the roaring engine noise, excited reminiscences were exchanged as they flew over Germany in perfect weather. Each city had its memories. A refueling stop in Schweinfurt started a flood of recollections. When the B-17 touched down finally at Kaufbeuren in Bavaria, it had been a remarkable flight.

At Kaufbeuren they were quartered in a large three-storied villa, the Landhaus, outside the grounds of the county mental hospital. Commanding this facility was Major van Rossum-Daum, Galland's first competent interrogator after the surrender. Staff studies on fighter control were to be carried out here, in an

Galland in Australia. Air Commodore Tony Tonkin of the Royal Australian Air Force watches as Galland sits in the cockpit of an Me-262 jet at Point Cook near Melbourne in September, 1974.

13 September 1968: Pathfinders Reunion at Biggin Hill. The RAF Pathfinders invited General Adolf Galland and other former Luftwaffe officers to their reunion in England. Left to right: GP Captain Johnnie Johnson, famed RAF ace; General Galland; Rudolf Schoenert (64 night victories); Gunther Radusch (64 at night); J. Hughes; Wolfgang Falch (8); and Wolfgang Thimmig (24).

Old foes, now friends, meet down under. On a visit to Auckland, New Zealand, in March, 1967, General Galland met once again his counterpart in the Battle of Brain, Air Marshal Sir Keith Park.

"Onkel" Theo Osterkamp, April 15, 1892, to January 2, 1975. A very famous personality in the Luftwaffe and an adored gentleman. The best "character" in the German Fighter Arm. After the war he had his business office with Galland.

atmosphere much more relaxed than at Latimer. There were no guards. The POWs were asked to give their parole (and none violated this undertaking).

A week after arrival at Kaufbeuren, Whitten and Galland drove to Hohenpeissenberg (beginning the search for his guns that would end in California nearly 40 years later). Galland was shocked to learn that his cache of prized shotguns and hunting rifles had been looted by a lieutenant colonel of the U.S. Army. Whitten readily learned his identity, but in the climate of those times nothing could be done.

Further disappointment awaited at Tegernsee, when they visited Haus Kathrein shortly afterwards. All Galland's personal belongings and papers had been looted from his final command post-cum-hospital by Counter Intelligence Corps personnel. His Knight's Cross with Diamonds and Award Certificates were gone (souvenirs that nobody could show to this day without embarrassment). His files of Tactical Regulations, invaluable to the current APWIU project and worthless to anyone else, had also been plundered.

APWIU prisoners were officially denied mail privileges. Whitten and his fellow officers nevertheless allowed Galland and the others to write letters, and they mailed them privately in town. Incoming mail was diverted around officialdom by having it all received by Colonel Walter Dahl, late of the Assault Fighters as a *Kommodore,* who had been released and resided at nearby Bad Wörrishofen. Families of POWs were traced and resettled near Kaufbeuren.

The *Luftwaffe*'s last General of the Ground Support Arm, Colonel Hubertus Hitschold, was among Galland's fellow prisoners. His captors found him to be a fine man. They obliged Hitschhold by locating his wife, bringing her to Bad Wörrishofen, and letting him spend the weekend with her. Such favors were appreciated by POWs living in an emotional desert. Trautloft was located in Munich and put on the APWIU payroll as a consultant. Similarly hired was Galland's wartime staff officer and almost constant traveling companion, Major Hans Schmoller-Haldy.

This improving scene was suddenly wrecked by orders to return Galland, Hitschhold, and Schmoller-Haldy to Camp Latimer. The German Air Force Personnel Holding Unit had taken over Latimer, which now housed almost the entire *Luftwaffe* High Command, including secretaries and office personnel. Staff studies continued at Latimer, a boring ordeal for Galland.

The kindnesses of Jack Whitten continually stretched and bent regulations, and often broke them entirely. Walks around Latimer Park helped offset the oppressive prison psychology that was inseparable from any confinement. Whitten went even further. The APWIU had a huge command and reconnaissance car. On the bumpers, Whitten had emblazoned MILITARY INTELLIGENCE SERVICE in letters eight inches high. This guaranteed free parking anywhere, anytime, even in front of military police HQ.

On 22 October 1945, Whitten told Galland and Hitschhold to dress in civilian clothes, and they went jolting into London in the towering vehicle. They made a sightseeing tour and lunched at the Cumberland Hotel with American fighter pilot Lt. Colonel Fred Kirtley. Afterwards they visited Selfridges, where Galland and Hitschhold bought coffee and tobacco. Clambering down out of the enormous car and strolling into Selfridges with the British public—who were now assuming he was with the Military Intelligence Service—was a caper that appealed to Galland. Something like the lobsters and champagne flight of a few years back, it lifted his spirits.

The Nuremberg Tribunal "war crimes" indictments were in progress at about this time. Many officers from the command hierarchies of all three German services were being indicted. Galland grew increasingly depressed. In the atmosphere of vengeance that prevailed at this time, he felt he might be indicted for doing his duty as a soldier.

The High Command of the *Luftwaffe* (OKL), was among the organizations indicted, and it was permitted to prepare an answer to the tribunal's charges. The Judge Advocate of the *Luftwaffe* High Command drew up a massive document that was passed around for all officers to sign. Eventually this document was brought into the room where Hitschhold and Galland were working, by a high-ranking OKL delegation. Word had gone around that the former General of the Fighter Arm had been disgusted and disaffected by what he had learned of Nazi excesses from General Halder, Whitten, and other sources in the postwar months.

The copy of the OKL response handed to Galland had already been signed by several high-ranking officers. Puffing on his cigar, Galland quietly read the document while the delegation waited. He then stood up, tore the document in half from top to bottom, and handed them the pieces.

"I personally welcome this trial, because from it we may learn who was responsible for these scandalous happenings."

Whitten learned of this incident from Hitschhold. Galland never mentioned it, and, to protect Hitschhold's confidence, Whitten never revealed to Galland that he knew of the former fighter general's "response to the response." Galland forgot it as well, until it surfaced again after 40 years in the draft of this book, the authors having obtained it independently from Jack Whitten.

By early December of 1945, Galland was back at Kaufbeuren, still working on the staff studies. Whitten brought him news of his parents, whom the kindly American had visited in Westerholt. They were well, and news of their famous son relieved them greatly. Life at the Landhaus was more tolerable than at Latimer, and, in January of 1946, everyone skiied frequently on the slopes behind the building.

Numerous U.S. fighter pilots came to visit. Lt. Colonels Fred Kirtley and Bob Delaney assisted for a time with the studies, and Colonel Ed Giller of the 55th Fighter Group became a frequent visitor, sometimes bringing young pilots with him. The staff studies served one good purpose for Galland. The systematic review of so many aspects of the war, conducted over such a long period, served to give him an organic grasp of the events and processes in which he had participated in high rank. (For the remainder of his life, he would be able to discuss these matters in amazing detail.)

On 21 January 1946, Galland and Whitten visited Herr Vollmer, one of the three cigar suppliers in Germany to whom Galland had granted "exclusive" rights to the specially manufactured *General der Jagdflieger* cigars. Vollmer had also served with JV-44 as a reserve officer doing staff work. He had owned a cigar factory in Karlsruhe but was now located at Hohenpeissenberg. A few boxes of the special cigars were still available, which pleased the man whose rank was on the label.

Through Jack Whitten's kindness and aid, he established a correspondence with the Baroness Gisela von Donner, widow of his former aide and friend, 1st Lt. Baron Conrad Hinrich von Donner. The latter had died in combat with U.S. heavy bombers in March of 1944. This attractive lady lived on the von Donner family farm in Schleswig-Holstein. She braved Germany's horrific postwar transportation system to make visits to see Galland. Whitten arranged for them to meet in town privately on weekends, a gesture of humanity best appreciated by those who have experienced protracted confinement.

Whitten's last extracurricular act with Galland as a POW was a visit to Counter Intelligence Corps HQ in Tegernsee. It was seeking a lead on Galland's missing property. It ran into a dead end. The NCO who had done the looting had been sent back to the United States, probably taking his loot with him. Three days after this, Captain John M. Whitten was advised that he was going back to the United States and ten days later was on a train out of Fürstenfeldbruck.

Losing his good friend reduced Galland's remaining POW time to a dreary routine. Whitten kept in touch by mail from the States and sent food packages to his favorite POW. (Correspondence continued, but the men did not meet personally again until 1950 in Frankfurt. Whitten was by then with the military government, and Galland was a prosperous consultant on vacation from the Argentine.)

Throughout 1946 and into 1947, Galland worked for the Historical Division, U.S. Forces, European Theater. He was kept busy at Kaufbeuren, Oberursel, and Allendorf until practically everything he knew had been pumped out of him and put down on paper. There were scores of interrogations behind him by 28 April 1947, when he was finally released in Heilbronn. Only now was his military career and the war itself concluded. He walked out into a Germany that was decisively changed—especially for former generals.

CHAPTER TWENTY-SEVEN

Although Galland had never at any time been mistreated while a POW, Allied occupation policies in postwar Germany were designed to make life hard for former high-ranking officers. Restrictions were imposed everywhere on these capable, trained leaders. Former generals were denied even middle-level posts in civilian life. Many high-ranking Allied officers were strongly opposed to this victimization of military professionals. They considered such actions to be wrong, shortsighted, and likely to boomerang—which they did in Korea and Vietnam. Politically conceived and imposed, the policies had to be enforced by the occupying military.

Renascent German civil life took its theme from the occupation policies. As a beaten, ravaged, and forcibly divided nation struggled to get back on its feet, professional officers were excluded from any kind of management, denied trade union membership, and barred from the universities. Outstanding *Luftwaffe* aces who had so recently won Germany's highest battle decorations in many cases lived from hand-to-mouth under these unfair policies. Doors were often slammed in their faces as they sought employment. They were turned away as "militarists." Allied politicians responsible for this punishment of honorable combat soldiers ignored the strict prewar prohibition against German officers joining political parties—including the Nazi Party.

The higher the former officer's rank, the tighter were the restrictions. Ex-generals who found employment with the occupation forces and in historical projects were the lucky ones. The others could live in peace if they became truck drivers, sold advertising, labored on farms, or otherwise worked far below their intellectual and administrative abilities. Galland had not the slightest intention of diminishing himself in this way. Once discharged in Heilbronn, he headed for Schleswig-Holstein in northern Germany and the large country estate of the Baroness Gisela von Donner.

Gisela had shown a remarkable devotion to Galland during his two years as a POW. She had ridden freight trains, sometimes loaded mainly with coal, to visit him in various POW camps. Car or passenger train travel was not available to ordinary Germans in those years. The attractive noblewoman endured the worst in his behalf. She was a primary force in strengthening Galland's spirit and morale. His prompt departure for her farm at Lehmkuhlen was therefore no mere whim but a well-considered and practical step.

Gisela was raising her three very small children on her own, like thousands of other war widows. As General of the Fighters, Galland had opposed fighter pilots' marriages because of this precise situation: a widow with no father for her children. Galland now could personally alleviate this problem with the widow of his former friend and aide. Listing himself as forest help, his "profile" sank low enough for him to be left alone by the occupation authorities. He helped Gisela run the farm, drawing on his own early years at Westerholt. He was at home in the country. An added joy was filling in as surrogate father to Gisela's children, who loved him.

As "forest help" he did little in the forest except help himself to game. This was strictly forbidden, as were all guns and ammunition. Galland hid a shotgun deep in the woods, wangled ammunition, and banged away out of official earshot. Even if he had to take constant care not to be caught, shooting game was infinitely preferable to the endless interrogations and stifling confinement. As a lifelong hunter and woodsman, he found these daily forest forays cleansing him of the prison psychology, and they were otherwise highly useful.

Even on a farm, food was short, and meat was hard to obtain all over Germany. At night he would return to the house laden with game. To eat what he had hunted and killed was an article of hunter Galland's faith. This fitted well with his current situation. Surplus game was excellent for trading, at a time when money was worth nothing. Other secret activities of the former general were growing tobacco and distilling his own schnaps. (He recalled that "both tasted terrible.")

This life in Schleswig-Holstein had many idyllic aspects, but the man of action began chafing for a wider challenge. Activities of former generals were still restricted, and Galland began to think of going abroad, illegally if need be. Air forces were developing overseas in many nations. Training assignments had been obtained by former German aces in countries like India, Egypt, and Syria. He felt that his speaking knowledge of English and Spanish might help him find similar work. Others in Germany were thinking and planning along the same lines.

Professor Kurt Tank contacted Galland in the summer of 1948. The former Focke-Wulf chief designer was living in an old castle near Minden and invited the former General of the Fighter Arm over for a visit. Three days of intensive discussions with Tank ensued, in which Tank detailed his plans to build a new fighter aircraft in Argentina, under contract to the Argentine Air Ministry. Galland agreed to become part of the overall package that Tank was to offer the Argentines. "It is going to be many years," said Tank, "before things are anything like normal in Germany again.''

Tank worked through a German named Siebrecht, who lived in Buenos Aires and knew his way around the Argentine Air Ministry. Always a man who favored direct action, Tank suddenly slipped out of Germany via Denmark, in defiance of Allied restrictions. Once in Argentina, Tank got things moving. A second group of engineers followed him, but they were intercepted on the Denmark route and sent back to Germany. Galland was in a third group, dispatched via Austria and Italy and thence by sea to Buenos Aires, that evaded the Allies.

Argentina was humming with action. Commercial life was booming. A new jet fighter force was in the making. As a recognized authority on jet fighter operations, Galland was given a three-year contract, with two extension options. He was to work under Brigadier General Juan Francisco Fabri, C.-in-C. of the Argentine Air Force. Fabri turned out to be a fine gentleman, as well as a skilled general and pilot.

Galland quickly developed a strong liking for the Argentine people, especially those who lived in the countryside. They were honest, open, hospitable, and friendly. Life here was uncomplicated and pleasant. When the Baroness von Donner joined him in due course, bringing her three children, life became thoroughly enjoyable. Social life, family picnics, and beach and country sightseeing tours became part of their lifestyle. The Argentine Air Force (AAF) found him a pleasant and roomy house, with servants' quarters and spacious grounds, outside Buenos Aires in the garden town of El Palomar.

The children went to school and rapidly acquired fluent Spanish. They were an integral part of Galland's happy scene. He watched over them, raising them as though he were their natural father and forging a bond of enduring love between them all. (They are now grown, married, and have families of their own.)

Galland's Spanish was passable for conversation but was inadequate for the considerable paper work involved with his job. An interpreter was assigned to him, to help him with his paper work and serve as an escort. Captain Luis Grieben was a native speaker and writer, with total fluency in Spanish and German. (He was to stay with Galland until 1953, at which time Grieben became accidentally involved in a plot against Peron and was jailed.)

Galland was to use his war experience to set up a modern jet fighter force for the AAF. About 100 British Gloster Meteor fighters had been acquired, but the Argentines did not know how to use them properly. There is a substantial gulf between the handling and servicing of piston-powered fighters and jet formations. Bridging that gulf was the essence of Galland's assignment. He was one of the few men living who had operated jets and jet formations in combat. He showed his hosts how to use the Meteors in formation flights and in combat and shooting exercises.

His drafting of training and tactical regulations was a loud echo of his work as General of the Fighters. The Argentine pilots were good but lacked experience. Galland had plenty of experience. The new jet AAF soon began taking shape.

Galland was asked to give lectures on his war experiences. Flying personnel in all ranks responded enthusiastically to the reports and descriptions Galland gave. They gained some idea of what it was like to be in the hot seat—in the air and on the ground. This enthusiasm for sound, solid guidance worked wonders. AAF efficiency rose.

A vast and pleasant difference between this work and his tasks as General of the Fighters impressed Galland deeply. The AAF eagerly took up his recommendations. There was no *Reich* Marshal, no *Reich* Marshal's kindergarten, no High Command to buck and battle. His proposals and recommendations were accepted and transformed promptly into workable regulations and procedures. Virtually everything Galland suggested was adopted and implemented in due course. He became, in effect, the father of the new AAF fighter force.

The Air Defense Command had many radars in storage—expensive sophisticated units that were not being used. Over a period of several months, Galland showed them how and where to install these units, to monitor national borders, and to provide fighter control. He also established the organization necessary to man and maintain these facilities.

This radar defense net and fighter control system required a comprehensive upgrading of communications. Galland's advice was again accepted. Within a short time, the AAF had dramatically improved its communications overall. Efficiency rose in consequence. The Air Defense Command was able to live up to its name and carry out its mission.

Great prestige and status came with Galland's unintentional role as father of the modern Argentine Air Force. When this force did so well against the British fleet in the Falkland Islands war, their good showing was not Galland's direct doing. The officers he had trained were by then retired. Several revolutions had also occurred in the interim, changing the AAF structure and hierarchy. The foundations of the modern AAF jet force, including its doctrine, spirit, and efficiency were nevertheless laid in Galland's time and rested mainly on the bedrock of his advice and guidance. Sound beginnings have enduring effects. No one would doubt that "Boom" Trenchard's vision lived in the RAF of World War II, even though the distinguished father of the RAF had left the scene.

Working with the Argentines was pleasant. Their cooperation and trust naturally produced harmony and progress. His professional life bordered on the joyful, without any of the pressures, intrigues, egotism, and ambition that distorted action in the high ranks of the *Luftwaffe*. Opportunities were plentiful to fly jet fighters and to cross the country by air. Galland enjoyed this to the full, comforted by the absence of projectiles in the air that might carry his name.

His job allowed him to take time off almost as he wished. This brought him full circle to sailplaning and his own beginnings as an airman. Sailplaning was an active sport in Argentina, and it was a first-love joy for Galland to soar again without an engine, casting himself on the whims of the wind.

Social life in Buenos Aires was also relaxed and enjoyable with his many Argentine friends. Galland made a special point of entering fully into Argentine life. He wanted to understand not just the customs and ways of Argentina but also the essence of contemporary Argentine thinking. Most of his friends during these years were local people.

Although he was among the most famous Germans in Buenos Aires, he avoided meeting too many German friends. He stayed out of organized German circles and clubs, because he was gratified by the rapport he had built with the Argentines. He did not wish to disturb such a constructive process. He kept in touch with Kurt Tank and Werner Baumbach, the onetime Inspector of the *Luftwaffe* Bomber Arm. Baumbach had also made a new start in Argentina, working with Construcciones Militares. (When Baumbach was killed in a guided bomb test-flying accident, Galland was a pallbearer at his Buenos Aires funeral.)

The AAF remained highly appreciative of his competence and wisdom. Twice his contract options were picked up. He felt like a member of a military family, with uniformed friends everywhere. In this spirit, he was invited to the Great Ball of the Military Club in Buenos Aires. His hosts asked him specifically to please wear his highest decoration with his tuxedo. Galland duly arrived at the ball wearing his Knight's Cross, with its Oak Leaves, Swords, and Diamonds. Everyone was happy—except the Soviet military delegation.

The warriors of the "world revolution" were presented by the Russian ambassador, who glanced at Galland's decorations with diplomatic disdain. The Russian officers were not diplomats. They scowled and glared angrily at the shiny Knight's Cross on Galland's neck. They did not believe that he would dare show himself with the highest German battle decoration.

Russia was talking peace in the world but still refused to end World War II. Scores of thousands of German officers and soldiers were still illegally imprisoned in Russia—including many hundreds of Galland's fighter pilots. To the Russian officers in Buenos Aires, Galland thus was still an enemy, and the focus of their hostile glares and remarks.

Galland had been glared at—and barked at—by the most terrible German personalities in the 20th century, so the Russian officers' conduct did not perturb him. The Argentine officers all rallied around their trusted German friend, supported him warmly, and soon calmed down the teacup tempest.

Galland had no illusions about himself as a partner for any woman, describing himself even in his 74th year as "a difficult and often terrible man in a marriage." His relationship with Gisela von Donner had been a good one, and in the Argentine they actually planned to get married. To Gisela's dismay, she was apprised of provisions in the late Baron von Donner's will that pertained to control of his estate in the event of her remarriage. Gisela found these severe restrictions unacceptable, and she and Galland were never married. Her decision to return to Germany with her children in 1953 meant the end of their de facto marriage, but their friendship continued warmly on through the decades.

Galland's Argentine years provided him with sufficient leisure to tackle writing a book about his war experiences. General Fabri, and others whose views he respected, predicted that such a book would be widely read in the world, and they encouraged him. Galland had many doubts that a book by a high-ranking German fighter pilot would be welcome at this time. Using his war notes as a guide, he assembled *The First and the Last,* an autobiographical account of his war experiences.

Although familiar with report writing and accustomed to composing directives and other official documents, writing a commercial book was a new field for the former general. He was helped by Captain Grieben, Gisela von Donner, and later by Captain Erich Bindert and Franz Schneekluth in Germany. Galland referred to the latter three as "my brain trust." Franz Schneekluth published *Die Ersten und Die Letzten* in Germany in 1953.

The book was well received, despite the strong antimilitary tenor of postwar German life. As a straightforward soldier's narrative, devoid of political justifications or propaganda, the book described the war from both fighter cockpit and high command. This uniquely broad perspective attracted the attention of British and French publishers. Translations were produced in 1955.

The British public has a strange and enduring passion for honorable enemies. *The First and The Last* became a big success in the British Commonwealth and was soon on its way to becoming an international classic. U.S., French, and Spanish editions followed. Galland's personal story was eventually translated into 14 languages. Sales eventually reached almost 3 million copies worldwide. The expatriate general's memoirs made him internationally famous.

After Gisela's return to Germany in 1953, Galland felt her loss sharply. He did some sailplaning in his leisure time, and, while pursuing this hobby, made the acquaintance of the Countess Sylvina von Dönhoff, an expatriate German noblewoman. From their common passion for sailplaning they quickly developed a passion for each other. Sylvina had been born in East Prussia and grew up partly in Bombay, where her father served as German ambassador. Sylvina's mother was Argentine-born and of landed lineage.

Galland married the countess in February of 1954, thereby beginning his official experience with marital blitz. He had always been drawn to pretty women, and they to him. To the astonishment of his numerous friends, he finally tied the knot with *one* lady—with whom he apparently expected to live happily ever after. In the Galland tradition, the countess was a beauty.

His Argentine idyll came to a close in 1955. His affection for the country and its people would last his lifetime, but all good things have a natural span. On 7 February 1955, the Argentine government invested him by presidential decree with the title of Military Pilot, *Honoris Causa.* A certificate of appreciation for his services in the birth of the new Argentine Air Force was presented to him in a big ceremony at Air Base Morón at Buenos Aires. His expatriate years ended on a high note.

The prodigal was returning home at a propitious time. Another new jet air force was about to be born, this one in his own country. Through his vacation visits to Germany and correspondence with old comrades, Galland was aware of this important development. Steinhoff, Panitzki, and others were laying the groundwork for the *Bundesluftwaffe* in Chancellor Konrad Adenauer's office.

Immediately upon his arrival in Germany, Galland was asked to see Herr Blank, later to be Germany's first postwar Defense Minister. Blank told him that those working with him on air force matters had recommended that Galland be appointed *Inspekteur*—the title that the *Bundesluftwaffe* was according its commander-in-chief. A similar recommendation had been made by his chief advisors, Generals Speidel and Heusinger.

Galland was eminently qualified for this post. His competence and capabilities were a matter of record. He was politically clean. Since the war, he had played a central role in creating a new jet air force for Argentina, the same task that was now to be carried out in Germany. No officer in Germany could match either his war record or this significant recent experience. Former *Luftwaffe* generals were aging. They had been idle or inconsequentially employed since 1945 in nonmilitary jobs. None had flown jets, organized them into modern formations, or organized a modern aerial defense system. Crowning all his other attributes, Galland was still a young man as generals go, being only 43 years old.

Blank asked for Galland's reaction to his offer of command of the new *Luftwaffe*.

"I cannot decide here and now, *Herr* Blank. I must think it over completely, and also examine what has been planned and done thus far. I want to know all the intentions in organization, personnel and technics—a complete briefing."

"Very well, General Galland. I will let you get a full briefing, and give you a week to decide. You can let me know."

As Galland walked out of Blank's office, he realized that a new zenith of his military career could lie ahead. Every young professional pilot dreams of becoming C.-in-C. of the air force. That is true all over the world. Blank's offer had not come as a surprise, but the actual event still carried an impact. Being offered the post of Commander-in-Chief produced a certain elation, like a sip of grand fine champagne cognac.

Galland spent most of the next seven days at Macky Steinhoff's house. His old comrade from JV-44 had been extensively involved with air force preparations for many months. In his analytical and methodical fashion, Steinhoff knew the bright spots and where all the knots and blocks lay. They talked, and Galland studied shoals of documents. His final decision was to tackle the job. He let *Herr* Blank know of his acceptance and awaited developments.

The new German forces shadow organization had been keyed to participation in the European Defense Community. France suddenly balked at this concept. France wanted its own national forces, and this became firm French policy. Another full year was accordingly required to prepare the political situation and reorganize the acceptance of the planned *Bundeswehr* forces.

During this additional year of preparations, political wheels kept turning. *Herr* Blank was replaced, and, when Franz Josef Strauss took over as Defense Minister, the latter claimed that General Josef Kammhuber had already been selected as the new *Inspekteur* of the *Bundesluftwaffe*. Kammhuber's service dated from the First World War, and Germany was about to enter the era of modern jet aviation.

When Kammhuber surfaced as the new C.-in-C., Galland could not help recollecting his many wartime flights with Kammhuber. There would be no possibility of serving under him now. Through politics and internal intrigue, the Adenauer government managed to rid itself of Germany's outstanding and best-qualified air general. (Adolf Galland would never hold another military appointment.)

Galland experienced severe disappointment over losing out to Kammhuber, but this did not last long. Events soon proved that the former General of the Fighters was better off out of the *Bundesluftwaffe* than in. Politics were plentiful. The prewar traditional law that kept politics out of the military was gone for good. Kammhuber had a rough time midwifing the *Bundesluftwaffe*, and Galland was glad it was not happening to him. He preferred that Kammhuber should have such troubles.

To rearm from the deepest national defamation, without a substantial period of rehabilitation, is an awkward procedure with inherent handicaps. German political leaders regarded the new forces as a *necessary evil*, and some said as much publicly. From all this, Galland had been delivered.

"I never cease to thank the French," he told the authors. "Without the delay they caused, and the reorganization they forced, I would have become the C.-in-C. I probably wouldn't have lasted 60 days in that political mill-race. I wouldn't have been able to stand it. Yes, I am very grateful to the French."

Shunted clear of military life, he was able to steer a completely different course. As a retired general, he knew personally every significant officer in the *Bundesluftwaffe*. His competence and technical abilities were established. Soldiers and politicians alike showed him the greatest respect. He was therefore in an excellent position to build himself a business career. Equipment of all kinds was going to be purchased by the *Bundesluftwaffe*, most of it from abroad. All he had to do was organize himself.

A gratifying extra dimension to his life was developing from his memoirs. Further military service would probably have cramped this unfoldment and blurred the clarity of his wartime achievements. His status among those who studied and relived aviation history was soaring like a sailplane. This international and worldwide community esteemed him as an historical figure. His former enemies clamored to meet him. His new life would send him traveling among these admirers. Between history and commerce, he was about to embark on a fulfilling 30-year joyride.

EPILOGUE

During the year that passed between Theodor Blank's proposal that Galland head the new *Luftwaffe* and the surprise emergence of Kammhuber as the actual appointee, Galland kept busy. Knowing what vast tasks awaited in building a new German Air Force from nothing, he turned his enforced wait to good account. Joining a private company in Düsseldorf that was already doing consulting and representative work for foreign armament firms, he took his first plunge into commercial life. Leasing a pleasant apartment across the Rhine in Neuss, he settled down happily with Sylvina. He was a businessman temporarily—or so he thought at the time.

Galland judged that insight into modern weapons procurement, from a commercial viewpoint, would help him when he assumed his new military role. (Without realizing it, he was embarking on the kind of business life that would occupy him for the remainder of his career and give him all the action he could handle.) Having just recently beaten Germany to the ground, and stripped her of all armaments, the Western Allies soon found themselves in a peculiar predicament. Naive wartime expectations about the altruism and rectitude of "Uncle Joe" Stalin became a gross political embarrassment. The Soviet world revolution rapidly proved itself the most relentless political movement in planetary history. Russia stood fully armed on the frontiers of Western Europe.

Soviet intransigence and political aims made the rearmament of West Germany strategically essential. Since even the manufacture of rifles had been prohibited in Germany during the postwar vengeance period, initial arms procurement for the *Bundeswehr* was to come from outside Germany. America donated the first aircraft weapons, obsolescent equipment from its own stocks. Arms makers of the Western world saw German rearmament as a business bonanza. All they had to do was gain access to this massive new weapons market.

Sellers of defense equipment did not not know the procurement procedures of the *Bundeswehr* or the special needs, requirements, and specifications of the

Galland's present home reflects the character of the famous Luftwaffe leader. Neat as a pin, everything in its place, the genteel Galland entertains often in his palatial residence. He is also a gourmet cook.

Karinhall West. Galland's spacious home in Oberwinter now has a large addition which his friends call "Karinhall." This photograph shows the fireplace and a few of his trophies.

1983, proud father. The retired Lt. General shows his affection for his two children, Andreas-Hubertus, born 7 November 1966, and Alexandra-Isabella, born 29 July, 1969.

Very proud parents. General Galland, a father for the first time on 7 November 1966 when his son Andreas-Hubertus was born, beams at his wife Hannalies.

ighter pilots flock gether. On 15 ecember 1967, ich Hartmann, top hter ace of WWII ith 352 victories, d co-author aymond F. Toliver et with General alland in his home Oberwinter.

new services. Overseas manufacturers did not know the key personalities of the new *Luftwaffe,* which was to be reconstructed from training planes upwards. A man with Adolf Galland's experience, contacts, and demonstrated capabilities fitted into this situation perfectly. Armaments suppliers overcame their marketing problems by using consultants—experienced, capable, and connected men who would provide the necessary liaison.

Through the contacts they had already developed, overseas and European manufacturers of aircraft and associated equipment knew that Galland was the proposed key man in the new *Luftwaffe.* This put him in demand. Extensive travel was required. He went all over Europe, and to Canada, Australia, South America, and the United States of America. His role was to keep abreast of aviation's rapid progress, to make recommendations and suggestions, and to bring together the corporate and governmental people who signed the actual contracts. Months raced past as Galland's workload approximated that of wartime days, until public announcement of Kammhuber's appointment upset Galland's vision of his own future.

Disappointment was quickly crowded out of his life by new offers of consulting contracts from numerous defense hardware firms. Once they knew that he would not be going into the new *Luftwaffe,* they competed with each other for his consulting services. Prosperity loomed. He had already come to enjoy his far-and-wide business travels, with their inevitable personal diversions into hunting and sport flying. Losing out on the *Luftwaffe* was setting him free, but there was a discordant personal note.

Galland had always wanted children of his own, which was part of his traditional outlook. With his 40s now draining away, it was time for a family. Unfortunately he could not have children with Sylvina. As long as he was anticipating joining the *Bundesluftwaffe,* furthermore, he did not consider divorce. Once the command assignment evaporated, he began to feel that he should take action towards having the family that he so much desired.

Substantial changes ensued in this period. His personal and business lives took new turns. He resigned from the Düsseldorf company. Taking up numerous offers to consult independently for substantial British, American, French, Italian, Canadian, and German companies, he opened his own office in Bonn. In that city, he would be on the scene of all major defense decisions in West Germany.

With him he took his secretary from Düsseldorf, Hannelies Ladwein. A tall, dark, and charming brunette, her efficiency, thoroughness, and ability to handle people had been a special strength to him in his first commercial activities. She was now to help significantly in his personal business success. They set up offices in a rambling high-ceilinged house on the Koblenzerstrasse, since renamed Adenauer Allee, a few minutes drive from the defense offices of the Federal Republic.

In addition to his consulting services, they made office space available, together with secretarial services, to representatives and visitors from various aerospace companies. For a period in the 1960s, Galland had "Onkel Theo"

Osterkamp—his old comrade of the champagne and lobsters incident during the war—as one of his tenants.

His memoirs had by now been read all over the world, and new translations were being made almost every year into yet another language. He enjoyed special fame in the aerospace field, where ace fighter pilots have always been accorded legend status. Overseas aerospace companies were eager to have such a man represent them in the huge new German armaments market.

Galland's book had another unusual consequence, unforeseen at the time he set down his memoirs. Businessmen in other countries recognized his direct soldier's narrative as the work of a man of integrity. Adding this quality to Galland's known capabilities, connections, and status in Germany made him the perfect representative. Competing companies hired him as a consultant without misgivings.

His former enemies paid him a practical compliment with this kind of trust; but for those who knew his character, it was really no risk. Any man who had stood his ground before Hitler and Goering on matters of principle would never compromise his integrity for mere commercial gain. As his friend Edu Neumann put it, "Galland was a man of courage before the Thrones of Kings." His courage guaranteed everything else in his character.

Galland admitted to the authors that it was "sometimes a delicate balancing act" to avoid conflicts of interest with the companies he represented. He nevertheless served them all well. His activities were lucrative. His personal life changed after his divorce from Sylvina, and he married Hannelies on 10 September 1963. After years of living in rented apartments, they built a splendid new hilltop home in suburban Oberwinter in May of 1965. Each working day thenceforth opened and closed with a pleasant 30-minute drive along the Rhine.

An English language capability beyond that acquired from Jack Whitten and others in POW days was essential to Galland's consulting work. He soon made the necessary improvements. He speaks an accented English, with the oft-voiced claim, "I didn't learn English, I only spoke it." The authors discovered in compiling this book that Adolf Galland is perfectly capable of grasping even subtle nuances of the English language, and especially the written language. He is fluent enough to address seminars in America and England, including the give and take of question and answer periods. He refers to it all slyly as "my Oxford English," but it carried him to success as a businessman and also made him an excellent technical advisor on this biography. With colloquial Spanish at his command as well, he experienced few language problems in his world travels.

Since boyhood Galland had dreamed of one day owning his own aircraft. His dream finally came true on his 50th birthday in 1962, when he purchased a Beechcraft Bonanza, registration D-EHEX, and nicknamed "Die Dicke"—the Fat One. The plane got the name because it was more portly than the planes he flew in WWII, as was Galland himself.

Reveling in the flying qualities of the Bonanza, he flew it all over Europe for both business and pleasure. Often he flew in *Rallyes,* sometimes with Erich Hartmann, the world's most successful fighter ace, as his copilot. They did well. When Galland took breaks from his consulting business, the Bonanza would be waiting to speed him to Austria or some other choice hunting site. His friends often flew with him.

On one business trip, he gave a lift to a fighter pilot from Israel. The youngster was a typical fighter jockey, boiling with gaiety and enthusiasm. He told Galland surprising tales of his aerial adventures in Israel's early struggles, when that country had to really scratch for armaments. "Believe it or not, General Galland, we got all your old ammunition from World War II, and we made good use of it. It was excellent ammunition, and we also made good use of your tactical combat advisories from 1942 through the end of 1944." Galland wondered at the twists of fate that would see the Israeli Air Force using tactical advice often resisted by the *Luftwaffe* High Command.

His Bonanza served him faithfully for 18 years. Failing vision forced him to give up piloting himself, after more than half a century in the pilot's seat. Turning away from the Bonanza for the last time was one of his hardest moments. Owning and flying Die Dicke had brought him the greatest joy of his life as a pilot.

Other joy had flooded in on him when Hannelies finally presented him with a son on 7 November 1966. Andreas Hubertus Galland provided his illustrious father with one of life's most exultant moments. Dolfo was now in his 55th year. Late though it was to be a daddy, the whole event recharged him with enthusiasm and *joie de vive.* On 29 July 1969, when Galland had already turned 57, Hannelies presented him with a daughter, Alexandra-Isabelle. His children were thenceforth the source of more late-in-life joy and fulfilment than any man can rationally anticipate. By the time this book was written his children had grown into arrow-straight young adults.

Alexandra favors her mother's looks. "Andus" is a near-replica of his father at the same time of life, a slender, loose-limbed young German with the thick, helmet-like hair of Galland senior. Andus is like the young Adolf also in his quickness, curiosity, and personal initiative. Acquiring English by working as a swimming pool serviceman in Florida one winter, he is a comfortable visitor to America on many occasions. With British ace Bob Stanford-Tuck as his godfather, and the immortal Dolfo as his dad, Andus embarked upon basic *Luftwaffe* training in 1985 with a heavy tradition to uphold.

When Hannelies retired from business to raise Andus and Alexandra, a replacement was necessary, and it was a tall order. Her services had been invaluable to his success. Galland's lifelong good luck held. He acquired the services of Frau Anne-Marie Drinhausen, a capable, energetic, and precise young lady. She has single-handedly almost equalled the efforts of his wartime staff for the past two decades. The trilingual Frau Drinhausen can shoot asides to a visitor in the office in English, while talking to someone else on the telephone in German. Every businessman should be so lucky as to find such a dedicated aide.

Interspersed with Galland's frequent business travels abroad were increasing numbers of invitations to attend reunions, seminars, and historical celebrations around the world. He was so mobile in business for 25 years that he became an international roving ambassador for the German fighter pilots of World War II. He enjoyed this "assignment" and represented Germany's airmen ably. Among German pilots in Germany, whether they were in *Bundesluftwaffe* uniform or civilian life, he remained "The Boss." As former Colonel Wolfgang Falck expressed things, "I never knew any German general who so vigorously stood up for his troops." Galland was honored, respected, and revered by the men he led in World War II. For those who rose to become generals in the *Bundeslufwaffe,* the ultimate honor remained an invitation to a social gathering at Galland's home in Oberwinter.

Galland developed a close personal friendship with retired RAF Wing Commander Robert Stanford-Tuck, credited with 30 victories in World War II. Galland and Stanford-Tuck were both master marksmen and hunters. Both were known for hoisting a few cocktails. On this basis, and because of their status as leading aces, they enjoyed a rollicking good time together down through the decades. They made good foils for each other, refighting the Battle of Britain and in after-dinner joshing.

Galland's best after-dinner story deals with his Diamonds decoration and never fails to delight guests. Galland's humor and German accent, combined with his abilities as a raconteur, give the story full flavor, hardly reproducible here. The tale begins some time after his Diamonds award, when he was sitting across from Goering in the *Reich* Marshal's personal train "Asia." Goering suddenly leaned forward, peering intensely at Galland's decoration. "Tell me," he said, "are those the Diamonds the *Fuehrer* gave you?" Assured that they were, Goering then asked Galland to take off the decoration, so he could examine it more closely.

The General of the Fighters kept the decoration around his neck with the aid of a lady's garter, and garter and all he handed it to the *Reich* Marshal. Goering held the decoration up to the light, and turned it back and forth with a look of disdain.

"The *Fuehrer* knows a lot about tanks and guns, General Galland, but he doesn't know anything about diamonds. Why, these are just *chips!*"

Galland knew nothing about diamonds, either, but he readily accepted the *Reich* Marshal's offer to have a superior copy of the decoration prepared by his personal jeweler. Goering appreciated jewels. The numerous rings encrusting his fingers attested to his passion. The *Reich* Marshal believed that the highest decoration should be of the highest quality. He promised to return Galland's decoration together with the superior Goering version in a few weeks.

The call duly came to visit Goering's HQ, and the beaming *Reich* Marshal met him with the new Diamonds decoration in one hand and Hitler's Diamonds in the other. Holding them up to the light, he turned on his heel and let the stones shimmer back, the decorations side by side in his hands.

"You see the difference, Galland? You see it?"

Galland had to agree that the *Reich* Marshal's Diamonds were bigger and much more brilliant and beautiful than those he had received from Hitler. Goering gave him both versions, so now he had a spare.

Goering and Hitler had a strange rivalry. There is no doubt that Hitler respected Goering's cultivated background and subtly tried to outdo him. Evidently Goering had said something to Hitler about improving the quality of the Diamonds to the Knight's Cross, for, soon after Galland had collected the Goering Diamonds, he was summoned to Hitler's HQ and was personally met by the *Fuehrer*.

"I can give you your proper Diamonds to your Knight's Cross now, General Galland," said Hitler. "The decoration you have was just a temporary copy. Would you take off your decoration, please?"

To Galland's amazement, Hitler took out a jewel case and produced a*nother* set of Diamonds. Taking Galland's decoration in one hand, the *Fuehrer* took his new Diamonds in the other and held them up to the light side by side, turning on his heel as he did so—and just as Galland had seen Goering do.

"You see the difference, General Galland? You see it? You see that the diamonds in your temporary decoration are just *chips!*" They were Goering's own words, but they shocked Galland, because the "temporary" set of Diamonds he had just handed Hitler were the *Reich* Marshal's custom-designed Diamonds. Galland thus finished up with three sets of Diamonds to his Knight's Cross. One set was destroyed in Berlin but replaced by Hitler, and Galland was able to retain this one set. The two other sets were stolen by an American NCO of the Counter Intelligence Corps at Tegernsee at war's end. Those decorations are no doubt somewhere in the United States today.

The former General of the Fighter Arm was several times the guest of NASA in the United States and at numerous USAF bases and facilities both in America and in Europe. In May of 1974, he gave a speech to the American High School Air Force Junior Reserve Officer Training Corps, on the occasion of their first annual dining out—at Bitburg. The U.S. Marine Corps invited him to Yuma, Arizona, in 1979, to join their Weapons and Tactics Instructor Course. Bob Stanford-Tuck went with him. So did General Gerhard Barkhorn of the *Bundesluftwaffe,* who had flown with Galland in JV-44 equipped with the Me-262 jet fighters.

The war days came closest of all in the years 1967 through 1969, when he was hired as a consultant by Spitfire Productions of London. They produced the epic film *The Battle of Britain,* released through United Artists. Many of the sequences in this film were shot in Spain. In addition to returning to familiar and little-changed scenes at Sevilla—including the Christina Hotel—Galland had the chance to once more fly the Me-109. Spain had built and used its own variants of the Me-109 long after World War II. Galland did not fly in scenes for the film; but for an old fighter pilot of 56, tooling around one last time in an Me-109 was an adventure in nostalgia.

Characters in the film were largely fictionalized. Representing Galland was the fictional "Major Falke," played by Manfred Reddemann. Dolfo's contemporaries chided him that it was indeed fiction, because he wasn't as handsome as Reddemann. A consoling factual touch was that Reddemann has a slightly bent nose. Heinz Riess as Goering was not as great in girth as the original Fat One but resembled him facially. The first time Galland saw the actor in the resplendent *Reich* Marshal's uniform, it was as though his old antagonist had been suddenly reincarnated—evoking memories of their wartime clashes.

Galland's lectures and appearances at seminars increased his popularity as the years passed. Nowhere was he more enthusiastically received than in Ireland. He was the honored guest of the Royal Aeronautical Society in Dublin, in March of 1980. His lecture subject was the Channel dash, the breakout of the German battleships from Brest in 1942. Galland had given a similar lecture in both the United States and Canada in earlier years. While his trans-Atlantic audiences were interested in the subject, his Irish hosts were openly enthusiastic.

Delivering his lecture in the direct, factual, and soldierly way normal to him, Galland was astonished by the mounting applause as he recounted the breakout details. As he told of each British error, miscalculation, or oversight, his Irish audience began reveling in the succession of British mishaps and failures. By the time Galland told of the successful return of the battleships to Germany, the Irish were on their feet. Twisting the British lion's tail was something that aroused their greatest enthusiasm and admiration. That night, he was one of the most popular men in Ireland.

Audiences never seemed to tire of Galland or of the other distinguished airmen who shared the podium with him in various countries. On the contrary, people with an historical bent realized increasingly how precious the sight and sound of these legendary warbirds in the flesh was becoming. When Galland appeared at a seminar in Long Beach, California, in December of 1983, his fellow panelists were America's General Jimmy Doolittle and Air Vice-Marshal "Johnny" Johnson, perhaps the RAF's top-scoring ace of World War II. The auditorium was packed, the people in the audience fully mindful that they might never again see so much living history in one place.

Galland found a lifelong friend in Sir Douglas Bader, when he treated his fallen foe chivalrously in 1941. Bader was a gentleman of renowned wit and humor. Quick with a quip and brilliant with badinage, Sir Douglas was ready for Galland when the latter was invited, in September of 1971, to attend the 1st Commonwealth Wartime Aircrew Reunion as a guest. The reunion was held in Winnipeg, Manitoba, Canada, a center of the enormous Empire Air Training Scheme. This enterprise had produced a flood of aircrew for the British bombing fleets, as well as many thousands of pilots.

During the introductory speeches, Bader greeted Galland and outlined for his audience how the organizers of the reunion had consulted with him about the propriety of inviting a former *Luftwaffe* general as an honored guest. Bader assured them that it was all perfectly proper.

"After all," said Bader artfully to his audience, *"if it weren't for chaps like him, we never would have had an Empire Air Training Scheme."*

Roaring laughter from the assembled veterans took ten minutes to subside, and Bader finally introduced their German guest. No one present enjoyed the joke more than Galland. The true dimension of a man is always revealed when a public joke is on himself.

Galland's business life was punctuated by numerous similar gatherings. Former foes like the Pathfinders Association, the men who marked targets for the RAF night bombers, and the reunion of the Royal Australian Air Force Europe invited him. In an especially loud echo of the past, he was the guest of the RAF Officers' Mess at No. 11 Group RAF. He sat down at a dining table in Bentley Priory at Stanmore, where Dowding and Park had out-generaled Goering, Kesselring, and Sperrle.

He was guest and often a participant in all kinds of fly-ins, *Rallyes,* and aviation social events. He remembered his own past. Always he found time for world youth interested in aviation. Wherever he went, his was a respected voice of encouragement. He was a pilot who had started in a sailplane, built with his own hands and those of other youngsters, and had flown on into history. He signed uncounted thousands of autographs. Requests continue to reach him from dozens of countries.

In September of 1969, he was the honorable guest at the fly-in of the German lady pilots at Ludwigsburg—a fateful occasion. The lady pilots were duly charmed and fascinated by their still-magnetic guest. Galland only had eyes for one. Retired *Luftwaffe* Colonel Wolfgang Falck, then-president of the German Fighter Pilots' Association, was with him on that occasion. Dolfo began nudging Falck, directing his attention to a tall and stunning brunette. Galland whispered an urgent request, using Wolf Falck's nickname.

"Fälkchen! Fälkchen! You must introduce me to *that girl.*"

"That girl" was Frau Heidi Horn, a successful businesswoman from Münster. Falck's introduction was the beginning of a long and often rocky romance. Those who knew Dolfo best were soon of the opinion that he had at last been "shot down"—fatally smitten by a woman. Galland and Hannelies were in due course divorced, but they remained warm friends. These accords continued over the raising of Andus and Alexandra and their joint parental responsibilities. Galland remained alone after the divorce, living in baronial solitude on his Oberwinter hilltop for many years. Heidi gave him Arrax, a scrappy wire-haired dachshund, for company.

One May night in 1983, co-author Constable sat with Galland discussing his attitude towards the fair sex throughout his life. "After the heat has died down,'' said the former general, ''I like to have friendship.'' No sooner had he said this than the telephone rang, and he withdrew for a few minutes. Returning with the broadest of Galland grins on his face, he was exultant.

''You see what I was just telling you? That was a girl friend of mine from 1927, just telephoning to see how my health is!''

History will not cease poking at him while he lives. In 1979, largely through the efforts of American aviation buff and historian Henry Sakaida, Galland was finally put in touch with the American P-47 pilot who clobbered him on his final Me-262 mission. Former Captain James Finnegan, now of San Rafael, California, was positively identified as the pilot who had fired on Galland's jet and put him out of the war with fragments in his knee. On one of Galland's subsequent visits to California, and later again in Oberwinter, they met in person and in friendship. The kindly Finnegan took no pride in injuring another human being, but putting Adolf Galland out of the war was the high point of his military career and an unforgettable distinction.

In 1983, Galland attended to another historical matter. Always he had wished to see again his crew chief Gerhard Meyer and his armorer Heinrich Olemotz. Both had been dedicated perfectionists in his glory days. Galland was deeply appreciative of the work of all ground crews and of their indispensable role in the whole air effort. For Meyer and Olemotz there was a special place in his heart. Attempting to trace Meyer through *Fighter News* (*Jägerblatt*), the magazine of the German Fighter Pilots' Association, he received replies from 18 Meyers. Many claimed to be his former crew chief. None of them was the real Meyer.

By June of 1983, Galland had finally traced them both. A reunion was arranged at his office in Bonn and later at his home in Oberwinter. The two veterans have entered their evening with the warmest respect and regard for their former C.O. They are now members of the Fighter Association, attending all important meetings; but their pilot-and-crew reunion with Galland has crowned their memories of military service.

The sudden passing of Sir Douglas Bader in 1983 saddened the world aviation community, Galland included. Their friendship had covered more than 42 years since Bader was brought down by JG-26 over France. Although he was in California on business at the time Bader died, Galland made sure to attend personally the later London memorial service held for the British ace at St. Clement Danes church in The Strand. The retired *Luftwaffe* general was hardly prepared for what happened, as described by Peter Tory in his *London Diary* newspaper column:

A curious and rather disturbing scene was enacted outside a London church yesterday, following the memorial service for our greatest derring-do air ace, Sir Douglas Bader.

There was nothing untoward about the buzz of excitement over the presence of Maggie Thatcher and such Battle of Britain legends as Bob Stanford-Tuck

Dolfo and Sir Roland. Galland and his friend, Robert Stanford-Tuck, a top RAF ace with 29 aerial victories over the Germans, had a rollicking good time together in post-war years, refighting the air war before rapt audiences all over the world. Galland nicknamed him "Sir Roland" to the amusement of both. Stanford-Tuck passed away 5 May 1987 at Sandwich Bay, England.

Long Beach, California, Co-authors Trevor Constable and Ray Toliver flank General Jimmy Doolittle while awaiting the arrival of General Adolf Galland. Hermann Boschet looks on.

Home from the honeymoon. General and Mrs. Adolf Galland pose for a photographer on 10 March 1984, just a month after their wedding day.

Adolf Galland, wife Heidi and John Whitten, Galland's American interrogator at the end of the war. This photo was taken at the Galland home in Oberwinter, Germany.

and "Laddie" Lucas. But the feverish attention paid by the public to a moustachioed, elderly man wearing a drab, black raincoat was just a little unsettling.

So who was this figure receiving such star treatment at an event which at once was mourning the death of an English hero, and celebrating our glorious victory over Germany in 1945? The stranger was none other than World War II *Luftwaffe* ace Adolf Galland, who scored an astonishing 104 victories over our own lads in the RAF.

General Galland, now 70, won Germany's highest decorations, most of which were pinned personally on his chest by the *Fuehrer*. Yet it was he more than any other celebrity at yesterday's service whom the public wanted to meet.

Almost pushing aside old British air force types bent low under the weight of their DFCs and Bars, the crowds assaulted the old *hun* with their requests for autographs. He signed his signature a dozen or more times and shook a hundred hands. One dignitary, with a glittering shield of medals, snapped testily: "Perhaps when the admirers have finished, we might move on."

Certainly Bader, had he been present, would have instantly recognized the stranger in the dark raincoat. Stomping over to his side, he would have banged him on the back and bellowed: "Bloody good show, glad you could come!"

Galland entered his eighth decade with every material comfort a man could require. His home in Oberwinter underwent successive expansions and additions, including a magnificent trophy hall reminiscent of the one at Goering's estate on the Schorfheide. Galland has had to suffer hearing his beautiful room called "Karinhall" by old comrades and friends.

For many years he enjoyed the apartment he owns at St. Gilgen on Lake Wolfgang in Austria. In Spain, he has an attractive summer villa near Benidorm. What else could his heart desire in the evening of his life, with his children grown and his life's work essentially concluded? What else? "That girl" Heidi to whom Wolf Falck introduced him in 1969.

On 10 February 1984, Adolf Galland and Heidi Horn were married. All their friends were astonished. This final foray into marital blitz did wonders for Galland's morale, as he battled against serious health problems and was hospitalized several times. At the reception they gave in Oberwinter, among old war comrades, friends, and dignitaries, was also his first wife, Sylvina. Upon seeing Galland together with Sylvina and Heidi, several old fighter pilots could not resist cracking, "Aha, Dolfo, the First and the Last, eh?"

According to Bob Stanford-Tuck, in the cricket vernacular, "Dolfo's had a bloody good innings, you know." Military men who have youthful, meteoric careers seldom survive the characteristic burnout that usually follows their early brilliance. Galland's career became long and brilliant, both military and civilian. Anton "Tonius" Weiler, the able head of the German Fighter Pilots' Association, characterized the Galland mystique in a 70th birthday message, publicly delivered in Cologne: "Glory and inactivity are two things that don't mix, and Galland has acted accordingly. He always left the slow ones behind, and never looked back."

Despite having his life's work behind him, Galland has reached in his 70s, and in retirement, an even higher glory. He has become a living legend. This is the culminating distinction for any man of action. Youngsters of today who may be inspired by his example, to be "number one" no matter what their present station or nation, will through their drive to achievement elevate the human condition. These young people will grace and not disgrace the earth. So be it with them, as it has been with him.

GLOSSARY

Abitur; Examinations given when graduating to qualify a student for admission to a university.

A/B *Schule;* Single-engine flight training school.

B-*Schule;* Blind-flying school.

BARBAROSSA; Code name for the German invasion of Russia in 1941.

Chaff; Narrow metalic strips dropped from aircraft to confuse and create false signals on radarscopes.

C-*Schule;* Multi-engine flight training school.

DLH; *Deutsche Lufthansa,* the German State airline.

DLV; *Deutscher Luftsportverband,* the German Aviation Sport Union.

Düppel; Town on Denmark border where chaff was first used.

DVS; *Duetsche Verkehrsfliegerschule,* the German Commercial Pilot's School.

EKdo; *Eprobungskommando;* Test or proving detachments

Ersatz; Substitute

Flieger; Flier or pilot or airman.

Fuhrungsstab; Operations staff.

General der Jagdflieger; General of fighters.

General der Kampfflieger; General of the bombers.

Geschwader; Air Force group.

Gruppe; Unit equivalent to a USAAF Squadron or an RAF Wing.

Gruppenkommandeur: Commander of a *Gruppe.*

Gymnasium; Grammar or Secondary School.

Hauptmann; Captain

Himmelbett; German system for ground controlled night interception of enemy aircraft.

Jabo; Jagdbomber or Fighter-bomber.

Jagd; Fighter

JG or *Jagdgeschwader;* Fighter Wing.

Jagdgruppe; Fighter *Gruppe.*

Jumo; Junkers Motorwerke.

Kampf; Battle

Kette; three-plane formation of aircraft.

Kettenfuhrer; Leader of a three-plane formation.

Knights Cross; see *Ritterkreuz.*

Kommodore; Commander of a *Luftwaffe* Wing.

Kriegsakadamie; War Academy.

Luftkriegsakademie; Air War Academy.

MK; *Maschinenkanone* or automatic canon.

OKH or *Oberkommando des Heeres;* Army High Command.

OKL or *Oberkommando der Luftwaffe;* Air Force High Command.

Ritterkreuz; Germany's highest decoration for bravery in WWII. It consists of
   five degrees, running from lowest to highest being the *Ritterkreuz,* the *Eichenlaub* or Oakleaves, the *Swertern* or Swords, the *Brillants* or Diamonds, and
   finally the Golden *Ritterkreus.*

Rotte; Two-plane formation.

Schlacht; Close support

Schlachtgeschwader; Close-support Wing.

Schwarm; Two *Rotten* or two pairs of aircraft in formation.

Stuka or *Sturzkampfflugzeug:* Dive bomber.

Verband; Formation.

Wehramt; Defense Office

Wehrmacht; Armed Forces

Wilde Sau; Wild Sow or Wild Boar. A night interception method employed by
   the *Luftwaffe* briefly.

X-*Gerät;* Known as X-Apparatus, an early blind-flying aid.

ZG; *Zerstörergeschwader* or Heavy Fighter Group.

GERMANY'S ACES WITH ONE HUNDRED OR MORE AERIAL VICTORIES

Name	Rank	Unit(s)	Born	Died	Score
Hartmann, Erich	Major	52	19.4.22		352
Barkhorn, Gerhard	Major	6,52,44	20 .3.19	6.1.83	301
Rall, Günther	Major	11,52,300	10.3.18		275
Kittel, Otto	1st. Lt.	54	21–2–17	16.2.45	267
Nowotny, Walter	Major	54,7	7.12.20	8.11.44	258
Batz, Wilhelm	Major	52	21.5.16	11.9.88	242
Rudorffer, Erich	Major	2,54,7	1.11.17		222
Bär, Heinrich	Lt. Col.	51,1,3,77	25.3 .13	28.4.57	220
Graf, Hermann	Colonel	52,53	24.10.12	4.11.88	212
Ehrler, Heinz	Major	5,77	14.9 .17	4.4.45	209
Weissenberger, Theo.	Major	5,7	21.12.14	10.6.50	208
Philipp, Hans	Lt. Col.	54,1	17.3.17	8.10.43	206
Schuck, Walter	Lt.	5,7	30.7.20		206
Hafner, Anton	1st. Lt.	51	2.6.18	17.10.44	204
Lipfert, Helmut	Capt.	52	6.8.16		203
Krupinski, Walter	Major	52,11,26,44	11.11.20		197
Hackl, Anton	Major	11,26,300	25 .3.15	1984	192
Brendel, Joachim	Capt.	53,51	27.4 .21		189
Stotz, Max	Capt.	54	13.2.12	19.8.43	189
Kirschner, Joachim	Capt.	3,27	7.6 .20	17.12.43	188
Brändle, Werner	Major	3	19.1.12	3.11.43	180
Josten, Günther	Lt.	52	7.11.21		178
Steinhoff, Johannes	Lt. Col.	7,77,52,44	15.9.13		176
Reinert, Ernst-W.	Capt.	27,77,7	2 .2.19		174
Schack, Günther	Capt.	51	12.11.17		174
Schmidt, Heinz	Capt.	52	20.4.20	5.9.43	173
Lang, Emil	Capt.	52,53,26	14 .1.09	3.9.44	173
Adameit, Horst	Major	54	8.2.12	8.8.44	166
Wilcke, Wolf-Diet,	Lt. Col.	53,3	11.3.13	23.3.44	162
Marseille, Hans-J.	Capt.	51,27	13.12.19	30.9.42	158
Sturm, Heinrich	Capt.	52	12.6.20	22.12.44	157
Thyben, Gerhardt	1st. Lt.	3,54	24.2.22		157
Beisswenger, Hans	1st. Lt	54	8.11.16	6.3.43	152
Düttmann, Peter	Lt.	52	23.5.23		150
McGollob, Gordon	Colonel	3,77	16.6 .12	17.9.87	150
Tegtmeier, Fritz	1st. Lt.	54,7	30.7.17		146
Wolf, Albin	1st. Lt.	54	28.10.20	2.4.44	144
Tanzer, Kurt	1st. Lt.	51	1.11.20	25.6.60	143
Müller, F-K. "Tutti"	Major	53,3	25.12.16	29.5.44	140

Gratz, Karl	1st Lt.	52	24.1.19		138
Setz, Heinrich	Major	52,77,27	12.3.15	13.3.43	138
Trenkel, Rudolf	Capt.	52,77	17.1.18		138
Schall, Franz	Capt.	52,7	1.6.18	10.4.45	137
Wolfrum, Walter	1st. Lt.	52	23.5.23		137
Dickfeld, Adolf	Lt. Col.	52,2,11	20.2.10		136
vonFassong, Horst-G.	Capt.	51,11	27.4.19	1.1.45	136
Fönnekold, Otto	1st. Lt.	52	15.2.20	31.8.44	136
Weber, Karl-Heinz	Major	51	30.1.22	7.6.44	136
Müncheberg, Joachim	Major	26,77	31.12.18	23.3.43	135
Waldmann, Hans	1st. Lt.	52,3,7	24.9.22	18.3.45	134
Grislawski, Alfred	Capt.	52,1,53	21.11.19		133
Wiese, Johannes	Major	52,77	7.3 .15		133
Borchers, Adolf	Major	52	10.2.13		132
Clausen, Erwin	Major	51	5.8.11	4.10.43	132
Lemke, Wilhelm	Capt.	3	27.9.20	4.12.43	131
Ihlefeld, Herbert	Colonel	52,11,77	1.6.14		130
Sterr, Heinrich	1st. Lt.	54	24.9.19	26.11.44	130
Hoffmann, Gerhard	Lt.	52	6.11.19	11.4.45	130
Eisenach, Franz	Major	54	11.8.18		129
Dahl, Walther	Colonel	3,300	27.3.16	25.11.85	128
Dörr, Franz	Capt.	5,77	10.2 .13		128
Obleser, Friedrich	1st. Lt.	52	21.2.23		128
Rademacher, Rudolf	Lt.	54,7	19.6.13	13.6.53	126
Zwernemann, Josef	1st. Lt.	52,77,11	26.3.16	8.4.44	126
Hrabak, Diether	Lt. Col.	52,54	19.12.14		125
Oesau, Walter	Lt. Col.	51,3,2	28.6.13	11.5.44	125
Ettel, Wolf-Udo	1st. Lt.	3,27	26.2.121	17.7.43	124
Tonne, Wolfgang	Capt.	53,27	28.2.18	20.4.43	122
Marquardt, Heinz	Sgt.	51	29.12.22		121
Schnaufer, Heinz-W.	Major	NJG4	16.2.22	13.7.50	121
Weiss, Robert	Capt.	54	21.4.20	29.12.44	121
Leie, Erich	1st. Lt.	2,51,77	10.9.16	7.3.45	118
Beerenbrock, Hans	Lt.	51	9.4.20		117
Birkner, Hans-J.	Lt.	52	22.10.21	14.12.44	117
Norz. Jakob	Lt.	77,5	20.12.20	16.9.44	117
Wernicke, Heinz	Lt.	54	17.10.20	27.12.44	117
Lambert, August	1st. Lt.	SG2-151	18.12.16	17.4.45	116
Mölders, Werner	Colonel	51,53	18.3.13	22.11.41	115
Crinius, Wilhelm	Lt.	27	2.12.20		114
Schröer, Werner	Major	27,3	12.12.18	10.2.85	114
Dammers, Hans	Lt.	52	8.12.13	17.3.44	113
Korts, Berthold	Lt.	52	21.5.12	28.8.43	113
Bühligen, Kurt	Lt. Col.	2	13.12.17	1985	112

Lent, Helmut	Lt. Col.	NJG3	13.6.18	7.10.44	110
Ubben, Kurt	Major	53,77	18.11.11	27.4.44	110
Woidich, Franz	Lt.	27,53	2.1.21		110
Seiler, Reinhard	Major	54	30.8.09		109
Bitsch, Emil	Capt.	3	14.6.16	15.3.44	108
Hahn, Hans "Assi"	Major	54,2	14.4.14	18.12.82	108
Lützow, Günther	Colonel	3,44	4.9.12	24.4.45	108
Vechtel, Bernard	Lt.	51	31.7.20	1975	108
Bauer, Viktor	Capt.	3	19.9.15		106
Lucas, Werner	Capt.	3	27.12.17	24.10.43	106
Galland, Adolf	Lt. Gen.	27,26,44	19.3.12		104
Sachsenberg, Heinz	Lt.	52	12.7.22	17.6.51	104
Grasser, Hartmann	Major	51,1,210	23.8.14	2.6.86	103
Freytag, Siegfried	Major	77,7	10.11.19		102
Geisshardt, Friedr.	Capt.	54,26	22.1.19	6.4.43	102
Mayer, Egon	Lt. Col.	2	19.8.17	2.3.44	102
Ostermann, Max-H.	1st. Lt.	54	11.12.17	9.8.42	102
Rollwage, Herbert	1st. Lt.	53	24.9.16	1980	102
Wurmheller, Josef	Major	53,2	4.5.17	22.6.44	102
Dähne, Paul-Heinrich	1st. Lt.	2,11,1	7.7.21	24.4.45	102
Miethig, Rudolf	1st. Lt.	52	17.10.21	10.6.43	101
Müller, Rudolf	Flt. Sgt.	5	21.11.20	unk.	101
Priller, Josef	Colonel	51,26	27.6.15	20.5.61	101
Wernitz, Ulrich	Lt.	54	23.1.21		101

APPENDIX

Surrender of JV-44

Here is the correct course of events: As you know, I was wounded in my last JV-44-mission and combat, on 26 April 1945, when I had downed two B-26 Marauders. Taking off from Munich-Riem, Col. Steinhoff crashed and was extremely badly burned. (Please see photo in my photo-book page 103).

Soon thereafter my JV-44 moved from Munich to Salzburg and a smaller part of the Me-262 was flown to Innsbruck. Since Col. Lützow was missed Lt. Col. Heinz Bär represented me as commander in the meantime. Two provided runways at the Autobahn Munich to Salzburg weren't used anymore because of the fast advancing Allied Forces. The Autobahn south of Munich and Ottobrunn crossing the Hofoldinger Forrest were used only for parking camouflaged Me-262 and He-162 in the woods. Here they were captured by the US troops.

The main part of the JV-44 with most of the personnel, aircraft and equipment was thereupon stationed at Salzburg Airport commanded by Lt. Col. Heinz Bär.

I transferred myself to the Luftwaffe-Hospital at Bad Wiessee, having my right leg in plaster. I was treated there and moved to a private villa at Tegernsee. From there I was in contact with my JV-44 at Salzburg and Innsbruck by means of telephone, Fieseler-Storch and Motorcycle messengers.

On the first of May I decided to make a last and desperate attempt to save and maintain—at the last possible instance—this unique and advanced operational jet fighter unit for a later use to be decided by the US authorities. I was completely aware of the highest danger and risks involved in case this action became known to any German military, SS, police, or political NS-party authority. This fact and the possibility of a misinterpretation of my final actions as commander of JV-44 (betrayer, deserter, etc.) prohibited me and a few involved officers around me to speak or to write about this attempt in any detail at a later time.

Up to now the whole correct historical story of this last minute action has remained virginal.

After some last-minute-consultations Major Wilhelm Herget volunteered to take-off with a "Storch" from a small spot next to my villa in order to cross the allied advanced troops and to land at Schleißheim. He was accompanied by my personal aid, Captain Hugo Kessler. They managed to land safely at the former Luftwaffen-airfield Schleißheim, north of Munich.

The following actions on both sides can best be seen and explained by the attached copies and translations in the correct temporal order:

1. My first message dated 1st May 1945, 0.15 hours,
2. The answer of Brig. General Pearson Menoher, dated 1st May 1945, with annexes 2a, 2b, 2c, 2d, and 2e (drawing for marking our Me-262),
3. My answer to Brig. General Menoher dated 2 May 1945,
4. Report of my first interrogation by Col. Newton, dated 6 May 1945 at Bad Tölz,

I believe this makes a very interesting story which has never been published before. When I was a P.O.W. I have been told that unfortunately the US Army officers approached by us did not understand the importance of my offer. All experts know that the operational jet-fighter-experience could only be gained by successful fighter-pilots and a highly skilled technical staff supported by a sufficient stock of manifold spareparts and specialised ground support equipment. All this was contained in the JV-44 and subject to my offer. Without a slightly satisfying response from the US side I did not have any other alternative, but to give the order for demolition, destruction and dissolution of the JV-44.

Best wishes,
yours,

c/c
Ray Toliver

Adolf Galland
Lt. General

I have sent Major Herget as well as my personal aid, Captain Kessler to the Commander in Chief of the Allied Forces, in order to discuss with him the possibilities and terms of a special surrender for the last entire and fully operational jet-fighter-unit. I therefore kindly ask you to have me approached in this regard at the earliest possible time without any delay, since the destruction of the aircraft and special equipment as well as the disbandment of the unit must be expected every hour.

The couriers have been informed with regard to further details.

signed Galland
Lt. General

Tegernsee, 2 May 1945
0.15 hours

sent with this order: signed : Herget (Major)
signed : Kessler (Captain)

Headquarters
XV Corps United States Army

1 May 1945

MEMORANDUM:
TO: Lieutenant General Adolf Galland.

I have authority to accept the surrender of Jagdverband 44, in accordance with the Rules of Land Warfare as prescribed by the Hague and Geneva Conventions.

I am returning Major Gerget and Captain Kessler to you with details of surrender attached. It is expected that they will return at 6PM, this date, with your decision. I will arrange for their return air escort at that time.

I am open to suggestion as to the surrender of the personnel other than pilots that you indicated in the attached memorandum.

PEARSON MENOHER
Brigadier General, GSC,
Chief of Staff.

Incl. 2

The following were present at the conference between American and German representatives for the surrender of "JAGDVERBAND 44" at 45th Infantry Division Command Post, at FELDMOCHING, at 1100, 1 May 1945:

American Representatives.
  Brig. Gen. Pearson Menoher, O-3805, C/S XV Corps.
  Brig. Gen. Jesse Auton, O-13798, 65th Fighter Wing, Eighth Air Force.
  Col. Dorr E. Newton, Jr., O-23396, Deputy Commander, XII TAC.

German Representatives.
  Maj. Wilhelm Herget, Jagdverband 44.
  Capt. Hugo Kessler, Jagdverband 44.

Interpreters.
  Capt. Rupert W. Guenthner, O-1302642, 45th Division CIC.
  1st Lt. John H. Brunswick, O-552530, G-2 Section, Hq XV Corps.
  Mr. Leonid Ruminoff, Special Agent, CIC, attached to 45th Infantry Division.

Stenographer.
  M/Sgt. Samuel L. Sack, 33314260, C/S Section, Hq XV Corps.

Incl. 1

> 45th Infantry Division
> FELDMOCHING, GERMANY
> (815645)
> 01 1300B May 1945

Notes On Conference With Emissaries of General Galland.

Q. When was this letter (letter brought by emissaries) written?

  A. Last night about 12:15 (300015B).

It was explained to the emissaries that according to the rules governing Land Warfare, when a man or a unit surrenders, neither the man nor the unit, or any of their equipment, is used against their own people. All surrenders are governed by the provisions of "Land Warfare" as set down by the Geneva Convention. The emissaries stated that this was fully understood.

Q. Does General Galland have the authority to surrender the "JAGDVERBAND 44"? What are the supporting units?

A. General Galland has that authority. It is a specialized unit; all 50 planes and all the personnel are one unit.

"As a subordinate commander, I have no authority to accept anything but a surrender as a prisoner of war. SHAEF policy is "Surrender"; all personnel become PWs. Would General Galland surrender?"

A. We would have to ask their Supreme Commander if Gen Galland would surrender. We would like to take this message to the general and come back. Could we do that?

Yes. And we would like to give you the details for bringing in the planes in the event General Galland accepts the surrender. How long does it take to fly to your place . . . is it at the field?

A. It would take about 45 minutes. It is not at the field as the general has been wounded and is in bed at a private place. We have no communications with the field but we have a motorcycle.

Q. How long would it take General Galland to say "Yes" or "No"? If you were to get back to him by 1530B, could you be back here by 1730B?

A. That is too quick. We could be back before dark tonight.

Details of Surrender

1. Marking of aircraft will be in accordance with the attached diagram.

2. One-half the aircraft will be landed at an airfield 8 kilometers Northwest of DARMSTADT (This will be the aircraft from INSBRUCK). The other one-half of the aircraft will be landed at GIEBELSTADT. (This will be the planes from SALZBURG). Alternate airfields will be LEIPHEIM and SCHABISH HALL.

3. Planes will proceed two at a time, five minutes apart, starting at 0700, 2 May 1945, weather permitting, or if not, as soon thereafter as possible.

4. A direct course from base to destination at 3000 meters altitude, or at 150 meters under any solid cloud layer, will be flown.

5. American fighter escort will patrol on either side of the two courses to be flown and will be above their aircraft.

6. German aircraft will not carry ammunition, but will leave guns and other equipment in the planes.

> PEARSON MENOHER
> Brigadier General, GSC
> Chief of Staff.

Incl. 3

The following discussion was made by the general and colonel from the Air Corps:

Q. Do the planes fly in formation?

A. No, only 2 or 3 together.

Q. Is it possible for the planes to reach the Rhine River?

A. I don't know. There is a shortage of fuel.

(Then followed a discussion of possible fields. The final decision was:) We would like the planes at Innesbruck to go to the field 8 Kms N.W. of DARM-STADT; the planes at SALSBURG will go to GIEBELSTADT. Alternate fields would be at LEIPSHEIM and SCHWABISCHALL. Start at 0700B tomorrow, weather permitting, or as soon thereafter as possible. Fly at 3000 meters or 150 meters under solid cloud cover. We will have a patrol escort along both courses and your planes will fly between them. (Other points, such as markings, etc., were also discussed.)

Emissary: If only unconditional surrender is acceptable, General Galland may order the planes destroyed on the ground. We also request that you do not use radio in discussing these details as they will be intercepted and the planes will be destroyed by the SS.

Gen Menoher: That is his decision to make. Surrender is all I have the authority to offer. We will comply as far as possible in not using radio. We are giving you these details for bringing in the planes in the event General Galland accepts.

I expect to send these two men back in their own plane. I will put 2 "Stork" type (Cubs) planes on each side of them as they take off. I would like General

Galland to let us know today as to the acceptance or the rejection of this plan. Our escort will go as far as the front line. If we can agree on a time, we will have 2 Cubs rendezvous at the place we leave them in order to pick them up when they come back.

A. We could do that. 1800B would be a good time for the rendezvous.

X X X X X X X X X X X

Incl. 4

Translation

2 May 1945

To
Brig. General, GSC
Chief of Staff
Pearson Menoher

I thank you for the receipt of my couriers and for your declaration.

The required execution of the action, however, does fail because of the very bad weather-conditions, the lack of fuel and additionally because of the technical problems with many Me-262 aircraft.

I therefore rather suggest to again fix the terms for the special surrender of the whole unit (aircraft, spare parts, special ground support equipment, pilots and specialized personnel.)

I am at your disposal in that regard.

signed: Adolf Galland
Lt. General

the following was written by hand below the text:

"Copy of General Galland's reply to surrender terms, sent back to XV. Corps by the General. Courier pilot, Major Herget was shot down, captured and evacuated through Army Medical channels to the rear having been burnt in the crash.

P. E. Menoher, GSC"

Headquarters
XII Tactical Air Command   **E-N-8**

APO 374, US Army,
6 May 1945

INTERVIEW WITH GENERAL GALLAND, CONDUCTED BY COL. NEWTON, XII TAC, THRU AN INTERPRETER, AT XXI CORPS C.P. AT BAD TOLZ, ON 5 MAY 1945.

My name is General Galland and I am from the Air Corps.
My unit is Jagdtverband 44.

Q. In view of your sending an emmisary to us on 1 May, we wonder if any of your unit is still in this area and if there is any that is not yet captured?

A. I don't know because I have had no communications since 1 May.

Q. Did your unit have instructions to evacuate the fields at Innsbruck and Salsburg or did they destroy their planes.

A. I did not give any instruction to anyone. I sent two officers to you on 1 May and they came back. They had until 1800 to give an answer. It was impossible to give an answer at 1800 because I could not get my plane off the ground because of heavy snow. The stipulations could not be carried out because most of the planes had no gas. On account of weather, in general, they could not get off the ground. The next day, I sent the same major back again with orders from me but he was shot down. The front moved so close to Salsburg that the conditions set forth made no further sense. I decided to stay right here where I was until I was overrun and then start communications again. I stayed of my own accord because I wanted to take up these communications—otherwise I could have gone back. I would like to know if you want to hear some of my personal feelings as to why I started these meetings.

Q. I was at the original meeting with General Menoher and know about your feelings. I also know the reply that was written to you in answer to them.

A. I am the outstanding specialist in jet-propelled aircraft and would like to assemble all the known lights in this subject and go on working on this with you.

Q. Any decision of that nature would have to be reached by a Commander of Higher Authority than me, but would you care to mention what would you do with the results of such work?

A. I am of the opinion that Germany has lost the war but the future of all Europe lies in the hands of the Allies.

Q. What units make up Jagdt 44?

A. That was a special unit put together in February this year by crack pilots.

Q. Was it made up of KG 51, 54 and JG 7?

A. No, they were different from them. That was the second largest that was left.

Q. Where are these other units now?

A. Around Prague. I don't know whether any of my pilots left the field to join them but they had very little gas. I have here a copy of the letter I transmitted with the Major who was shot down, in reply to your surrender terms. Translated, it reads:

"I thank you for your reception of my courier and your acceptance of him. The carrying through of the stipulations was impossible because of weather and gasoline and the fact that a certain number of the planes were not usable. I propose, however, that the transfer of all planes, troops and surrounding installations will be carried forward immediately. In this respect, I am at your command.

Q. What is your address?

A. 147 Neureut Street, Tegernsee. This is Dr. Ernest S. Schubert, my physician. He is staying at the same address.

Q. If we permit you to return and remain, at least temporarily, would you give your parole to stay and remain at our disposal until we want you again?

A. Yes. You may post guards but it won't be necessary. I have to report to the hospital near there every day. I only have to report twice weekly, but I go every day.

Q. Our main mission at present was to find out about your unit and where they were. If you will give us your word to remain, we will send others to return there and they will take up the matter of your specialty and other details.

A. I gladly give my word because I have no place to go and no desire to go anywheres. I will be at your wishes at all times.

Above is a literal translation of the interview as cited.

DORR E. NEWTON JR.
Colonel, G.S.C.
Acting Deputy Commander.

INDEX